CREATING AGILE ORGANIZATIONS

CREATING AGILE ORGANIZATIONS

A SYSTEMIC APPROACH

Cesário Oliveira Ramos

Ilia Pavlichenko

✦✦ Addison-Wesley

Boston • Columbus • New York • San Francisco • Amsterdam • Cape Town
Dubai • London • Madrid • Milan • Munich • Paris • Montreal • Toronto • Delhi • Mexico City
São Paulo • Sydney • Hong Kong • Seoul • Singapore • Taipei • Tokyo

Cover image: Sukpaiboonwat/Shutterstock

Figures 3.9, 3.11: Adapted from *This is Lean: Resolving the Efficiency Paradox* by Niklas Modig and Par Ahlstrom (2012).

Figures A.1, A.2, A.3, A.4: Adapted from *A Scrum Book* by Jeff Sutherland and James O. Coplien (2019).

Figure A.15: Adapted from *Thomas-Kilmann Conflict Mode Instrument* by Kenneth Thomas and R. Kilmann (2002).

For information about buying this title in bulk quantities, or for special sales opportunities (which may include electronic versions; custom cover designs; and content particular to your business, training goals, marketing focus, or branding interests), please contact our corporate sales department at corpsales@pearsoned.com or (800) 382-3419.

For government sales inquiries, please contact governmentsales@pearsoned.com.

For questions about sales outside the U.S., please contact intlcs@pearson.com.

Visit us on the Web: informit.com/aw

Library of Congress Control Number: 2022938926

ISBN-13: 978-0-13-585319-1
ISBN-10: 0-13-585319-2

1 2022

Pearson's Commitment to Diversity, Equity, and Inclusion

Pearson is dedicated to creating bias-free content that reflects the diversity of all learners. We embrace the many dimensions of diversity, including but not limited to race, ethnicity, gender, socioeconomic status, ability, age, sexual orientation, and religious or political beliefs.

Education is a powerful force for equity and change in our world. It has the potential to deliver opportunities that improve lives and enable economic mobility. As we work with authors to create content for every product and service, we acknowledge our responsibility to demonstrate inclusivity and incorporate diverse scholarship so that everyone can achieve their potential through learning. As the world's leading learning company, we have a duty to help drive change and live up to our purpose to help more people create a better life for themselves and to create a better world.

Our ambition is to purposefully contribute to a world where:

- Everyone has an equitable and lifelong opportunity to succeed through learning.

- Our educational products and services are inclusive and represent the rich diversity of learners.

- Our educational content accurately reflects the histories and experiences of the learners we serve.

- Our educational content prompts deeper discussions with learners and motivates them to expand their own learning (and worldview).

While we work hard to present unbiased content, we want to hear from you about any concerns or needs with this Pearson product so that we can investigate and address them.

- Please contact us with concerns about any potential bias at https://www.pearson.com/report-bias.html.

To Jacqueline, whose patience and love continue to amaze me.
—Cesário Ramos

To my precious Olga and beloved children, Gordei and Evaliya, whose
support I felt so much throughout the writing.
—Ilia Pavlichenko

Contents

Foreword

Perhaps the greatest misunderstanding about Agile—especially at scale—is that it's just a new *process or way of working* or *mindset* or *culture*. Senior management then incorrectly thinks, "Since this is just a change of practices and processes and mindset, our role is to *support* it with education for the hands-on people. And . . . these new practices and culture can be introduced into the *existing organization*."

From this ignorance flows a world of dysfunction, disruption, and degradation, leading to the widespread failure of Agile to provide high-impact and lasting benefits.

Cesário and Ilia are among a small group of coaches who really understand both this mistake and its remedy, focusing on a key element of successful change to being adaptive at scale.

Organizational Design

Cesário and Ilia also understand that organizational design (OD) is *not* something that senior managers should *support*. Rather, that OD is something senior managers need to themselves own, master, create, and lead—rather than something delegated to middle management or consultants. In that sense, this book is a practical primer on OD for senior management.

Also, near the top of the list in Agile misunderstandings is the *incorrect* belief that *Agile equals deliver fast*. Sure, early, and frequent delivery is important for learning, reducing risks, and making an impact (or not). But especially at scale, consider this scenario: There are two fast-delivery *feature teams*, each specialized in a different domain: one in bond trading and the other in equities trading. Suppose they both deliver fast, and it's discovered that there's little money (this quarter) in bond trading, but lots in equity trading. But—and this is the key point—as long as there exists a formal team called the Bond Trading feature team, and probably a Bond Trading software development manager, then even though they have learned "bonds currently suck," the team is likely to keep doing the same kind of work, because the *organizational design has formally locked them into working on that subject*, often under the local-optimization thinking mistake of "local efficiency."

So, fast delivery and learning aren't enough at scale. Without other adaptive OD elements in place—such as teams not formally dedicated to one specialist domain—there might not be any concrete change.

Cesário and Ilia understand that. And they help us understand all that in this wonderful book from two passionate people with years in the trenches involved in large-scale adaptive development.

—*Craig Larman*

Foreword

If surviving in the 21st century had a theme, it would be agility. As an organization, as a team, and as a human being, the need to be able to respond to an ever-changing environment is crucial to survive and thrive. Perhaps that has always been the case, but what is different about the 21st century is the speed at which you need to change. The combination of globalization, climate change, and the digital revolution have made life ever-changing, unpredictable, and complex. But the 21st century is not all doom and gloom. We have at our disposal technology that we have never had before—if only we can get out of our own way and use it effectively. Human beings are amazing at solving problems if you give them the right tools, and a clear unobstructed view of the problem they need to solve.

And therein lies the rub. The reality is that organizations are constructed to support a very different paradigm. A paradigm where change is slow and efficiency is more important than effectiveness. Where solving problems is the province of the few. And where trust will never outweigh risk. This paradigm is rooted in the ideas of mass production, a model that has done amazing things but in which flexibility is never the priority. But things can change. For example, Tesla changes its production process so frequently that every car is considered to be unique, requiring automated crash testing and external sign-off for every car. Imagine building a car production line where change is normal, where cars continue to change even when they have left the factory. How does that affect the organization? What do the processes look like? What are the roles and responsibilities? How are risk and compliance handled?

Building an organization for change is difficult enough, but it is made 1000 times harder when you have an existing structure, servicing an existing set of customers, with existing products, all while not forgetting the legacy of existing systems, software, processes, and job structures. Not only do you have to create a new approach, but you also have to create the right environment for change.

Over the last 25 years, I have been lucky to spend time with hundreds of organizations at different stages in this change process. I have seen innovation studios, product factories, and tribes. I have seen companies acquire the change. I have witnessed companies aligned to OKRs, value streams, business processes, customer segments, and product lines. All of these approaches had good and bad elements, and their ultimate success hinged not on the approach but rather on the nature of the people who drove the change and whom the change was affecting. It was neither the approach nor the people alone that were a barometer of success, but instead the combination of those two things.

In this book, Cesário and Ilia have provided a unique view of organizational agility. They first describe the foundational ideas that enable someone to approach the problem. These are the tools and vocabulary needed to think about Agile enterprise-level change. The second section is a practical approach to adoption. It marries the foundational elements into a people- and customer-centric approach to change. The book is epic in scope, and some ideas have to be handled at a high level, but it manages to present a cookbook for Agile adoption and change. In fact, the authors' initial motivation for the book was driven by the need to bring consultants up to speed on their Agile enterprise change engagements. For some, this book will be a roadmap for future research and learnings; for others, it will serve as a guidebook for their own organization. Whatever your motivation for reading this book, it provides a great resource as we embark on transforming our organizations to thrive in the 21st century.

Good luck with your transformation and enjoy the journey (with this book in hand).

— Dave West, CEO Scrum.org
Boston, Massachusetts

Preface

Welcome to *Creating Agile Organizations*, a book that explains how to guide a successful Agile transformation in your organization.

The term "Agile," as we use it in this book, is defined in the Agile Manifesto, which first appeared in 2001 and defined a set of software development values and principles. The Agile Manifesto was a reaction to the unsuccessful linear development process—the dominant way of working at that time. The people who created the Agile Manifesto all had their own Agile approaches, such as Scrum, DSDM, FDD, Extreme Programming, Adaptive Agile Development, and Crystal, among others, but nonetheless agreed on 5 values and 12 principles.

The popularity of the Agile approach has since grown rapidly across the software development world and beyond. One of the most popular approaches to Agile today is known as Scrum. The Scrum framework was created in 1993—eight years before the Agile Manifesto—and introduced to the broader public in 1995. This book uses the Scrum framework as the foundation to create agility. But we go far beyond the Scrum framework and add the practices and guides needed to become an Agile organization.

Most Agile approaches like Scrum are easy to understand. Actually applying them, though, implies changes to the structure, processes, and policies of an organization.

Once an organization understands and envisions what it wants to become, it is usually still a very long and painful journey to get there. There are many obstacles on the road to agility, including power politics, hidden agendas, resistance, lack of skills and competences, and many more.

Why This Book?

The concepts in this book are based on decades of guiding large- and small-scale Agile adoptions around the world. During those years, we observed many organizations that struggled to scale Agile to bigger product groups. We came to realize that the biggest pitfall is that of local optimization and its implications for the resulting organization design.

In a nutshell, the Agile adoption approach we encounter is this: Organizations typically start with a few Agile teams in a bottom-up manner. As these teams become successful individually, their successes draw the attention of the larger organization. And, as a result, the broader organization wants to apply what works so well for individual teams, with bigger development groups inside and outside software development. Copying what works for a single team to the larger organization is unlikely to succeed. Most attempted adoptions use some level of Scrum at the team level only and leave the rest of the organization design intact. The teams are responsible for a narrow part of the product and focus on increasing their individual team performance. The false assumption is that the performance of the entire group will increase because the separate teams improve their performance. Contrary to what many might think at first, improving the teams independently will often not improve the group's performance as a whole. The whole group's performance depends on how the teams interact with each other and how they are tuned, not on how they perform separately. What is needed is an approach that optimizes the entire group, which we share with you in this book.

In this book, we share coaching techniques and practices that we applied in successful change initiatives and found helpful to most organizations. We describe how to work at the level of organizational design, senior and middle management, the product group, and the team.

What Makes an Organization "Agile"?

An Agile organization can adapt to changing market demands both rapidly and at a low cost. It aims to learn faster than its competitors and uses that learning to invest in the important work and to avoid wasting resources on low-value work.

Organizational agility comes from the following capabilities:

- Work is completed in short iterations in which ideas are turned into value, each time providing the opportunity to effectively change direction.

- Short feedback loops enable fast learning about the offered products, services, user needs, technology, and internal processes.

- Teams can solve a broad range of user problems, thereby minimizing specialization bottlenecks and improving time-to-market.

At the heart of Agile organizations are self-managing, cross-functional teams that solve end-user needs and create value for the company. In Agile organizations, the teams self-organize to use their full intellectual potential. And, if they organize suboptimally, they correct and continually adjust as they find out more—that is, through bottom-up intelligence.

Yet having many Agile teams is not sufficient for achieving agility at scale—you also need the right organizational design that enables those teams to be successful. Many traditional organizational designs based on the principles of Taylorism optimize more for control, predictability, and resource utilization than for adaptability and learning. Delayed learning makes it difficult to decide on the right product and process improvements, and rigidity makes reacting to new insights costly. Management faces the task of redesigning the organization so that agility at scale becomes possible.

Typically, this means:

- Organizing teams around products to optimize for satisfying customer needs

- Developing groups that can work across the whole product value stream to meet business objectives and market needs

- Moving to a management system that values adaptability and learning over control and predictability

Coaching organizations for adaptability starts with understanding the impact an Agile setup has on the current organizational design. Once an organization understands and accepts the design implications, the next step is to discover and develop an organizational structure that works in its specific context. People who create their own process will feel ownership of it, and therefore are more likely to evolve and improve it over time.

Intended Audience

We wrote this book with several audiences in mind. First are Scrum Masters and Agile coaches who guide teams and organizations in Agile adoptions. To them, this book offers not only practical coaching techniques but also deep insights into organizational dynamics and design implications.

We also wrote this book for managers who want to scale agility to their broader organization. They can change the organizational dynamics and interactions required for adaptability by redesigning organizational structure, policies, processes, human operations, and management behavior.

In general, this book will be helpful for anyone looking to improve their current Agile setup.

We hope that you, the reader of this book, will enjoy the benefits of *Creating Agile Organizations* and will be inspired to face your organizational design challenges head-on.

—Cesário A. Oliveira Ramos
Hengelo, The Netherlands

—Ilia Pavlichenko
Istanbul, Turkey

Introduction

This book is about transforming an organization into one that can respond effectively to market changes and delight the customer. It is about redesigning the organization into an Agile one as effectively and painlessly as possible to create continuous innovation and customer value.

Bringing agility into an organization is hard work, and it requires patience, humor, and long-term commitment. It can take many years to simplify your organization and discover how to make agility work in your organization. But once you have been through all that, you ought to be able to react more effectively to changing market conditions. Unfortunately, there is no magic wand you can wave to complete this transformation, nor is there an oracle you can consult who has all the answers to your problems. Instead, you must find *your* answers and discover your organizational model one step at a time.

Agility at the Organization Level

Many problems at the workplace are not the fault of the individual managers or teams. Instead, they are often the result of the organizational design in which those managers and teams work. According to Jay Galbraith, an organizational design consists of five major interrelated components[1]:

- **Strategy**: The primary direction of the company. The goals and objectives, values and mission, products or services to be provided, markets to be served, value offered, and sources of competitive advantage.

- **Structures**: The units, roles, responsibilities, and relationships.

- **Processes**: The flow of information, both horizontal (workflows, product development, value delivery) and vertical (business planning, budgeting), as well as the coordination between units.

- **Reward systems**: The alignment of employee goals with the goals of organization through salaries, promotions, bonuses, profit sharing, stock options, recognition, and challenging assignments.

- **People practices**: How to develop, rotate, and recruit people. Which capabilities and mindsets are needed.

Galbraith created the Star Model for thinking holistically about these components. When all components are aligned and reinforce each other, the organization is most effective because people get a consistent message about the appropriate behavior. In an Agile organization, this component alignment means that the organizational design supports—rather than limits—the people's ability to effectively adapt to customer demands.

For an organization to be effective, all the policies must be aligned and interacting harmoniously with one another.[2]

To implement this strategy, a company requires certain capabilities. These capabilities can be developed by ensuring the organization has the right processes, structures, people practices, and reward system in place. The reward system should be congruent with the structure and processes to influence the strategic direction. The challenge is to design each of these components into a system of work that allows the required Agile capabilities to be developed over time.

A Systems Thinking Approach to Adopting Agility

Why do people repeat the same unsuccessful behavior in organizations? Why do certain problems in organizations seem to appear again and again? Why aren't improvement actions leading to the expected results? What is probably going on is that the improvement actions are anti-systemic, acting on independent problem events without paying close attention to their relationships and deeper causes.

An organizational design includes, among other things, decisions about the division of work and the assignment of responsibility among units. When units coordinate to get the job done, they create complex interactions and feedback loops—the system's structure—that generate the observable recurring problems. You address these problems by understanding the system's structure and then redesigning the organization to create new interactions at the workplace.

> A classic example of system effects: We observe a slight decrease in productivity in a software development team and the team gets behind schedule. As a quick fix, project management pressures the developers to step up and "just make it happen." This quick fix solves the problem for the upcoming release because the developers take shortcuts and lower quality to meet the schedule. For the next release, the team works with a lower-quality system, so their productivity is worse than before owing to the accumulation of the technical debt. What will likely happen is project management pressuring the development team again, worsening the situation. Both parties behave "rationally" from their point of view with good intentions.

When you see how the system of work constrains people's behavior, you realize that the recurring problems are mainly due to the system, not to the people themselves. Thus, working on the people when the problem is actually systemic in nature is not the right path to go down. You can achieve minor improvements at best.

> Continuing the preceding example: Release after release, management notices that the product quality is decreasing over time; there are many bugs and multiple user complaints. They decide to send the team to train on software quality. This action will likely help only in the very short term. Why? Because project management still pressures the team to meet the schedule. Eventually, the team is forced to cut corners again, even though they know how to write quality software: The system's dynamics are left intact and generate the same behavior patterns.

The system of work determines, to a large extent, how people cooperate, what the prevailing mental models are, and how work gets done. It also determines what is valued, which leadership style is employed, and even which color paint is used on the walls. To change all this takes time and requires that people unlearn old lessons and relearn new ones. The current organizational design decisions result from how the designers think the world works—their mental models. Thus, in Agile adoption, it's important to help the organization become aware of how the current system of work supports or obstructs achieving their agility goals. It can then use that understanding to make improvements to its systems.

The Importance of Self-Organization for Agility

The basis for agility is an environment of exploring new possibilities for improvement. Such an environment cannot overly constrain people's exploration with detailed procedures and rules because that reduces the space for innovative ideas—precisely the opposite of what is needed. Instead, management needs to support self-organization by establishing a few simple rules, a clear goal, and short feedback loops.

A classic example that shows how self-organization works is a flock of birds. How do they keep flying in the V-formation while they change direction and reach their goal? The answer lies in self-organization based on simple rules and frequent feedback. Although the flock of birds seems centrally organized, the individual behavior of the birds is not. Each bird organizes itself so that it does not lose sight of the others but also does not bump into the others. If we had to simulate this, we would have some simple rules. One of those rules could be something like: Always keep a distance between 30 and 50 cm from each other. The emergent behavior of the flock is the result. If we try to control the V-formation by managing the individual behavior of each bird, we will not be effective. There are too many interactions happening to be able to understand what is going on. Moreover, the emergent V-formation cannot be understood by studying each bird individually because it emerges from the interactions and feedback loops.

In our organizational context, by necessity, no single person can understand or know everything about the transformation and solve all the problems. You cannot have one person telling a large group of people exactly what to do. But you also cannot have a large group of people doing whatever they want when they want to. What you *can* do is provide clear focus and direction, ensure that people take responsibility for solving the problems that they own, and provide the support they deserve. Such an approach provides control and makes better use of the individuals' intellect, but also simultaneously gives them flexibility to explore solutions.

A New Role for Management

The role of operational management is likely to change. From our experience, many Agile organizations end up with fewer operational management roles. Why? Because a lot of the operational work becomes the responsibility of the teams. For example, a product person now makes decisions about the product, and the self-managing teams take care of coordination and decide how to do their work. Therefore, operational managers no longer need to divide the work, decide what people should do, or coordinate between people or teams. Instead, they can devote their whole intellect to making it possible for the teams to be successful. Improving the organizational system of work and mentoring people on problem solving is the new reality for them.

A Learning Organization

A large part of Agile adoption focuses on learning how to work with self-managing teams in short iterations of learning. People need to learn new things—for example, new work practices, team-work, and ways to lead Agile teams. Also, the decision-making process, communication structures, and measures of progress are subject to change. A second part of Agile adoption is the change to a mindset of continual improvement. This covers a broad spectrum of people—from R&D, business, and management to sales, marketing, and other disciplines.

There are roughly two ways to begin the transformation: either the organization is starting from scratch, or it has already been working with Agile for some time. In the former case, you have the benefit that you can start with a greenfield. A downside is that you are at the start line, and a long bumpy road lies ahead. But the latter case might be even worse! The organization might have been doing Agile for a long time—just doing it wrong and not getting the expected benefits. You will need to repair misunderstandings and facilitate relearning to help it take the next step.

When people immerse themselves in a new experience and uncover better ways of doing their work, the new experiences influence a person's mental model about how things work. Gradually new practices become "the way we do things here," and new patterns of behaviors emerge in the organization.

Ownership for Continual Improvement

In an article published in *The Journal of Personality and Social Psychology*,[3] Ellen J. Langer of Yale University described an experiment with lottery tickets to illustrate the phenomenon known as the illusion of control. Two groups were involved in this experiment. The people in the first group received lottery tickets that were preselected for them, while the people in the second group got to choose their tickets and numbers. When they had their tickets, the experimenter asked people in both groups to sell back their tickets. As predicted, the people who got to choose their tickets wanted to receive a higher amount of money than the ones who got a ticket assigned. Why does this happen? To quote the paper:

> [W]hen a chance situation mimics a skill situation, people behave as if they have control over the uncontrollable event even when the fact that success or failure depends on chance is salient.[3]

The people who chose their tickets also felt more ownership of them, which is an essential observation for us. When you create something yourself, you feel ownership of it, and once you own it, you might care enough to improve it. You can say the same thing about teams that create their work process: They feel ownership of their approach, which makes them take responsibility for improving it. Once teams discover and learn what works for them, they can share that learning with other teams across the organization. This process of lateral learning enables the organization to discover which changes it needs to make to build a model that works in its context.

Empirical Process Control

Successfully bringing agility into an organization is a journey of discovery and learning. There is no fixed end-state when you can say, "The transformation is done." Instead, the end-state is a dynamic one, in which new insights are continually used to improve the product, processes, and organizational design.

An organization needs to change itself to become Agile. The challenge is that one cannot know upfront exactly what needs to change or precisely how the future state should look; it is a complex problem of innovation. Such a problem cannot be solved by centralized control, imposed order, and prediction. Instead, you must use an empirical process in which you take an informed step forward, inspect the results, and then adapt your plan based on what was learned. This approach is not only useful for the adoption of an Agile organizational design, but also an essential part of running an Agile business.

The Scrum Framework

The Scrum[4] framework enables empiricism through transparency, inspection, and adaptation—and that is why we use the Scrum framework as the basis for the transformation process. Scrum is a framework that you can use to build your process; it is not a framework that builds your product. Methods give a sequence of steps to build a product—they are a procedure for accomplishing something—and tell you how to do things. However, Scrum makes you aware of problems that are preventing you from reaching your goals. Once these problems become clear, you have the opportunity to do something about them.

How to Start?

Having an inspiring or urgent reason to change is a precondition for a successful transformation. Without it, the chances of lasting change are slim. After all, why would we change if all is running perfectly? Once the reason is there, then the hard work begins.

A Quick Tour of the Book

This book shares how we applied many research findings to our Agile transformations as effectively and painlessly as possible. Readers will find the book most valuable if they have a good understanding of the Scrum framework. We don't intend for this book to be an introduction to Scrum.

The book can be roughly divided into two parts. The first part, *Foundational Concepts*, includes systems thinking, basics of flow and resource efficiency, guidelines for organizational design, preferred coaching approach, and guidelines for productive change. The second half of the book, *Applying the Concepts*, offers practical tools for large-scale organizational Agile adoption—for example, defining a product workshop, tools for preparing and facilitating large-scale Agile events, and guides for working with teams and leadership. The tools are explained using various real-life examples of organizations, Product Owners, and teams on their journey to becoming an Agile company.

The examples show how to prepare, structure, and guide large-scale Agile adoptions. They provide real-life examples of organizational designs, challenges, solutions, and pitfalls that you can learn from.

Finally, we share a few case studies that illustrate how Scrum can be used to apply agility successfully at a large scale.

Part I: Foundational Concepts

Chapter 1: Organizing for Adaptability focuses on the problems that organizations face when adopting agility at scale. It describes typical problems, organizational design flaws, and what must change if the organization is to be successful.

Chapter 2: Systems Thinking describes the overarching approach to improve on organization. We introduce the basic concepts and techniques and lay the foundation for the rest of the book.

Chapter 3: Optimize for Adaptiveness is about the strategic choices regarding optimization goals. It provides the basics of lean thinking and queueing theory to enable managers to make informed trade-offs between flow and resource efficiency.

Chapter 4: Agile Organizational Design describes organizational design principles for use when working at the leadership level of an organization.

Chapter 5: An Agile Adoption Approach provides an overview of the adoption approach. We share a bird's-eye view of the activities we found crucial for a large-scale adoption.

Chapter 6: Coaching for Change provides guiding principles on how to make the change successful in your organization.

Part II: Applying the Concepts

Chapter 7: Group Facilitation covers the many occasions in which you need to facilitate a group of people. In this chapter, we share how to prepare, design, and facilitate workshops.

Chapter 8: Preparing the Product Group describes how to do just enough preparation to successfully start your transformation. We explain how to align management around their objectives, identify what needs to change, define your product, and identify the organizational elements to form the product group.

Chapter 9: Launching the Product Group focuses on how to successfully launch the product group and prepare to work in the new organizational design. We provide a set of activities and techniques you can consider in your launch.

Chapter 10: Coaching Teams is about working with teams in a large group. We delve into what teams are and what you as a coach can do to guide team development. We discuss techniques you can use for coaching, and explore productive team relationships.

Chapter 11: Guiding the Product Ownership focuses on ways to create and service product ownership within a large product group. Who is the right person to lead the group? How you can move away from output and to outcome-based measures and how you can work with multiple teams are other topics covered in this chapter.

The book concludes with the **Appendix: Workshop Examples**, which highlight real-life examples to guide you on your own Agile transformation journey.

It is our hope that you, the reader of this book, will enjoy the benefits of *Creating Agile Organizations*, and be inspired to discover your path to agility.

References

1. Jay Galbraith et al. *Designing Dynamic Organizations: A Hands-on Guide for Leaders at All Levels* (Amacom, 2001).

2. Jay R. Galbraith. "Star Model." www.jaygalbraith.com/services/star-model.

3. Ellen J. Langer. "The Illusion of Control." *Journal of Personality and Social Psychology* 32, no. 2 (1975): 311–328. https://doi.org/10.1037/0022-3514.32.2.311.

4. "The 2020 Scrum Guide." https://scrumguides.org/scrum-guide.htm.

Acknowledgments

A very special thanks to our manuscript reviewers, who worked through the early versions of the manuscript to give us feedback. Thanks to Rick Ijspeerd, Craig Larman, Martin Mandischer, Hannes Eickmann, Annebeth van Hall, Elisabeth Geyer-Schall, Ademar Aguiar, Roman Lobus, Vincent Wensink, Arjen Uittenbogaard, Leise Astrid Passer Jensen, Denis Sunny, Venkatesh N. Krishnamurthy, Simon Reindl, Pascal Dufour, and Jowen Mei for their all their effort to point out mistakes, vague sections, missing parts, plain old errors, and opportunities for improvement.

We want to make a special mention of Jim Coplien, who spent many days providing detailed feedback. His brilliant and detailed comments, concrete suggestions, and provocative statements made us critically examine our manuscript and helped us dramatically improve its structure and content. Many of his remarks made us laugh and cry simultaneously; we want to share two of such comments:

> "This is not an experiment. It's just let's-fart-around-and-see-what-happens."

> "Again, this can be the topic of a whole university degree. Thank heavens you have dedicated a whole chapter to it. I will really feel prepared—almost as much as if I had a coaching certificate."

Thank you, Sensei, for being so hard on us; we humbly appreciate it!

Many thanks to Dave West and Kurt Bittner, who got us started writing this book. Our warmest thanks go to our editor from Pearson, Menka Mehta, who worked patiently with us through many missed deadlines to get this book to done.

And last, many thanks to our graphical artist Arqam ul Hassan for turning our sketches into outstanding graphics.

About the Authors

Cesário Oliveira Ramos works worldwide as a senior management consultant on large-scale Agile adoptions in the financial and high-tech industries. His international experience, strong background in technology, and passion for people make him an influential partner in organization design and in leading the adoption of Agile. Cesário has a MSc in mathematics and computing science from the University of Eindhoven and is also a Certified LeSS (Large-Scale Scrum) Trainer and Professional Scrum Trainer from Scrum.org. Outside of his consulting work, Cesário has served as a Java/C# developer, lead software architect, CTO, and product manager. He is also the author of *Create Agile Organizations, A Scrum Book,* and *EMERGENT: Lean & Agile Adoption for an Innovative Workplace.*

Ilia Pavlichenko leads Agile transformations in companies around the world. He is an organization design consultant with a rigorous focus on coaching senior management. Ilia regularly speaks at international Agile/Scrum conferences. Ilia is also a Certified LeSS (Large-Scale Scrum) Trainer and a Professional Scrum Trainer from Scrum.org. In the past he was a programmer, project manager, Scrum Master, and Agile Coach at multiple product organizations. Ilia is a candidate for Master of Sports in table tennis and streetlifting, and is a fan of Queen and Brian May.

PART I
FOUNDATIONAL CONCEPTS

1

Organizing for Adaptability

Agility is the ability of an organization to adapt to new conditions and to change its direction while creating maximum value and customer experience.
—Mike Beedle

The basic building blocks of an Agile organization are self-managing cross-functional teams that can create customer value. When you combine many such teams, you can create larger groups that self-organize effectively around the ever-changing market needs. To make that possible, you need to understand the typical problems and pitfalls that organizations face when adopting agility at scale, and what to change so that your organization can be successful.

Hello, VUCA World!

We live in exponential times—that is, a time when the speed of change is increasing exponentially. VUCA is an acronym used to describe or reflect on the volatility, uncertainty, complexity, and ambiguity of general conditions and situations.

Here are just a few facts to get us started:

- A business cycle that was 75 years long 50 years ago was only 7 years in 2017.

- As many as 93% of U.S. multinational enterprises are changing their business models.[1]

- A higher "percentage of profit and Revenue [have come] from NEW products and services in the last five years"—50% on average, and 70% in more competitive industries.[2]

- Half of the companies in the *Fortune* 500 have disappeared since the year 2000 (according to Pierre Nanteme, CEO of Accenture).

To cope with this fast-changing environment, it is not a surprise that organizations are striving for agility these days. Indeed, many organizations are now asking this question: How can we become sufficiently Agile to reach our goals? Although agility might help the organization to achieve some of those goals, it is not a silver bullet, and "responding to change" is not enough. The Agile approach is to work in customer-driven iterations that frequently deliver value to the end user or customer. Adopting Agile at scale requires a supporting organization design.

What Is an Agile Organization Design?

An organization has a design, just like a car. Likewise, software systems have designs, too. Each design has specific optimization goals it intends to achieve. For example, a key optimization goal when Toyota was developing its Prius car model was fuel efficiency and aerodynamics—but not maneuverability at top speed. You could try to win a Formula 1 race with a Prius, but that probably won't work.

The architecture that Amazon.com uses has as an optimization goal to be able to build many software components rapidly and independently. To make this possible, the company uses a service-oriented architecture.[3]

Another example is the Formula 1 pitstop team: Their configuration and process enable them to change the tires and refuel a Formula 1 car in less than 2 seconds (Figure 1.1).

Figure 1.1
Formula 1 pitstop team.

Many people are needed to achieve that goal. If you look closely at a pitstop in action, you will realize that each person spends most of the time waiting on others. You can observe that one person waits for the wheel nut to be removed so that he can then remove the old tire. Another person waits for the old tire to be removed so that he can then place the new tire; meanwhile, the person who removed the wheel nut is waiting for the new tire to be placed so that he can tighten the wheel nut again. The Formula 1 pitstop team process and the car it services are designed for speed, not for resource efficiency. But what happens if you bring a Formula 1 pitstop team and process to a big truck and ask them to change four tires in less than 2 seconds? You can try, but that probably will not work because the truck's design is not optimized for doing that; instead, it is optimized to meet other goals.

What Does Your Organization Optimize For?

Organizational designs have optimizing goals, too. An organizational design is a combination of roles, responsibilities, reward systems, coordination and reporting lines, structures, processes, and policies intended to execute the business strategy. A few examples of possible optimizing goals could be the following:

- **Resource efficiency:** Efficient use of people and other resources.
- **Ideation:** Maximize the number of innovative ideas and creativity.
- **Learning:** Gain knowledge about customers and their needs, the market, and new technology.
- **Security:** Critical information protection.
- **Speed:** Shortest time from idea to delivery.
- **Adaptability:** Ability for an organization to change direction fast and at a low cost.
- **Reliability:** Delivery with low deviations from the plan.
- **Safety:** Protection from danger, risk, or injury.
- **Quality:** Conformance to standards, product excellence.

Senior managers are organizational designers. They should pick a few optimization goals they believe are crucial for their organization to pursue so that it can reach its business objectives and communicate those goals to the whole organization. Alignment around optimization goals facilitates decision making and reduces ambiguity. In such a case, many management decisions about organizational design can be verified to see if they are in line with the chosen optimization goals.

Optimization Goals and Indirect Wishes

An organization should be aware of the difference between its optimization goals and its indirect wishes or business goals. Here are a few examples of the latter: reduce operational costs, increase revenue, or increase market share. Indirect desires are not influenced by the system of work directly, but rather are the intended outcome of working in such a system. For example, organizations often optimize for agility because they assume it will help them achieve their business objectives; agility itself is not the business objective, but rather the means to reach it. When an organization wants to optimize for agility, it needs a proper organizational design for that. But what does it mean to optimize for agility?

Optimizing Goals of an Agile Organization

According to Mike Beedle, agility is the capability of an organization to adapt to new conditions and to change its direction while creating maximum value and customer experience. We love this definition. This definition impacts an organization at two different levels. First, it addresses agility at the overall organizational level:

> *Flexibility is the ability and capacity to reposition resources and functions of the organisation in a manner consistent with the evolving strategy of management as they respond, proactively or reactively, to change in the environment.*[4]

Such flexibility is useful for reacting to opportunities by starting, combining, or ending products or services in an organization.

The second level is about the adaptability of products or services themselves and addresses the following question:

> *How can we effectively adapt our product to changing market demands fast to cope with changing user needs?*

An Agile organization can do both; however, in this book, we focus on the latter. An Agile organization is able to switch between working on one job to another both quickly and at low cost.

Changing direction is key, but you must also decide in which direction to go. How do you know in which direction to adapt? You need to have a feedback loop. Short feedback loops increase learning, so if you want to be Agile, you need an organizational design that optimizes for the following:

- **Learning about the value stream:** Learning quickly about users' needs, product features, and market trends. Speed of delivery is necessary but not sufficient. After shipment, you still need to gather feedback from the market, reflect on it, and act on it.

- **Learning about the product organization:** Having short feedback loops for the processes used, organizational design, technologies, and team capabilities.

- **Adaptability:** Being able to use both types of learning to change direction at the level of the product group by switching between jobs quickly and at a low cost while creating maximum value.

Typical Problems When Adopting Agility

It is relatively simple to achieve agility with one team that has all the needed competencies and technical skills; however, many larger organizations usually have multiple teams that need to work together on a single value proposition or product. They need to scale Agile across all those teams so that they can become adaptable at scale. But scaling what works so well for individual teams working separately to larger groups working together turns out to be a different and more difficult problem to solve. While each separate team might be Agile locally, that doesn't mean the group will also be Agile. An important reason for this difference is that the more teams there are, the more likely it becomes that they will specialize in a single function, skill, or technology—for example, product management teams, marketing teams, IT teams, development teams, or manufacturing teams. In an organization with such a structure, interdependencies typically exist between the teams. The unfinished product moves from one group to the other, with each group adding something before the product is delivered to the customer.

Specializing the teams facilitates integration within the specialization but complicates integration across the groups. Why? The teams are responsible for completing their part and then handing the product over to the next unit; therefore, they do not feel the need to communicate frequently with other teams. When they do communicate, they might even have difficulty understanding the other teams' perspectives. Numerous problems can follow from that. For example:

- A lack of customer and market information from the business teams makes it difficult for development teams to deliver successful products.

- The development teams might not necessarily focus on the requirements that the business department believes are the most important.

- The development teams might ignore requirements regarding manufacturability that increase manufacturing time and cost.

The more the teams specialize, the more likely it becomes that they cannot deliver end-customer value, but only provide a part of the desired value. All these parts need to be identified, planned, integrated, and coordinated to yield the complete end-to-end value before an organization can comprehensively understand what is going on. Much of this activity is unnecessary and delays learning and, therefore, the ability to adapt in the right direction.

Systems Thinking theory focuses on the complete picture to improve the end-to-end process; it involves studying the broader system behavior over time and using that understanding to improve. The important insight from Systems Thinking theory is that the performance of an interdependent group of teams depends primarily on how the teams are tuned, not on individual team autonomy or how the teams perform as separate entities. In Chapter 2, "Systems Thinking," we cover in more detail how to use this approach in Agile organizations.

The Functional Hierarchy Organization Design

Typical organization design is the functional hierarchy. As Peter Scholtes described in *The Leaders' Handbook*,[5] a severe accident between passenger trains in the year 1841 heavily influenced how we design our organizations today. According to Scholtes, the railroad company wanted to ensure that such an accident could not happen again. A decision had to be made about how to reorganize the railroad management system. The railroad had a choice between the two most well-known organization designs at the time—the military and the church. The military was a top-down hierarchical structure, whereas the church used a distributed structure. After careful consideration, the railroad opted for the top-down hierarchy because it optimized for control and enabled the company to find the cause of problems quickly. Its decision still influences current-day organizations, as illustrated in Figure 1.2.

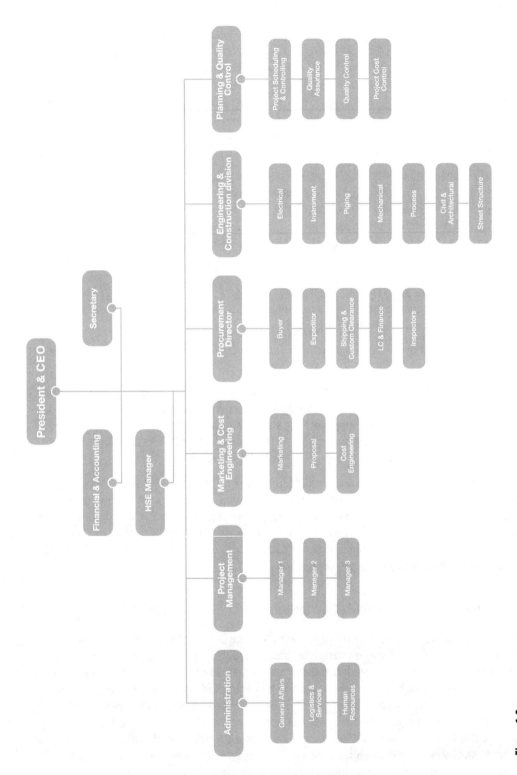

Figure 1.2
Hierarchy organization design.

Specializing the Work

In the first half of the 1900s, Henry Ford and Frederick Winslow Taylor heavily influenced management thinking. Ford introduced the very successful automobile production line, while Taylor focused on his scientific management approach. Both liked to specialize the work and divide work into separate functional tasks. Narrow functional tasks enabled people to concentrate on doing a simple job, so that people with poor or no education could work efficiently.

Separate the Head from the Hand

Taylor also introduced the concept of *separating the head from the hands*. Educated people would design the process and partition the work into dumbed-down tasks, and then people could be attached to those tasks. Furthermore, Taylor stated that there was a best way of doing the work and that management's job was to find that one best way and then let the workers do it. Along with the best way came measures, and later key performance indicators, and standard times for each of the tasks.

Ford had a similarly dim view of workers' capabilities, complaining, "Why is it every time I ask for a pair of hands, they come with a brain attached?" In Ford's system, people were only as valuable as the simple, repetitive tasks that they could perform. In essence, they were viewed as "interchangeable, nameless, and faceless."

Fast Forward to Present Times

In organizations that do large-scale development, much of the thinking advocated by Taylor and Ford still prevails today. These organizations are designed as a series of functional groups, with the aim being that each of the groups work individually at maximum efficiency. The resulting silos are managed by single-function managers and have measures—key performance indicators—to assess how well they are performing. Figure 1.3 illustrates a typical example of such an organizational design in the context of software development.

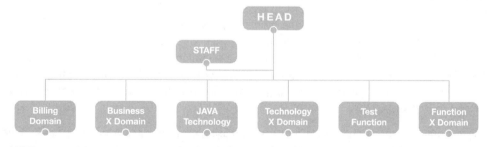

Figure 1.3
Typical silo organizational design in modern times.

You can see domain groups that specialize in a part of the business—for example, billing. Next to that, you can see specialization in technology such as Java, as well as specialization along with functions such as testing or marketing. There is nothing wrong with this kind of functional hierarchy as long as its optimizing goals are in line with your organization's goals and it helps you in reaching your business objectives. John Kotter, Professor of Leadership, Emeritus, at the Harvard Business School, highlights some important goals of this kind of hierarchy:

> [A]t both a philosophical and a practical level, the Hierarchy (with its management processes) opposes change. It strives to eliminate anomaly, standardize processes, solve short-term problems, and achieve stopwatch efficiency within its current mode of operating.[6]

The Agile optimizing goals are not in line with the purpose of the functional hierarchy. This organizational design invites managers to optimize the silos separately, but customer value flows horizontally across silos—not vertically across the hierarchy. So, if you want the organization to learn fast and use that learning to correct its direction, you need to focus on how the silos interact, not on how they perform separately. This implies minimizing costs when switching between jobs and getting the work through your organization as effectively as required. But how do you do that? By minimizing task switching costs and transitioning from resource efficiency to flow efficiency. In the context of software development, for resource efficiency it is more important to ensure each team always has a feature to work on. For flow efficiency, it is more important that a feature is always being worked on. So, in an organization focused on resource efficiency, the work is likely queued before each team with the goal of always keeping them busy. In contrast, in an organization that emphasizes flow efficiency, the goal is for teams to always be ready to pick up work, which implies that teams are expected to learn to understand and work effectively on multiple topics; if there is nothing to work on, then the teams must be idle sometimes.

An excellent way to achieve agility is by redesigning your organization. If you are not willing to make this effort, then scaling Agile in an organization with a functional hierarchy design will get you into trouble quickly, as we will show next.

Avoid Copy–Paste Scaling: A Typical Scaling Approach

Scaling is about increasing in size. Fire departments, for example, scale their operations depending on the severity of the fire. Depending on the scenario, they may increase the size of the trucks, the number of vehicles, the number of people, and the coordination and communication process as needed. This approach is what Cesário Ramos calls *copy–paste scaling*.[7] You "copy" the trucks and people needed and "paste" them to form a larger group while adding extra processes for communication and coordination.

When you apply this approach to Agile, it means increasing capacity by copying and pasting Agile teams in your development group. To support and coordinate this growth, organizations typically augment their teams with special roles such as *project managers* or *feature owners*. They also add extra layers of coordination, such as *release management*; extra process steps, such as *integration test phase*; and even additional artifacts, such as *system specifications* and *team work packages*.

Unfortunately, this results in reduced team–customer collaboration because the teams start to focus on the added coordination roles, the intermediate artifacts, and the revised processes. As a result, you are now decreasing the feedback loops and slowing down rather than speeding up.

Let us provide an example.

One of our clients operates in the energy trading business and has a distributed development group across three sites. It initially started with a few Scrum teams, but quickly scaled up to 16 teams due to market demands over a couple of months.

The development group supports a business process that consists of several steps and technical components, including User Interface, Database, and Workflow. aturally, following a copy–paste scaling approach, they formed their Scrum teams around the steps and components. Each Scrum team had its team Product Backlog, Scrum Master, and team Product Owner. To serve the teams, they had to divide each feature into separate parts corresponding to their specialty. Hence, each team could only deliver a feature part, even though feature delivery mainly required work across multiple business process steps and components. As a result, the teams needed extensive planning and coordination to try to align their work and deliver an integrated product.

In this organizational design, the teams delivered their feature parts out of sync. Why? Because the work that each needed to do for a feature part was not equal. For example, a feature might require a lot of work on the User Interface and very little work on the Database. This imbalance in teamwork meant delayed testing and customer validation until all teams completed their part. Hence, this approach led to long feedback loops and opaque measures of progress. The result was low productivity, high defect rates, and unhappy customers.

Overview of an Agile Organization Design

Many Agile teams use the Scrum framework to get their work done. Scrum was first presented to the broader audience at the 1995 OOPSLA conference as an enhancement of the iterative and incremental approach to software development. Just like many other Agile approaches, Scrum was designed to work with small self-managing cross-functional teams; initially, those teams were defined as including no more than six people.[8]

A Scrum team works in short cycles called *Sprints* that enable feedback about progress toward a goal:

Scrum is a lightweight framework that helps people, teams, and organizations generate value through adaptive solutions for complex problems.[9] —**The 2020 Scrum Guide**

In this book, we use the Agile team as the basic building block of an Agile organization. When you combine many such teams, you can create larger Agile groups that solve complex problems in short cycles.

What Is an Agile Team?

In the book *Creating Effective Teams*, the authors distinguished between a group of people and a team:

> *A work group is composed of members who are striving to create a shared view of goals and to develop an efficient and effective organizational structure in which to accomplish those goals. A work group becomes a team when shared goals have been established and effective methods to accomplish those goals are in place.*[10]

A very important characteristic of Agile teams is that they feel collective ownership of their work and problems. In such a team, its members work on shared goals, and tasks apply to the whole team rather than to individuals. The members also understand and accept their team roles and regularly put team goals above their personal work goals.

The definition of a team provided by Peter G. Northouse, a professor emeritus at Western Michigan University, provides us with a description that applies closely to a team in Scrum:

> *A team is a type of organizational group that is composed of members who are interdependent, who share common goals, and who must coordinate their activities to accomplish these goals.*[11]

Just as on a Scrum team, the members of an Agile team are interdependent and must coordinate to get results. One can expect to find trust, an environment of psychological safety, and confidence among team members regarding their capabilities. Everyone in the team participates in decision making and owns the team decisions; decisions are made based on knowledge, not on hierarchical position.

Another definition provided by Jon R. Katzenbach, highlights the fact that team members have complementary skills and hold themselves accountable:

> *A team is a small number of people with complementary skills who are committed to a common purpose, performance goals, and approach for which they hold themselves mutually accountable.*[12]

Although each of these definitions is slightly different, they agree that a team is a group of people who depend on each other's skills to accomplish shared goals. The critical point is that team members do not have an independent job to do, but rather must work together to produce some value—like a product.

How do these small teams work together at scale? We will answer these questions throughout the entirety of this book. For now, we start with an overview of the organizational characteristics you can expect to find in any Agile organizational design.

Structural Characteristics

One can consider a single Scrum team as a small product organization and value stream design. The team design is such that it has all the competencies required to turn its work into increments of customer value delivered in short cycles. You can give the most valuable feature—a complex problem—to such a team, and they can independently deliver a solution into the customer's hands. Working with such a team offers various Agile benefits to an organization, including the following:

- The team can always work on the most valuable work.

- Team independence decreases the time to deliver an increment of value—that is, it increases flow.

- Working in short cycles allows for the possibility of changing direction.

- Team autonomy promotes ownership of team results and team processes.

- Working directly on an end-user problem improves understanding of the customer problem domain.

How can you get the same benefits when you have many teams working on a common goal? When each team can independently deliver the most valuable work into the hands of the customer at least every cycle. We call such a team a *feature team*[13] and consider it to be a key element of an Agile organization (Figure 1.4).

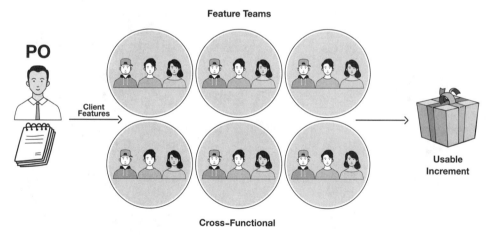

Figure 1.4
Feature teams.

Agility at Scale

A standard view is that scaling agility represents a change for teams only. Therefore, the system of management, the organizational structure, and the policies remain the same. Working in an organizational design like the functional hierarchy, however, makes it almost impossible to achieve agility at scale. Therefore, management faces the task of redesigning the organization so that agility at scale becomes possible. Typically, this means:

- Organizing a product group around your product or services to optimize for solving customer needs.

- Developing teams that can deliver end-user value that meet business objectives and market needs.

- Moving to a management system that values transparency, learning, and adapting to new realities over detailed planning and measuring performance against them.

What would such an Agile organization look like? The prototype of this organization would have a few shared functions along with the strategic management. The rest of the organization is mainly organized around semi-independent product groups, as illustrated in Figure 1.5.

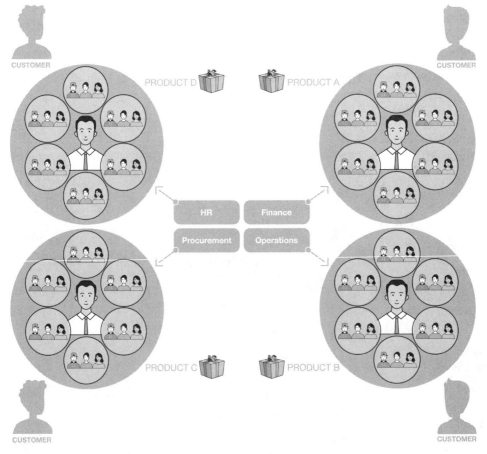

Figure 1.5
Prototype of an Agile organization.

When a product group consists mainly of feature teams, then coordination costs go down. Why? Teams that belong to the same product unit coordinate effectively because they report to the same manager, adopt the same goals and priorities, and share the same resources. The flow of work also increases because by grouping interdependent roles in the product units and in the teams, the teams waste less time on alignment and coordination activities. Over time, members of the product group are likely to develop a shared culture, further facilitating collaboration.

In general, you would expect to see the following structures and responsibilities in an Agile organization:

- Semi-independent product groups with separate leadership, finances, resources, and people, which may be augmented with shared services such as purchasing, sales, human operations, and finance.

- A person at the senior management level with a deep understanding of the product and process leading the product group.

- Operational management that is responsible for developing people through mentoring and improving the system of work.

- Teams that are responsible for delivering quality products. Working in such a team encourages shared team responsibility instead of individual responsibility for doing a specialized task. The teams are organized so that they have all the skills required to provide end-to-end value for customers without depending on people outside the team. Independence enables autonomous and fast-moving organizations.

- People who take responsibility for their process improvement. They own and solve the problems that occur in their daily work to improve agility.

Characteristics of Processes and People Practices

Which processes, people practices, and measures can you observe in an Agile organization? In Chapter 4, "Agile Organizational Design," we share an extensive overview. For now, Table 1.1 provides a brief summary.

Table 1.1   Typical Agile Organization Characteristics

Key Processes	People Practices	Measures
Teams are kept stable to allow them to develop into high-performing teams. It takes time for a team to grow and for people to develop a feeling of ownership of their process and product.	Operating in cross-functional teams means that the team members are willing and able to pick up work outside of their main expertise so as to always make progress as a team. Individuals have their deep expertise but also develop skills in different disciplines to become multifunctional specialists. Multifunctional specialists reduce bottlenecks created by the work imbalance across the different functions.	Team success is measured based on business outcome measures, not delivery outputs. The measures are derived from the purpose of the product or service and are expressed in terms of customer value and business impact.

Key Processes	People Practices	Measures
The teams work closely with the end users or (internal) customers to thoroughly understand their problems and needs. They use that learning to decide how to develop and improve their product or service.	People receive frequent feedback on their work. They use this feedback to develop their competence as well as their skills. Developing people is considered a key management focus.	The group is aware of their process effectiveness so that they can improve it. A more effective process will free up resources that can be either reinvested, relocated, or removed from the fixed cost.
Teams frequently validate the business and development assumptions made during development. The short feedback loops reduce risks and increase the possibilities to adapt effectively toward new insights.	People feel safe to fail, and there is room to learn. A two-year study by Google came to the following conclusion: "The highest-performing teams have one thing in common: psychological safety, the belief that you won't be punished when you make a mistake."[14]	
	Most people have a growth mindset and a passion for learning; they seek mastery of their abilities. The people value challenges and use them to put in the effort to learn and grow.[15]	

The organization's top management should clearly and unambiguously define what the optimization goals are and communicate those to members of the organization. Otherwise, the inconsistency between stated optimization goals and supporting organizational design decisions will create tensions and frustration in the field.

> *All teams will henceforth expose their data and functionality through services interfaces. Anyone who doesn't do this will be fired. Have a nice day.* —**Jeff Bezos, 2002 architecture mandate for Amazon.com**

Summary

Working with people who understand the *why* behind the new way of working is a crucial ingredient and lays the foundations for success. Management alignment on the optimization goals as well as co-creating an understanding of Agile principles and practices is an excellent first step to take.

The organizational design used severely impacts the organization's agility at the overall product level. The espoused optimizing goals must be supported by the organizational design to scale agility successfully. Unfortunately, when your current organizational design is based on a functional hierarchy, then you are likely optimizing for predictability, control, and resource utilization, and maintaining the status quo.

In contrast, agility at scale requires an organizational redesign so that you optimize for the right optimization goals. A senior manager who fills the role of organizational designer is needed.

References

1. KPMG. "Business Transformation and the Corporate Agenda." https://advisory.kpmg.us/articles/2017/business-transformation-and-the-corporate-agenda.html.

2. Robert G. Cooper, Scott J. Edgett, and Elko J. Kleinschmidt. *Best Practices in Product Innovation: What Distinguishes Top Performers* (Stage-Gate, 2003).

3. Peter Vosshall and Werner Vogels. "Dynamo: Amazon's Highly Available Key–Value Store." *ACM SIGOPS Operating Systems Review*, October 2007.

4. C. Koornhof. "Financial Flexibility and the Assessment of Future Cash Flows." *Investment Analyst Journal* 31 (1988): 13–19.

5. Peter Scholtes. *The Leader's Handbook: Making Things Happen, Getting Things Done* (McGraw-Hill Education, 1997), 2.

6. John Kotter. "Hierarchy and Network: Two Structures, One Organization." *Harvard Business Review*. https://hbr.org/2011/05/two-structures-one-organizatio.

7. Cesário Ramos. "Scale Your Product NOT Your Scrum." February 2016. https://www.agilix.nl/resources/ScaleYourProductNotYourScrum.pdf.

8. K. Schwaber. "SCRUM Development Process." In J. Sutherland, C, Casanave, J. Miller, P. Patel, and G. Hollowell, eds. *Business Object Design and Implementation* (Springer, 1997). https://doi.org/10.1007/978-1-4471-0947-1_11

9. "The 2020 Scrum Guide." https://scrumguides.org/scrum-guide.html.

10. Susan A. Wheelan. *Creating Effective Teams: A Guide for Members and Leaders*, 5th ed. (Sage, 2021), Chapter 1, p. 2.

11. Peter G. Northouse. *Leadership: Theory and Practice* (Sage Publications, 1997).

12. Jon R. Katzenbach. *The Wisdom of Teams: Creating the High-Performance Organization* (Harvard Business Review Press, October 13, 2015), 45.

13. Craig Larman and Bas Vodde. "Feature Team Primer." 2010. https://featureteams.org/feature_team_primer.pdf.

14. ReWork. "Guide: Understand Team Effectiveness." https://rework.withgoogle.com/guides/understanding-team-effectiveness/steps/introduction/.

15. Carol S. Dweck. *Mindset: The New Psychology of Success* (Ballantine Books, 2007).

2

Systems Thinking

Someone's sitting in the shade today because someone planted a tree a long time ago.
—Warren Buffett

How many times have you "improved" something in your organization, but the improvements didn't last long? Or how about those times when your quick fixes ended up having the opposite effect? And when was the last time you improved something and went far beyond your usual experience and thinking?

In this chapter, we introduce you to the world of *systems thinking*. In our humble opinion, having a systems view is an important skill for any learning organization that aspires to be vision-driven.

Systems thinking is a language and set of tools meant to illuminate our thinking about how the systems we are all part of actually operate.[1]

Several conceptual models are presented in this chapter: a framework for organizational learning, an iceberg model, creative tension, Causal Loop Diagrams (CLDs), and typical system stories that are called "archetypes." Theoretical concepts are accompanied by examples from organizational coaching.

Basics of Systems Thinking

Two Systems

In his book *Stumbling on Happiness*,[2] Dan Gilbert presented the results of interesting neurobiological research that showed our ability to think about the future developed at some point within the last 3 million years and is explained by the rapid growth of our frontal lobe (neocortex). Before this development, our ancestors lived in the "eternal present moment." By considering the relatively young age of our "thinking brain" in comparison to the "reptilian brain," it becomes clear why we want things now and not later. In his book *Thinking, Fast and Slow*,[3] Daniel Kahneman writes about the two different ways the brain forms thoughts:

- **System 1** works automatically and quickly. It is switched on by default and operates according to the "fight or flight" principle. It is the oldest part of the brain.

- **System 2** has to be switched on consciously, works slowly, and is responsible for the complex analysis of situations. In people, it is associated with prudent choices and concentration. It is located in the neocortex and developed recently.

Thousands of years ago, our ancestors fought for survival and any rustling or shadow in the bushes could become a mortal danger. The "fight or flight" principle helped us to quickly make life-or-death decisions. If our ancestors did not have a rapid and well-developed System 1, it is possible that you would not be reading this sentence. Our environment has changed, however. By contrast with our ancestors, who were concerned with the present and how to meet their own basic needs, we live in a world of digital technologies in a global postindustrial society. The majority of issues in our complex social systems cannot be best solved effectively using System 1.

The fixation on events, supported by System 1, distracts us from seeing longer-term trends or recurring patterns of system behavior. We are likely to address current problems with quick fixes, and do not ask ourselves what causes these patterns to emerge. Without an understanding of these patterns, which requires us to apply System 2, we cannot learn to create new structures that generate new patterns of behavior to solve these problems. To better understand such behavior, we use systems thinking.

When to Apply Systems Thinking and Which Problem Does It Solve?

Systems thinking broadens the number of available solutions and helps us to understand how these solutions impact other parts of the system. Problems that are perfect for systems thinking tend to have the following common characteristics:

- The issue is a significant one.

- The problem is chronic and not a one-off event.

- The problem is familiar and has a well-known history.

- People have previously tried to solve the problem to no avail.

With systems thinking, we apply methods and tools that help us to discover a better understanding of dynamic complexity. This approach also provokes discovery and learning. People gain knowledge from their experience, by trying new things and getting feedback on whether and how it works. The speed of the feedback plays an important role for motivation and learning.

Feedback is the breakfast of champions.[4]

For example, imagine that you want to learn how to play the piano, but you are only allowed to hear the sound of your keystrokes a week later. How would that affect your learning? It will make it much harder, if not practically impossible, for most people to learn to play the piano. Nevertheless, some great discoveries in history evolve as slow hunches,[5] maturing and connecting to other ideas over time.

In organizations, the feedback loop is often broken or severely delayed. In consequence, learning at the system level is problematic. This kind of problem happens when people have a narrow set of accountabilities and are able to make decisions only locally. Peter M. Senge, an American systems scientist and the author of the seminal book *Fifth Discipline*,[6] speaks about a limited "decision horizon," where people have a narrow horizon to observe the effects of their decisions. People end up fixing problems locally and, at the same time, degrade the situation for their colleagues.

> *Over 90% of the problems that arise in a corporation are better solved somewhere other than where they appear.*[7]

Systems and Collections

The simplest definition of a system that we have found is this:

> *A group of **interrelated** and **interdependent** parts, which form a complex and unified whole that has a specific purpose.*[8]

The words "interrelated" and "interdependent" appear in this definition in bold font, since without interdependencies, it is a collection and not a system. For example, a grain of sand on a beach, forks and spoons laying on the table, and books in a library are well-known examples of collections.

> *Without interdependencies, it is a collection and not a system.*[8]

When a cook enters the kitchen, then they, in a sense, unite the ingredients using cooking tools and a recipe into a meal. Through the act of cooking, these parts become a system. Often, it is only by adding a person to the collection of parts that its purpose emerges and the system is born. Of course, the context is king. From one perspective, something might be a system; from another, it might not.

Organizations as Complex Social Systems

In his book *Re-creating the Corporation*,[7] Russell Ackoff categorizes systems according to several types. The critical classifying variable is the purpose that exists where there is choice:

- **Deterministic:** A clock, a toaster, a car, a thermostat, an airplane, Neither the parts nor the whole is purposeful.

- **Animate:** Animals, a person, living organisms. The whole is purposeful, but not the parts.

- **Social:** A team, family, product group, organization, university, society. Both the whole and the parts are purposeful.

- **Ecological:** A forest, jungle, planet. The parts are purposeful, but not the whole.

An entity is purposeful if it can select both means and ends in two or more environments.[7]

The four types of systems are nested and form a hierarchy, as illustrated in Figure 2.1. For example, a human being (animate system) consists of deterministic systems (heart, kidneys, brain). An autopilot algorithm (a deterministic system) carries out an objective that is inherent to it and cannot abandon it. Social systems consist of animate systems (people) and are part of larger social systems. Understanding the types of systems is important, as different types of systems require the use of different tools and approaches to understand them.

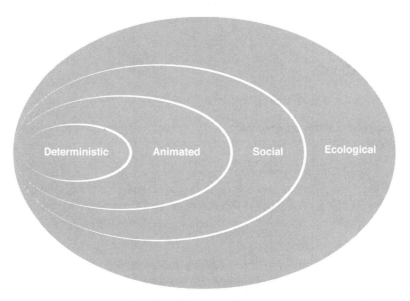

Figure 2.1
Nested systems.

A product development effort is a system, and it is part of a larger system, which might be a product area, a product organization, or the whole company. In turn, we need to regard software development as a social system in which the needs and purpose of the whole and parts influence its performance. Only then can we address the underlying problems and achieve long-lasting improvements, because only then can we learn at the system level and use that understanding to improve the whole.

Linear and Systems Thinking

Some life situations do not demand a systemic approach. We know how to strike a nail into the wall, pack a suitcase, or get to our friend's house on their birthday. From our childhood, we have been accustomed to perceiving the world in a linear fashion and seeking a clear connection between cause and effect. We see the world as a sequence of linear events, each of which is a consequence of the previous event (Figure 2.2).

$$A \longrightarrow B \longrightarrow C \longrightarrow D$$

Figure 2.2
Linear sequence.

This kind of approach works well with deterministic systems. We know what to do with a broken clock, car, or mechanism, even if it is very complicated. We must find an expert who will discover the cause of the malfunction and fix it.

But in complex social systems, the situation is quite different. Human behavior is more complex, unpredictable, and often irrational. Social systems consist of elements that affect one another and have feedback cycles (Figure 2.3).

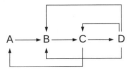

Figure 2.3
Feedback cycles.

Here's a simple example. A team complains that it doesn't devote enough effort to writing automated tests. The manual testing that is required takes a lot of time and effort, and there is no time left for writing automated tests. Where do the cause and effect lie? Cause and effect could be shown as a cycle, as in Figure 2.4.

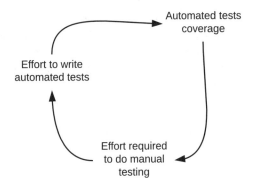

Figure 2.4
What are the cause and effect?

Define the Boundary of the System Wisely

The system boundary is a conceptual line that divides the system that you want to study from "everything else." It is a critical decision that affects what you optimize afterward. If you have an issue in understanding influences and relationships within the system, probably you defined the boundaries too loosely. Conversely, if you find too many influences exist outside of the boundaries, probably you set the boundaries too tightly. The following example describes a situation in which the boundary of our coaching intervention was set unwisely and prevented us from making a better impact in organizational coaching.

We worked with a company with an R&D office in eastern Europe and sales and marketing departments in California. Although we had good contacts and a certain level of influence on the U.S. part of the organization, we focused more on the R&D office. There were so many things to do there! The product group chronically committed to highly ambitious quarterly goals and never reached them. Because of these unrealistic goals, much more work than could be handled was pulled into the Sprints. That increased both average work-in-progress (WIP) and average cycle times. The long cycle times resulted in further unrealized commitments to the customers, affecting the sales and marketing departments. Therefore, the next quarter the product group strived for even more ambitious goals—and, again, didn't reach them. Teams knew that their goals were unrealistic and constantly complained that the head of the product group pushed them to overcommit.

We decided to help the product group to balance capacity with the incoming work. As we were invited to facilitate the quarterly planning, we decided to intervene and implement planning based on empirical data—we aimed to help the product group to draft realistic product goals and pull work based on their past performance.

The head of the product group agreed with our proposal. After a day of intensive planning, nine teams had a high-level plan that was very realistic according to a closed voting session. When managers at the U.S. office saw the plan the next day, they were shocked, to say the least. They were very angry and actively protested. We didn't take into account the fact that the company depended on external investment. The company was preparing for a Series-C funding round, and its external commitments were at least twice more ambitious than the plan we had developed with the teams. Unfortunately, our efforts were solely focused on the R&D office and didn't take into account the sales and marketing departments, key stakeholders, and external company commitments.

This principle is not limited to the boundary of a coaching. It applies to:

- Definition of the product
- The size of the value areas (see the Scrum pattern Value Area)
- Speed of Agile transformation and number of product groups you launch

Definition of the product and value areas are discussed in detail in Chapter 8, "Preparing the Product Group." Speed of Agile transformation is addressed in Chapter 5, "An Agile Adoption Approach."

Work on the System

We often show a picture that depicts the organizational design of the product group that we collaborated with. Have a look at the diagram in Figure 2.5. What do you notice?

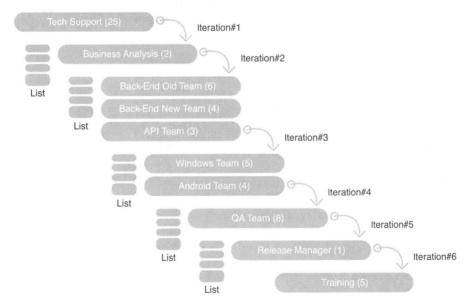

Figure 2.5
Sequential development.

- The work is organized around teams with a narrow work focus: analytics, backend, Android, Windows, and so on.
- Due to the multiple dependencies, the teams transfer their part of work that has been completed from iteration to iteration to the next team.
- The chain is completed by the "release manager," who outputs the new functionality as a large package to production for the clients.
- When measuring the lead time, we noticed that it is long and spans several Sprints (2–3 months).

Which major factors influence the performance of the whole system? Usually, we pose this question to the group and then give them a few minutes to generate as many factors as they can. We ask to place the factors into two columns: system and people. Figure 2.6 shows the typical result that emerges from this exercise.

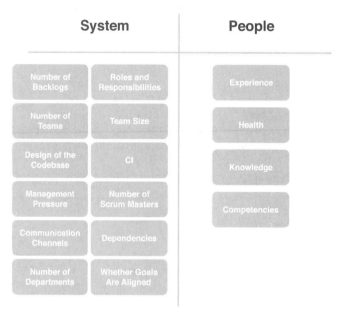

Figure 2.6
System and people.

We have conducted this experiment with top managers, developers, middle management, sales department staff, and market experts, but the result is always predictable: The majority of the stickers end up in the "system" column. Why is that?

> *The fact is that the system that people work in and the interaction with people may account for 90 or 95 percent of performance.*[9]

Deming wanted management to optimize an organization's system as a whole and not according to its parts. His seminal book *Out of the Crisis*[9] is a critique of the widely accepted model of management at that time, which is based on the principles of *scientific management*[10] (Taylorism). Systems thinking explains why this is not the best approach to maximize system performance: The system actually depends on the interaction of its parts, rather than on how effectively they work in isolation.

In Figure 2.6, you might notice that the entries describe an organizational design in which teams and people work in specialized fields. Dependencies between teams cause massive queues between teams because each team is focused on maximizing its local performance. As Donald G. Reinertsen stated in his book *The Principles of Product Development Flow*,[11] queues are the main cause of the majority of economic waste in product development. Queues increase cycle time, risks, variability, and costs. They also reduce quality by delaying feedback from the downstream process. That usually results in unsatisfactory time-to-market and organizational stress (the business is upset, customers are unhappy, developers get delayed feedback) for the system, as depicted in Figure 2.7.

Figure 2.7
Organizational stress.

Managers are often amazed that people in different departments, whose efficiency is determined by local key performance indicators (KPIs), interact poorly. They don't understand why people are not willing to learn things outside their current expertise within the existing reward system. Likewise, they can't fathom why clients do not receive high-quality support if a maximum time limit has been placed for processing the request. But is it really a surprise that a sales department staff member does everything possible to close a sale (even if it is not in the client's interests) when their KPI and quarterly bonus are tied to the number of sales?

People do not wake up in the morning with the idea of how to get their company into trouble. The overwhelming majority honestly carry out their work, but are constrained by the system and organizational structures. In systems thinking, the primary "switch" for a change in the organization is in the system. Attempts to change an organizational culture while keeping the organizational design intact are naive and doomed to failure.

> *People's behavior is a product of their system. Changing the system gives rise to a change in people's behavior.*[12]

Iceberg of Systems Thinking

People have different life experiences. Our childhood experiences, family values, and social environment all contribute to our beliefs, convictions, and values, which are then refined during the course of our lives. Organizational structures are the product of the mental models of their constructors—that is to say, of the managers of the organizations. They reflect what those managers believe and what their life experiences tell them.

Systems and their structures shape the sustained patterns of behavior in companies. They contribute a lot to what we call a "culture." Behavior that is consistently demonstrated three times or more is called a *pattern*. Separate, unrelated incidents are called *events*. Figure 2.8 illustrates how experience, mental models, systems structures, patterns of behavior, and events are connected in a model called the *iceberg of systems thinking*.

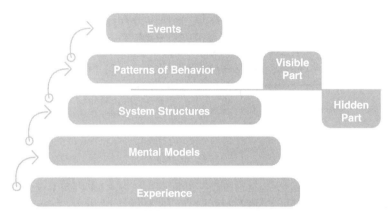

Figure 2.8
Iceberg of systems thinking.

To understand is to perceive patterns.—**Isaiah Berlin**

For example, in one company we noticed that the Scrum Masters often resigned in early January. The structure that supported this pattern was hidden—namely, a bonus that was given only at the end of the year. People were incentivized to stay for a while at the company even if they made a decision for themselves to leave the organization. Individual events were at the top of this particular iceberg.

Figure 2.5 showed an organizational design identified by our clients. We studied this system from the inside and mapped our findings onto the system iceberg as follows:

- **Events:** Delay in delivering value to the market on January 14, with 23 bugs identified in the production environment after release.

- **Patterns:** Multiple buggy and delayed releases over time, dependencies between teams, people blaming each other, developers not willing to learn new skills. The problems got worse over time.

- **Structures:** Functional and component teams created local identities and made people focus on improving the performance of the separate parts. The human resources (HR) policies encouraged individual efficiency and limited people in their multi-skill development.

- **Mental models:** It is "productive" and "efficient" to have narrow specialists in the organization; everyone should be busy to maximize success.

Problems in an organization can observed in the form of events. If you try to resolve such events in isolation, you might miss their deeper causes. When you take a step back and look at how the events unfold over time, you might recognize patterns of system behavior—that is, recurring events. The structures of the system generate these patterns. So, if you make interventions at the structure level, you are generating new patterns of system behaviors—in essence, you are creating a new future. Interventions at the event level are reactive. The structures remain intact, so the events will likely keep repeating. In contrast, interventions at the structure level are generative.

Analyzing the Current Situation

The questions in Table 2.1 are useful to discover events, patterns, and structures in organizations. We prefer to use them in workshops to jointly create an understanding of what is happening.

Table 2.1   Questions for Discovering Events, Patterns, and Structures

Events	What happened?
	What are some of the notable events?
Patterns	What's been happening?
	How has performance changed over time?
	What are other important trends?
	What is changing? and why is it changing?
Structure: Identify cause–effect relationships	What has caused this change in performance?
	What are some of the tangible or physical factors contributing to these patterns?
	What are some of the intangible factors (including beliefs, values, and mental models) that may be contributing to these patterns?
	What are some of the consequences of changes in performance?
	Do any of the consequences become causes of further erosion or stagnation of performance?

The answers to these questions help you to move from reactive to generative intervention mode. Generative mode brings something new into being that did not exist before. As we move down the levels, our focus changes from being present-oriented to being future-oriented. Consequently, the actions that we take on lower levels are more impactful on future outcomes.

A useful technique to focus on patterns of change over time, rather than on isolated events, is a behavior over time graph (BOTG). Drawing these graphs, in combination with the questions from Table 2.1, creates engagement and lively discussion in workshops. It helps people think more deeply about what is happening and why.

A BOTG shows how your variables of interest behave over time. In the theoretical example in Figure 2.9, the key variables are *time-to-market*, *release quality*, and *number of people*.

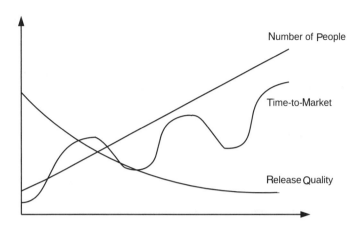

Figure 2.9
Behavior Over Time Graph.

The BOTG shows that the time-to-market keeps increasing while the quality of releases declines despite the hiring of more and more people. The graph also shows periodic improvements in the time-to-market, especially after the company hires new developers. We know that it is very unlikely that time-to-market will decrease if we simply add more people (see the book *The Mythical Man Month*[13]). So, there is likely something deeper going on—namely, taking shortcuts on quality, as shown by the "release quality" curve. The BOTG helps us build an initial theory about the current reality.

Organizational Learning and Creative Tension

Organizational learning is the ability to "continually expand the capacity for creating the future."[6] In other words, reliably producing desired results is evidence of organizational learning. Peter Senge describes the ability to produce results as a mastery of "creative tension" or maintaining clarity and attention on both the desired results (vision) and reality.[6] Actions that are taken because of an awareness of this tension tend to produce results that are more consistent with our vision, or aspirations, than actions that are simply a reaction to our circumstances.

> *The vision (what we want) and a clear picture of current reality (where we are relative to what we want) generates what we call "creative tension": a force to bring them together, caused by the natural tendency of tension to seek resolution.*[6]

To resolve creative tension, people either lower their vision to meet their current reality or take steps to change their current reality to match their vision. This decision-making process can be described in terms of the *responsibility process*[14] model. Lowering the vision is actually avoiding responsibility and may take several different forms: denial, laying blame, justification, shame, and obligation. Upholding a creative tension and making steps to change the current reality denote taking responsibility. We find that typically people lower their vision, so they do not have to experience the emotional stress that often accompanies living with a gap between their vision and the current reality. In part, this choice is driven by a desire for efficiency.

Figure 2.10
Creative tension.

Everyone who has Scrum experience knows how difficult it is to comply with the rules of this simple framework. Usually there is a gap between the current reality in the organization and the vision of Scrum. For example, the Scrum team needs to be cross-functional and able to create a useful increment at least once per Sprint. In practice, this simple rule is quite difficult to achieve, due to multiple impediments: functional and component teams' organizational design, lack of skills, internal politics, different kinds of dependencies, lack of modern engineering practices, and so on. Thus, many practitioners and novice Scrum Masters eventually give up and adapt the Scrum to reality, which results in a large number of shortcomings that are sometimes called *Scrum-Buts*.[15] The fundamental solution would be coaching the teams, the product owner, and the organization, which in time will lead to closing the gap. Ken Schwaber, the co-creator of Scrum, famously said:

> *Scrum professionals do not redefine Scrum itself or "tailor" it to their organizations; Scrum is Scrum.*

Leaders need to help people stay focused on their visions. Commitment to those visions offers the best proof that the future can become a product of our dreams and not merely a reaffirmation of the status quo.

Leaders need to be aware when teams and organizations are about to lower their vision and aim to bring them back. The next step would be confronting the current reality and facilitating the next steps to change it.

Applying Systems Thinking

In the previous sections, we've learned the basics of systems thinking. With the iceberg model, we can analyze the current situation and establish creative tension, thereby helping the organization learn. The next step is to take a deep dive into understanding the system structures using a Causal Loop Diagram (CLD).

Causal Loop Diagram

The CLD is one of the most widely used tools in systems thinking. It is a visual representation of the system structure that illuminates the relationships between key factors. Just like any other model, however, it is a simplification of reality. The CLD is qualitative and subjective and might not be based on hard facts.

*We always rely on models as all our decisions are based on a mental, incomplete understanding
of reality.*—**Forrester, 1961**

On the other hand, the CLD makes assumptions explicit and provides people with a space where
they can learn from each other. CLD creates a foundation for a dialogue.

We model to have a conversation. The output is shared understanding, not the model.[16]

By creating a CLD, people externalize their internal thinking processes. Now they can create a shared
understanding of reality and build an integrated model together. When system relationships are dis-
played on the wall, you as a coach are now able to ask powerful questions and coach the system.

The main elements of the diagrams in Figure 2.11 are as follows:

- Variables (behavior, condition)
- Cause–effect relationships (direct and opposite)
- Reinforcing and balancing loops (indicated by "R" and "B," respectively)
- Time delay
- Quick fix (QF)—that is, a non-fundamental solution
- A strong deterministic cause–effect relationship (the bold arrow)
- A short-term cause–effect relationship
- Mental models (the cloud icon) that stay behind the cause–effect relationships

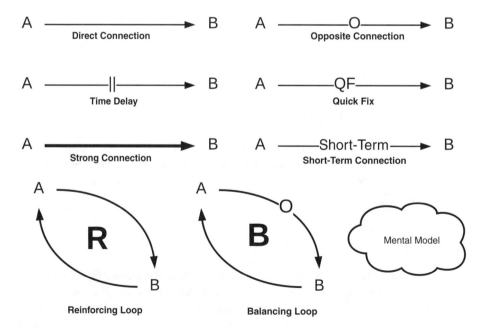

Figure 2.11
Organizational stress.

The variables are the core of the CLD. Correctly named variables help create a clear understanding of the situation at hand and allow the viewers to easily grasp the story. We recommend using neutral nouns or noun phrases—for instance, "time of delay," "return on investment," and "refined backlogs" instead of "more delay," "higher costs," and "refining backlogs," respectively.

A CLD Example

Let's construct our first system diagram. It will illustrate the story that we observed in one particular company. This company operated in the financial industry, and the team was developing a mortgage product. The actual speed of development caused a deviation with the upfront "committed schedule." System 1 had provided a quick fix, but it put pressure on the team. The greater the pressure, the less time the team spent on writing tests and refactoring code because they were focused on creating features as fast as possible, albeit at the expense of quality. The speed of development increased for a while, and deviation from the "committed" schedule decreased. Meanwhile, the temporary increase in velocity reinforced the mental model "We need to put pressure on a team to get results." Figure 2.12 illustrates the balancing loop (B1) in this scenario.

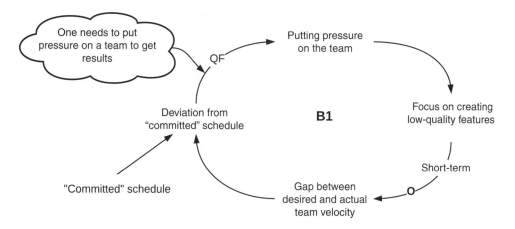

Figure 2.12
Pressuring the team.

Balancing loops always have an inherent goal, whether it is visible or not. The basic structure of a balancing loop involves a gap between the goal (or desired level) and the actual level. In this case, it is a gap between the desired and actual team velocity. Balancing processes try to bring conditions into equilibrium. Let's have a look at how the events progressed at our example company.

In time, the focus on creating features at the cost of the quality led to a large technical debt that seriously hindered the team. In turn, the team velocity noticeably declined. The pressure remained, however, because the mental model had not changed. Why? Because pressuring the team got a quick result and this cause–effect relationship is easily remembered. The cause and effect between pressuring the teams and the slow accumulation of technical debt is harder to see because of the time delay, which could be many weeks. Figure 2.13 shows the reinforcing loop (R2), which in time became the dominant one in the system.

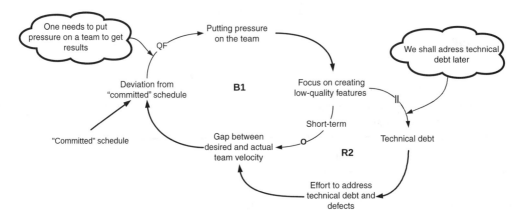

Figure 2.13
Technical debt.

Reinforcing loops are self-reinforcing, which means they compound change in one direction with yet more change. If not stopped, they continue to reinforce a particular behavior. One quick method to determine if the loop is reinforcing or balancing is to count the number of O's. If there are an even number of O's (or zero), the loop is reinforcing; if there are an odd number, it is balancing.

Figure 2.13 illustrates nonlinear effects and delays that hinder understanding the system. The story represents a familiar archetype in systems thinking: "fixes that backfire."[17] Similar stories are commonplace in product development. The organization believes that it can demand anything from development; developers unfortunately reinforce this conviction with a reduction in quality.

Shared Responsibility

Who is responsible for the system dynamic described in the previous section—management or development? The truth is, it's everyone, because they are all part of the same system. As we figured out earlier, patterns of behavior are the product of the structures and mental models. In this particular case, management was concerned with meeting the schedule to which it had committed upfront. The company was covered by a network of such "commitments" that cascaded from above. Top managers had made commitments to the board of directors, and then required similar commitments from their subordinates, and so on.

> *The primary purpose of mapping a system is to stimulate catalytic conversations that lead to shared insights and shared responsibility, which in turn provide the foundation for coordinated action.*[1]

Summing up, there are several valid benefits for using CLDs:

- They involve the slow and higher-quality System 2, which is necessary for analysis, and, subsequently, the adoption of well-considered solutions in complex social systems. To achieve this outcome, large group facilitation is helpful.

- Systemic diagrams help to unfold the structures and mental models that generate patterns.

- If CLDs are created in a group setting, people are more likely to take responsibility for suggested improvements, because everyone understands that they are part of the same system. As a result, people come up with better decisions.

Doom Loop Technique

We are often asked how to become experienced in creating CLDs. It takes some time to develop decent skills, and the secret is practicing a lot.

We would like to introduce you to a nice starter technique, called the "doom loop." This technique consists of several steps to help you build your first CLDs, as illustrated in Figure 2.14 and described here:

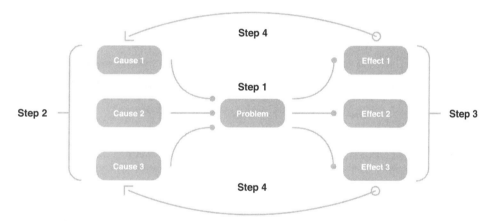

Figure 2.14
Doom loop technique.

Step 1. Put the key variable that reflects the problem in the center of the diagram.

Step 2. Generate one to three variables that might be the cause or severely affect the problem. Place them to the left of the key variable and link them with it. Additionally, you can apply the "five whys"[18] technique.

Step 3. Generate one to three variables that are the effects of the problem. Place them to the right and link them with the key variable.

Step 4. Try to identify connections between effects and causes.

If necessary, add additional variables to refine the diagram.

Example: Using the Doom Loop Technique

We used the doom loop technique at a bank and invited Scrum Masters, Product Owners, and management to the workshop. We were eager to dig deeper into a problem that everyone understood: postponed releases. We started with an introduction to systems thinking and taught the workshop participants the basic language of CLDs.

Throughout the workshop, participants worked in small groups of no more than five people, creating their own CLDs. We alternated cycles of convergence and divergence, giving them the opportunity to synchronize their diagrams. You can use techniques: *Shift and Share,*[19] *World Café,*[20] and *roulette*[21] for effective facilitation. The workshop resulted in the diagram shown in Figure 2.15. By the end of the workshop, participants agreed on a few improvement actions.

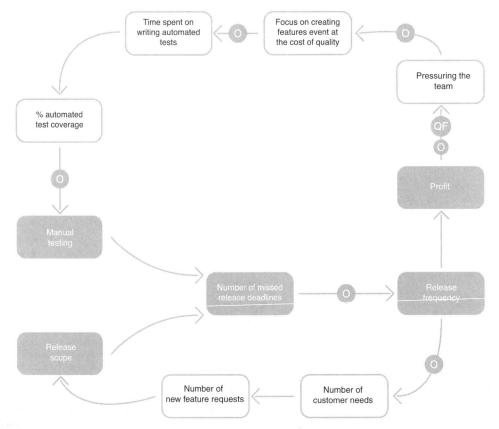

Figure 2.15
Doom loop technique.

Optimize the Whole

People quite often unknowingly create local optimizations—an increase in the performance of the separate parts at the cost of the performance of the whole. In Figure 2.15, local optimizations might mean, for example, finding a new tool for writing automated tests faster. Another example would be handling the customer requests more efficiently. The system's behavior over time remains the same because the system structure stays intact. So, for example, improving the efficiency of writing automated tests will only temporarily improve the number of missed release deadlines, as you can see in Figure 2.16.

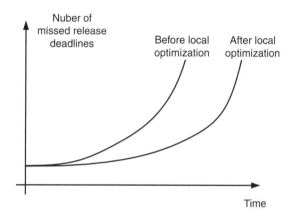

Figure 2.16
Local optimization.

Instead of an action that is optimized locally, you need an activity that optimizes the whole—a redesign of the system structure. Think about the following interventions:

- **Breaking a loop by removing a variable:** For example, remove "focus on creating low-quality features even at the cost of quality" or "pressuring the team."

- **Taking actions to reduce the delay, so you learn faster:** For example, implement continuous deployment to your customers. Although you might like to deploy every day, you might find that you cannot because of the amount of manual testing required. That was previously hidden.

- **Adding a balancing loop to weaken the negative reinforcing loop:** For example, connect "% of automated tests" to lower "pressuring the team." You would probably need to introduce a new policy, rule, or process change.

- **Adding a new external variable as the goal of performance:** For example, add "desired release time." This variable upholds the creative tension, focuses on the vision, and confronts the current reality.

Figure 2.17 illustrates proposed interventions that result in liberating actions and changes in behavior. That leads to new outcomes and new experiences for people from which new mental models might emerge.

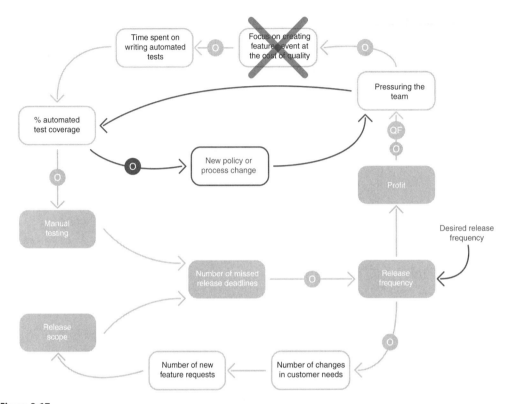

Figure 2.17
Possible interventions.

System Archetypes

Multiple loops may interact to form certain patterns. Some patterns were observed to keep recurring in many different contexts and organizations. In systems thinking, those patterns are called *system archetypes.*[22] There are about a dozen system archetypes, and some of them appear quite often in product development. Archetypes have been thoroughly applied in practice for decades. Strategies for solving the problems they depict are well known. By learning the most common archetypes, you can get better at diagnosing the system and suggesting effective solutions for a product organization. In this way, you can become a better change agent. The sections that follow describe the most common archetypes, including an example of each:

- Fixes that backfire
- Limits to growth

- Shifting the burden

- Drifting goals

Fixes That Backfire

Archetype Structure

"Fixes that backfire" consist of one balancing loop (B1) and one reinforcing loop (R2), as illustrated in Figure 2.18. A problem symptom needs resolution. A solution is quickly implemented that alleviates the symptom (loop B1). The relief is temporary, however. The symptom eventually returns and is worse than before because unintended consequences unfold over a period of time.

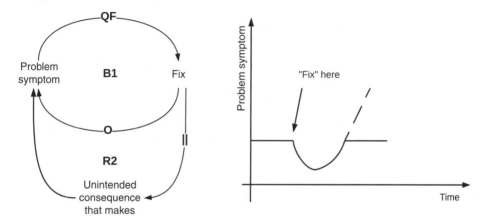

Figure 2.18
Fixes that backfire.

Let's illustrate this archetype with an example from our coaching practice

Management complained that two Scrum teams working on the single corporate product chronically failed to meet the Sprint goals. Customers suffered from system instability and poor quality. At the same time, management wanted to increase the number of sales. Stakeholder and customer dissatisfaction was readily evident.

We started investigating the situation to clarify the picture. Figure 2.19 depicts what we found. The bonuses of the sales department personnel were tied to the number of renewed contracts. The drop in sales motivated them to close deals by any means necessary—in particular, by promising customers that the company would customize the product for them. We discovered the balancing loop B1 with the "fix." At the same time, the quarterly product goal was related to the system's stability and quality improvement. The sales staff put pressure on the teams, giving them the tasks and bypassing the Product Owner. Developers, trying to close unplanned tasks, reduced quality by cutting the corners (R1). Everyone wondered why the Sprint goals were chronically not reached. This irritated customers, and sales declined (R2).

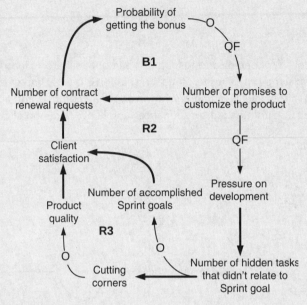

Figure 2.19
Example of fixes that backfire CLD.

We organized several collaborative workshops with stakeholders with the goal of redesigning the system. We did our best to create an atmosphere of psychological safety at the beginning of each workshop by stating the principles of systems thinking:

- There is no one to blame in the system.

- Everyone is right, but only partially.

Complex social systems are capable of self-regulation. Thus, the job of the organizational coach is not to "fix" the system, but rather to create awareness and understanding of the dynamics of what is happening for everyone.

By drawing CLDs with stakeholders, we created shared responsibility. Ultimately, the participants were able to work out several solutions, which eventually solved the problem:

- An agreement was reached that all changes go through the Product Owner only.

- New tariffs were developed for customers. For small customers, product customization was restricted.

- The sales staff started participating in Sprint reviews and Product Backlog Refinement (PBR) activities.

Leverage Points and Strategies

To manage the "fixes that backfire" dynamic, consider the following suggestions:

1. Point out the tendency to focus on immediate issues and solutions. Clarify the real goal with respect to the problem.

2. Create an awareness of negative, unintended consequences of the quick fix solutions.

3. Identify and address the underlying problem, not its symptoms.

4. If it is not possible to address the underlying problem, identify an alternative fix that doesn't make the symptom worse in the long term.

5. Try to apply the fix in a way that limits the consequences.

6. Measure the unintended consequences as well as the intended impact of the solutions.

7. Use retrospectives to determine whether the fix had negative side effects.

Limits to Growth

Archetype Structure

A "limits to growth" structure consists of a reinforcing loop (R1), whose growth, after some success, is offset by an action of a balancing loop (B2). Figure 2.20 shows the structure of this archetype.

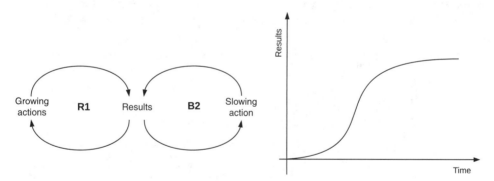

Figure 2.20
Limits to growth.

We were consulting for a large retail bank and did our best to ensure a successful start of the first product teams. We thought that we had launched an endless reinforcing loop: The more teams we kicked off, the more people felt enthusiastic about the change and made a buzz around the initiative. Seeing that so many people were inspired by the change, management asked us to launch more teams. Unexpectedly, we found ourselves working in a repeating mode: training Monday–Tuesday, team kickoff Wednesday–Friday. We kicked off so many Scrum teams that one of the Agile coaches came up with a tool called a Scrum Traffic Light, which helped us to track the progress and health of the launched teams every two weeks.

At the same time, our own resources were limited. Our productivity dropped significantly over time, and we felt exhausted. The quality of our work declined, too. Unfortunately, we spent little time supporting recently kicked-off teams and mentoring Scrum Masters. Teams and Scrum Masters faced many organizational impediments that were not addressed properly and were just accumulating over the time. That eventually decreased the initial enthusiasm about the change because everyone felt the transformation was slipping.

In a few months, we painfully realized that we had fallen into the trap of the "limits to growth" archetype. That was the time to stop and try something different. No matter how painful and uncomfortable it felt, we initiated a series of meetings with top management and a transformation team. We admitted that we had failed. By discussing and visualizing the current situation with the CLD, we created an awareness of what had been happening. The outcome was several decisions. The first one was to stop launching new pilots and limit the number of pilots per every senior Agile coach. Another decision was to start actively mentoring internal Scrum Masters [the Scrum (Master) Coach pattern[26]]. We believed that over time they would grow their abilities and be able to work on an organizational level and launch the teams themselves. Figure 2.21 shows the resulting diagram.

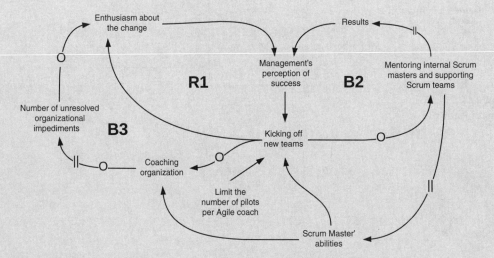

Figure 2.21
Example of limits to growth.

There was an overall frustration and disappointment in the company after these decisions were announced. But after a few months, we finally saw the effects of the decisions made earlier. Agile transformation got back on track.

The story told here is not unique, and we are not the only Agile coaches who have fallen into this trap. The "limits to growth" archetype shows that being successful and being unsuccessful can be equally dangerous. Success stresses and overburdens the current system. It can also trap people in a mentality of "what worked in the past will continue to work in the future."

Leverage Points and Strategies

To manage or change the "limits to success" dynamic, use the following suggestions as guidelines:

1. Anticipate the limiting forces and address them early, before they gain momentum.

2. Minimize limiting actions and their consequences.

3. Stop pushing harder on the growing action when it's no longer giving you the results you expect.

4. Consider adding a balancing loop to provide protection from a vicious spiral because reinforcing processes are inherently unstable.

Shifting the Burden

Archetype Structure

The "shifting the burden"[23] structure is composed of two balancing loops and a reinforcing one, as illustrated in Figure 2.22. It is one of the most pervasive structures in product development. It begins with a symptom that is "solved" with a symptomatic solution that relieves the problem for a while; however, this approach has two negative effects:

- It diverts attention away from the fundamental source of the problem and the fundamental solution.

- The capability of the system to implement the fundamental solution deteriorates over time, reinforcing the perceived need for symptomatic solution.

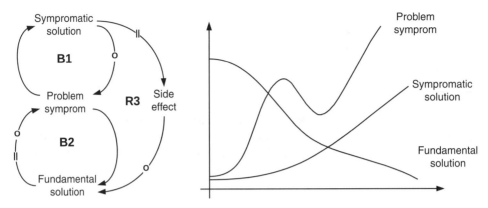

Figure 2.22
Shifting the burden.

"A short-term "solution" is used to correct a problem, with seemingly positive immediate results. Over time, the capabilities for the fundamental solution may atrophy or become disabled, leading to an even greater reliance on the symptomatic solution" [6]

The "shifting the burden" archetype is similar to "fixes that backfire." The key difference is that in "shifting the burden," people are often aware of the fundamental solution, but still stick to the symptomatic one. Table 2.2 outlines just a few examples of "shifting the burden" in product development.

Table 2.2   Examples of Shifting the Burden in Product Development

Symptom	Symptomatic Solution	Fundamental Solution	Side Effect(s)
Dependencies between teams	Managing dependencies by adding specialized roles and techniques	Getting rid of the dependencies by forming feature teams	Specialized roles resist attempts to implement the fundamental solution
Immature team	Adding a specialized role of the team lead	Coaching the team to make it more self-organizing	Responsibility is shifted to the team lead
Knowledge gap in a team	Hire a new developer	Learning a new skill	Culture of narrow specialists
Slipping schedule	Incentives and bribes to make people work harder	Cutting the scope	Displacement of internal motivation by external motivation
Product Owner stress working with multiple teams	Introduce additional Product Owners and Product Backlogs	Let teams clarify the requirements directly with customers	Responsibility is shifted to the fake Product Owners

Learning disability |

Let's investigate the commonly used example of "shifting the burden" with multiple team Product Owners and local Product Backlogs.

In this case, the problem symptom is the Product Owner having much stress managing a single Product Backlog for several teams. This occurs when all the work related to the Product Backlog in Scrum—including ordering, clarification, product discovery, and collaborating with stakeholders—is done by one person. The symptomatic solution is increasing the number of Product Owners and local backlogs to decrease the stress on the one Product Owner. The prevailing mental models that stand behind this are "Scrum is a team-based framework" and "the Product Owner solely manages the Product Backlog."

 The first one is wrong because regardless of the number of Scrum teams working on the product, they have a single Product Owner and single Product Backlog. This is vital for keeping the optimizing goals "working on the highest-value items," "speed of learning," and "adaptability" intact.

The second mental model is inaccurate because in Scrum, the Product Owner may delegate any work to the developers. Rather than doing all the work alone, the Product Owner can have many helpers, and the best candidates for the helpers are the teams. Thus, the fundamental solution is delegating clarification of Product Backlog items to the developers. By doing so, developers learn more about the actual needs of the customers.

By implementing the symptomatic solution, the organization embeds unnecessary additional roles in the system. The negative effects are twofold. First, once installed in these roles, the team Product Owners are not interested in a systemic solution, as their roles would be abolished. Second, developers are separated from stakeholders and customers, and are fed the detailed requirements by the team Product Owners. Therefore, their knowledge of the business domain and communication skills do not evolve, as they are forced to focus on just part of the value stream (e.g., coding, testing, design, architecture). Figure 2.23 illustrates this dynamic.

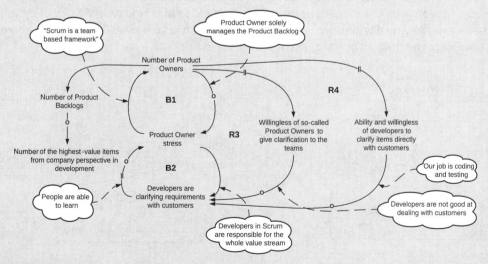

Figure 2.23
Example of shifting the burden.

Leverage Points and Strategies

To manage or change the "shifting the burden" dynamic, use the following suggestions as guidelines:

1. Create an awareness of the system to focus on immediate quick fixes. Clarify the real goal with respect to the problem. It may be necessary to establish a perfection vision.

2. Uncover and address mental models that perpetuate dependence on the quick fix.

3. Implement a "cold turkey" strategy if possible—in other words, complete and immediate rejection of using the symptomatic solution.

4. Weaken the link between the symptom and the quick fix.

5. If addressing the symptom is necessary, identify an alternative fix that doesn't generate so many side effects.

6. Look for ways to balance short- and long-term approaches.

Drifting Goals

Archetype Structure

The "drifting goals" archetype demonstrates the difficulty of confronting reality. It starts with a gap between desired and actual performance, as illustrated in Figure 2.24. Under pressure, the quick fix is to lower and strive to meet a less ambitious goal to reduce the gap. If we don't get what we want, we start to want what we get (balancing loop B1). But there's another way to take corrective action and, after a while, to reduce the gap without compromising the initial goal (balancing loop B2). It is hard because there is a delay in time, and many organizations are not willing to wait so long. There is also a fear that the corrective action won't generate increased performance. The "drifting goals" archetype reveals deteriorating performance over a long period of time in case of a vicious cycle, and vice versa. Total quality improvement (TQI), *Kaizen*, and other continuous improvement efforts are examples of the "drifting goals" structure being used in a positive manner.

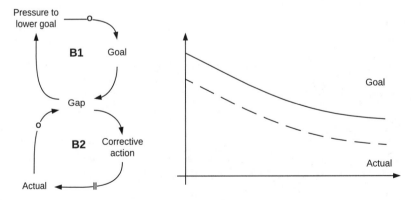

Figure 2.24
Drifting goals.

The "drifting goals" structure underlies several similar dynamics that we have observed in many product organizations. People get more specialized over time and eventually become single specialists. This archetype causes organizations to create dynamic teams to exactly match the concrete features or projects. Likewise, the organization grows to include more and more people. This dynamic is illustrated in Figure 2.25.

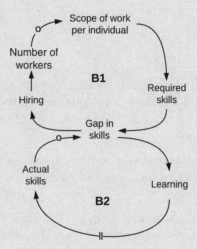

Figure 2.25
Example of drifting goals.

One of the best tools to help you maintain your focus on the goal and keep it intact is crafting a perfection vision. This concept, which stems from lean thinking, is based on the principle of continual improvement. The ultimate goal for a product organization is to provide perfect value to the customer through a perfect value creation process that has zero waste. An example of the perfection vision for a product organization is as follows:

- The perfection goal is to have a releasable product all the time.

- There is no branching in development.

- All tests are automated except for (1) exploratory tests, (2) usability tests, and (3) tests that require physical movement. All people must learn test automation skills.

- Special coordination roles (such as project managers) are avoided, and teams are responsible for coordination.

- Most of the teams are customer-centric feature teams.

Leverage Points and Strategies

To manage or change the "drifting goals" dynamic, use the following suggestions as guidelines:

1. Hold the goal steady and intact.
2. If current performance is low, focus on designing and implementing the corrective action.
3. Find and address the mental models.

Summary

Systems thinking is a language and set of tools meant to illuminate thinking about how the systems of which we are part operate. It reveals the reasons for chronic problems in complex organizational contexts. It is an essential thinking approach for creating a general picture of reality by engaging individuals with different viewpoints.

Organizational coaches can benefit from using a systems thinking approach. When systems thinking is applied in this context, it is vital to identify patterns of behavior, system structures, and mental models.

Creative tension is a gap between the current reality and the vision. Commitment to the vision offers the best proof that the future can become a product of the dreams and not merely a reaffirmation of the status quo.

Causal Loop Diagrams are one of the most popular tools for systems thinking. By using them, we can tell "stories" about the behavior within a system. It takes time to become skillful in creating CLDs, so practice a lot. The doom loop technique is an excellent starting point.

When preparing a system intervention, be aware of local optimizations. There are many ways of intervening in a system: breaking a loop, reducing a delay to improve learning, adding a balancing loop, and introducing an external variable with a new performance goal.

We do not recommend compiling a CLD yourself and imposing it on an organization. There is a big difference between the insights that people obtain as a result of creating models themselves versus the one-way transmission of information. The outcome of a system intervention is improvement experiments.

Optimize the whole system and avoid local optimizations, and agree and hold to the optimization goal upfront. Look for the conflicting system goals and resolve the conflicts.

Typical system stories are called archetypes. Some of the most frequently observed archetypes one can find in product development are "fixes that backfire," "shifting the burden," "limits to growth," and "drifting goals."

References

1. David Peter Stroh. *Systems Thinking for Social Change: A Practical Guide to Solving Complex Problems, Avoiding Unintended Consequences, and Achieving Lasting Results* (Chelsea Green Publishing, 2015).

2. Daniel Gilbert. *Stumbling on Happiness* (Vintage, 2007).

3. Daniel Kahneman. *Thinking Fast and Slow* (Farrar, Straus and Giroux, 2011).

4. Kenneth H. Blanchard and Spencer Johnson. *The New One Minute Manager* (Harper Collins India, 2016).

5. Steven Johnson. *Where Good Ideas Come From: The Natural History of Innovation* (Riverhead Books, 2010).

6. Peter M. Senge. *Fifth Discipline: The Art and Practice of the Learning Organization* (Doubleday, 2006).

7. Russell L. Ackoff, *Re-creating the Corporation: A Design of Organizations for the 21st Century* (Oxford University Press, 1999).

8. Daniel H. Kim. "Introduction to Systems Thinking." Pegasus Communications. https://thesystemsthinker.com/wp-content/uploads/2016/03/Introduction-to-Systems-Thinking-IMS013Epk.pdf.

9. W. Edwards Deming. *Out of the Crisis* (MIT Press, 1982).

10. Frederick Taylor Winslow. *The Principles of Scientific Management* (Martino Fine Books, 2014).

11. Donald G. Reinertsen, *The Principles of Product Development Flow: Second Generation Lean Product Development* (Celeritas Publishing, 2014).

12. John Seddon. *Freedom from Command and Control: Rethinking Management for Lean Service* (Productivity Press, 2005).

13. Frederick P. Brooks Jr. *The Mythical Man-Month: Essays on Software Engineering, Anniversary Edition* (Addison-Wesley Professional, 1995).

14. Christopher Avery. *The Responsibility Process: Unlocking Your Natural Ability to Live and Lead with Power* (Parnerwerks, 2016).

15. Ken Schwaber. "Scrum But Replaced by Scrum And" [Blog post]. April 5, 2012. https://kenschwaber.word-press.com/2012/04/05/scrum-but-replaced-by-scrum-and/.

16. Craig Larman and Bas Vodde. *Large-Scale Scrum: More with LeSS* (Addison-Wesley Professional, 2016).

17. William Braun. "The System Archetypes." 2002. www.albany.edu/faculty/gpr/PAD724/724WebArticles/sys_archetypes.pdf.

18. "Five Whys." Wikipedia. https://en.wikipedia.org/wiki/Five_whys.

19. "Shift and Share." Liberating Structures. www.liberatingstructures.com/11-shift-share/.

20. "World Cafe Method." The World Cafe. www.theworldcafe.com/key-concepts-resources/world-cafe-method/.

21. "Multi-team Backlog Refinement" [Blog post]. Agilix, February 11, 2019. https://agilix.nl/blog/how-to-do-multi-team-backlog-refinement/.

22. The pioneering work on codifying system archetypes and making them accessible was done by Michael Goodman, Jennifer Kemeny, and Charlie Kiefer at Innovation Associates. See William Braun. "The System Archetypes." 2002. www.albany.edu/faculty/gpr/PAD724/724WebArticles/sys_archetypes.pdf.

23. "Scrum (Master) Coach." https://sites.google.com/a/scrumplop.org/published-patterns/product-organization-pattern-language/scrummaster/scrum-master-coach?authuser=0.

3

Optimize for Adaptiveness

Management is efficiency in climbing the ladder of success; leadership determines
whether the ladder is leaning against the right wall.
—Stephen Covey

According to Craig Larman, co-creator of the LeSS framework and renowned consultant, reducing switching costs by learning is resisted most by any organization.

We can hardly disagree with that. Indeed, this is something that we observe during our own work quite often. Speed of delivery can be easily "sold" to management. But speed is not enough to be Agile at the organizational level.

Once, we consulted for a product company in eastern Europe. It was building a portal with an innovative fintech system that processed payments among tens of countries. The organizational design consisted of several feature teams that were able to deliver usable increments to the market every couple of weeks. Despite the fact that teams were feature teams, they specialized around tiny business domains to "maximize focus and thus speed of delivery." All teams could only pick up items corresponding to their business knowledge. Suddenly, when a crash happened in the market, one of the teams got overloaded with the number of changes they had to deal with. Figure 3.1 illustrates the trap that the organization fell into. On the left of the figure, you can see that each team specializes in a narrow domain. On the right side, you can see that the highest-value work exceeds the capacity of Team 1, and no other team can help.

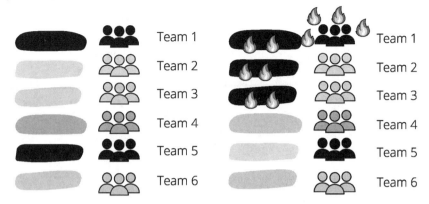

Figure 3.1
Changes overloading the narrowly specialized Team 1.

This organization turned out to be fragile, unable to absorb significant change. At that time, the product organization was like the *Titanic*—moving fast toward the iceberg but unable to avoid colliding with it.

From a Systems Thinking perspective, we can recognize the "fixes that backfire" archetype. The causal loop diagram in Figure 3.2 illustrates how management's focus on speed of delivery over learning led to specialized teams. In the long run, that decreased teams' ability to work on the most critical work at the organizational level and blocked the product group from quickly responding to change.

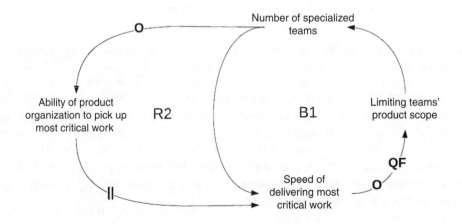

Figure 3.2
"Fixes that backfire" systems archetype for narrowly specialized teams.

What It Means to Be Adaptable

Imagine a product group with 10 cross-functional teams. Each team can pick up any feature that comes into the product group, which means that all teams in the product group can always work on the most critical work. Also, imagine that all teams optimize for delivering a feature in short cycles (e.g., two weeks) from an idea into the hands of the end user, which means that they have fast feedback for learning. As a final step, imagine that the teams split large work items into small items,[1] which they then work on during each cycle. Such a product group has the conditions to be maximally Agile as defined in Chapter 1, "Organizing for Adaptability." Why?

- A big piece of work—for example, a project in a traditional project organization—is split into small items of end-user value. Now, instead of assuming that the entire big item is "required," the teams only deliver the high-value items in short iterations and ditch the low-value ones altogether. Large items convey lots of information, are full of assumptions, and therefore carry high risks. So, the product group does not focus on the question "How can we deliver all the 'requirements' in this big item?" but instead avoids a fixed work scope and replans during every cycle.

- All cross-functional teams can pick up the most important work, so the product group can react to the work that comes in with 100% of the teams. Contrast this with the specialized teams in Figure 3.1, which have a limited work scope based on their area of expertise. When the most crucial work exceeds the capacity of the specialist teams, no other team can help, so the product group cannot react and focus on the highest-value work with all teams.

- The group learns from short feedback loops and puts that learning back into the plan on what to work on next. In this way, the group can react to changing conditions as more is learned and discovered.

Creating such a product group implies that certain organizational design elements (which is the scope of this whole book) must be in place. All product group teams have the skills to work across all domains, technical components, applications, and all tools. How can the organization create such a group? There are three main concerns:

1. Minimize switching costs from moving from one work item to another. These include learning costs, cognitive costs, and the cost of a team stopping existing work and starting new work. Chapter 10, "Coaching Teams," discusses optimizing value and multifunctional learning in detail.

2. Minimize transaction costs—that is, the costs of overhead activities. In lean thinking, these are activities that either are necessary but non-value-adding waste (temporarily necessary waste[2]) or are unnecessary and could be eliminated (pure waste[2]). In Agile software development, transaction costs arise in activities other than software design, programming, and verification, including communication, coordination, and repeating manual activities such as manual deployment or testing. The key point is that your software must be soft enough so that you can change it quickly, at low cost, and can validate that it delivers what is expected. The way to lower the transaction costs for software development is to use appropriate engineering practices, including effective automation of the build and test process, for starters, and

eventually complete automation of the entire delivery pipeline. Also, the product being built must have a decoupled architecture that is grown iteratively so that any part can be easily changed or replaced. The version control practices matter, too. Trunk-based development, especially the elimination of feature branching and continuous integration, is essential for teams to coordinate effectively and keep technical debt from growing invisibly and insidiously. And these areas are just a starting point—there are lots more ways to minimize transaction costs.

3. The final concern is the learning speed of the product group—that is, the ability of fast delivery to create short feedback combined with the quality of measuring to decide what is most important to work on next.

Throughout the book, we share many ideas on addressing these concerns. In this chapter, we start with concern 3: increasing the speed of learning by focusing on flow efficiency.

Flow Efficiency

In coaching engagements, we often encounter the objection "But this is not efficient" as a reaction when we propose using Agile principles and tools. Each such conversation is an opportunity for coaching and figuring out what people mean by *efficiency*. Are we talking about *flow efficiency* or *resource efficiency*? Senior management should make a strategic choice about the relative importance of the two types of efficiencies in their organization, because the organizational design decisions (structure, coordination, integration, and people practices) heavily depend on that and largely define the level of agility. To make informed decisions, organizations need to be well educated regarding the behavior and nature of queues in product development and how they impact flow and economics. We'll start here with the basics of queueing theory and discuss flow and resource efficiency afterward.

Behavior of Queues

We'll start considering the behavior and nature of queues by equipping ourselves with a little vocabulary. A simple queueing system consists of a *queue, unit arrival rate, unit departure rate*, and a *server*. The queue consists of *units* of work.

Imagine a supermarket clerk at the checkout (server) and a line of shoppers in front of this clerk (queue), as illustrated in Figure 3.3. The time shoppers spend waiting in line is called *waiting time (WT)*. The time while they are being served is called *service time (ST)*. The total time from the moment they arrive until they finish buying their groceries is called *cycle time (CT)*. The *unit* of work is an individual shopper. The number of units/shoppers waiting to be served is the *work-in-progress (WIP)*. The number of goods that an individual shopper carries in their cart defines the *batch size* of the unit. The more goods that reside in the cart, the larger the batch size is.

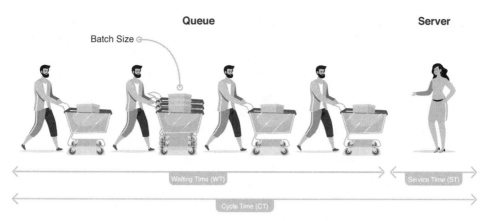

Figure 3.3
Queueing system.

Relationships Among Utilization, Cycle Time, and Variability

Resource utilization is the percentage of the time when a resource (server) is busy processing units. Let's investigate how resource utilization affects the length of the queue and overall cycle time. Contrary to conventional wisdom, a linear increase in resource utilization leads to a super-linear increase in the queues and cycle times. This is perfectly illustrated by *Kingman's formula*.[3] Figure 3.4 shows how cycle time (vertical axis) is a function of resource utilization (horizontal axis).

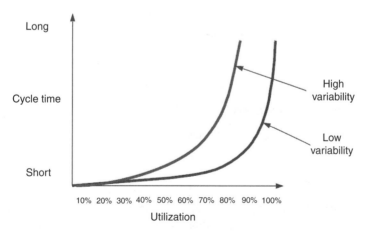

Figure 3.4
Resource utilization, cycle time, and variability.

As we move from 60% to 80%, we double the cycle time. As we move from 80% to 90%, we double it again. As we move from 90% to 95%, we double it yet again. This is exactly the opposite of what an average person's intuition might indicate. Thus, pushing a 90% busy team to take on an additional 5% of work might severely increase the length of the development cycle!

You can also see that the increase in cycle time is further amplified by variability, which is anything that causes the system to depart from its regular, predictable behavior. The more variability that is present in the queue, the more dramatic the increase in cycle time that is observed.

Variability shows up as uncertainty either in the arrival rate of the tasks or in the duration of the tasks.[4]

Let's return to our example of the clerk and shoppers. The rate at which shoppers join the line is unpredictable (arrival rate). The duration of the time over which a clerk processes an individual shopper varies, too. For example, if a barcode on one of the food boxes is unreadable, the clerk needs to enter the code manually. That increases the average waiting time for the other shoppers in the queue.

The world of product development is even more complex, as development in this setting is a one-time activity and contains more variability. For instance, in software development, when writing code, the programmer most often creates a new design, a new "recipe" that has never existed before; there is no value in doing the same development twice. In contrast, manufacturing work implies doing something that has been done before many times; there is equal value in doing the same thing multiple times.

Since product development is normally a one-time activity, it can contain great uncertainty in task arrival times and task durations. We are almost certain to see queues in the product development process.[4]

Product development is exposed to numerous sources of variability:

- Variations in customer demand (seasoning, changing trends)
- Work that arrives in different sizes and at different speeds (small and big feature requests)
- Differences in processing times (employees with junior and senior skills)
- Rework, bugs, and change requests
- People getting sick, joining the organization, and leaving it
- The environment and tools (crashes, unpredictable behavior)
- Interruptions to handle high-priority work

In product development, it's very easy to overload the system—a team, for example—and to create delays by putting it in a high utilization state. Then the team will have no time to absorb variability in its work. So, when the workload of the team exceeds their capacity, a queue of work emerges in front of the team.

Queues Create Waste

Queues are the main cause of the long cycle times in product development and have profound economic consequences. Is it possible to quantify the impact of the queues? Many organizations are using *cost of delay*, a concept that has gained traction over the years, for this purpose. Cost of delay means the loss of a benefit due to the delay and/or penalty. In product development, we aspire to get some benefit from the result of our work. Therefore, postponing the delivery of an important feature or delaying a release might incur unnecessary costs. (Cost of delay is described in more detail in section N, "Cost of Delay," in the Appendix.)

> *If you are going to quantify one thing, quantify the cost of delay.*[5]

Donald G. Reinertsen, in *The Principles of Product Development Flow*,[5] writes about six different sources of waste that queues create:

- **Longer cycle times:** By quantifying the cost of delay, we can attach a financial cost to the queues. As a rule of thumb, delay cost rises proportionally to queue size.

- **More risks:** When a feature request goes through the development pipeline, the product organization becomes vulnerable to changes in customer preferences and shifts in technologies. When code is developed and tested but not yet put into production, this risk still remains. The risk grows exponentially with cycle time.

- **More variability:** Variability is amplified when a system operates at high levels of utilization. In such a case, even small deviations in loading can cause large deviations in cycle time.

- **Secondary needs and overhead:** Queues raise the costs of product development by generating secondary needs that can be taken for granted but are not truly necessary. For example, if it has too much WIP, a team will be forced to introduce additional processes, meetings, and methods to deal with queues.

- **Reduced quality:** Queues delay feedback from downstream processes. If developers get feedback instantly, they can fix a bug really quickly. If they must wait a week for this feedback, they will continue making a false assumption and putting it into the code. That causes more rework later.

- **Low morale:** Queues demotivate employees because knowing that your work will stay in a queue for a couple of months isn't very inspiring and doesn't create a sense of urgency.

Balancing Excess Capacity with the Cost of Delay

Being systems thinkers, we should consider both the costs of queues and the costs of having resources that stay idle. The optimal utilization rate should balance these expenses. To see how this balance works, consider the graph in Figure 3.5, which was taken from Reinertsen's *Managing the Design Factory*.[4]

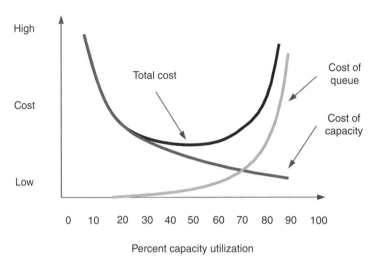

Figure 3.5
Total cost vs. capacity cost.

By increasing capacity utilization, we achieve a super-linear increase in the cycle time and, as a rule of thumb, proportionally delay costs. As you can see, the total cost takes the form of a U-curve. It has a flat bottom, and the optimal resource utilization rate lies somewhere between 30% and 70%. Does that mean we need to control resource utilization to make sure it doesn't approach critical values? Unfortunately, such an effort isn't very practical because it's hard to estimate resource utilization with sufficient accuracy. The better alternative is focusing on queues: eliminating them or controlling their size (WIP), given that the size of the queue directly controls the cycle time by reducing waiting time. We'll return to the algorithm for dealing with queues later in this chapter.

Relationships Among Utilization, Batch Size, and Cycle Time

Another important relationship we need to investigate is how batch size affects the queue size and cycle time. Let's get back to our example of the shoppers in a supermarket. The batch size is the number of goods that reside in the cart. More goods increase the batch size and directly affect the size of the shopper queue. Imagine you're standing behind a shopper who has a huge number of goods in their cart. You might become upset, especially if your batch size is small—you hold a single bottle of beer in your hand and that's the only reason why you entered the supermarket. Here are a few examples of batches in product development:

- The size of the Product Backlog Items (PBIs)
- The forecast created during the Sprint planning

- The number of features to be tested at once

- The big pile of code ready to be integrated with other developers/teams

- The amount of detailed requirements waiting to be designed together

- The number of PBIs being discussed during a refinement session

- The number of issues being discussed during Sprint retrospective

Does the batch size impact the queue size and cycle time? Definitely, because it increases variability. Just imagine picking up a big requirement that will mean 6 months of work—it will have lots of uncertainty and surprises. Figure 3.6 illustrates the relationships among utilization level, batch size, and cycle time.

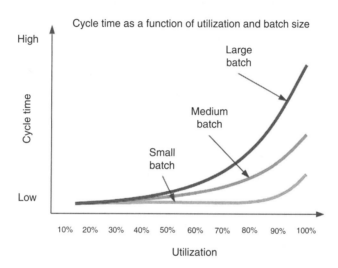

Figure 3.6
Cycle time as a function of utilization and batch size.

In Figure 3.6, notice that large batches increase the cycle time super-linearly. Why? Large batches contain more variability and more uncertainty. Remember that really big requirement that will need 6 months of work, and that will provide lots of surprises during development? In fact, it's not a single requirement or feature, but rather a bunch of sub-requirements and smaller features. That's why it's recommended to split large PBIs into smaller and roughly equal-sized items—to reduce average cycle time. By splitting a big feature, you reduce variability by removing uncertainty and surprises during the Sprint as you learn more. Don't be surprised, then, that the estimated amount of work on smaller items can be vastly more than the original estimate of the parent feature. The difference arises because you've uncovered previously unnoticed work and learned from that.

One-Piece Continuous Flow

As discussed in the previous section, it's economically beneficial to work with smaller batches. By radically reducing batch sizes, organizations can achieve dramatic decreases in their cycle times. Does this mean that in product development we should strive to work with the smallest batch that is equal to one? Not at all, because we need to consider the transaction costs, which grow in parallel with reducing the batch size and usually accompany product development.

Suppose you live in Europe and bought a new book, *Queueing Theory*, that was printed and stored in the United States. Would it be profitable to charter a plane, put a single book on that plane, and fly it to you immediately? Of course not. The transaction costs would be enormous despite the fact that the cycle time is as short as possible.

Figure 3.7 (from Reinertsen's *The Principles of Product Development Flow*[5]) illustrates the economic feasibility of the batch size, which entails a U-curve optimization. We don't need to find the exact optimal point on this curve to capture most of the value because the curve has a flat bottom.

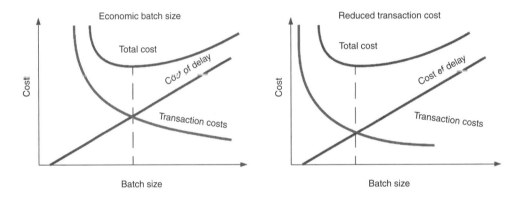

Figure 3.7
Economic batch size and reducing transaction costs.

Do high transaction costs imply we have to forget about small batches? No, to expand opportunities to work with smaller batches, the organization needs to reduce the transaction costs so that the U-curve is moved to the left. The good news is that in product development, and especially in software development, it's possible to get rid of most of the transaction costs by using engineering practices such as automated testing and continuous integration. Continuous integration is a practice that uses queueing theory to its advantage by limiting the batch size of the code integrated into the system to, for example, a single day. All the tests except for the exploratory tests and ones that need physical movement can be automated and transaction costs can be reduced in this way. In software development, one-piece continuous flow (pattern Swarming: One-Piece Continuous Flow[6]) is a useful approach and one that we strongly recommend.

When the batch size is reduced, transaction costs rise, which tends to make the organization uncomfortable. Small batches make the impediments to flow transparent. By overcoming these impediments, it is possible to improve the flow.

Here are some of the challenges related to the batch size reduction that a Scrum Master might consider presenting to a Scrum team. These challenges will inevitably uncover internal organizational weaknesses that need to be addressed. The potential benefit is a shortened average cycle time in the long run:

- Decreasing the length of the Sprint

- Decreasing the average size of the PBIs

- Decreasing the average WIP in a Sprint

- Developers learning secondary skills

In Chapter 4, "Agile Organizational Design," we introduce multi-skill organizational design options. Chapter 10, "Coaching Teams," devotes more time to the topic of how to coach the team in multi-functionality and how to work in a one-piece flow style.

Queueing System Structures

Until now, we have considered the simplest queue system, which features a one-to-one relationship between a server and a queue. In practice, multiple servers and multiple queues may be linked. You might observe this kind of system in an airport, when several lines of passengers stay in parallel lines waiting to be processed by different passport control stations. In contrast, some airports organize the passenger lines differently by creating multiple passport desks that are fed by a single queue of passengers. Figure 3.8 illustrates these queueing system structures.

One server per queue   **One queue and multiple servers**

Figure 3.8
Queueing system structures.

From queueing theory, we know that the structure with multiple servers and a single queue linked to it is more predictable. Why? Even if one of the servers is halted temporarily or processing one of the units takes more time than anticipated, the queue doesn't stop: The units continue to be processed by other servers. This queueing structure decreases variability in waiting times and, therefore, decreases average cycle time for the units of work.

Applying Queueing Structure to Agile Product Development

Let's apply our knowledge about the behavior of queueing systems with a single queue attached to multiple servers to Agile product development. The Sprint Backlog is a queue that is often decomposed into smaller pieces of work called Sprint Backlog Items (SBIs; see pattern Sprint Backlog Item[7]) that support the Sprint Goal (pattern Sprint Goal[8]). If developers have narrow specializations, don't develop their skills over time, and are unwilling to work in a collaborative manner and help each other, multiple queues of SBIs will be created with corresponding multiple servers (developers). Such a team is fragile and highly vulnerable to peak workloads, so cycle time increases.

The same thinking applies at the product group level. Often management designs a system with multiple teams that are organized around parts of the product with numerous local team backlogs—a practice that Cesário Ramos calls *copy–paste scaling*.[9] The path to more predictable delivery and flow entails designing a product group with a single Product Backlog and cross-functional Scrum teams that can pull any PBI from the single queue and help each other if such a need arises.

Algorithm for Dealing with Queues

When an organization is aware of queues' impact on the cycle times and economics, it can use strategies to mitigate the negative effects that queues have on flow. In *Scaling Lean and Agile Development*,[10] Craig Larman and Bas Vodde brilliantly write about plan "A" and plan "B" for dealing with queues. We support this approach.

Plan "A" is redesigning the system of work so as to completely eradicate the queues by removing bottlenecks and other forces that create the queues. That implies:

- Eliminating single-specialist workers working in sequential development and forming cross-functional teams

- Applying automated acceptance test-driven development and moving from serial to parallel development

Plan "B" would be:

- Visualizing the queues that are left

- Implementing queue management to reduce batch size and variability and to limit WIP

Start with plan "A" and move to plan "B" only after you have already exhausted opportunities from the first step.

Choose an Operational Strategy

Niklas Modig, author of the book *This Is Lean*,[11] proposes a simple but powerful model with four areas that can help senior management make choices regarding the primary operational focus of the organization. In this model, which is illustrated in Figure 3.9, the horizontal axis is the level of flow efficiency (from low to high), defined as the amount of time that passes from identifying a need to satisfying a need. The vertical axis is the level of resource efficiency (from low to high), defined as the percentage of the time that resources stay busy.

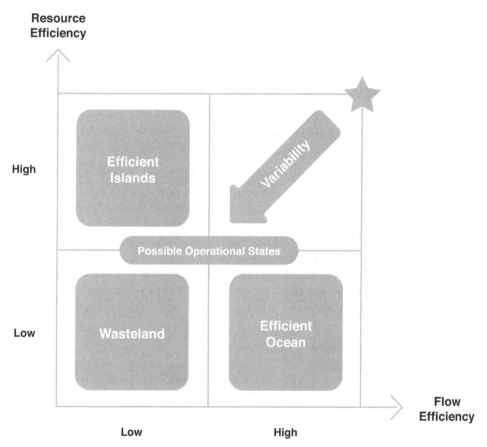

Figure 3.9
Flow vs. resource efficiency.

In the top right-hand corner of Figure 3.9 is the perfect state, which is characterized by high resource and flow efficiencies. The challenge to reaching this state is the variability in product development. Another challenge is that it requires perfectly flexible resources, such that capacity and competence can be easily adjusted. Thus, it's extremely difficult to rank high on both flow and resource efficiencies simultaneously. In turn, an organization needs to make a strategic choice about the relative importance of two types of efficiencies.

Resource Efficiency

In a resource efficiency paradigm, organizations strive to "attach work to resources" to maximize the amount of time that a resource stays busy. The goal is to find economies of scale, so that increasing resource efficiency leads to decreased unit costs. Therefore, work is divided into smaller tasks that are carried out by different individuals and organizational functions. In organizations that stick to this strategy, one could find the following organizational elements:

- Resource management

- Employees assigned to several projects/products concurrently

- Narrow specialization supported by corresponding HR practices

- Functional hierarchy organizational design

- Lots of started but not finished work (WIP)

Unfortunately, because of the relationships among utilization levels, cycle time, and variability, this strategy likely causes an exponential increase in end-to-end cycle times in delivering value to the customer in complex systems with interdependent tasks—for example, product development.

A typical functional organization operates as shown in Figure 3.10. In this example, three organizational functions are working at high levels of utilization, and each has a local queue of work. Each function has corresponding local performance measures (KPIs). To calculate the total time (cycle time) for the request "A" to go through the system and get into the hands of the customer, we sum up the waiting times (WT1 + WT2 + WT3) and service times (ST1 + ST2 + ST3). For simplicity, we consider the first in, first out (FIFO) type of queue. Of course, in development, we could reprioritize the queues for each function so that they handle item A with the highest priority. In reality, this prioritization goal is very hard to realize because of system effects, as we will explain throughout this book. And even if we do this, other work will be halted and kept waiting until item A has been processed, increasing the average cycle time.

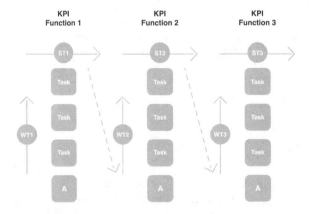

WT = Waiting time, ST = Service Time
Cycle Time = (WT1 + WT3 + WT3) + (ST1 + ST2 + ST3)

Figure 3.10
Organization entangled by queues.

In most product organizations with which we have collaborated, waiting times before Agile adoption consumed most of the total time, while each team was working at full capacity. This situation becomes apparent when we visualize the flow using the *value stream mapping*[12] technique. We will discuss this technique in more detail in Chapter 8, "Preparing the Product Group." Thus, such an organization is resource-efficient but not flow-efficient, because all work goes through some kind of flow.

> *Controlling work through functional measures can only be harmful to flow. All work goes through some kind of flow, so we would be better having measures of it. Managers worry about this idea because they assume it may threaten costs. They cannot see the costs associated with the waste caused by functional management. Only by managing costs end-to-end, associating costs with the flow, can you reduce costs in a sustainable manner.*[13]

A few years ago, we were involved in a massive transformation effort in a big bank. We were sitting in the office of the CEO and discussing the first steps for Agile adoption. We asked the CEO, what was the reason, from his point of view, why it took so long to create new products and services?

The CEO sighed loudly and answered, "IT department. It seems like everything they are involved in becomes even slower. We could move so much faster, but right now, we don't have enough capacity in IT." It was an interesting point. A few months later, we had another conversation with the CEO, and now we had hard facts based on data that we took from the value stream mapping analysis. The problem was not the IT department or, to put it more accurately, not just the IT department. The current organizational design of the bank opted for resource utilization, which created lots of queues. It was a typical functional hierarchy of power. Each silo stayed busy working on their local stuff and making local KPIs.

Flow Efficiency

Flow efficiency is a strategy of focusing on the amount of time it takes to move from identifying a customer need to satisfying that need. Flow efficiency focuses on the unit that is processed—for example, a product feature—in the organization. To improve flow efficiency, instead of ensuring that the servers always have work to do, you should ensure that the work is always being worked on. That means creating an organization that is organized around a specific need (product feature) and requires all staff to work together. A cross-functional Scrum team ensures the feature is always being worked on and does not wait in a queue. That is why we consider the heart of any Agile organization to be self-managing, cross-functional teams that solve end-user needs and create value for the organization, while also having fun.

> *Agile organizations prioritize flow efficiency over resource efficiency.*

Product organizations that make a choice to seek flow efficiency typically have the journey illustrated in Figure 3.11. The starting point could be A or B. The first move is focused on establishing the flow, so that the organizational system transfers to point C.

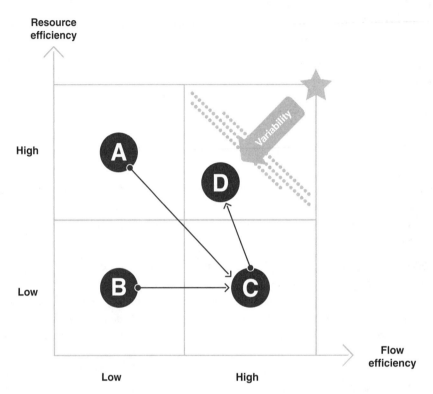

Figure 3.11
Journey to flow efficiency.

At point C, the organization has reached a good flow efficiency, and average cycles times are significantly decreased. The next step is optimizing the resource efficiency and thus moving to point D. That can be done by training and developing people, by introducing standards, and by attacking sources of variability. Finally, with continual improvement, the organization strives to reach the perfect state and to become proficient in both flow and resource efficiency. We'll stick to this approach in our coming discussions, and the book navigates you through this route. Here's an example that illustrates this journey.

We started working with a product group that consisted of 40 developers spread over seven component teams. Each team was focusing on local efficiency, which inevitably led to queues between teams and long cycle times. Teams were managing the queues through complicated *Kanban* systems and were limiting WIP (plan "B"). This approach showed some benefits and everyone noticed gains, but management was still not satisfied with the average development cycle time.

After initial training and a set of preparation activities, we redesigned the system into six cross-functional teams that had all the competencies needed to deliver end-to-end value. The Product Owner and management asked the teams to focus on developing "releasable" increments and not to pay attention to individual workloads. The office layout and environment were changed to enable pair programming and swarming. The Product Owner showed up at the first Sprint planning meeting carrying sox feature cards in his hands and saying that was all he had for the teams. He asked them to bring those features to the releasable state; when that happened, he promised to give them more work.

There was much stress during the first Sprints, and developers felt underutilized. People complained that it was an uncomfortable and unusual style of work. Nevertheless, the new system of work made them swarm and collaborate. The decrease in cycle time was immediate and dramatic—four times just in several weeks. At this point in time, the organization moved from point A to point C in Figure 3.11.

Next, the organization started the movement toward point D. Much attention was paid to training and developing multifunctional skills to improve resource utilization. Scrum Masters did a great job of involving the HR director in this process, and eventually new people practices were introduced. Developers were incentivized to develop broad skills because those affected their salary.

In several months, a few teams were able to split into smaller ones while continuing to deliver value independently. Resource utilization improved as the developers became more flexible. And that was the point D that was finally reached. The product group is still improving and on its way to a perfection state.

Summary

This chapter introduced the basics of queueing theory. Both utilization rate and batch size affect the lengths of the queues nonlinearly, and this effect is further amplified by variability. Product development is a one-time activity with high variability, and queues are expected to exist in such an environment.

The optimal resource utilization rate lies somewhere between 30% and 70%. Nevertheless, it's not practical to control people's utilization because it's hard to estimate this rate with sufficient accuracy. The better alternative is focusing on queues: eliminating them or controlling their size, as that characteristic directly controls the cycle time. Queues are associated with six different sources of waste: longer cycle times, more risks, more variability, secondary needs and overhead, reduced quality, and low morale.

The preferred approach to dealing with queues is to redesign the system of work so as to completely eradicate them. A less preferable approach is visualizing the queues that are left and implementing queue management to reduce batch size and variability, and to limit WIP.

An organization needs to make a strategic choice about the relative importance of two types of efficiencies: flow efficiency and resource efficiency. In the resource efficiency paradigm, organizations strive to "attach work to resources" to maximize the amount of time that a resource stays busy. Flow efficiency is the strategy of focusing on the amount of time it takes to move from identifying a need to satisfying that need. Flow efficiency emphasizes the unit that is processed in the organization keeps flowing until completion. Agile organizations prioritize flow efficiency over resource efficiency. This choice impacts organizational design decisions: structure, coordination, integration, and people practices.

References

1. "Small Items." https://sites.google.com/a/scrumplop.org/published-patterns/value-stream/small-items.

2. Craig Larman and Bas Vodde. "Lean Primer." www.leanprimer.com/downloads/lean_primer.pdf.

3. "Kingman's Formula." Wikipedia. https://en.wikipedia.org/wiki/Kingman%27s_formula.

4. Donald G. Reinertsen. *Managing the Design Factory* (Free Press, 1997).

5. Donald G. Reinertsen. *The Principles of Product Development Flow* (Celeritas, 2009).

6. "Swarming: One-Piece Continuous Flow." https://sites.google.com/a/scrumplop.org/published-patterns/product-organization-pattern-language/development-team/swarming--one-piece-continuous-flow.

7. "Sprint Backlog Item." https://sites.google.com/a/scrumplop.org/published-patterns/value-stream/sprint-backlog/sprint-backlog-item?authuser=0.

8. "Sprint Goal." https://sites.google.com/a/scrumplop.org/published-patterns/value-stream/sprint-goal?authuser=0.

9. Cesário Ramos. "Copy Paste Scaling." DZone. https://dzone.com/articles/common-mistakes-when-scaling-scrum.

10. Craig Larman and Bas Vodde. *Scaling Lean and Agile Development: Thinking and Organizational Tools for Large-Scale Scrum* (Addison-Wesley, 2009).

11. Niklas Modig. *This Is Lean* (Rheologica Publishing, 2013).

12. Karen Martin and Mike Osterling. *Value Stream Mapping* (McGraw-Hill Education, 2014).

13. John Seddon. *Freedom from Command and Control* (Vanguard Consulting, 2003).

4

Agile Organizational Design

The organization is not an end in itself; it is simply a vehicle for accomplishing the strategic tasks of the business.
—Amy Kates and Jay R. Galbraith[1]

Organizational design is a topic about which writings could fill an entire library. Even so, we decided to include it in this book because it strongly influences the level of agility in an organization. Many decisions in an Agile transformation affect the organizational design—from product definition, team composition, and roles and responsibilities to the appraisal system. However, an Agile setup probably isn't needed everywhere in the organization—Agile is not a silver bullet. Instead, we recommend evaluating a focus and practice that are appropriate for an organization's specific ambition.

An Agile approach is very effective in the context of innovation and development—or, as Ken Schwaber once said, "in situations where more is unknown than known."[2] In some places, Agile will be less appropriate.

In the previous chapters, we described the optimizing goals of an Agile organizational design. We shared typical reasons for adopting agility in an organization and shared common adoption challenges. In this chapter, we share Agile organizational design guidelines that build on the previous discussions. We start with a design process overview that you can use as a guide.

Why Organizational Redesign?

A proper organizational design is one that enables the organization to execute its business strategy effectively. The business strategy sets out the primary plan for a company to succeed. Typically, it specifies not only the products, services, and markets to serve, but also the goals to attain, required behaviors, and values to pursue. To realize the strategy, an organization must have supporting capabilities. According to Jay Galbraith, an organizational capability is defined as "the skills, competencies, and alignment of the people that create a competitive advantage"[3]—the things the organization needs to be able to do to execute the strategy. At the level of the overall organization, capabilities are more general, such as "Produce leading-edge products." At the unit level, a capability could be more specific, such as "Having autonomous teams that solve end-user problems."

When its strategy and its capabilities are incompatible, the organization becomes less effective. Let us share two simple examples.

- One of our clients decided that it needed to respond quickly to customer requests to be successful. Its existing department structure and processes made even a small change to a product take months of decision making and development. This company's current capabilities did not support its new strategy.

- A company that is a low-cost producer of standardized products needs different capabilities than a company that focuses on innovation and fast new-product development. The former will benefit from process efficiency and standardized processes, while the latter requires experimentation, creativity, and innovation.

When an organization concludes (based on industry trends, competitor analyses, or current performance) that it needs to become an Agile organization, many of its current capabilities might no longer be needed or sufficient for success. In that case, the employees need to redesign the organization into one that allows it to build the necessary capabilities over time. A redesign includes rethinking:

- **Structure:** Which organizational units, such as departments, groups, and teams, are required? How are work and responsibilities divided among those units? Which roles are required, and how are accountability and decision-making authority allocated among roles?

- **Processes and integration:** How do the units and roles relate to each other and collaborate? How do they share information, allocate budgets, coordinate, and make decisions?

- **People:** Which behaviors and values bring the structure to life? Which team and employee skills and capabilities are needed? What do we value in people? Which rewards and reward systems are required?

Business Strategy Drives Organizational Design

Figure 4.1 provides an overview of how the business strategy drives the organizational design. The required capabilities follow from the business strategy, and the goal is to design an organization that allows the required capabilities to emerge over time.

Figure 4.1
Business strategy drives organizational design.

Working in a new design helps the people unlearn what worked previously but is no longer appropriate, and learn what is needed to build the new capabilities.

Some examples of how design decisions can facilitate the development of capabilities are as follows:

- For fast adaptation to customer insights, consider creating a short feedback delivery process that allows fast learning about the customer. Allow decision making by people who work closely with the customers.

- For teams to take ownership of delivering customer value, consider designing autonomous teams that include all the skills necessary to finish their work independently of other teams.

- For efficient product development flow, consider designing a reward system and career path that values people for developing multiple skills. Multi-skilled specialists can reduce bottlenecks in the delivery process (see Chapter 3, "Optimize for Adaptiveness").

Caution

Some companies might want to adopt Agile to reduce costs by reducing headcount. We do **not** recommend this approach because when the bulk of your costs are fixed costs, you don't profit through cost reduction. Many times, the core reasons for high costs are overly complex processes, work in process, and slow delivery (inventory). In those cases, you can best reduce costs by improving flow.

Cost is in Flow of work, not in the workers' Activity. Improve Flow and reduce costs.[4]

Overview of a Design Process

Until the people start working in the new organizational design and experience its effects, most of the design decisions made will merely be speculations; it is not clear if these will yield the expected results. Therefore, it is crucial to reflect frequently and learn about what works and what does not. Then you can feed that learning back into the process to improve and let the details of the change emerge. Apply Agile to the adoption process itself: Collaborate, Act, Reflect, and Improve—actions coined "the heart of Agile" by Alistair Cockburn, co-author of the *Manifesto for Agile Software Development*.[5]

Aim to involve all relevant and impacted people in all aspects of the organizational design. Design a process for *the ongoing evolution of the organizational design* and a culture of challenging the status quo, and regularly revisit the process, structure, and required capabilities.

We like to visualize the design process as unfolding in multiple overlapping phases, as shown in Figure 4.2.

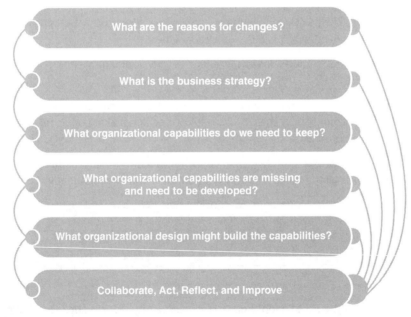

Figure 4.2
Overview of the design process.

In the first phase, you clarify the reasons for change and the business strategy. You answer these questions:

- What are the reasons for change?
- What is the (new)business strategy?

The answers to these two questions provide the context to determine the required organizational capabilities. Questions to consider answering next are:

- Which organization capabilities are missing and need to be developed?

- Which, if any, of the current organizational capabilities do we need to keep?

You'll need to assess the current organization and determine which current organizational capabilities support or obstruct the changed strategy. See Chapter 8, "Preparing the Product Group," and Chapter 9, "Launching the Product Group," for details on how to do this.

You'll probably want to keep some of the current capabilities and augment them with any missing capabilities to obtain a complete list of what you think is needed to succeed. You can then create a first organizational design that helps you build these capabilities. The question to answer next is this:

- Which organizational design will provide the required capabilities?

The design guidelines described in this chapter help in making these design decisions.

Finally, you arrive at the last essential step:

- Work in the new design, frequently reflect, and feed insights into the previous steps to improve.

With this process to guide you—and the list of required capabilities in your hand—you are ready to start designing the Agile organization that fits your context. The next section shares some design guidelines for meeting the typical challenges encountered in the design process of an Agile organization.

Agile Organization Design Guidelines

We organized these guidelines around the areas of structure, processes and integration, and people.

Structural Guidelines

The way people and work are grouped into units is called the structure of an organization. When the work is more than a single team can handle, the work needs to be divided among different units; this includes assigning responsibilities, defining reporting relations, and allocating resources. The following section provides guidelines for structuring an organization for agility.

Guideline 1: Organize in Product Groups

In the book *The Toyota Way*,[6(p. 304)] Jeffrey Liker, Professor of Industrial and Operations Engineering at the University of Michigan, recommends organizing around product families. Each product family should have a senior manager who is responsible for the product family and has control over all the resources needed to create those products, including maintenance, engineering, and quality. According to James O. Coplien, co-author of *A Scrum Book*,[7] the key structural unit of an Agile organization is the collection of people playing roles that interact along the flow of value from an idea to use.

In this book we use the term *product group* to denote the key structural unit; it is defined by the following criteria:

- Its purpose or function within the organization

- The organizational elements required to achieve its purpose or function, such as cross-functional teams, shared functions, systems, roles, accountabilities, and responsibilities

- The senior manager who leads the product group—a person with a deep understanding of the product and process, who is responsible for creating value to users and is accountable for product success to the customer and organization

- A market focus and/or profit and loss responsibility

- Product decision-making autonomy

Avoid Designing the Product Group from the Inside Out

As mentioned in Chapter 1, "Organizing for Adaptability," in a functional hierarchy, many different units are required to deliver customer value. Typically, such a design results from thinking from the inside out. An inside-out design is based on an internal business process or the system architecture.

Here are two examples of design from the inside out:

- One of our clients developed a trading system. The process from registration, trading, and billing consists of 23 process steps. How did they design their structure? They had 17 teams, and each team worked on one or two business process steps, even though a feature largely required multiple business process steps to deliver value to a customer.

- Another client developed x-ray analysis systems. The system architecture consisted of components such as Motion Control, Data Extraction, Data Analysis, and many more. How did they structure the organization? They had one or more teams per architectural component, although 80% of customer features required changing most of the components together.

Such designs make it hard to focus on adding customer value; instead, they emphasize concentrating on and locally optimizing the performance of the component teams. As discussed previously, such a design introduces long feedback loops and hence low agility.

Prefer Designing the Product Group from the Outside In

To design the product group from the outside in, start with the customer problems that need to be solved. Study how solving those problems for your customer works in your organization. Determine which organizational elements, such as units, processes, and people, are needed to create customer value. Then combine them into a product group, as outlined in the previous criteria for a product group. In Chapter 8, "Preparing the Product Group," we discuss in detail how you can define your product group. For now, we provide an example of a product group that was defined from the outside in.

A product group was organized around a banking product that targeted small and medium entrepreneurs (SME), who needed the following services: opening accounts; maintaining them; and supporting basic operations such as payments, paying taxes, and reporting. This product group was led by a vice president of the bank who reported directly to the CEO. This person was also the Product Owner. The core digital solution was developed by five feature teams fed from the shared Product Backlog. Important to note here is that the product group also included non-software development teams that made the unit autonomous. Figure 4.3 shows the structure of the Product Group.

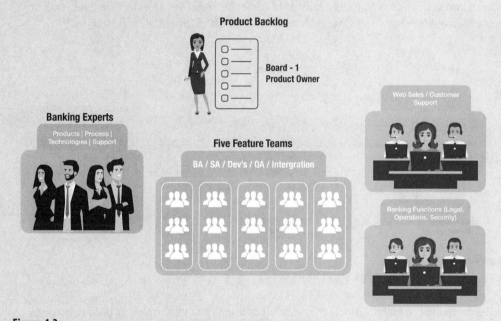

Figure 4.3
An example outside-in design for an SME digital structure.

The Product Owner was also supported by a group of banking experts who had rich domain knowledge and did not do software development. Instead, they were responsible for creating customer support and sales processes, and assisted the Product Owner with marketing research. The product group also contained functions such as sales, customer support, security, legal oversight, and daily banking operations. These functions were not included in the feature teams because their interdependency with the features teams was weak and pooled (see Guideline 5). This product group had a high level of autonomy and showed excellent business results that were recognized at the company level.

Guideline 2: Decouple Unit Functions

For an organization to fulfill its purpose, it needs to perform various activities. For example, in a typical product organization, you can expect to see functions such as product development, sales, marketing, and IT, as well as supportive administrative functions such as staffing, planning, and budgeting. From an organizational design perspective, the question is: "How do we allocate these functions to units in our organization to best achieve our purpose?"

The most straightforward organizational design is to allocate each of these functions to a separate unit. Figure 4.4 illustrates this process. Nicolay Worren, Associate Professor in Leadership and Organization at the Norwegian University of Life Sciences, provides an extensive discussion of decoupling unit functions in his paper "Functional Analysis of Organizational Designs."[8]

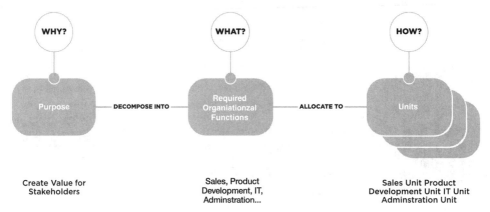

Figure 4.4
Functional decomposition of organizational units.

Ideally, each unit can fulfill its function by making decisions and performing its tasks to reach its goals, without negatively affecting the ability of other units to fulfill their own functions and attain their own particular goals. However, when the functions are coupled, this can lead to serious problems.

Here's a classic example seen in development organizations: To maximize revenue, the sales department sells more products than the development department can deliver. The sales department attempts to achieve its sales targets, negatively impacting the product development's ability to achieve its goal of timely delivery.

Such coupling between the unit's functions can severely hamper the performance of the larger organization. According to Worren, coupling between unit functions is associated with increased coordination costs, goal conflicts, ineffective or dysfunctional government, loss of productivity, and, most importantly, lower ability to respond to change.

Therefore, we advise that you decouple unit functions so that you prevent attempts to achieve a particular unit function at the expense of negatively impacting the ability to perform one or more other unit functions.

How to Discover Coupling Between Unit Functions

To determine whether there are couplings between units' functions, you can use a design structure matrix (DSM)[6] to visualize the relationships between units and functions. Figure 4.5 shows a simplified DSM for one of our clients. An "R" indicates a strong contribution to a unit function, and an "r" means a small contribution. If all the unit functions are decoupled, there will be only "R"s along the diagonal in the matrix.

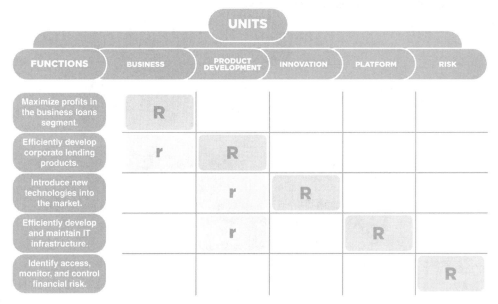

Figure 4.5
Design structure matrix with coupled functions between units.

In this example, the lowercase "r"s show, for example, that the Product Development and Innovation units are coupled. We noticed this in many discussions, and here is one example: When the Innovation unit wanted to experiment with innovative technology to meet its goals related to *Introduce new technologies into the market*, it came in conflict with the Product Development unit. The Product Development unit had to choose between investing time and effort into new, unproven technologies and its primary objective of *Efficiently developing corporate lending products*. What happened is that Product Development gave requests from the Innovation unit a low priority, because addressing them would negatively impact the short-term benefits of the Product Development unit. The result was that the Innovation unit was seriously impeded in achieving its goal—the unit functions were coupled incorrectly.

How to Handle Coupling of Unit Requirements

In general, there are three ways to resolve the coupling:

- Restructure and transfer responsibilities between units or to a separate unit—this approach is described in Figure 4.6 and the text that follows.

- Merge units so that they share measures of success or customer outcomes (see Guideline 3).

- Remove overlapping or conflicting function goals between units by redefining them (see Guideline 4).

Our client chose the first option and structurally separated the Innovation unit from the Product Development, as shown in Figure 4.6. The Innovation unit got its resources, people, and management. Although not perfect yet, both units could now achieve their objectives with more autonomy without negatively impacting each other's functions.

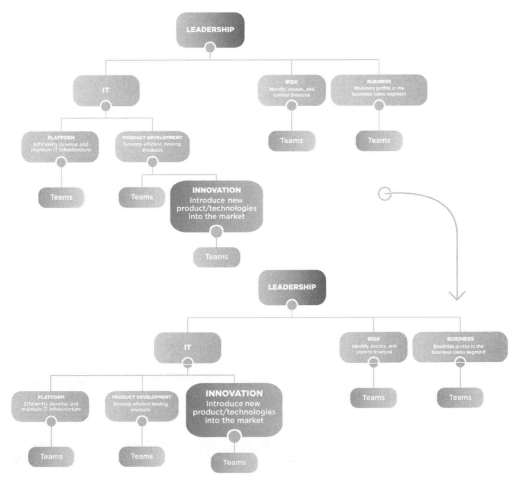

Figure 4.6
A solution to decouple the unit functions.

A potential future side effect of this new structure could be that Product Development will view Innovation as a competitive threat. Also, Innovation could "throw" new products over to Product Development that they cannot develop effectively. To address this issue, the organization would need a process for technology transfer to effectively take innovations into the market.

Independence of functions does not mean that there are no operational dependencies between the units. Our client's Development and Innovation units still need to collaborate. So, they are operationally dependent but have no functional coupling.

Guideline 3: Merge Units with Essential Interdependencies

Another way to reduce the coupling between unit functions is to merge them and assign them to a larger unit. But which unit functions should be merged? We take a systems view and consider merging those unit functions that are essential parts of the broader product.

R. A. Ackoff, Professor Emeritus of Management Science at the Wharton School, University of Pennsylvania, provides a general approach to identify the broader system (a product group in our case) of which units are a part:

Step 1. Start with any unit and then identify the containing whole by asking for each unit: What is this unit a part of?

Step 2. Identify the purpose or defining function of this containing whole, usually a product group with profit and loss responsibility. (The great cybernetician, Stafford Beer, coined the phrase, "The purpose of a system is what it does." So, the purpose of a product group should be to output successful products. See also Chapter 8, "Preparing the Product Group" for a real-life example for defining your product.)

Step 3. Identify the role or function each unit has in this containing whole with respect to the function or purpose of the broader product group.

Step 4. Analyze whether the identified roles or functions manifest as essential interdependencies between the unit and the product group. A unit provides an essential capability if that capability is required for the product group to carry out its purpose. If a unit can be omitted and the product group can still output successful product, then the unit is a nonessential part. (See Chapter 1 in Ackoff's book *Re-creating the Corporation*[9] for further details on how to define a system and its essential parts.)

Suppose you conclude that a separate unit has essential interdependencies with other units in the product group. In that case, you probably do not want to keep them as separate independent units—with independent management goals and objectives—but instead should merge them into a larger unit. Why? Because essential interdependencies create unnecessary coordination costs and slow the organization down when two or more subunits need to coordinate and adjust to each other's actions. More importantly, they reduce organizational flexibility, because changes cannot be made independently in one unit without affecting the work performed by other units.

> *In software development most of the dependencies between component teams are essential interdependencies. That is, decisions made in one team may affect the decisions in one or more other team, and vice versa.*

Let's go through a real-life example using the context in Figure 4.5. The Product Development unit wanted to improve their test automation environment to achieve their assigned unit function: *Efficiently develop corporate lending products*. The Business unit decided against going that route because that would delay the release date of their product and negatively impact their assigned unit function: *Maximize profit in the business segment*. These two unit requirements seem to conflict, in which case Guideline 3 suggests separating them. But are they really conflicting functions?

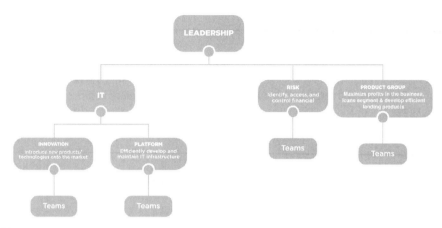

Figure 4.7
A Product Group structure.

Let's apply Ackoff's steps to determine if they are essential parts or the same larger whole:

1. Identify the containing whole by asking for each unit: What is this a part of?
   Both the Product Development unit and the Business unit were part of a 500-plus member product group.

2. Identify the purpose or defining function of this containing whole.
   The purpose of the product group was: *Empower entrepreneurs to stay a step ahead by offering corporate lending products and services.*

3. Identify the role or function each unit has in this containing whole.
   For the Business unit: *Efficiently develop corporate lending products*; for the Development unit: *Maximize profit in the business segment.*

Now the question is: Are both units essential parts for the product group to carry out its purpose?

Let's analyze this scenario. To *maximize profits*, the Business unit needs *efficient development*, and to *develop efficiently,* the Product Development unit needs to *develop the most profitable features*. So, the capability to *maximize profits* by the Business unit is affected by the capability to *develop efficiently* by the Product Development unit, and vice versa—the units are interdependent. Consequently, both units are required to carry out the product group's purpose, and none of the units can achieve that purpose independently. Therefore, both units are interdependent and essential parts of the product group and should be assigned to the same larger unit, the product group.

In Figure 4.7, you can see that the Product Development unit and the Business unit were merged into a Product Group. Additional benefits of this design are as follows:

- Business and Development people now belong to the same unit and are more likely to coordinate effectively because they work for the same management.

- They also share goals and priorities and want to achieve the same purpose.

- Over time, the people in a unit are likely to develop a shared process that further improves collaboration.

In contrast, if one unit is dependent upon other independent units to perform its work, it will require coordination with people who usually report to another manager, pursue different goals and priorities, and may work with incompatible processes. In an Agile organization, this is the wrong path to go down.

In Chapter 8, "Preparing the Product Group," we'll share a detailed example of how to perform this merger by capitalizing on the types and strengths of dependencies. For now, we'll limit the discussion to explaining the principle in general terms.

The System Boundaries Determine the Types of Dependencies Between the Units

Let's discuss two situations that might arise in the organization. As mentioned in Chapter 2, "Systems Thinking," boundaries divide the system you want to study from "everything else." A broad boundary can determine that a unit is an essential part, while a narrow boundary can determine that the unit is not an essential part. For example, in Figure 4.7, we see a Risk unit. Should that Risk unit be merged with the product group?

- **First situation:** Let's narrow down the boundary of the whole to be only the Product Development unit. In this case, the question becomes: Is the Risk unit an essential part of the Product Development unit and necessary to achieve its function?

  Using the DSM in figure 4.5, the answer is no: To *Efficiently develop corporate lending products*, the Product Development unit does not depend on the capability of the Risk unit: *Identify, assess, monitor, and control financial risk*. Thus, the Risk unit should not be part of the same larger unit because the Risk unit is a nonessential part of the Product Development unit. The product group does not need the Risk unit to carry out its purpose of product development.

- **Second situation:** Let's broaden the boundary of the whole to be the product group. In this case, the question becomes: Is the Risk unit an essential part of the product group unit and necessary to achieve its purpose? The answer is yes: For the product group to carry out its purpose of *Empowering entrepreneurs to stay a step ahead by offering corporate lending products and services*, it depends on the Risk unit performing its function of *Identify, assess, monitor, and control financial risk*. In this case, the Risk unit should be part of the same larger unit because it is an essential part of the product group. (If this is legally possible in banking is another story that we do not discuss here.)

Guideline 4: Combine Authority with Responsibility

A traditional organizational chart shows two main ways of dividing work: horizontally and vertically. Horizontal division divides responsibility between units, and vertical division divides authority.

For example, a classic approach is to divide responsibility for software development between IT and business units—a horizontal division of work. The IT department is responsible for the timely delivery of software, while the business is responsible for financial success. The authority to manage the development effort is delegated to a manager role, such as a project manager—a vertical division of work. In such a setup, both the IT and the business units are responsible for their parts, but the control to make development decisions remains with the project manager. Typically, the business (the front-end units) identifies customer requirements, close sale contracts, and then requests products from the IT department (the back-end units). This kind of design is an example of a front–back model.[10] , as illustrated in Figure 4.8.

Product development resources are consolidated in back-end units and; the front-end units specialize around customers, so one can easily get benefits of scale and specialization. Furthermore, a front-back organization allocates distinct responsibilities to each unit, and that allows for independent goals and performance indicators. So, one also gets reduced coupling of unit functions. Unfortunately, in complex product development, such a setup of the front-back model gets the Agile organization into problems easily.

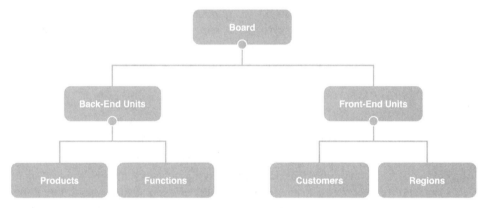

Figure 4.8
Example of a front–back model.

Problems with a Front–Back Model Setup in Agile Development

Although not intended by the front-back model, we usually see that the front-end units are profit centers, while the back-end unit is a cost center. Revenue-related goals are assigned only to the front-end units (e.g., business or sales unit), which leaves the back-end units (e.g., IT or R&D) with productivity and cost goals. The front-end units want to be fast and Agile and to develop customer solutions, while the back-end focuses on cost reduction, efficiency, stability of requirements, and standardization. In such an implementation of the front-back model, you likely will find coupling among unit functions and the associated problems discussed earlier. For example, when the back-end has the most power, it will push technology to the market units to sell. This separation of objectives raises the risks of producing products that do not meet customer needs. When the front-end unit has the most power, the back-end is reactive to the "pull" from the front-end units, and has a tendency to optimize for predictability and efficiency, not flow of value. Furthermore, such a setup often leads to the "contract game,"[11] in which each unit locally optimizes for its own performance at the cost of the overall performance of the organization. It gets even worse when the organization uses internal contracts between the front-end and back-end units to deliver functionality on time, on budget and within scope. The back-end unit wants to avoid making commitments it cannot meet and so pushes for accepting less work and for more delivery time, while the front-end units push for getting more work done.

> *The focus is not on optimizing the system to quickly deliver the best customer value, in the context of learning and a changing world.* —**Craig Larman and Bas Vodde, Practices for Scaling Lean and Agile Development**[11]

The fundamental problem in this setup is the separation between authority and responsibility for product success. The front-end units are responsible for requirements but not responsible for developing them. And the back-end units are responsible for developing the requirements but not for product success. In Agile development of complex products, front-end and back-end units need mutually replan scope, delivery dates and budgets continually as more is learned. The separation of authority and responsibility as expressed above doesn't support such a dialogue. Therefore, it is essential to combine the authority to make development decisions with the responsibility to achieve the value outcomes. In Scrum, this combination is expressed in the Product Owner role. *The Scrum Guide*[12] states:

> *The Product Owner is responsible for maximizing the value of the product ...*

In addition, the Product Owner has the sole authority to decide:

> *For the Product Owner to succeed, the entire organization must respect his or her decisions.*

The end result is a Product Group with a senior manager playing the role of the Product Owner.

The senior manager leading the product group, as defined in Guideline 1, is an excellent candidate for playing the role of the Product Owner.

Here's an example from one of our clients that illustrates some of the problems from introducing a front–back model. Our client was a large telecommunication company; it had been a market leader for many years and had a well-functioning portfolio of classic telecommunication products—telephone, Internet, and so on. The company introduced a few innovation products and created dedicated product groups for them. One of the new products was a "Cloud Service" similar to Amazon Cloud. Its customers were B2B and B2G organizations that wanted highly customizable cloud service solutions from their local provider.

We had been contacted by the company's top management and met with the CEO, who told us they needed help and wanted to be educated in modern management approaches. We agreed to have a two-day introductory training session for the board of directors and top management of the organization. First, however, we suggested conducting a Go See session for one of the value streams (see Chapter 6, "Coaching for Change," for details on how to perform a Go See). Usually, you can obtain a good understanding of the flow efficiency of the whole company by going through only one of its value streams. Because a value stream usually spans most of the functions and units, the CEO suggested taking the "Cloud Service" product as an example (see Figure 4.9).

We found a cross-functional product group called "Cloud Service" in which most of the development and engineering functions were tightly co-located in the head office. That was definitely a good thing to find. Still, the product group itself was just a part of the whole value stream. The "front" part was found in two other organizational units. First, we found so-called value-added services (VAS) experts who belonged to the corporate sales department. Those people worked in the regions and were in close contact with the clients (B2B, B2G). They generated leads and then transferred them to the product group. Second, we found another "front" part located in a marketing function. They did all the marketing research and performed all branding and marketing activities.

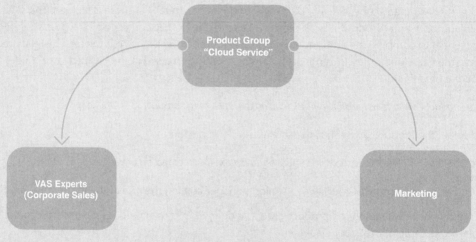

Figure 4.9
Example of front–back model.

It turned out that the marketing role also owned the business case for the product. It was so easy to see two areas of tension: between the product group and sales function, and between the product group and marketing. Why? VAS experts were given individual KPIs and bonuses that made them generate fake sales. The product group employees claimed that most of the leads they received were of poor quality. Another problem was that salespeople were disconnected from the back-end and sold features that did not exist yet. Here are some relevant quotes from individual interviews that we conducted:

- "The current system motivates VAS experts to generate low-quality customers who start using the service and soon refuse it since the VAS expert receives a bonus from the number of leads and is interested in increasing their number."

- "Sellers sell something that doesn't yet exist."

- "Salespeople receive very high bonuses, 40% of 3 months' sales."

Now to the issues between the product group and marketing. The product group employees didn't like the branding that marketing provided and claimed the latter was disconnected from the reality of the product. Here are some pertinent quotes from individual interviews:

- "It is profitable for marketing to understate forecasts in order to achieve KPIs. This puts us in a bad position, because we do not have enough resources."

- "We're out of touch with customers" (product marketing).

- "The client left because it took a long time to coordinate between the departments."

- "Marketers lack qualifications; they have to live next to technology/"

This example highlights some of the issues a company might encounter when client-oriented units (sales, marketing) are separated from the product organization in a front–back model and the value proposition needs to be highly customizable and unique for every paying customer.

Guideline 5: Contain Reciprocal Task Interdependencies

In his book *Organizations in Action*,[13] James D. Thompson describes three types of unit interdependencies:

- **Pooled interdependence:** The weakest interdependence, which is based on shared resources. For example, different teams share the same resources, such as a single test environment, or dependency on a person with a scarce skill.

- **Sequential interdependence:** When a team is dependent upon the work done by another team. For example, an assembly team is dependent upon input from a team producing the parts. It is an asymmetrical dependency. This type of dependency is also observed when one organizes work according to value streams or customer journeys, and teams focus on only a part of them.

- **Reciprocal interdependence:** When there is a frequent two-way dependency between the work of the teams. It is a symmetrical dependency. The work of one team is input for the other team, and vice versa, and there is uncertainty about how to accomplish the work, which makes frequent alignment necessary.[14]

A study about the implications of these types of dependencies was published in a paper by Alba N. Nuñez, Ronald E. Giachetti, and Giacomo Boria.[15] They concluded—as shown in Figure 4.10—that "the experiments find no significant difference between pooled and sequential interdependence and the resulting coordination load." Moreover, "coordination load increases significantly when interdependence changes from sequential to reciprocal." Working with reciprocal interdependencies takes twice as much time to coordinate compared to work with the other types of dependencies.

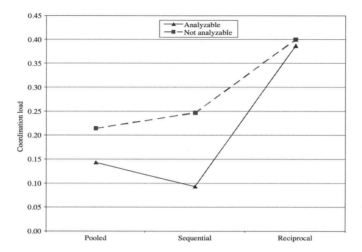

Figure 4.10
Coordination load as a function of interdependence and analyzability. (Adapted from Ronald E. Giachetti et al.[15])

The reciprocal interdependency very much resembles the dependencies between software development teams that work on a single product. These teams have either a mutual functional dependency—when a feature is divided into independent technical parts to be developed by different teams—or a mutual technical dependency—when each team picks up a complete feature but works on the same software components.

Redesign to Contain Reciprocal Dependencies

James D. Thompson suggested that we should design work based on the intensity of interdependence and then introduce specific coordination techniques for each.[13] In the case of pooled interdependence, one could use rules as the coordination mechanism. For example, a shared testing environment can be coordinated using a simple set of reservation rules. Sequential interdependence can be organized by proper planning, for instance. For reciprocal interdependence, it is recommended to manage the dependencies through constant information sharing and mutual adjustments. An excellent way to do so is with an organizational design that contains the reciprocal interdependencies within the same formal unit—as Nicolay Worren describes in his book *Organization Design*.[16]

The key idea is to first design the organization to minimize reciprocal interdependencies between units related to producing value. Then a way to handle the sequential and pooled interdependencies can be devised.

When you group the necessary functions and skills to produce value, coordination becomes easier, flow increases, and rework decreases. This design also facilitates team accountability for a complete work item instead of for just a part of the item. The teams can now become autonomous[17] and can manage their work. The organization can stop giving work packages to a team to execute and instead provide customer problems for a team to solve.

Guideline 6: Group by Common Customer

In Guideline 4: Combine Authority with Responsibility we introduced the effects of separating authority and responsibility between front-end and back-end units. In this guideline we provide a related but distinct problem and a specific solution. Separating the front-end units and back-end units in Agile development is generally not recommended. Why? Because it is not enough for the front-end units to identify customer needs and then hand them over to the back-end units. Instead, people within the product units benefit from a good customer understanding so that they can develop the right solutions. When the back-end units work closely with customers, they learn about the customer domain, needs, and problems. Better customer understanding will not only result in better solutions, but also increase the autonomy of the units because they can make more correct and fine-grained decisions on their own; this also increases your organization's flow and adaptability.

Also, when the salespeople estimate the costs for a product release in response to customer requests, is it enough to rely on historical data? Do they need to understand technology? Is it possible to design a process in which the independent front-end and back-end units come to a suitable, reliable solution about costs, duration, and functionality? From the perspective of becoming an Agile organization, the answer to these questions is "no." Therefore, the Agile organization considers two options to globally optimize for adaptability and flow:

- Merging front-end units with back-end units into a larger unit, the product group, that builds the complex product, brings it to the market, and leverages feedback. The product group might include product marketing, sales and development in the same unit, and that unit is responsible for the success of the product or service in the market. Please note the subtle difference with Guideline 3: Merge Units with Essential Interdependencies. In this guideline we are not merging because of interdependencies, but rather because of broad learning about the customer.

- Creating shared customers and shared performance indicators for the different units' managers. As a result, the front-end unit's manager is no longer the customer of the back-end unit. Instead, managers from e.g. the market and product departments become responsible for the benefits their common customers generate. This coupling creates the conditions for each manager to do what is best for the shared customer (optimize the whole) instead of locally optimizing its unit. An elaborate discussion about this approach can be found in a paper by J. Strikwerda and J. W. Stoelhorst.[18]

Guideline 7: Derive Required Capabilities from the Strategic Focus

Chapter 1, "Organizing for Adaptability," introduced the Agile organization characteristics; these are necessary but insufficient to make all design decisions. For example, you still need to answer typical questions such as the following:

- How do you structure the organization for value delivery and how do you divide the work?

- Which roles are needed, and how do you distribute authority and responsibility among the units and roles?

- Which processes are needed within the units, and how do you coordinate between different units?

- Which human resources policies should be used to promote multi-skilled people working in teams?

- Which specific outcomes and output measures are relevant for the organization?

How can you make these decisions? The strategic focus of your organization points in the right direction.

Strategic Focus

As in most design problems, you must make trade-offs between alternative design options in organizational design. The strategic focus of your organization helps determine the appropriate trade-offs. Combine the characteristics of the Agile organization with the organization's strategic focus to identify the required capabilities. Figure 4.11 illustrates an overview of determining the required organizational capabilities.

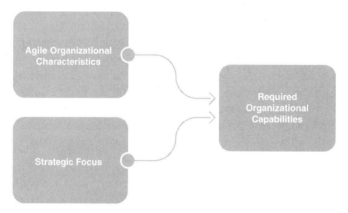

Figure 4.11
Determining the required organizational capabilities.

Jay R. Galbraith and his co-authors[3] distinguish between three types of strategic foci:

- **A product-centric organization** typically focuses on the capabilities of innovation, new-product development, or time-to-market. Value is identified as new products, new applications, and features that competitors cannot offer yet. The organization is structured around its products. Employees specialize in research and development and are striving to be the best. In a commercial context, success could be measured in product releases or profit from new products. Technology companies such as Microsoft, Intel, ASML, and Apple offer these kinds of products and can be considered product companies. Agility lies in discovering and addressing changing customer needs faster and more effectively than the competitors can.

- **An operations-centric organization** mainly focuses on the capabilities of low cost, reliability, automation, and quality. Value is identified based on price, efficiency, consistent quality, cost to serve, or cost per transaction. The organization structures itself around key processes, works to standards, and aims for high resource utilization and operational excellence. Examples are companies that need to handle high volumes of customer transactions such as insurance claims or settlements in banks. Companies like McDonald's and Dodo Pizza are also examples of organizations that focus on operational excellence. Perhaps customers do not get the "best" hamburger or pizza in the world, but service is predictable, fast, and reliable. Decision making about the products and processes is handled by specialists and standardization units. The need for agility is mostly cast in terms of reacting to variations in volume.

- **A customer-centric organization** has the capabilities of delivering high customer satisfaction and nurturing long-term relationships with their customers. Value lies in customer retention and long-term customer satisfaction. The value proposition centers on deep customer understanding and creating tailored solutions for customers. Such an organization is likely structured around customers and has customer- or market-segment-specific units. Employees have the skills to build long-term relationships with customers and show passion for assisting with customer implementations and providing aftercare. An example is a consultancy with units for a specific large customer. Decision making resides with the units that work closest to the customers. Agility is mostly about adjusting to specific customer needs.

Each focus asks for specific capabilities, resulting in differences in the Agile organizational design. However, we typically see a need for a mix of foci at our customers, where different units have different foci and therefore different Agile setups.

Process and Integration Guidelines

A new structure also brings new ways of collaboration between units. How will the units coordinate? Which roles, processes, and reporting relationships are required to work effectively in the new structure? The following section provides guidelines for designing processes and coordination mechanisms.

Guideline 8: Create Conditions for Emergent Coordination

Once you have identified the units to include in your group, the next question is how they should coordinate. For example, how can we ensure that different units agree on the same goals, maintain alignment, avoid work duplication, share knowledge, or coordinate their activities?

In Agile organizations, the teams are responsible for their interteam coordination. Why? Because the people who do the work understand best what needs to be coordinated and how to perform coordination work. So, instead of asking "Which coordination technique should the different units use?", we instead ask "How can we create the conditions so that people know about what, with whom, and when they need to coordinate?"

A networked organizational structure directly links self-organizing teams within and across groups and departments. This enables the teams to coordinate directly with each other when needed. It is different from a hierarchical structure, where interaction and coordination follow the hierarchy. A networked design also allows for faster learning and problem solving because the teams know where to find expertise when they need it.

You can create emergent coordination conditions by introducing the following elements:

- Communities

- Temporary coordination roles

- Co-location

Communities

In an Agile organization, the units still have to attend to cross-unit concerns, including alignment on functional and other skills, standards, shared tools, and processes. For example, a product group needs to align architectural standards or consistent user experience (UX). A way to coordinate its efforts is to form communities of people from different units who share an interest in a topic and like to coordinate on cross-cutting concerns with peers. They should meet regularly to align and share their learnings and experiences. In this way, they can help the product group avoid unnecessary duplication of work and promote standardization and alignment across units.

To successfully launch and nurture communities, consider the following:

- Communities should be easy to start and stop; therefore, communities are informal and do not appear on the organizational chart. Organizational policy should make it easy to form and terminate communities.

- A flourishing community benefits from a proactive organization and attention. Therefore, it's best to have a community coordinator with a desire to cultivate a strong community that cares, preferably someone who is an active, hands-on practitioner. The coordinator facilitates discussions and meetings, promotes participation, and bakes (or buys) the cake to bring to the meetings.

- Communities of practice rely on voluntary participation. Anyone with a passion for the topic should be able to join and leave, not just experts.

- The community might be supported by providing meeting space, tooling that records their work, shares information, and offers the ability to contact community mentors for further questions and clarification.

One of our clients in the energy market redesigned a large group of teams. The people worked in single-function teams such as business analyst, testing, programming, reporting, database, and architecture teams. They were asked to form new cross-functional teams so that each team had all the skills necessary to develop customer features. With the elimination of the single-function teams, no unit was responsible for ensuring architectural consistency and integrity. The organization introduced an architecture community, among others, to handle these cross-cutting concerns (Chapter 8, "Preparing the Product Group," provides more details about creating communities).

Use the following questions to think about what you can do to promote communities:

- Which concerns in your organization might benefit from communities?
- What formal support is already in place to support communities in your organization?
- What, if any, redesign is needed in policies, rewards, processes, or measures to improve your organization's communities?

Chapter 9, "Launching the Product Group," provides more detail on how to form communities.

Temporary Coordination Roles

One specific area of coordination is how to learn about unfamiliar but necessary skills and components. The teams should own their coordination; therefore, you do not want to assign coordination to a specialized role. Instead, introduce temporal roles that can help the group learn to eliminate the roles eventually.

Here's a simple example of the problem. In the start situation, there are three teams, each specializing in a single skill and working on a single component. We still have three teams in the new situation, but now each team works across all the components. Not all new teams might have enough expertise to complete work at an acceptable pace. For example, teams 2 and 3 only have junior Java programmers. How can we deal with this situation?

Craig Larman and Bas Vodde introduce the roles of Traveler and Mentor in their brilliant book *Large Scale Scrum*.[19] Both roles help address the problem of teams learning to work across skills and components.

Traveler

The Traveler role addresses the problem of scarce experts, whose knowledge is critical to all teams. The experts temporarily become Travelers and do not have a final team yet. During planning, they join a team that needs their expertise the most. During the iteration, a Traveler works as a regular team member. But Travelers have a secondary goal of reducing the dependency on them by ensuring that the team knows a little more about the subject at the end of the iteration. Typically, this knowledge transfer is done by teaching, pairing, and mobbing. At the end of an iteration, the Traveler is free to join another team. Over time, the teams learn more and more about the subject, and eventually the Traveler role is no longer needed. At that point, the person joins one of the teams as a stable member.

Mentor

The Mentor role solves the problem of teams that have to work in unfamiliar areas of the product. Mentors are full-time team members, but they reserve time to mentor others. Mentoring is done in many ways, such as joining other teams' design sessions, paying extra attention to answering questions, and holding workshops.

Co-location

Galbraith stated that "the greater the task uncertainty, the greater the amount of information that must be processed among decision-makers during task execution to achieve a given level of performance."[17] Task uncertainty is related to the predictability and variability of the work. Development work is characterized by high variability and usually low predictability, which requires frequent adaptation and often unplanned coordination. The likelihood that people will engage in discussions with each other becomes far higher when they work closer to each other and are more likely to meet each other. Therefore, it's a good idea to co-locate interdependent units within the same floor space so that they can easily have ad hoc discussions.

Design collaborative working spaces of various sizes that:

- Are effortless to find and reserve.
- Are open, allowing others to notice and quickly join a discussion.
- Encourage interactive discussions.
- Provide tools such as a vast number of whiteboards, flipcharts, and reconfigurable table setting.

Create opportunities for diverse interaction such as the following:

- Regularly holding open space events (see *Open Space Technology: A User's Guide*[20]) to include everyone in constructing agendas and addressing important issues. Having co-created the agenda and when free to follow their passion, people will take the responsibility very quickly.
- Having spaces that provide small snacks, coffee, and beverages so that it is easier to approach people. See the pattern Snack Shrine in the book *A Scrum Book*.[7]
- Introducing open work spaces instead of closed offices so that it is easier to approach people. However, you also need private spaces for sensitive conversations, to avoid disturbing colleagues in a discussion, or just for working privately for some time.

Guideline 9: Commodity Platform

A platform, in our context, is a software environment that provides functionality to its users and allows them to build products on it. On the one hand, an organization might use external platforms such as iOS, Android, or browsers as a foundation on which to develop software. On the other hand, an organization might have internal platform groups that develop shared platforms such as infrastructure, databases, or delivery and development tools. When a product group's teams can consume the shared platform functionality on a self-service basis, that supports autonomy and improves product delivery flow. In contrast, when a shared platform contains product-specific functionality that can only be updated regularly by the platform group, it can quickly become a bottleneck in development.

> Let us share an example. One of our clients had a platform called the "Internet channel" that was intended to increase user conversion and usability. The problem was that many product groups could not deliver functionality to their customer without the platform performing work to expose the functionality to the outside world. The Internet channel became overloaded by all the requests and bottlenecked the development process.

A common reason for these problems is the many reciprocal dependencies between the product groups and the platform group. As previously stated, you would like to contain reciprocal interdependencies within the same unit, either within the shared platform group or within the product group. But how? The recommended way out of this dilemma is to eliminate the platform group. But in the case of an 800-person platform group, eliminating the platform group might not be possible or might take many years to realize. Sometimes a more realistic approach is to minimize the dependencies through a redesign. Some redesign ideas were already discussed in Guidelines 2, 3, 4, 5, and 6. In the case of a platform group, we like to add the specific suggestion of eliminating interdependencies by creating a commodity platform.

What Is a Commodity Platform?

A commodity platform contains no product-specific functionality, only functionality that is the same for all product groups. For example. all applications that run on your smartphone have access to the same platform (e.g., iOS/Android) functionality. The application's unique value does not derive from the platform functionality. From the application's perspective, the platform functionality is a commodity—it is the same for all—and does not help to differentiate it from other applications in the marketplace. Developers can create their applications without requiring any change in the platform because all product-specific functionality resides in the application itself. Product groups rarely require changes from a commodity platform.

Therefore, to eliminate the interdependencies between platform and product groups, the organization can move all of the product-specific functionality out of the platform and into the product units. It can accomplish this either by physically removing the functionality and implementing it elsewhere under the control of the product units, or by allocating the ownership of the product-specific part to the product units. In this way, the platform is reduced to a commodity platform; all product-specific/differentiating functionality is removed from it (see Figure 4.12).

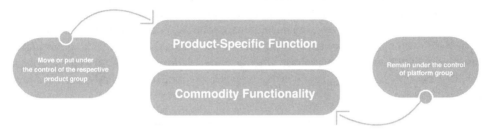

Figure 4.12
The platform contains only common functionality.

In the end situation, the product groups still have a dependency upon the commodity platform, but the dependencies are likely to be sequential, instead of reciprocal. You can manage these dependencies by collaboration, planning, and strict processes using techniques such as continuous integration and deployment.

Guideline 10: Design Shared Services for Support

On the one hand, the product group structure (Guideline 1) creates semi-independent units with separate leadership, finances, resources, and people. This independency reduces the need for coordination with other units in the broader organization. The product group can be fast, effectively adapt to customer demands, and focus on the success of its product. On the other hand, independent product groups duplicate roles and functions, meaning that the organization can lose the benefits of centralized units such as economies of scale (e.g., from corporate financial resources) and economies of scope (e.g., from cross-selling). An Agile organization might want to balance its design between independence and centralization and introduce some shared services such as purchasing, sales, human operations, or marketing, to name a few. But be very suspicious about shared service activities that directly affect the product development outputs—for example, a "platform service," "UX service," or "quality assurance service."

Designing a Service Unit

A service unit's purpose is to support the product group's operations. When designing services, the typical questions to answer are:

- Should a service be a shared service or be duplicated across product groups?

- Which activities, if any, should be part of a service and which, if any, should be included in the product group?

Once again, you can study the dependencies between units to make informed decisions about shared services. We already discussed the following types of dependencies:

- Coupling between unit functions are on the level of the unit's goals (Guideline 3).

- Essential interdependencies determine which units should not be independent but instead be merged into the product group because they are essential parts of it (Guideline 4).

- Reciprocal task dependencies should be contained in the product group (Guideline 7).

In this guideline, we consider regular operational dependencies between units. For example, when a product group asks the human resources (HR) department to hire new people, then there is an operational dependency between the product group and the HR department. This dependency is not essential and not reciprocal, and there is no coupling between unit functions. So, probably the product group should not include HR capability to be Agile. Or should it? To make a more informed decision, consider the following additional dependency perspectives:

- The cost of development delay when the unit is a shared service

- The criticality and uncertainty of the dependency between the product group and the unit

Uncertain Dependency

A dependency is uncertain when the shared service introduces uncertainty about proper, timely, or reliable product delivery. This happens when the successful completion of work is dependent upon a service delivery external to the product group. You can discover uncertain dependencies when there is a need for constant collaboration and adjustment between the product unit and the shared service unit. For example, having a shared service that discovers customer needs and problems is likely not a good idea. Why? Because the product groups' subsequent solutions will have significant uncertainty. How does the product group know that they are solving the right problem? And how do they know that they correctly solved the problem? Reducing the development risks requires fast and frequent feedback, collaboration, and adjustments with the shared service. Therefore, a service that creates uncertain dependencies is a candidate to be duplicated in a product group and not designed as a stand-alone shared service.

Critical Dependency

A dependency is critical when the shared service's actions affect the product group's important outcomes, such as customer satisfaction, revenue, or quality.

Let's return to the "Internet channel" example (which we often encounter in banks) to illustrate the idea. As users interact with the products through the Internet channel, it has a significant effect on the customer experience. In this case, customer experience is critical for product success, so the organization should consider designing the "internal channel" as part of the product group and not as a shared service. Why? First, a shared service can easily become disconnected from product revenue concerns, where the real value lies. Second, designing the Internet channel as a shared service puts a critical product success factor outside the product group's direct control.

Figure 4.13 provides an overview of the dependency types and suggested design decisions.

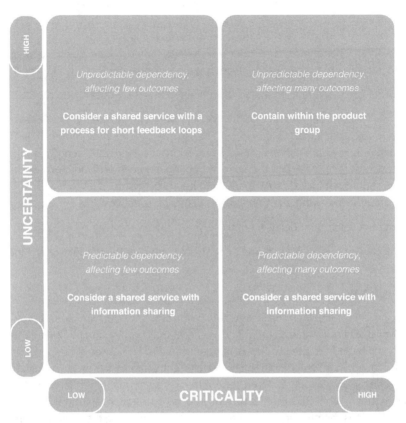

Figure 4.13
Shared services dependencies.

Cost of Development Delay

A third variable to consider is the cost of development delay (see also the discussion of cost of delay in Chapter 3, "Optimize for Adaptiveness"). A focus on resource efficiency often leads to low flow efficiency, which in turn increases costs. Let us explain why by returning to the "Internet channel" example once again. Suppose a product group needs "internal channel" expertise regularly but has to wait six weeks, on average, for the Internet channel service to deliver their work. What is the cost of this delay?

What if you can eliminate that delay by duplicating the shared service function across the product units? Would that better support your strategy and build your required capabilities?

To summarize: The decision to turn a function into a shared service depends on the cost of delay and the type of dependency between a product group and the function. In general, you should study the impact of dependencies of high uncertainty and high criticality outside the product group and then redesign, if needed, by following Guidelines 2, 3, 4, and 5.

People Guidelines

The people guidelines help develop people skills and capabilities that align with the structure and processes. To help your people develop the capabilities that support Agility, consider designing a supportive appraisal system, career paths, and performance management policies. The following guidelines can assist you in creating a system that develops people who support the Agile organization's capabilities.

Guideline 11: Separate Product Management from Line Management

The matrix organizational design emerged during the 1960s, and its primary purpose was to synchronize operations across different sites. It does so by having dual reporting lines, in which employees report to a local manager to develop local business and also report to a global product or technology group manager. Today, many organizations still use such design ideas to increase alignment across independent units and encourage people to consider multiple perspectives when making decisions.

The matrix design introduces numerous problems,[21] but two are of specific importance to an Agile organization:

- The problem of emphasizing individual skill development over whole team development
- The problem of line management decisions conflicting with product decisions

Let us illustrate these using an example from one of our clients. Figure 4.14 offers a simplified view of their organizational setup.

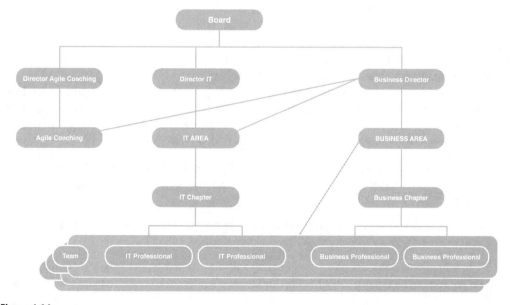

Figure 4.14
AVOID: Example of dual reporting relationships.

At the top of Figure 4.14, you see the business, IT, and Agile coaching departments, each headed by a director. At the bottom, you see cross-functional teams that include people from the business and IT departments. You also see a structure the client called "chapters" in the IT and business departments. These chapters are a configuration of people who share a common topic of interest in business or IT. Persons with the role of "chapter lead" were responsible for skill and competency development of the people in their chapter. The chapters were further grouped into "areas." Note that the people in the teams in this matrix have two reporting lines: one to their chapter lead and one to the area lead.

Problem: Line Management Decisions Conflicting with Product Decisions

On the one hand, the people in the teams in this organization report to their chapter lead for individual performance. On the other hand, they report to a business area lead for product development. The two managers would often set different goals, which led to conflicts in priorities that the people were expected to handle themselves. More often than not, dual reporting did not work because the reality was that the people prioritized the goals of the chapter lead—who did their performance appraisals—over the product goals laid down by the area lead. A typical remark heard from area leads in this group was that the teams had a lot of "side steering," meaning that the teams worked on many things next to what was necessary for the product. In the end, the dual reporting lines reduced the focus on the product group's priorities, introduced task switching, and made it hard for the teams to focus on product group priorities.

Problem: Emphasizing Individual Skill Development Over Whole Team Development

The chapter leads also acted as line managers for their people and were responsible for appraisals and people development. For example, there were IT chapter leads for specific technologies like Java and UX, and their goal was to help people develop in that skill. This kind of single-skill approach encourages people to grow in narrow, single-skill career paths, optimizing the performance of individuals, but not necessarily the performance of the team in which they work. To develop the team's performance, there needs to be a focus on developing individuals in such a way that they improve the performance of the team, too. In cross-functional teams, this means that the teams have the right balance of multi-skilled specialists (as we explain in detail in Chapter 10, "Coaching Teams"). So, instead of having single-skill line managers focusing on individual performances, prefer a cross-functional line manager who focuses on the whole team.

To remedy this problem, design the product group so that line management decisions are separated from product management decisions and cross-functional teams receive priorities from a single source. Such a design should lead to:

- A single person—the product group lead—who focuses on product success and has final say over the priority of all work for the cross-functional teams.

- Cross-functional line managers—without any authority to give work to the teams—who focus on improving the organizational design and team effectiveness. They also help individuals to develop in service of overall team performance. Performance appraisals can be handled by these managers, as will be discussed in Guideline 12.

- Expert leads (otherwise regular team members) who facilitate the development of employees. These individuals have no HR responsibility or authority for giving work to the teams.

Note

Many times, we get this question: To whom do the cross-functional line managers report? In our opinion, this does not really matter. They could report to the product group lead or to some separate line. The key point is that these line managers have no authority over the people, as all work comes from a single source.

Guideline 12: Multi-skill Development

A successful team works together toward serving the business goals. The team skills required to do that are always changing. For example, a top technology today will likely not be so highly regarded in a couple of years. New technologies emerge, and your product groups need to acquire a deep understanding of them to stay competitive. To adapt to this changing world, people who frequently obtain a deep understanding of new areas are the standard rather than the exception.

Balance Proficiency and Expertise for Adaptability

When an organization focuses on maximizing the efficiency of single-skill experts, it becomes difficult for those experts to help others outside their area of expertise. When there is too much work in their area of expertise, they become a single-point bottleneck; when there is not enough work for these specialists to do, they likely start to work ahead. Both situations slow down the development process.

Generalists understand multiple skills, but likely not all of them at an expert level. They can help others in the team and, therefore, are less likely to start to work ahead and more likely to help alleviate bottlenecks in the team. But now and then, a team needs a specialist understanding in an area. If you have only generalists with average expertise, the team cannot handle this expert work in the short term. So, you would want a balance between deeply specialized people and generalist people. Note that we are not talking about proficiency here—both the expert and the generalist will benefit from being proficient at their expertise level.

In our experience, expert understanding is needed less frequently than average understanding. Just consider the work that your team did last week. What percentage of that work required expert knowledge that the average team member could not provide?

You are likely to conclude that there is more work that requires average understanding than expert understanding. The question then becomes how to find the right balance of experts, generalists, and the skills they need to develop.

Create the Conditions to Develop Multi-skilled Specialists

Ideally, you would have people in your teams who are experts in multiple skills, but unfortunately these people are hard to find. As an alternative, you can create the conditions that encourage people to develop into multi-skilled specialists over time.

To do so, create a system of human operations that:

- Values employees by a combination of personal and team accomplishments.
- Values people who become multi-skilled specialists.
- Maintains a balance between deep specialists and generalists in the teams.

An organization can accomplish this goal by creating a multi-skilled growth system that allows people to create their own job paths. Figure 4.15 shows such a value system.

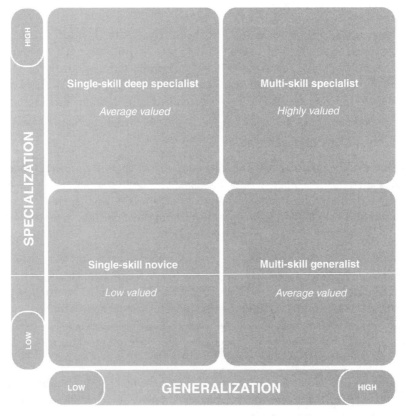

Figure 4.15
Multi-skilled value system.

The most valued members are the rare multi-skilled specialists. People with a deep single-skill proficiency are valued as much as people who have average proficiency in multiple skills. The role descriptions are left generic in Figure 4.15 so that they are decoupled from specific skills and technology—because success is about the skills people want to learn, rather than about the skills people currently have.

How to Find the Balance

The exact skills needed within a team will inevitably change over time, so the specific skills are better not fixed. Also, the exact balance between deep specialists and generalists depends upon the team context and the skills required to develop the product. Therefore, the human operations systems let the teams figure out:

- What is the best balance?
- Which team members should develop which skills?

The teams have the responsibility to ensure that they grow into effective Agile teams, and management is there to support them in doing so.

Agile vs. Traditional Human Resources Management

We want to share a short overview of the principles of HR in an Agile setting. Why? Because once the principles are understood, you can then work with the HR personnel to fill in the details. After all, the HR people study for this. In our experience, they know the details very well but were instructed to create an HR system for a non-Agile setting.

Performance Appraisal in a Traditional Setting

Why do we need a performance appraisal? The classis answer is:

> To retain employees, treat low performers, reward high performers, identify employees' potentials, offer perspectives, develop employees, motivate through objectives, and learn through feedback.

What is the general process?

- The manager and employee speak about what happened in the past and what to do in the future.
- This conversation takes place once or twice a year.
- Results are always decisions about the future and judgments about the past.
- The manager and employees make judgments.
- Feedback is quantitative and closed.
- The manager sets objectives.
- The meeting is initiated by the manager because of the mandatory process.

- Performance is evaluated against job descriptions with many criteria.
- This process is related to other procedures such as compensation, talent management, learning, and retention.
- HR owns the process.

Appraisal processes like these are known to be counterproductive and should be avoided. A focus on judgment instead of learning, long feedback loops on behavior, and—even worse—individual performance in a complex environment stand in the way of developing an Agile organization. It gets worse when an organization uses forced ranking.

> [In one study,] 62% of the variance in the ratings could be accounted for by individual raters' peculiarities of perception. Actual performance accounted for only 21% of the variance. . . . Thus ratings reveal more about the rater than they do about the ratee.[22]

The traditional HR principles do not apply very well in the context of an Agile setting that requires teamwork and work is unpredictable. Some of the guiding principles in a traditional setting are as follows:

- Work and associated results are predictable.
- The work environment is static.
- Employees have control over their performance and can do their work independently.
- Autonomy is low.
- Employees are motivated by extrinsic motivators.
- The manager is responsible for employee development.
- We need a formal process.
- Learning is about bringing in understanding/skills from outside the company.
- Learning is individual, and you learn from managers and trainers.

> [F]orced ranking results in lower productivity, inequity and scepticism, negative effects on employee engagement, reduced collaboration, and damage to morale and mistrust of leadership.[23]

All of these points do not apply in the context of Agile product development. Let's see how a performance appraisal could work in an Agile setting.

Performance Appraisal in an Agile Setting

Why do we need a performance appraisal in an Agile setting? The answer is:

> Performance appraisal is not needed. It is considered potentially harmful.

The lesson is that the organization must learn and adapt to changing conditions in technology, market, and so on. Learning through feedback is essential.

How is the context different in an Agile setting?

- There is high uncertainty in the work the teams do.

- People collaborate in teams with highly interdependent tasks.

- Setting objectives in uncertain work does not make sense. You do not know what is needed in a year or what you will be working on.

- Work is interrelated. It is not fair to judge people on their outcomes in interrelated work teams. Results depend on many people.

- The team skills required to add value to the customers are always changing. For example, a top technology now will likely fall out of favor in a couple of years. New technologies emerge, and your product groups need to acquire a deep understanding of them to stay competitive. To adapt to this changing world, people who frequently learn a deep understanding of new areas are the standard rather than the exception.

- Autonomy is high.

- The manager cannot evaluate employees' performance because they know much more about the subject than the manager does.

- Experts learn from each other, not from the manager.

- Learning is about creating a solution to a problem.

- Only the social recognition/team can determine if an employee is a top performer. Top performers are the ones who make the team win, and who can adapt to the changing world. The same goes for low performers.

- One cannot combine a power relationship with providing feedback for learning. So, the SM, coach, and team leaders cannot have a power relationship with the employees. They cannot be their "boss."

Therefore, the general process in an Agile setting is based on the following principles:

- Employees receive frequent feedback from their social surroundings (social sessions) that drives them to improve their skills and competencies.

- Feedback is informal and not a judgment. That is, it is not written down and given to a manager or HR staff. Instead, it is exclusively given to the employees themselves.

- The team lead, team members, and other direct collaborators provide feedback as partners or coaches, not as the "boss." There is no power relationship between the people who give feedback and the people who receive the feedback.

- Feedback is qualitative and open.

- The employees determine what is needed. The employees initiate feedback sessions or contact talent management.

- The focus is on employee expectations and company expectations.

Summary

The chapter provides an overview of one approach and several guidelines for Agile organizational design to guide the reader in coaching the organizational (re)design process.

When an organization's capabilities no longer support its strategic objectives, it needs to develop new capabilities. Organizational capabilities cannot be bought, but rather need to be developed by working in a new design.

In an Agile organization, the product group is first established as the central unit, and then the particulars evolve through continual improvement. The teams reflect frequently and improve the details as they go.

To figure out the details, we provided 12 guidelines organized around structure, process and integration, and people.

The structure guidelines explain how to divide work, allocate responsibilities, and group different functions. The basis of the organizational structure is a product group that creates end-user value and economic impact. Units should be able to reach their goals without negatively affecting the ability of other units to fulfill their goals. The three main ways to achieve decoupling are transferring responsibilities, merging units with essential interdependencies, and combining authority with responsibility in the same unit. To avoid rigidity and slow, expensive adaptation to changes, the product group should contain reciprocal task interdependencies.

The process and integration guidelines focus on coordination and decision making among teams and product groups. Fast and effective coordination is about creating the conditions for people to understand when they need to coordinate, with whom, and about what. Contrary to common belief, this means lightweight processes and very few coordination rules.

A common problem is dealing with shared platforms. When product groups share a platform, it can become a bottleneck in development. Organizations are advised to eliminate this problem by moving all product-specific functionality to the product groups. The platform is then reduced to a commodity, and eventually no product-specific/differentiating functionality is contained on the platform.

Independent product groups can lead to duplication of services. For example, each might have its separate call center or Internet channel group. As a result, the organization can lose its economies of scale and scope. How can you decide whether to include or exclude a service? We suggest basing the decision to include or exclude a unit in a product group on criticality, uncertainty, and cost of delay of the interdependencies.

In terms of the people guidelines, organizations are recommended to develop cross-functional teams by having a cross-functional line manager. In addition, they should create an appropriate reward system and development system that encourages continual learning and balances single-skill and multi-skill specialists.

References

1. Jay R. Galbraith and Amy Kates. *Designing Your Organization: Using the STAR Model to Solve 5 Critical Design Challenges* (Jossey-Bass, 2007).

2. Ken Schwaber and Jeff Sutherland. "The Scrum Guide." https://scrumguides.org/docs/scrumguide/v2020/2020-Scrum-Guide-US.pdf.

3. Jay Galbraith et al. *Designing Dynamic Organizations: A Hands-on Guide for Leaders at All Levels* (Amacom, 2001).

4. John Seddon. *Freedom from Command and Control: Rethinking Management for Lean Service* (Productivity Press, 2005).

5. "Manifesto for Agile Software Development." https://agilemanifesto.org/.

6. Jeffrey Liker. *The Toyota Way: 14 Management Principles from the World's Greatest Manufacturer* (McGraw-Hill, 2004).

7. Scrum Patterns Group. *A Scrum Book* (2019). www.scrumbook.org.

8. Nicolay Worren. "Functional Analysis of Organizational Designs." Revised December 2015. www.researchgate.net/publication/286922936_Functional_analysis_of_organizational_designs_Revised_December_2015.

9. Russell L. Ackoff, *Re-creating the Corporation: A Design of Organizations for the 21st Century* (Oxford University Press, 1999).

10. Galbraith Management Consultants. "The Front–Back Model: How Does It Work?" December 20, 2012. www.jaygalbraith.com/resources/white-papers/57-the-front-back-model-how-does-it-work

11. Craig Larman and Bas Vodde. *Scaling Lean and Agile Development: Thinking and Organizational Tools for Large-Scale Scrum* (Addison-Wesley, 2009).

12. "The 2020 Scrum Guide." https://scrumguides.org/scrum-guide.html.

13. James D. Thompson. *Organizations in Action* (Routledge, 2003).

14. Taiichi Ohno. *Taiichi Ohno's Workplace Management: Special 100th Birthday Edition* (McGraw-Hill, 2012).

15. Alba N. Nuñez, Ronald E. Giachetti, and Giacomo Boria. "Quantifying Coordination Work as a Function of the Task Uncertainty and Interdependence." *Journal of Enterprise Information Management* 22, no. 3 (2009): 361–376. www.researchgate.net/publication/220306294_Quantifying_coordination_work_as_a_function_of_the_task_uncertainty_and_interdependence.

16. Nicolay Worren. *Organization Design: Simplifying Complex Systems*, 2nd ed. (Routledge: 2018).

17. Jay R. Galbraith. "Organization Design: An Information Processing View." *Interfaces* 4, no. 3 (1974): 28–36.

18. J. Strikwerda and J. W. Stoelhorst. "The Emergence and Evolution of the Multidimensional Organization." *California Management Review* 51, no. 4 (2009): 11–31. www.researchgate.net/publication/264948078_The_Emergence_and_Evolution_of_the_Multidimensional_ Organization.

19. Craig Larman and Bas Vodde. *Large-Scale Scrum: More with LeSS* (Addison-Wesley, 2016).

20. Harrison H. Owen. *Open Space Technology: A User's Guide* (Berrett-Koehler, 2008).

21. Stanley M. Davis and Paul R. Lawrence. "Problems of Matrix Organizations." *Harvard Business Review*, May 1978. https://hbr.org/1978/05/problems-of-matrix-organizations.

22. S. E. Scullen, M. K. Mount, and M. Goff. "Understanding the Latent Structure of Job Performance Ratings." *Journal of Applied Psychology* 85 (2000): 956–970.

23. Jeffrey Pfeffer and Robert L. Sutton. "Hard Facts, Dangerous Half-Truths, and Total Nonsense Profiting from Evidence-Based Management." *Strategy and Leadership* 34, no. 2 (2006): 35–42. doi: 10.1108/10878570610652617

5

An Agile Adoption Approach

The effort required to adopt Scrum is huge, and only enterprises with compelling reasons will make the effort.
—Ken Schwaber

One of the big mistakes many companies made in Agile adoption was to view Agile as a set of techniques and tools for Agile teams. Agile teams are powerful for getting work done but are just a tiny part of a more extensive system. Unfortunately, your efforts will be mostly lacking in impact if the adoption ends with a few workshops and a handful of cross-functional teams. Without a real culture change, your teams will start to slow down, and before you know it, all will be much like where you started. The issue is not about tools, techniques, or following the rules of Scrum. The culture needs to change so that delighting the customer and improving the process, product, and organization become a way of life.

Principles of an Agile Adoption

Over many years we have worked with several organizations interested in developing an Agile setup. Some of these organizations started many years ago, while others were relatively new to their journey. All have discovered that a transformation requires radical change. While working with these organizations, we have also learned a few things, including some basic principles of Agile adoption. The following is a brief summary of the adoption principles we have come to value:

- **Start with your customer.** Understand the nature of your market and define your product accordingly. Then design the organization as a product group to learn fast about the customer needs in service of adapting to change. Identify customer value to improve the product and the process of product development.

- **Change the system of work.** People working in Agile organizations possess different behavior patterns and thinking. As Jay Galbraith points out, "Leaders cannot directly control the culture."[1] Instead, they change the culture by changing the system of work. John Seddon also observes this: "Attempting to change an organization's culture is a folly, it always fails. People's behavior (the culture) is a product of the system; when you change the system, people's behavior changes."[2]

- **Leadership from top down.** Because implementing change is a journey filled with complexities, risk, and far-reaching organizational impact, the committed participation of senior management is essential. They practice *Go See* to understand what is happening in the organization, decide on optimization goals, and make vital decisions regarding organizational design, thereby changing the system of work.

- **Agile from bottom up.** Ask the teams to take full responsibility for their process and provide the freedom to create and improve their product to delight the customer.

- **Manage knowledge.** Finally, manage knowledge to learn how and what to change within the organization. The teams create valuable knowledge by solving impediments in their specific setting. That knowledge needs to be shared and further developed to prevent re-inventing the same things over again.

All of these principles are detailed throughout the book.

Agile adoption has so many variables, parallel activities, paths, and feedback loops that it is impossible to create a detailed plan upfront. This does not mean that planning is a futile task; rather, it is simply an activity that needs to be repeated. So plan to replan! Figure 5.1 illustrates a typical sequence of steps you need to take to launch the adoption.

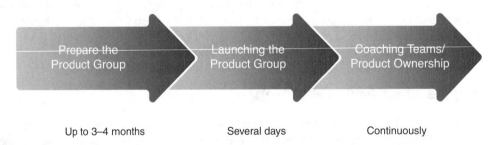

Prepare the Product Group	Launching the Product Group	Coaching Teams/ Product Ownership
Up to 3–4 months	Several days	Continuously

Figure 5.1
Typical adoption steps.

It can take from a few weeks to a few months to get from the first meeting with management until the first product group launch. The reason is that the people involved need to participate in the preparation while they keep doing their usual jobs. If you can halt the people's work, you could probably finish the whole preparation within two weeks.

Why not longer than a few months? From experience, we have learned that overly long preparation drains too much energy, resulting in people losing enthusiasm and their impulse for a change. Also, all the time that is spent in preparation meetings is time that the group is not really learning anything in practice. For these reasons, we prefer starting with an imperfect product group in a few months, and starting learning rather than losing too much time trying to achieve the perfect conditions. After the product group launch, the focus turns to supporting the teams and product ownership in the new way of working.

Overview of an Adoption Approach

To provide an overview of the adoption approach, we start with a bird's-eye view of the activities crucial for large-scale adoption and reference the chapters where you can find the activity details. After that, we provide overarching adoption guidelines.

A Bird's-Eye View of Adoption Activities

We have found the following topics crucial for an Agile transformation. We don't presume you'll follow a hierarchical, order-specific process because you're dealing with a complex system. Many of the activities occur in parallel, some of them happen before the product group launch, and some may happen mid-transformation. In some contexts, you may consider some activities irrelevant.

Prepare the Product Group (Chapter 8):

- **Involve the managers.** It is difficult to grow effective Scrum teams without senior management involvement. That is because these executives have the authority to resolve organizational impediments and change the system of work. Avoid starting your adoption without making sure senior leadership is onboard and involved. Don't expect senior management to be committed yet, as they have likely not experienced real Agile development yet.

- **Understand the current reality.** Often people start an Agile transformation without a deep appreciation of the current reality. To find the areas of highest leverage, you need to carefully understand the current reality first. This includes a brutally honest understanding of your current development process and management system.

- **Create a vision of what to become.** It is crucial to align everyone involved on the vision of what you want to achieve with the transformation: The path: Business objectives → Optimization goals → Teams' expectations. Alignment creates a clear goal and focus. It can also be improved with change stories.

- **Identify the product.** The product definition determines which organizational elements (people, components, processes, and systems) will be part of the first step in the transformation.

- **Hold awareness sessions.** Organize sessions that people can attend to discover and learn about adopting the Agile way of working. For example, you might organize periodic sessions on Tuesdays and Thursdays, where people are free to walk in and attend. In these sessions, management and you can engage with the participants on the reasons, objectives, and ideas for the adoption.

- **Practice nonviolent education.** Teach the *why* behind the Agile processes, structure, and values to create deep understanding. Invite people and teach whoever comes in. If the workshop is good enough, there will be a word-of-mouth effect and new volunteers will show up soon.

- **Volunteer to participate in the product group.** It is not fair to ask people to volunteer for something they do not understand yet. People outside the product group might want to join, and people inside the product group might want to leave it. Facilitate a volunteering session after educating the people about the implications of working in the product group.

- **Co-create the change.** Invite the people impacted by transformation to co-create the change, to share ideas, hopes, and dreams. Co-creation increases the chances of success for any change or product initiative.

- **Hold mobbing workshops.** People might want to learn about new product work areas before the first iteration. The current functional teams should organize mobbing workshops that people can join to learn more about their functions and product work areas.

Launch the Product Group (Chapter 9):

- **Create the product definition of done (DoD).** DoD is everything a team must do to a feature so that the product is still ready for delivery to end users with the new feature added to it.

- **Hold a feature team adoption map workshop.** Aligning on feature team adoption is the first step and a potential next step toward creating the perfect feature team.

- **Hold a self-designing teams' workshop.** Facilitate a workshop where people volunteer to be part of a specific team.

- **Hold team lift-off workshops.** Facilitate lift-off workshops to lay a solid foundation for team success.

- **Identify and launch communities.** Create conditions for communities to emerge that address cross-cutting concerns within the product group.

- **Identify coordination mechanisms.** With the elimination of single-function teams, determine which coordination mechanisms and team roles are required.

- **Facilitate decision making.** Create decision rules that will guide teams in their work.

- **Create useful checklists.** Reduce uncertainty by creating checklists that address typical problems in a large-scale environment.

Coaching Teams (Chapter 10):

- **Implement Agile engineering.** Agile development works only with the right development practices in place. In the context of software development, moving to Agile development means delivering high-quality software during every iteration. The teams involved will learn where they need skills to operate in a more Agile manner.

- **Help a group to become a team.** Reward behaviors that build healthy team dynamic and communicate the purpose.

- **Provide coaching for multifunctional learning.** Create a team whose members can work on multiple kinds of tasks—that is, a team of multi-skilled individuals.

- **Provide systems team coaching.** Improve the performance of a team by improving how the team members interact.

- **Improve team dynamics.** Create a culture of trust and psychological safety—one that's characterized by radical candor and facilitated conflict.

- **Emphasize continuous learning.** Define measures that drive learning.

Guide the Product Ownership (Chapter 11):

- **The Product Owner:** Find a person with the right capabilities to drive product development, manage stakeholder relationships, and ensure deep understanding of the market and customer needs.

- **Customer understanding:** If you don't understand whether you are solving the right problems, you can end up with a lot of quality features that have no customer value.

- **Product ownership measures:** Measure business impact and team performance.

- **Stakeholder alignment:** Prepare end users and stakeholders for working closer with the teams on requirements clarification.

- **Leadership:** Know how to lead and guide teams at scale through visioning and style.

Overarching Adoption Guidelines

Through our years of collaborating with so many companies, we've identified several guidelines that worked for us in most of the contexts. You can apply them to enhance your chances of successful adoption.

Form a Leading Group

The adoption needs a group of people who start and run the change initiative. This group can be called anything, but in this book, we call it the *leading group*. The main reason for having a leading group is to connect bottom-up intelligence with top-down support. To achieve that, the group should include a mix of people from different levels of the organization, from senior management to people who do hands-on value work. A combination of people from different levels of the organization will improve the understanding of the problems and make you more effective in solving them. The main goal of the leading group is to support the teams by removing organizational impediments and making the necessary organizational design changes possible.

Networks and leadership from the diverse many are at the core of driving strategic initiatives. This dual system is critical in reinforcing, sustaining, and embedding business outcomes and new ways of working associated with a successful change effort.[3]

The change group may maintain a backlog of change goals, actions, and impediments that they need to work on.

How the Change Group Creates a Bottom-Up Feedback Loop

In a product group, various teams are discovering how to be Agile in their current workplace. The teams do experiments to learn and implement the needed changes in their daily work. The bottom-up flow of feedback consists of the change results the teams have made and requests for help to the leadership to solve organizational impediments that the teams encounter.

How the Change Group Creates a Top-Down Feedback Loop

The top-down feedback loop ensures the correct change group support can take place. To understand what is needed on the work floor, you will need to have a feedback loop that stretches from the people doing direct work up to the leadership. The mix of people in the change group ensures this bottom-up feedback takes place. After inspection of the input received from the teams, the top-down flow of feedback consists of senior management organizational impediment solving and the subsequent formulation of the necessary change goal(s).

Caution

The leading group role is temporary. Why? The adoption is not a project with a start date and an end date. The adoption end goal is a state in which changing the status quo is business as usual and changes should happen without the need for a leading group.

Align Leadership on the Strategic Focus

As in all design problems, you have to make trade-offs between alternative organizational design options. Work with the leadership to produce a prioritized list of capabilities they think are needed to execute their strategy—the strategic focus. You can use this list to evaluate design decisions and facilitate trade-off discussions during the Agile adoption.

Table 5.1 serves as a starting point for aligning on the strategic focus. It shows three main areas of strategic focus, and corresponding capabilities and measures.

Table 5.1   Guide to Determine Priority in Strategic Focus

	Importance	Rationale
Customer focus on:		
Building long-term relationships		
Increasing customer satisfaction		
Customizing products at customers' request		
Cross-selling and bundling products		
Increasing customer retention		
Operations focus on:		
Low-cost producer		
Operational excellence and process efficiency		
Standardization		
Cost per transaction		
Predictability		
Product focus on:		
Encouraging innovation		
Turning speed in development time into an advantage		
In-depth expertise in research and development		
Having product features be first in the market		
Product market share		
Product revenue		

Within each of these focus areas, the Agile characteristics are implemented differently, so it is important to understand which are most important.

Each focus area asks for specific capabilities that will result in differences in the Agile organizational design. Typically, however, we see a need for a mix of focus areas at our clients, where different levels in the hierarchy have different foci.

Create Basic Conditions for Success

Numerous challenges will surface during the adoption of an Agile organizational design, and many important decisions need to be made along the way to ensure that the organization becomes truly Agile. It's important to create ownership and tap into the intrinsic motivation of the organization's people. This keeps the adoption productive and engaging.

Have a Senior Manager as a Change Leader

When adopting Agile, impediments will pop up that need to be handled. Agile teams can handle lots of the impediments by themselves; however, some impediments that require organizational redesign will need senior management support and approval. When these impediments are not removed, the teams just try to work around them. They become like a pebble in your shoe. After a while, you don't notice it's there anymore. If you're not able to solve these impediments, the organization stops improving. Therefore, find a senior manager to play the role of a change leader.

> *Even if you make some gains, the overwhelming tendency is to go right back to the old way. It can be overcome only by a strongly determined leader with a clear set of goals (vision) who is actively driving the change.*[4]

The change leader should be a person who benefits from global optimization and has the authority to get the right people together to tackle the impediments that will arise.

One of our clients, from our point of view, defined restrictively narrow boundaries for its retail business products. For instance, it viewed "transactional business" and "debit cards" as separate products, but we advocated for one customer-centric product group. The problem was resolved only after getting support of the board members, as they were interested in the success of the whole retail business, not separate products. In *A Scrum Book*, you can find the pattern Greatest Value:

Create the greatest overall value at the greatest scale and scope within the enterprise's span of influence, and continuously strive to expand that scope. Manage work locally with a view to the Whole, using effective engagement and feedback, to eliminate local optimizations.[5]

Sometimes it turns out that even a CEO does not have enough power because that person is constrained in some way by other individuals—for instance, a board of directors or central office in case it's a multinational corporation.

Chapter 8, "Preparing the Product Group," provides more detail about engaging senior leaders and getting their support.

Formulate a Clear Problem to Solve

To successfully implement Agile, you have to realize that just implementing the mechanics of your favorite Agile process (Scrum for example) is not going to make life better. Implementing Agile cannot be your goal. Therefore, before you start to implement any organizational change, you should ask yourself the following questions:

- What is the problem we need to solve?
- What is the business objective?

- Why can't I reach my goal with the current organizational structure/culture?

- How will I know I am making progress?

Answering these questions is not easy, but taking the time to answer them sets you up for success. Chapter 8, "Preparing the Product Group," provides detailed guidance on this topic.

Use Feedback from the Work Floor to Improve

It is important to set up feedback loops for providing information about how the adoption is progressing—for example, acting in line with the Agile values, employee satisfaction, product quality, created value, customer satisfaction, and progress toward the goal. Once you have set up the feedback loops, the challenge becomes to use them properly. What we frequently see in adoption journeys is that the information coming from the feedback loops is often in vain. We see teams that raise organizational impediment after impediment, but the change leaders do not take the time or have the skills to listen thoroughly and respond to them. Therefore, if you are not able to inspect your adoption progress or cannot improve the generated feedback, you are throwing away your most valuable opportunity to guide the adoption.

Create a Safe Space

An organization adopting Agile is learning, and you can learn by making mistakes. If the organization does not create a safe environment, people will act using a CYA (cover your a**) strategy. People will try to avoid experimenting and will hide their mistakes. A safe environment makes it possible for people to make mistakes and learn from them. Trust and respect alleviate the fear of embarrassment, support an "inspect and adapt" culture, and improve the decision-making process. You start developing your environment of trust by taking these steps:

- Create a shared change vision.

- Create shared values.

- Establish clear working agreements.

- Clarify the purpose of the change.

Chapter 10, "Coaching Teams," touches on the importance of trust in a little more depth.

Learn Fast and Expand Change

An organization needs to learn what works in its specific context. We recommend that organizations start analyzing failures and opportunities as soon as possible. Let teams and individuals explore the space and get feedback.

Organizations learn only through individuals who learn. Individual learning does not guarantee organizational learning. But without it no organizational learning occurs.[6]

We do not recommend all-at-once enterprise transformation; it involves too much preparation time and high risks. At the same time, starting too quickly without proper preparation or explicit goals makes it hard to assess whether you're making progress in the desired direction—learning becomes goalless.

Therefore, start with one product group and a maximum number of around ten teams (see the "limits to growth" archetype in Chapter 2, "Systems Thinking"). Provide top coaching to that group to maximize their chance of success. Then, as the group becomes more capable, expand by starting other product groups.

Working incrementally with groups:

- Reduces risk at the enterprise level as you focus on a small part of the organization.
- Reduces the time needed to plan and prepare the group so you start learning earlier.
- Allows putting what you learn in one group into the coaching of the following groups.
- Provides focus so that you can give full attention to the group to succeed.
- Allows you to educate internal coaches who can then guide more product groups in parallel.

Large products might consist of hundreds of teams. In that case, we recommend starting with one Value Area.

> A Value Area is a valuable product part that addresses the needs of a customer segment but which has no useful value or identity apart from its inclusion in the product.[7]

Then make that area capable and expand to other areas.

How Many Product Groups in Parallel?

We often get questions about how many product groups the organization should launch in parallel after the first pilot. We recommend starting a new group only if you can provide top coaching and full support to the group. For a 10-team group, we recommend five full-time coaches during the preparation and guidance of those teams during the first few months. Usually, organizations do not have enough Scrum Masters available with the right experience in large-scale coaching. To meet this need, we recommend providing mentors for the internal Scrum Masters (see the Scrum Master Coach pattern[8]) during the initial launches so that they can start their product groups on their own.

> The key constraint is the people, resources, and focus you can bring to maintain and even improve the support for each product.[9]

Beware of launching too many product groups in parallel especially if they are interdependent. Get inspiration from the pattern [1]*One Step at a Time*.

Collaboration Between the Product Group and the Rest of the Organization

A product group acts as a parallel unit within the larger organization. The people within the product group practice the new way of working. The people outside the group still work as usual, which typically creates an interface problem between the two. For example, there are likely still projects that require people from the product group to do things. Most of these issues are solved by just following the rules of the group. In this case, the project can no longer access people or teams directly, but instead needs to go through the Product Owner to get their work on the Product Backlog. The Product Owner will do a lot of stakeholder management in the early months of the adoption.

Only the Product Owner gives work to the teams.[10]

Other issues are context-specific and will require your intellect and Agile understanding to fix.

Start with a Discontinuous Improvement Step

According to Lesley Kuhn's *Adventures in Complexity: For Organizations Near the Edge of Chaos*,[11] organizational systems change according to two principles

1. Organizational change is a reaction to the changes in the system environment.

2. Organizational change is a result of local interactions.

In keeping with the first principle, we propose to start with a radical redesign of the work environment and to follow up on that with incremental improvement steps (see Guideline 8 in Chapter 6, "Coaching for Change," for more details). Why? Two reasons. The first reason is that when you take only small, incremental steps of improvement, you risk getting stuck in a local optimum. Such dynamics are illustrated in Figure 5.2.

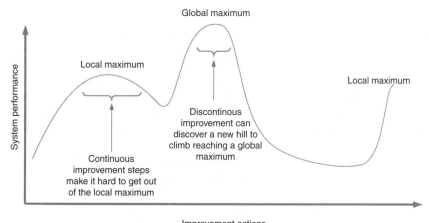

Figure 5.2
Radical change action to discover a global maximum.

To get out of the local optimum, you must make a discontinuous improvement and break with your current approach (see Chapter 8 in Russell Ackoff's *Re-creating the Corporation*[12]). Such a radical change might mean eliminating single-function departments and redesigning them to become cross-functional product groups.

From the systems thinking view, leaving the organization design intact will likely not address the root causes of the problems you see. So, the structures that generate the problems remain, and the local changes will have little to no effect.

Follow with Continual Improvement Steps

Once the people are successfully working in the new organizational design, the conditions are set to gradually unlearn past practices and replace them with new approaches. Over time, a new way of working can be discovered, and a new culture emerges. However, some people will likely feel uncomfortable and show all kinds of concerns or even resistance to the changes. To maximize the chances of success in this phase, the group requires all the learning support they deserve. Chapter 6, "Coaching for Change," provides additional details on specific coaching guidelines and techniques.

Note

A useful source of guidance for building a Scrum organization one step at a time are the Scrum patterns.[13] The decision to use Scrum patterns corresponds to a radical change. Once that decision has been made and those foundations are in place, then you can work incrementally. Scrum patterns explain how to solve problems in a specific context. See also "System Improvements with Scrum Patterns" in the Appendix.

Avoid Providing the Answer Before You Know the Question

A large bank asked us to help roll out the bank's standard way of working across all of its branches in Europe. The idea was that the bank's managers had invented the best way of working over the last five years, and now the other branches just needed to implement their method. We asked them, How do you know that this method will work in other contexts as well? Many things may be different: Maybe their customers are different? Perhaps the market is different? Maybe solutions that work here will not work very well in the other offices? Maybe they have different problems to solve? The bank managers assured us that their way was the best way after all these years of tailoring it and did not want to start the whole discussion again.

Assuming that the best way of working is known, the only thing left to do is to ensure that all branches and teams work according to it. The result is what we call "spreadsheet Agile adoption," and the approach usually goes like this:

Step 1. Smart people come up with the best process that the teams, groups, and branches should implement.

Step 2. They create a model for measuring compliance with this process/method.

Step 3. They create spreadsheets with questions, measures, and checkboxes to assess how well these teams, groups, and branches are complying with the standard way of working. Figure 5.3 shows an example of the spreadsheet that that we found at one of our clients

Step 4. They send out Agile coaches to assess, train, and coach the teams, groups, and branches to work according to the standard process.

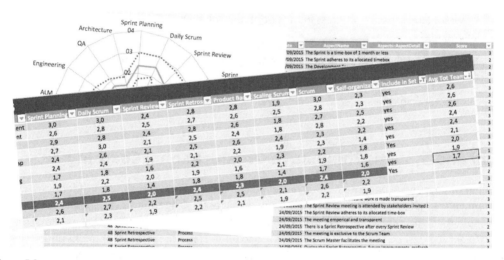

Figure 5.3
Spreadsheet Agile adoption.

There are some objections you can raise to this approach, but probably the most important concern is the potential lack of ownership by the teams and branches. In an Agile organization, we need the people to own and improve their processes, and that is more likely to happen if they can create their process. Handing them the "best" process will very likely not create the feeling of ownership, and if it is already the "best" process, why bother improving it anyway? Also, the "solution" is likely to be rejected and to not work effectively because people probably know their own environment better. So, instead of prescribing the way of working in detail, give them a goal and let them build their own process.

Standards are useful in many cases. They are necessary as a baseline against which improvement experiments can be compared.

There is something called standard work, but standards should be changed constantly.[14]

In this case, treating all groups that do similar work in the same way and measuring compliance with the one standard process is ineffective. It also creates some undesirable effects:

- It creates a focus on spreadsheet compliance with the "best" way of working, instead of a focus on ownership of the process.

- It does not lead to engaged problem solvers who create and improve their products and processes—quite the opposite, in fact.

- It ignores the local environment of teams, groups, and products, and instead proposes a quick fix.

- It gives a false sense of progress in the adoption—what we call "progress by checkbox measurements."

- Most importantly, it signals that you do not expect workers to think and solve problems in their process.

You likely do not want these outcomes for your organization.

Applying Systems Thinking in Organizational Coaching

Multiple surveys and experience reports reveal quite a low rate of successful Agile adoptions. Efforts to improve the system often result in organizations that essentially continue to operate as if the new input made no difference. The reason for such failures is that organizations have a life of their own. To get the desired breakthrough, one needs to understand the forces that might undermine the change and work with them. Our premise is that applying systems thinking principles and tools helps to achieve better results. We would like you to be smart and learn to think systemically about an Agile adoption.

Agree on a Common System Optimization Goal

One of the major reasons why most change initiatives are resisted and then fail is because the proposed changes conflict with the implicit goal of the system. Thus, the system pushes back, in an effort to retain the stable state and undo the changes.

We observed an interesting dynamic in a finance company. It was designed as a typical functional organization with silos led by functional managers. Those managers speculated that the implicit goal of the system was efficiency (loop B1 in Figure 5.4). We've learned that by listening attentively to the stories told and by having conversations with management, assumptions can be uncovered. Narrow specialization was highly valued in this company. The Agile transformation was delegated to the local Agile coach, who did his best to reduce the average work-in-progress (WIP) in the system, knowing that it would positively impact the average cycle time (CT). He was smart and used visualization and WIP limits to improve the flow. As a result, the core systems' elements remained the same while the existing system goal (efficiency) remained intact—but started to conflict with the aspirational goal (speed). The system quickly reverted back to the stable state: Developers started making themselves busy taking new work and secretly breaking WIP limits.

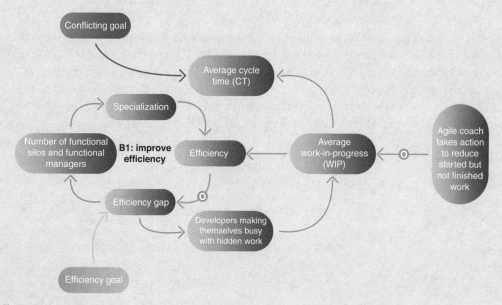

Figure 5.4
Conflicting system goals CLD.

As this example suggests, if you want the system to pursue a different optimization goal, you need first to involve critical stakeholders and let them agree on the desired optimization goal. Then, with their support, you change the system's structure to pursue a different goal and thus resolve the conflict. In this finance company, the functional silos were eventually disbanded and the product organization's structure became a cross-functional one. Chapter 4, "Agile Organizational Design," provides more information about some of the more useful ideas on how to redesign the organization to achieve goals of agility.

Address Secondary Concerns Without Compromising the System Goal

System optimization goal(s) should be defined early in a change vision; otherwise, there is no solid foundation to guide the change. Chapter 8, "Preparing the Product Group," provides a detailed description of how to conduct a workshop on defining system goals. Besides the system goal, you will have to face and address secondary concerns that stay in the way of reaching the system goal. (There is a great blog post by Lv Yi on this topic that you might read.[15]) Let's illustrate the importance of such an alignment with an example.

We coach Scrum teams to define the DoD that is "releasable" from the start. With this product, undone work is minimized and business is capable of shipping the product early, which in turn means learning fast about customer needs. We are accustomed to receiving lots of pushback from less mature teams at this point. The reason is that often companies have high transaction costs due to lack of automation, which reduces their efficiency and significantly increases their costs. The second typical objection is the utilization of developers during the Sprint. So, it's hard to say if the decision to start from a point of "DoD = releasable" is right until you define the system optimization goal and ask people to support it. For instance, if the goal is learning fast and delivering the highest value, the answer becomes obvious. Figure 5.5 illustrates how resource utilization and efficiency remain important secondary concerns and need to be addressed—for example, through automation activities and by acquiring secondary skills by developers.

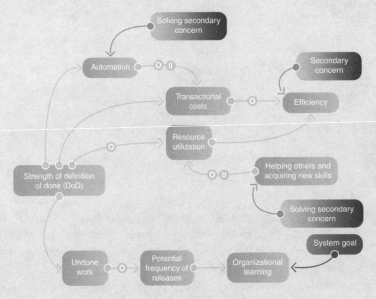

Figure 5.5
Addressing secondary concerns CLD.

In summary, it's critical to understand that we cannot resolve secondary concerns at the expense of system-optimizing goals.

Have an Intermediate Improvement Goal and Perfection Vision

Over time, without explicit attention, processes and discipline will inevitably decay. Improvement can happen only accidentally. Make sure that your change initiative has a clear intermediate improvement goal that drives the changes and is supported by people. It can be derived from the perfection vision, whose goal is to help you improve endlessly (as illustrated in Figure 5.6). Chapter 8, "Preparing the Product Group," explains how to create a perfection vision in more detail.

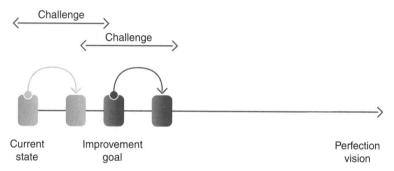

Figure 5.6
The intermediate improvement goal becomes more ambitious over time.

Daniel Pink, in *Drive: The Surprising Truth About What Motivates Us,*[16] tells us that it is natural for humans to seek mastery and to pursue increasingly more ambitious goals. That's why keeping the improvement goal moving forward creates the necessary challenge that motivates people to implement improvements. Co-creating the changes is also important because it creates a sense of ownership; in turn, people are more likely to absorb the changes (as you will learn about in more detail in Chapter 6, "Coaching for Change").

Of course, if the improvement goal is overly ambitious, it creates stress and overburden. In response, people gravitate toward addressing problem symptoms rather than their source, and improvement stops. That is why it's important to keep the balance between overly ambitious and too mundane goals to be in a flow. Over time, as the current state is enhanced, you can raise the bar and update the intermediate improvement goal, making it more ambitious, thereby keeping the tension between the desired and the actual. You keep the challenge; you continuously improve. Figure 5.7 illustrates this dynamic.

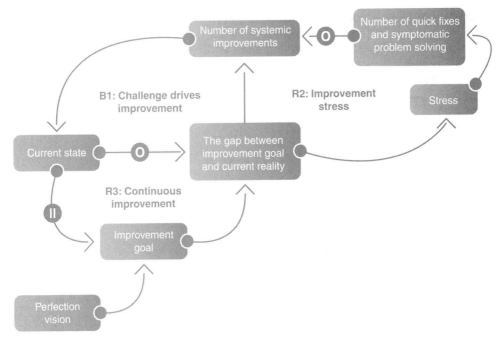

Figure 5.7
Continuous improvement dynamic.

In a large-scale initiative, there were so many things to improve that Scrum Masters felt helpless. They were intensely focused on the upcoming work (facilitation, reacting to teams' immediate requests) and almost forgot about the essentials. We asked them if they had a list of impediments and a goal to improve towards. They replied that they didn't. After explaining why it is important to have a goal, we coached them and collaboratively created an improvement goal for the next quarter: "To bring all Scrum artifacts to the transparent state and make the product flow (Product → Vision → Product Goal → Product Backlog → Refinement → Sprint Goal) effective."

Planning Organizational Interventions

To impact organizational performance, we suggest implementing a six-step process to redesign the system and plan effective organizational interventions (see Figure 5.8):

1. Create a story of the issue at hand by involving critical stakeholders.

2. Sketch the behavior of critical factors on a behavior over time (BOT) diagram.

3. Create a Causal Loop Diagram (CLD) with stakeholders.

4. Find high-leverage interventions: breaking loops, strengthening/weakening connections, reducing delays, adding new variables.

5. Run small experiments, track them, and use them as learning opportunities.

6. Inspect and adapt.

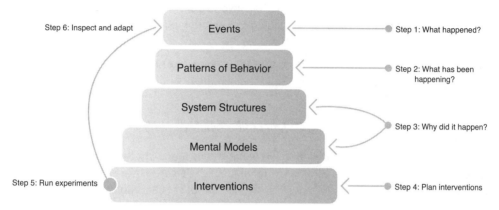

Figure 5.8
Systems thinking in organizational coaching.

We think it's best to illustrate this algorithm with a concrete example.

Step 1: Create a Story ("What Happened?")

We started working with a group of Scrum Masters in a large service organization. During multiple interviews, we asked how much time they spent on coaching organization beyond the team. The Scrum Masters gave evasive answers while agreeing that it was an essential part of the role. They complained of a significant lack of time. In their words, team activities were absorbing all of the time. We were wondering why that happened because in Scrum, the Scrum Master should provide service to the whole organization.[15]

Even so, the company understood the importance of the full-time Scrum Master role in their unique context. Each Scrum Master was working with one team only. We became fascinated by their lack of time for organizational coaching and conducted an investigation. We observed how the Scrum Masters worked with their teams and discovered that teams were highly dependent on their Scrum Masters. For example, the Scrum Masters conducted all the Daily Scrums, even though the teams had been working together for more than a year and could have learned to do this themselves (see the Scrum Master Incognito pattern[17]).

> As the owner of the Scrum process, it is the Scrum Master's job to ensure the team takes ownership of the Daily Scrum.[18]

A Daily Scrum is an event for the developers. The Scrum Master's job (see the Scrum Master pattern[19]) is to teach the team to conduct it effectively within a timebox. At this company, the teams were also unable to facilitate other Scrum events independently. There was no discussion among the team members about who should address challenges or internal conflicts. The Scrum Master was expected to pitch in everywhere.

Generally, a Scrum Master has two options: getting involved and solving the problem directly, or coaching the team, making it more self-managing and autonomous (see the Autonomous Team pattern[20]).

The teams and management regarded the Scrum Masters' roles as being exclusive to serve the teams. In many interviews, we came across this mental model: "Scrum Master is a team-level role."

Step 2: Draw the Behavior of Key Factors ("What Has Been Happening?")

As illustrated in Figure 5.9, when we plotted key variables, we found out that the level of teams' self-organization and ability to handle challenges gradually decreased over time. Meanwhile, Scrum Masters' involvement dramatically increased, as did the number of challenges.

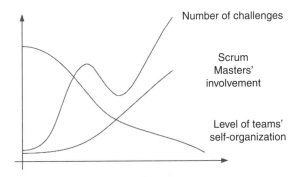

Figure 5.9
Behavior over time diagram.

Step 3: Create a CLD ("Why Did That Happen?")

Together with key stakeholders, we visualized the story in a systems model diagram (see Figure 5.10) and identified a "shifting the burden" system archetype, which explained the dependence on the Scrum Masters. The result was two balancing loops and one reinforcing loop:

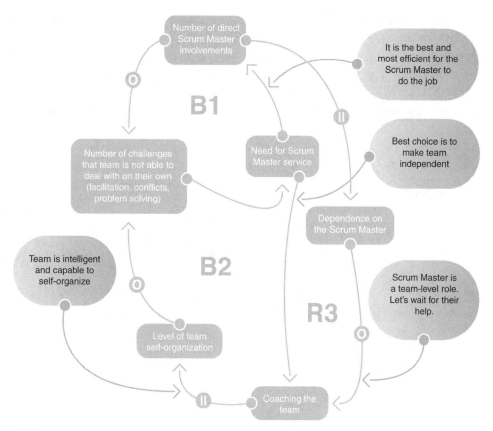

Figure 5.10
Dependence on the Scrum Master.

- **B1 (quick fix):** The more challenges that the team members are not able to deal with on their own, the more the Scrum Master's service is needed, and the more often the Scrum Master is directly involved to solve the team's problems. With this approach, the problem temporarily goes away. The mental model that supports this behavior is "It is the best and most efficient for the Scrum Master to do the job."

- **B2 (fundamental solution):** The more challenges that the team cannot deal with on its own, the more the Scrum Master's service is needed, and the more often that person decides to coach the team. From a long-term perspective, the team becomes more self-managing and can handle more challenges on their own. The mental models that support this behavior are "The best choice is to make the team independent" and "The team is intelligent and capable of self-organization."

- **R3 (dependence on the Scrum Master):** The more often the Scrum Master decides to be directly involved, the more often the team anticipates receiving this person's help, and the less likely it is that the Scrum Master will be able to apply fundamental solutions and coach the team.

The mental model that supports this behavior is "Scrum Master is a team-level role. Let's wait for their help."

In the example company, because the Scrum Masters had been entirely absorbed by the "operational stuff" on the team level, they had not devoted time to coaching the organization; however, the organizational dysfunctions and impediments were still present. They were the cause of many team challenges, which the Scrum Masters subsequently had to deal with locally (see Figure 5.11).

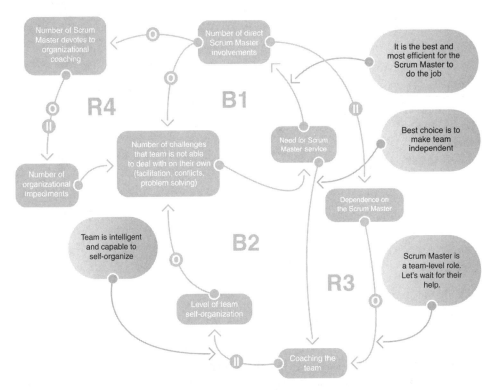

Figure 5.11
Organizational impediments create new challenges.

Examples of impediments include dependencies between teams due to silos, insufficient authority for Product Owners, handoffs between teams, poor cross-functionality, and so on. By visualizing this on a system diagram (Figure 5.11), we obtain reinforcing loop R4:

- **R4:** The more challenges that the team cannot deal with on their own, the more the Scrum Master's service is needed. The more the Scrum Master is directly involved, the less time that person devotes to coaching the organization, increasing the number of organizational impediments that stand in the way of self-organization.

The management at the example company was practicing the Gemba Walks approach from lean thinking. Thus, organizational-level dysfunctions and impediments were on the radar. But because of management's mental model (i.e., that the Scrum Masters were not suited to coaching the organization as a whole), the company had engaged external coaches for many years. The latter did not work in tandem with the Scrum Masters and were not interested in developing them [see the Scrum (Master) Coach pattern[21]]. Thus, over time, dependence on external consultancy grew. We indicate this on the system diagram in Figure 5.12 with the three loops—B5, B6, and R7—that depict together the second archetype, "shifting the burden":

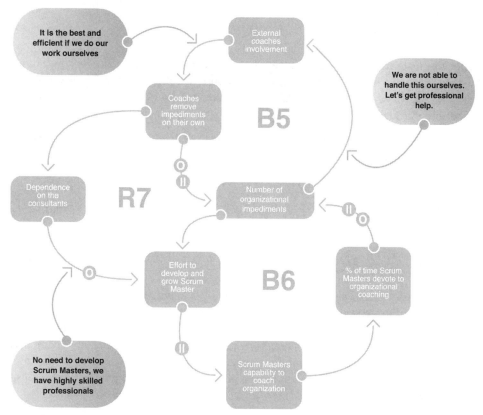

Figure 5.12

Dependence on the external consultants.

- **B5 (quick fix):** The more organizational impediments, the more the organization needs to involve external expertise, and the more consultants remove barriers on their own, which temporarily clears up the issue. The mental model underlying the manager's behavior is "We cannot handle it ourselves. Let's get professional help." The mental model underlying the consultants' behavior is "It is the best and most efficient if we do our work ourselves."

- **B6 (fundamental solution):** The more organizational impediments there are, the more the effort is devoted to developing and growing Scrum Masters in time. Then, the greater the

Scrum Masters' capability to coach the organization, the more time Scrum Masters devote to organizational coaching, and the smaller the number of organizational impediments becomes.

- **R7 (dependence):** The more dependence on external consultancy, the less likely it becomes that the organization will put effort into developing and growing Scrum Masters. The mental model that supports this behavior is "There's no need to develop Scrum Masters; we have highly skilled professionals."

Step 4: Find High-Leverage Interventions

When people create an image of reality together and collectively own the solution, they are significantly more inclined to support it. Working in small groups at our client, participants came up with several CLDs, each of which told a story differently. After some discussions, participants merged their work into the final diagram. The outcomes of this step were several improvement experiments:

- The Scrum Masters start coaching the teams how to conduct events, resolve conflicts, and facilitate Scrum events themselves.

- Scrum Masters begin working in tandem with consultants at the organization level.

- Senior management communicated the message that the role of a Scrum Master is not limited to the teams only.

Steps 5 and 6: Run Experiments, Inspect, and Adapt

Some time has passed since we worked with this client. The Scrum Masters were encouraged to facilitate a critical strategy workshop along with the consultants. The CEO is having a regular bimonthly meeting with Scrum Masters and is in constant dialogue with them. A group of Scrum Masters is now teaching Scrum Basic training instead of relying on external trainers. Scrum Masters are still being mentored and guided by more experienced trainers and organizational coaches. Every Scrum Master has a dedicated mentor and a personal development plan, which they inspect and adapt quarterly.

From what we have observed, the Scrum Masters indeed became more independent, skillful, and capable. We believe that the systems thinking approach helped them to create this change.

Summary

In this chapter, we provided an overview of all the activities (to be explained in detail in the next chapters) to consider for successful Agile Adoption. We then provided overarching adoption guidelines.

The starting point is a leading group consisting of people from all levels of the organization who facilitate the change. To start learning fast and put that learning back in the adoption, the recommended approach is to avoid enterprise-wide adoption, but instead work with a single product group at a time. It is important to perform a radical discontinuous improvement step and establish the complete product group at the start. Then you should give that product group all the support they deserve and create the basic conditions for them to be successful.

To ensure ownership of the new way of working, the teams themselves should create their process while you avoid the "spreadsheet Agile adoption" pitfalls. You can avoid local optimizations by taking a systems view toward the organizational coaching and use Scrum patterns to solve problems that optimize the goals of the product group.

References

1. Jay Galbraith et al. *Designing Dynamic Organizations: A Hands-on Guide for Leaders at All Levels* (Amacom, 2001).

2. John Seddon. *Freedom from Command and Control: Rethinking Management for Lean Service* (Productivity Press, 2005).

3. John P. Kotter, Vanessa Akhtar, and Gaurav Gupta. *Change: How Organizations Achieve Hard-to-Imagine Results in Uncertain and Volatile Times* (Wiley, 2021).

4. Art Byrne and James P. Womack. *The Lean Turnaround : How Business Leaders Use Lean Principles to Create Value and Transform Their Company* (McGraw-Hill, 2012).

5. "Greatest Value." https://sites.google.com/a/scrumplop.org/published-patterns/value-stream/greatest-value.

6. Peter Senge. *The Fifth Discipline: The Art and Practice of the Learning Organization* (Doubleday, 1994).

7. "Value Areas." https://sites.google.com/a/scrumplop.org/published-patterns/value-stream/value-areas.

8. "Scrum (Master) Coach." https://tinyurl.com/ScrumMastCoach.

9. Craig Larman and Bas Vodde. *Large-Scale Scrum: More with LeSS* (Addison-Wesley, 2016).

10. Ken Schwaber and Jeff Sutherland. "The Scrum Guide." https://scrumguides.org/docs/scrumguide/v2020/2020-Scrum-Guide-US.pdf.

11. Lesley Kuhn. *Adventures in Complexity: For Organizations Near the Edge of Chaos* (Triarchy Press, 2009), 26–28.

12. Russell L. Ackoff, *Re-creating the Corporation: A Design of Organizations for the 21st Century* (Oxford University Press, 1999)..

13. "One Step at a Time." https://tinyurl.com/yc4bn9my.

14. Taiichi Ohno. *Taiichi Ohno's Workplace Management: Special 100th Birthday Edition* (McGraw-Hill, 2012).

15. Lv Yi. "System Goals and Secondary Concerns." https://blog.odd-e.com/yilv/2018/07/seeing-system-dynamics-in-organizational-change-2-local-optimization-and-system-optimizing-goal.html.

16. Daniel Pink. *Drive: The Surprising Truth About What Motivates Us* (Riverhead Books, 2001).

17. "Scrum Master Incognito." https://tinyurl.com/4v5r6pub.

18. Scrum Patterns Group. *A Scrum Book* (2019). www.scrumbook.org.

19. "ScrumMaster." https://tinyurl.com/2p8nd6sf.

20. "Autonomous Team." https://tinyurl.com/35b3zene.

6

Coaching for Change

The ability to design and implement change easily and realize its benefits quickly is at the core of survival and competitive advantage.
—Melanie Franklin[1]

Resisting change during adoption is a normal human reaction. It is not a sign that a team or a particular department lacks courage or abilities. Likewise, it is not necessarily a sign that a particular framework or method is bad. Resisting change is not only inevitable, but actually necessary for a change to become successful. A change agent needs to be well prepared to work with resistance and have knowledge and skills in change management. In this chapter, we share guidelines and techniques that we use during change initiatives of any size.

We decided to devote a separate chapter to change management because of its transactional nature. You may need to apply it at any time during the life cycle of the adoption (from the initial Go See sessions to coaching teams) and at any system level (individual, team, product, or company).

We don't present a new theory of change. There are plenty of books with the word "change" in their title and, of course, plenty of scientific research on this topic. The guidelines that we lay down here are based on our personal experience. We analyzed past failure and success stories, identified patterns, and found a few guidelines that stood behind what we had done. This chapter highlights those guidelines that we found essential for a successful change. They can be used separately but also can be combined to enhance each other.

Guideline 1: Influence People

Presentations, training, and collaborative workshops are useful and arouse curiosity. But change means dealing with people individually. People have deeply ingrained habits and personal needs. What every change agent needs is the human touch.

> People aren't likely to change just because someone shows up with a good idea or a snappy presentation. It comes down to making a human connection—understanding where people are coming from and what their challenges and aspirations are.[2]

There are a number of approaches and techniques that we use during the change process. Some of them we had learned from the book *Fearless Change: Patterns for Introducing New Ideas*.[3]

Use Corridor Politics

Before an important vote or decision-making session, work individually with the critical stakeholders so as to increase the chances of the decision being made in favor of the change initiative. If you go into such a critical session without having an idea what may happen, you can have an unfavorable outcome that is difficult to change.

After a Go See session in a product company, we had a meeting with the senior management and presented the results of our assessment. The presentation was well received. One of the recommendations was to adopt Professional Scrum. Among other things, that implied getting rid of multiple Product Backlogs' fake "Product Owners." Senior management wanted the final decision to be supported by a majority of employees. Therefore, we worked individually with the most influential stakeholders before the final vote. Those were mostly the team leads and ex-Product Owners, to whom we personally explained the benefits of the new organizational design. In one-on-one conversations, we heard lots of concerns and did our best to address them. We made sure people were aware of the consequences of the decision. The large group meeting was a success and went smoothly.

Show Personal Benefits

Changes impact the way people work and change their habitual environments and routines. Changes essentially can be felt locally. For this reason, it's important to help people understand how the change will benefit them personally.

In a large bank, we observed team leads working under stress due to lots of coordination activities for which they were responsible. From our point of view, that was the result of non-optimal organizational design based on component teams and lots of functional silos. The management burden gradually increased and senior developers spent less time coding. We knew that was their passion and vocation, the reason they chose the profession of software developer. Therefore, one of the arguments when deliberating about forming feature teams was a more sustainable pace and releasing the time for writing code. Of course, we made sure they understood the anticipated benefits we expected from the middle- and long-term perspectives as well.

Build Rapport

We are more likely inclined to support the proposed changes if we know and wholly trust the person. Taking advantage of early opportunities to make human connections during or even before introducing a change is indispensable. Change agents become more effective when they deliberately take time to learn and build rapport with people.

In early 2020, we signed a contract and dived into a large initiative with a telecommunication company. The product group was developing on a media platform (similar to Netflix) and at that moment consisted of seven semi-component teams with a typical "copy–paste Scrum" setup. We conducted a Go See session in early spring, but then faced a COVID-19 lockdown. The Go See session was the last face-to-face event. The rest of the consulting work (preparation activities, the actual organizational change and teams' lift-off, coaching and supporting teams after the change) was conducted online through Zoom and Miro. It felt very exhausting and we were emotionally drained.

That was a change that led to lots of resistance and pain. Why? Our interpretation is that we didn't build enough trust. In a usual setting, we used to have lots of private talks throughout the day with developers, say hello to newcomers in the office, mingle here and there, and enjoy random small talks. We used to personally thank teams for their contribution and have sporadic lunches with different companions. We didn't have a chance to just pat someone on the shoulder and say, "Would you love to have a cup of tea with me in a corporate kitchen?" We really missed that.

In early 2021, the lockdown ended and we got back to offline work again. And how wonderful that felt! At that time we worked with another company and conducted all activities in the office. That contrast was amazing. We were back again to building connections and trust with people.

Reach for Connectors

The so-called connectors are of particular value for a change agent. Those are the people in a system who possess many social links. Because of their extensive social networks, they have power to transmit messages and behaviors through a system. Connectors have wide social circles. Research on social networks says that there is more influence in having many weak ties with people than just a few strong ones, because more people are exposed to what is being spread in the former case. So, your strategic goal is to find those people, convert them into supporters, and exploit their social influence rather than approach everyone individually.

Another conclusion here is that it's beneficial becoming a connector yourself. Get to know the accountants, human resources personnel, finance staff, and people filling other functions in your organization. Expand your social circle by communicating with a broad range of people beyond your immediate colleagues.

Now we have two questions for you:

- Who are the "connectors" in your current change initiative and how can you use their social power?
- What can you do to become a social connector with lots of social ties yourself?

Guideline 2: Co-Create the Change

For many years, management used the top-down and plan-based approach for change. They decided on a change and handed it to the change team. The slightly better way was developing a plan and then selling it to the employees. Neither approach worked very well. When the organizational change strategy and its execution are run by different people, encountering strong resistance during execution is very likely. To avoid that pitfall, we prefer a different approach. We invite everyone to co-create the change with us, to share ideas, hopes, and dreams. Co-creation increases the chances of success for any change or product initiative. When people actively participate from the start and their feedback is used to improve the solution, resistance is much lower and adoption higher. Thus, usually change is best to be introduced in both the bottom-up and top-down directions. Peter Senge, author of *The Fifth Discipline: The Art and Practice of the Learning Organization*, seems to agree:

> During the last few years, a new understanding of the process of organizational change has emerged. It is not top-down or bottom-up, but participative at all levels—aligned through a common understanding of a system.[4]

There are three forms of co-creation that we often use: facilitated sessions, surveys, and instant feedback techniques. We'll provide you with a few examples.

The founders of the company that we helped with Agile adoption were serious about involving employees in a change. We invited the whole office to a series of workshops whose purpose was to define the metrics of Agile adoption. During the first workshop, we decided on the optimizing goals. We had 20-plus participants working in small groups. Each group was developing their version of the Causal Loop Diagram (CLD) from variables that we provided. After each round, we discussed the resulting diagram to create a shared understanding. Chapter 8, "Preparing the Product Group," provides more information about how to facilitate such a workshop.

When the participants understood how organizational design and processes relate to optimizing goals, they came up with an ordered list of three such goals that, from their collective point of view, best fit their organizational context and current business goals: *highest value*, *predictability*, and *speed*. The next two workshops were dedicated to defining perfect states, learning goals, and metrics for each optimizing goal. You can read more on this topic in Chapter 10, "Coaching Teams." It took us several weeks to conduct a series of workshops, but the result was profound. The employees collaboratively defined the optimizing goals, learning goals, and metrics for Agile adoption. They did it themselves, and from that moment felt responsible for the change.

Co-creation is also a great approach in any product management activities. Co-creating the vision, business model, roadmap, and other strategic artifacts creates buy-in from teams and increases their intrinsic motivation (see Chapter 11, "Guiding the Product Ownership," for more details). Now let us share another example of co-creation.

The CEO of one product company approached us and asked us to help in planning and facilitating a collaborative product workshop, the purpose of which was to prioritize the list of potential long-term products. The discovery of each product was led by a subject-matter expert. The CEO wanted this workshop to be very participative. He asked the whole product group (more than 70 employees) to join it.

We kicked off the workshop by stating the purpose and agenda. Then we proceeded to short product presentations. Each expert had 5 minutes to present their product, using 5 slides maximum. We created a template for each presentation. Each presentation was followed by a 10-minute Lean Coffee session with shorter timeboxes for each question (2 minutes). In an hour and a half, we were done and went for a short break.

After the break, we asked senior managers to introduce 10 criteria that were important for prioritizing the products. At that time, we had approximately 50 participants on the video call with us. The next step was the hundred-dollar test, which we used to get the relative weights of the criteria. It is a lighthearted method that uses fictional money as a voting tool. It's a fun technique that keeps participants engaged in the process. We randomly created small groups (3 to 5 members) and sent them to the breakout rooms. Each group received a fictional 100 dollars and had to reach a consensus on how to "spend" them on 10 criteria based on their importance. For instance, the group might decide to give each criterion an equal amount of dollars if they were equally important. When that was done, we calculated the final weight of each criterion by summing up numbers from each group.

At this moment we had criteria with relative weights. The last exercise was the weighted scoring model to prioritize the products. We created 6 groups around subject-matter experts and asked them with the help of their group to put down the numbers on a scale from 1 to 5 (from low to high) that assessed how the product impacted each criterion.

The next morning, we received an unexpected audio message from one of the workshop participants saying how cool that was and how well structured the session felt. We think it's a nice example of product co-creation.

We immediately recognized the short-term value. We noticed a different attitude among employees toward the changes after the session. From our point of view, people became more receptive to the changes proposed and gained trust in the process.

Sometimes we use surveys to get feedback on how the change goes. Use this tool with extreme care. It can be amazing if you have someone who is decently trained in developing surveys. But it's also easy to get bad data and fall into a self-deception. Here's a quick example.

Before undertaking the change, we agreed with the founders of the company that we would collect data and work constantly on obtaining feedback from employees regarding the adoption. We used Google Forms for that purpose. Also, we had a paragraph in the contract saying that a minimum of 70% of the staff should consider the results successful to continue the contract. The survey focused on how well the product group was progressing on major issues that were brought to the surface during the initial Go See session:

- Dependencies between teams
- Long lead times
- Low adaptiveness
- Lack of focus

You can get immediate feedback that supports co-creation using the *perfection game*[5] or the *happiness door*.[6] The perfection game is one of the core protocols[7] (which also include both qualitative and quantitative feedback), and is highly actionable. For instance, you might ask participants to rate the Refinement session on a scale from 1 to 10, where 10 is perfection (see Figure 6.1).

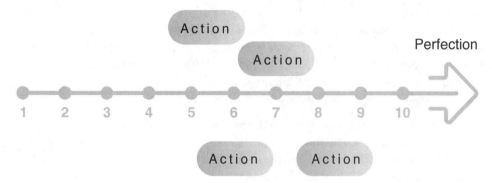

Figure 6.1
The perfection game.

If someone gives something an 8, that person is saying that it is 80% perfect and should write on a sticky note exactly what is needed to gain the missing 20%.

Guideline 3: Voluntary Participation

Change creates anxiety. The status quo has a tremendous hold on individuals, and the possibility of losing what people have grown accustomed to creates worry and uncertainty. The future state is often unknown and brings fear. Agile approaches demand new types of behaviors that are contrary to those with which most people are familiar. Mandating participation reduces enthusiasm, and imposing Agile makes no allowance for what people want or what they think and feel. The intelligent and creative people may "check out" and disengage. That results in failed change initiatives, poor morale, and employee turnover. Mandating also creates artificial problems, such as these:

- "X is not participating in the Daily Scrum and sabotages the process."
- "Team members don't see value in Sprint Retrospectives."
- "Z is not respecting the WIP limits."

We want to share a story in which we let the non-volunteers stay within a product group. This story describes the problem of having unsupportive people inside a change perimeter.

In one product group, we had a component team structure at the beginning of the adoption. After the preparation period, we had a team self-design workshop (see Chapter 8, "Preparing the Product Group") and redesigned the structure into four feature teams. In the old structure, there was a separate business analyst team with four people in it. Those guys knew the product and its domain really well. They spent most of their time writing the specs and pushing them onto the component teams. We recommended putting business analysts inside the teams. They got an invitation to join the transformation, but actively resisted the new process. We left them outside the teams, but they were still part of the product group. They also represented the Product Owner during the multi-team Product Backlog Refinement events; that was an unskillful idea and a fundamental failure in our adoption.

Now we had "anti-adoption" people within the product group. That caused lots of pain and frustration because the "anti-adoption" people tried to undo the changes. They were trying to revert the system back to the previous status quo and component teams' structure. What exactly were they doing? They talked to the developers here and there and urged them to leave the company or at least protest against the change. They spread bad news and made sure even tiny setbacks were known to everyone.

We were lucky to have strong support from the senior leadership and Scrum Masters. By not taking the volunteering guideline seriously, we created conditions in which resisters could easily undermine the changes. Many of them finally quit the company. But a great deal of energy was wasted on dealing with them, instead of supporting those people who helped the change.

The lesson we learned is that in a change process, it's a really bad idea to let people join the product group unless they fully understand the new way of working and have volunteered to follow it. Also remember that a Scrum Master has a direct power to remove a disruptive person (Remove the Shade pattern[8]).

Get the Right People on the Bus and off the Bus

In his research, Jim Collins, the author of *Good to Great*,[9] discovered and proposed factors that differentiate great companies. Collins uses the phrase "getting right people on the bus AND getting wrong people off the bus" to describe these factors—and it is the "wrong people off the bus" part that is very important in Agile transformation. Who are the right people? In a context of Agile change. they are the people who support Agile/Scrum values or are at least ready to give it a try. They might not have the best competencies and skills, but the right mindset is the key. Skills and competencies can be improved along the way, but *now* is also very important during such a change! Pay attention to highly skilled individuals who actively resist Agile values.

The high-performance, low-values match players are poison in your team or organization. Lovingly set them free, as fast as you can. Their very existence in your team or organization erodes your leadership integrity and erodes trust among staff as well as customers.[10]

Such people usually have strong social ties and influence across the network, which can undermine your efforts. You need to get them out of the way and keep them away from the change.

What It Means to Be a Volunteer

Is there a way to avoid the resistance and achieve enthusiasm instead of demotivation? The fundamental solution is voluntary participation. We find it helpful to think of a change as a game. All games share four defining traits: a goal, rules, a feedback system, and voluntary participation.

Voluntary participation requires that everyone who is playing the game knowingly and willingly accepts the goal, the rules, and the feedback. Knowingness establishes common ground for multiple people to play together. And the freedom to enter or leave a game at will ensures that intentionally stressful and challenging work is experienced as a safe and pleasurable activity.[11]

Famous scholar James P. Carse distinguishes between finite and infinite games:

A finite game is played for the purpose of winning, an infinite game for the purpose of continuing the play. The infinite game—there is only one—includes any authentic interaction, from touching to culture, that changes rules, plays with boundaries and exists solely for the purpose of continuing the game.[12]

In this sense, Scrum is an infinite collaborative game as well as Agile adoption. In this context, the volunteer is the person who accepts the goal of the change and its rules and is ready to use the internal feedback mechanism to improve. In the case of Scrum, voluntary participation would translate into the following behaviors and attitudes (see Figure 6.2):

- Accepting the goal of "delivering the highest value during each Sprint" and its main implication, working outside your main specialty

- Conforming to the rules of the game co-created with your product group and described in the *Scrum Guide*

- Actively participating in the Scrum events for inspection and adaptation

- Readiness to conform to Scrum values: openness, courage, respect, focus, and commitment

Figure 6.2
What it means to be a volunteer.

What happens to people who do not accept the change? Do they have to leave the company? Of course not. One of the pillars of lean thinking is "respect for people," and the first value espoused in the *Agile Manifesto* is "Individuals and interactions over processes and tools." We respect their choice. We kindly ask non-volunteers to stay outside the product group because they don't accept the rules of the game, and that disagreement would create a conflict within the system. For example, if your organization has 3000 employees and your product group is 500 people, then there is a lot of work to do outside the product group to pick up.

> *You do not have to spend a lot of time and effort on those who strongly resist change. You only have to help and protect those who want to change, so that they are able to succeed. This does not mean that you can afford to ignore the existence of committed and influential opponents of change. You may have to find ways to prevent these individuals from sabotaging the process. However, once you have figured out who cannot be converted, you should not waste more time trying to persuade them.*[13]

The next story describes how we took the voluntary participation guideline seriously in a large-scale context.

In a middle-size product company, after holding the initial Go See session, we presented our major observations and recommendations to the senior managers. We observed typical copy–paste Scrum adoption with multiple local optimizations. Then we shared the digital version of the Go See document with everyone.

The next step was organizing a meeting and patiently responding to all emerging questions. We used the UX Fishbowl structure as the core facilitation structure. The goal of the presentation was to pop the happy bubble (Pop the Happy Bubble pattern[14]) and invite people into a change. One of the existing Scrum Masters responded promptly and rather aggressively to our recommendations. She held very strongly to her opinion and denied any possibility of collaborating. The mutual decision, after private discussion among us, the Scrum Master, and senior management, was to transfer her to a different business division. She moved there the very next day.

After a while, some people who did not volunteer initially might see that this Agile way of working works and agree to voluntarily join. On the one hand, this is perfectly okay. However, the teams may be wary, and then the Scrum Master might have a repatriation issue to nurture. On the other hand, some people are just early adopters and others are laggards, and both types of people are useful in your organization. You can give them a chance.

Nonviolent Education

The main prerequisite of voluntary participation is education that creates awareness about new ways of working. People need to know what they are volunteering for. By *education*, we mean taking a deep dive into the principles behind the proposed change. The classic approach is organizing a formal training 2 or 3 days in a row. People are often "encouraged" to participate in the class by their management.

We prefer a different approach. We divide the class into several 3- to 4-hour workshops and roll them over one by one during a month or so. Each workshop is taught 3 or 4 times, depending on the size of the product group. Why do we do this? A few reasons. First, if we take the volunteering guideline seriously, we cannot force people to learn, no matter how awesome the class is and how pure our intentions are. Instead, we invite people and teach whoever comes in. We believe that if the workshop is good enough, there will be a word-of-mouth effect and new volunteers will show up soon. We call this approach a *nonviolent education*.

In one product group at a client, we had 10 Scrum teams with one shared Product Owner who didn't have full cross-functionality due to some constraints in knowledge and skills. We believed that using principles of lean and *Kanban* would help the teams to improve the flow and shorten the average cycle time. Thus, we knew we needed to decrease the work-in-progress (WIP) in the system. We divided our training class into three workshops and delivered each three times during a 2-month period. On average, we had 15 to 20 participants in each class. After that, teams approached us to ask for help in creating *Kanban* systems, establishing basic flow metrics, and limiting WIP. In addition, during the Overall Retrospective, team representatives decided to limit WIP on a product group level.

What If You Don't Have Volunteers?

We frequently get the question: What if there are no volunteers? Well, the answer is that it's good that you learned about this potential problem before you rolled out the change and dropped into an unproductive atmosphere with lots of resistance and low chances of success. Besides, that's very useful information and you have a golden opportunity to seize upon it. Dig deeper, ask why, search for the truth, and find deeper causes. Now you know that your most important goal is finding volunteers. This implies continuing to persuade people, reaching out to them, educating, and having a lot of patience. Another choice could be recruiting new employees who would accept the rules of the game from the start.

Senior managers at one retail bank with which we worked took the voluntary participation guideline very seriously. They wanted to kick off a LeSS product group, but despite their best efforts found only a few volunteers in the whole company. That didn't stop them, though. It took them almost half a year to recruit new developers who accepted the rules of LeSS, including its emphasis on multifunctional learning.

Guideline 4: Acknowledge the Loss

We are convinced that every change comes with its own price. Always. Without exceptions. People are holding on tightly to the past because there is something that they value.

With respect to motivation, change is accompanied by loss of some kind and by uncertainty. Resistance to loss and uncertainty is easy to understand; that is, one is motivated to reduce the loss and uncertainty.[15]

When people make a transition, this process involves loss, confusion, and grief. When we have a solid understanding of what is being lost, we are better prepared for the pressure during a change. The following questions can help you to assess the volume of loss:

- Does the change involve a change in identity?

- Is the individuals' status affected?

- Is it necessary to acquire new skills and competencies?

- Will the familiar routines change?

- What about autonomy?

- Will those involved in change experience more work pressure?

- Will any relationships change or suffer?

It is a paradox of change that respectful acknowledgment of the loss is necessary for people to move forward. Do not pretend that change is painless or effortless. An open conversation with teams and acknowledgment of what they are saying goodbye to is more helpful.

During the kick-off of a large product group with nine teams, we spent a significant amount of time working with the loss and emotions that people experienced. We used a sequence of exercises. The first one was about expressing emotions. We gave participants a list of basic human emotions (happiness, sadness, fear, disgust, anger, surprise) proposed by Paul Ekman,[16] and asked them to share that in small groups.

Next, we presented them with an adapted version of the *Griefwalking* exercise.[17] It helps to tap into social support while moving through a loss or profound transition. We first invited participants to respond to four open-ended sentences using the *Spiral Journal* technique[18]:

- Yes, it is true that …

- It is hard because …

- I will always remember and never forget …

- Now that I have shared my grief, it may be possible to …

Once everyone completed the journal, we created eight stations and asked people to evenly distribute themselves among them. At each station, they read sentences from their journals one by one. That was a way to make a space for a group to process, support, and attend to the experience of loss and transition together. The final step was implementing a *Conversation Cafe*[19] to debrief their experience together.

Beware of the Loss Aversion Bias

Change agents should be aware of the loss aversion cognitive bias. It explains why individuals feel the pain of loss twice as intensely as the equivalent pleasure of gain. It also means that sticking to the status quo is often a more preferable option to seeking out the potential benefits associated with change. Loss aversion impacts decisions and may lead to bad decision making. It prevents teams and corporations from making riskier decisions even if those risks are accurately calculated and have the potential to bring positive returns.

How can you avoid a loss aversion bias when implementing an Agile transformation? A nice way to deal with this challenge is by imagining the worst scenario that could have happened and then creating risk mitigation strategies. That decreases the fear of the unknown and helps participants accept a more rational decision.

When working with a client, while preparing for a shift from components to a feature teams organizational design, we noticed lots of complaints regarding a potential drop in quality. That was an important voice of the system that we could not neglect. Also, we knew we had to deal with loss aversion bias. We suggested arranging several workshops to identify and quantify future risks so that the product group could develop appropriate strategies for addressing them.

First, we asked the team representatives to come up with all potential risks they could think of connected with shifting to feature teams. When they were done, we categorized the risks (see Figure 6.3).

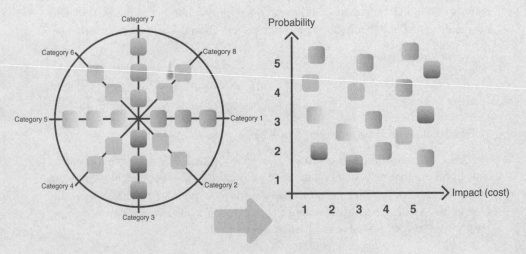

Figure 6.3
Risk management activities.

The next step was qualifying identified risks. We introduced Probability/Impact (cost) axes and asked participants to rank all the risks. The conversations among team members helped them reach consensus on how to place sticky notes relative to each other. Finally, we converted the risks into actionable Product Backlog Items and included them in the Product Backlog. To do this, we first explained the four strategies for addressing risks:

- **Avoidance:** Eliminate the risk

- **Mitigation:** Reduce the probability

- **Transference:** Insurance, outsource, etc.

- **Acceptance:** Accept and communicate to stakeholders

After that, participants, working in small groups, found appropriate strategies for each risk and created Product Backlog Items for them. In this way, we decreased the fear of the unknown, uncovered a few important risks we had not noticed before, and reduced the loss aversion bias.

Guideline 5: Deliver the Message Continually

The human brain is resistant to change. But why? Tobore Onojighofia makes an argument based on a neurological perspective.[20] He suggests that the core of the brain's resistance to change is its energy efficiency mechanisms. The brain accounts for only 2% of the body's mass but consumes more than 20% of its energy. It is a metabolically expensive tissue by nature. Each unit of brain tissue requires 25 times the amount of energy of a similar muscle unit. The brain manages its energy resources very efficiently with the help of internal simplified pictures of reality called "mental models." Mental models help to conserve energy; otherwise, the brain would have to consume much more than 20% of the body's energy, because it would need to relearn and re-store similar information continuously.

Knowledge or information that is congruent with existing knowledge tends to be absorbed quickly. In contrast, contrary knowledge tends to be rejected. For instance, if you truly believe in *Agile Manifesto* values and principles, you are less likely to consider information that contradicts this belief.

In a change process, this model suggests that you will often need to deliver the same information many times. That's because the new information goes against the mental models of many people. Sometimes the same message may need to be delivered three or four times before it is understood and accepted. A few examples follow.

In a big change initiative, seven component teams (composed of more than 70 people) were transformed into feature teams. We had been preparing the product group for almost four months. The preparation period included, but was not limited to, lots of training on Scrum, training on product ownership, and an engineering school for developers. Many people had visited several training sessions, but the majority were still concerned about the same controversial topics. They popped up so often that we had to create a FAQ guide and share it over the intranet. Some of the questions it covered:

- Why is there just one Product Backlog for many teams?
- Isn't it more productive for every team member to work on "their own" work? Why swarming and mobbing?
- How will multifunctional learning be supported?
- How do we deal with the rare specialists who have been developing their skills for years?
- How do we enable collective ownership without creating massive technical debt?
- How will the Product Backlog be ordered?
- How will the technical debt be handled in one shared Product Backlog?

After creating the FAQs and holding a series of formal training sessions, we continued changing the collective mental models of the product group by organizing regular *Lean Coffee*[21] events each Thursday. During each session, we collected the questions from participants, then grouped them into the themes, voted, and discussed them one by one during 5-minute slots that ended with consensus voting (support from 1 to 5).

During the first events, the number of participants was stable and fluctuated around 10 to 15. Over time, the number gradually decreased (see Figure 6.4). We stopped conducting the Lean Coffee events after four months when one day nobody showed up.

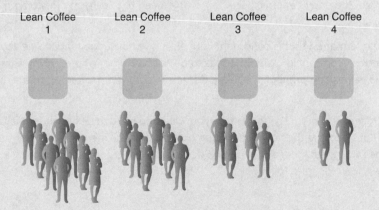

Figure 6.4
Lean Coffee events.

When we approached people and asked them why they were no longer visiting Lean Coffee, they said that now after so many sessions the principles and ideas behind the change were clear and they didn't need more explanation.

The same guideline applies to delivering the message about the necessity of the change and the *why* behind it.

After we conducted and presented the results of the Go See session, senior management and volunteers collaboratively created the "change story" (see Chapter 8, "Preparing the Product Group"). It described the current and future states of the change, success metrics, the scope of the change, and its urgency. After that, we conducted several workshops in the span of several weeks and invited everyone to join them. During these workshops, management presented the reason behind the change based on the "change story" and answered questions. Thus, we didn't deliver the message once, but patiently did it many times in a row. More than that, we returned periodically to the "change story" during important adoption events.

Guideline 6: Help People to Cross the Edge

We have learned a very useful model called the edge model, depicted in Figure 6.5. We utilize it when working with teams that are about to go through a change.

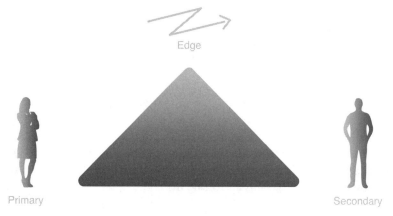

Figure 6.5
The edge model.

The edge model is easy to understand. Before any change, people are located in their primary state. They have some familiar routines, acquired skills, and identity. This is the status quo. The secondary state is the state after the change where you invite people to go to what is probably an unfamiliar and uncomfortable place with lots of unknowns. To reach the secondary state, people need to pass the edge.

Let's consider an example. Suppose that you are an Agile coach working with a product organization with typical copy–paste Scrum adoption, where teams are organized around components and functions. Management has decided to reorganize and adopt feature teams to optimize the system for learning and adaptability. The probable primary state of most developers might be summarized this way:

- The feeling of safety ("Everything runs quite stably here; there's no need for change.")
- Feelings of competence ("I am doing a good job working within my component and technology.")
- Frustration ("The development and technical debt drives me crazy.")

The secondary state might be as follows:

- Fear ("No one will take care of the code quality; that will inevitably cause a failure.")
- Feelings of incompetence ("I will have to learn new technologies and components.")
- Expectation ("Finally we will be able to ship something fast and become more competitive.")

The primary state is not better than the secondary state. It is just information about where people are in relation to the point of the edge. When they are about to cross the edge, you will often detect the following types of behaviors:

- Exaggerated body language
- A high-pitched voice
- Changing the subject
- Fidgeting
- Low energy levels
- Staring
- "Fight or flight"

As an Agile coach, your job is to help teams uncover these behaviors and make the system aware of them. We'll provide more details on this topic in Chapter 10, "Coaching Teams." For now, we'll focus on a few strategies for supporting teams in crossing the edge.

Guest Visit

A guest visit is an invitation to visit the secondary state for a short time and then return to the primary state safely. Thus, you do not force anyone to commit to change, just kindly ask them to investigate the secondary state through nonbinding travel as a tourist. Let us share an example of how we did this.

We were two months into a LeSS adoption with newly formed feature teams when the CEO suddenly called us. He was very frustrated because after the last low-quality release, the support team was overwhelmed with phone calls from angry customers. The teams rolled back the changes and conducted a Retrospective. The main reason for a recent accident was recognized to be a lack of test coverage in most of the architectural components and a lack of continuous integration.

We helped to organize a trip to one of our clients that had adopted many modern engineering practices—teams were continuously working in pairs, using mob programming, and following test-driven development (TDD) practices. High-quality code was the norm there. During the guest trip, team representatives observed and directly communicated with feature teams that integrated code continuously and were able to ship a quality product to the market. Developers asked lots of questions and looked rather puzzled, but returned to their own company quite motivated.

Two years passed after that trip. Over that period, the product group removed most of the technical debt and was capable of continuously delivering value with high quality to their clients.

Create Edge Awareness

Another strategy is creating awareness regarding where people are relative to the edge. By doing this, we make people responsible for acting according to what they think is best for them now. We believe people are intelligent and capable of making informed decisions. The proven method of creating awareness is using constellations (you can find more detailed description of this exercise in Chapter 10, "Coaching Teams"). Let us share an example of how we did this.

In a product group of more than 70 people, we got a message from management that they could not afford to work exclusively with volunteers. That message was delivered just before dissolving component teams and transitioning to feature teams. Unfortunately, that was the situation we always try to avoid. But despite the best efforts, we could not change the managerial decision and went into the adoption with a diverse group and different levels of support. To further complicate matters, we were conducting the change during the COVID-19 lockdown and entirely online.

During the kick-off, which lasted for five consecutive days, we introduced constellations that revealed where teams were related to the edge. As the kick-off workshops were done through Zoom and Miro exclusively, we created graphics on a board that described the edge model. After quickly explaining what it meant, we asked developers to show where they were at by placing icons on a frame. Then we randomly created small groups and asked people to answer two questions:

- Where am I now in relation to the edge?

- What do I feel?

We did it twice—at the beginning of the kick-off and at the end. The constellations were followed by structured reflection and discussion using the *What, So What, Now What*[22] and *15% Solutions*[23] structures.

In half a year, the product group had finally reached the main optimization goal of "delivering highest value." How did we know that? Feature teams were able to work on the most important Product Backlog Items from a single Product Backlog regardless of their ordering and the channels (iOS, Android, Web, Linux) to which features were bound. Scrum Masters conducted the constellation exercise with teams' representatives during an overall Retrospective once again. As you can see in Figure 6.6, the situation had drastically changed.

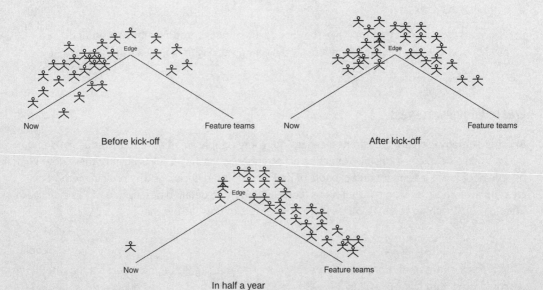

Figure 6.6
Constellations over the time.

Honor the Past

The past may be imperfect, but people are standing on its foundation. There were successes in the past. It is important to honor and celebrate where an organization has been, because it helps establish a transition to the future. And, by doing this, we recognize the contributions to the change of those people who sacrificed to make it possible. This can be the single most important factor in making a successful change.

> *Paradoxically, honoring the past helps people let go of it.*[2]

We often organize a special workshop to celebrate the successes and honor the past. Here is the detailed facilitation plan.

Preparation. Ask attendees to bring as many photos from the past as they can to the workshop. Bring markers, plenty of colorful sticky notes, and transparent tape, and make sure you have a long wall with paper on it. Alternatively, place several whiteboards next to each other. Draw the timeline on the paper and put dates on it. Agree with attendees on how far back in time you would like to look beforehand.

Step 1.   Remember the past. Form small groups of 3 to 5 people and ask them to write down all significant events they can recall. Put the sticky notes on the wall along with photos (20 minutes).

Step 2.   Discussion. When Step 1 is finished, ask the groups to walk along the wall while reading and discussing other groups' sticky notes. Post clarifying questions using sticky notes if any topic needs to be clarified (10–20 minutes).

Step 3.   Clarification. Collect any clarifying questions that were posted on the wall and initiate a whole-group discussion. Each clarifying question is directed to the group that generated and/or created the corresponding topic on the wall.

Step 4.   Conversation café. Invite all participants to gather in small groups to listen to one another's thoughts and reflect together on the past using the Conversation Café format. State the theme of the conversation in the form of a question—for instance, "What do we appreciate about the past?" (30–40 minutes).

Guideline 7: Axes of Change

The Axes of Change is a change model for coaches. We use it by default when working with people and teams because it provides so much structure and support during our coaching conversations. Next, we'll explain what it is and how we use it.

The model is described in the book *Coaching Change* by Michael Hall.[24] The model provides for:

- Structured conversations so that you do not get lost in the stories of the people and teams

- An understanding of the essential aspects for successful change

- Clear guidance for asking powerful questions that trigger the teams
- A process that leaves all the content work for the team and operates only at the structural level of the change process

Michael Hall modeled the change strategy of people with a talent to change themselves. He discovered that for all these experts, change consists of several components:

1. Negative emotions that tell us what we want to avoid

2. Positive emotions that tell us what we want to achieve

3. Insight into what needs to change and why

4. Deciding to change

5. Creation of a new strategy, new mental models, motivations, associations, and feelings

6. Practice of the new behavior

7. Celebration of achievements

8. Monitoring of progress and making changes to improve

All Components of the Strategy Are Important

Think back to an unsuccessful personal change. You likely will recognize that you did not pay proper attention to all the components. You might have experienced component 1, the negative emotions that correspond to your behavior. You also may have experienced component 2, understanding why it is good to change, but the change was unsuccessful.

For example, suppose you felt guilty for not spending enough time with your family and understood that more time with your family would make life much better. Based on these two components, you tried to change your behavior for a while. You did not plan 100% of your agenda and may not have brought work home with you, but you fell back into your old behavior before you knew it. Now your schedule is again filled, and you find yourself sending work emails at 10 p.m.

This happens a lot, and the reason is that all components need to receive the proper attention if a change is to be successful. You might not deeply understand what needs to change and why (component 3), and you might not profoundly believe that your new strategy can work.

The Four Axes of Change Model

From the eight change components in the preceding list, you can identify four phases that Michael Hall visualizes as forming four axes, as illustrated in Figure 6.7.

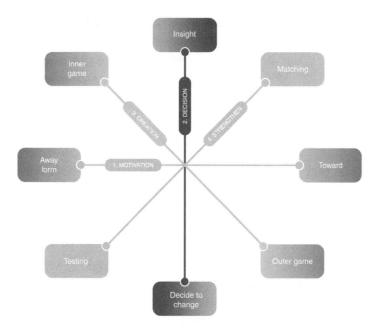

Figure 6.7
Axes of change.

The Motivation, Decision, Creation, and Strengthen phases of change can serve as your navigational guide. You can dance with the team around the axes, listening intently to what is being said and aligning your questions with their preference. You can ensure all of the axes are covered by asking the right questions.

Kirsten Schults introduced us to her soup metaphor as a means to explain how to use the axis. We share it in the sections that follow and add some sample questions.

Axis 1: Motivation

Change starts with motivation. Motivation has two sides: negative and positive. The negative part motivates people to move away from the current situation:

- Focused on problems
- Avoiding mistakes
- "Not wanting" plays a central role

Meanwhile, the positive side motivates people to move toward a better situation:

- Focused on goals
- Wanting to achieve objectives
- "Wanting" plays a central role.

Away from: You have a soup that you do not like, and you want a better one.

- What don't you like about it?
- What bad things will happen if you keep eating that soup?
- What have you had enough of?

Toward: You want a better-tasting soup, one that you really enjoy and makes life a whole lot better.

- How does this better soup taste?
- Why would you make a new soup?
- What will be possible with the new soup?

Axis 2: Decision

Choosing to change involves deciding to say goodbye to the old and welcome the new. This decision becomes stronger when there is a deep understanding in mental models, thinking, and feelings that feed the old behaviors. People and teams need to understand how they got into the current situation, what keeps them there, and why it doesn't work for them.

Insight: You currently use a recipe to make your own bad soup, but which recipe do you use?

- If I wanted to have the same bad soup, what should I think and do?
- Which thoughts keep you making the same soup?
- What are you convinced of that makes you create your bad soup?

Decide to change: You decide to create a new recipe and make your dream soup.

- What are you waiting for?
- Are you going to change?
- Now that you hear yourself talking, what do you realize about yourself?

Axis 3: Creation

On this axis, you create new mental models with new associations, thoughts, feelings, and beliefs. Our mental models give meaning to ourselves and the world in relation to our goals.

Inner game: Let's create a new soup recipe.

- What can you also think about your current recipe so that change becomes possible?
- Which positive associations about the new thinking come to mind?
- What should become important in the recipe?

- What other meaning can you give to steps in your bad soup recipe?
- What would you need to believe to make the new recipe?

Outer game: Let's change the old recipe into the new recipe.

- What is the first thing you are going to do?
- What needs to happen to make this work?
- With whom and when are you going to do it?
- What are you going to do today? Tomorrow?

Axis 4: Strengthen

To make change stick, it is important to acknowledge progress; change becomes a positive experience that way. In addition, it is important to test how well the change works and what could be improved.

Matching: The changes you already notice and improve the soup.

- Which changes do you already recognize?
- In what way does it strengthen you?
- What plans do you have to continue this?

Testing: Testing the new recipe.

- How well does the new recipe work?
- Which parts need improvement?
- What excuses do you have to not do it right now?

Applying the Axes of Change to Teams

We use the Axes of Change model in two modes: centralized coaching or decentralized coaching. In the centralized approach, we dance with the teams along the axis; that is, we keep the model in our head and use the questions to move around the axes. In the decentralized approach, we facilitate a workshop in single- or multi-team format. We facilitate a workshop using the canvas in Figure 6.8.

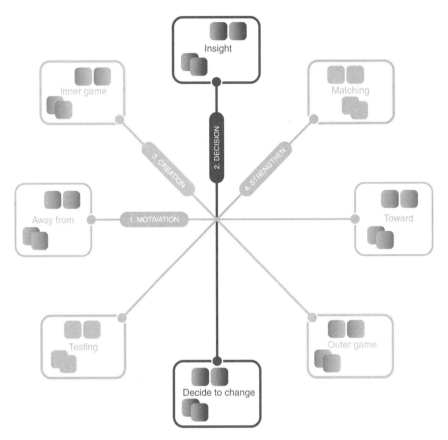

Figure 6.8
Axes of Change team canvas.

We facilitate this workshop by using the retrospective format from Esther Derby and Diana Larsen's *Agile Retrospectives*[25] as follows:

- **Set the stage.** Explain the model and share the soup metaphor.

- **Gather data.** First in pairs, and then as a team, answer the questions on the Motivation axis first, and discuss your answers. Then repeat this process for the questions on the Decision axis.

- **Generate insights.** First in pairs, and then as a team, answer the questions on the Creation–Inner Game axis, and discuss your answers. Think creatively; look for patterns, themes, and connections.

- **Decide what to do.** First in pairs, and then as a team, answer the questions on the Creation–Outer Game axis, and discuss your answers.

- **Close.** Summarize and end the meeting.

In a follow-up session, you start with the Strengthen axis to do matching and testing.

Guideline 8: Find the Right Balance of Radical/Incremental Change

There is a myth that one needs to choose either radical change or incremental change. This is a typical false dichotomy—that is, a simplistic, binary approach. In nature, the change occurs both incrementally *and* radically. This is true for all social systems: individuals, teams, and organizations.

> *It is interesting to note that Darwin's theory of evolution has been characterized for many years as a slow, incremental process of change, but more recently, scholars have challenged this view, stating that changes in living organisms actually occur in spurts, or leaps, as perturbations.*[15]

Punctuated equilibrium theory has changed the way biologists and scientists think about evolution. Punctuated equilibrium proposes that a stable state exists for a period of time, during which small, incremental adjustments are made to adjust for environmental changes without significantly affecting the status quo (Figure 6.9). It is followed by a short period of a radical change, in which the deep, underlying structures change. That enables the system to evolve to a new status quo.

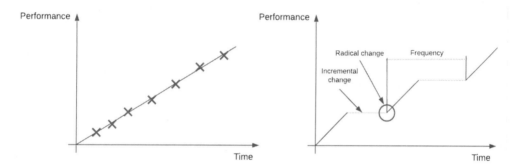

Figure 6.9
Evolution over time.

Incremental change is inevitable. People need time to absorb change and make the new processes and rules deeply ingrained and habitual. Most of the work happens during flat periods, including preparation for radical change. The problem with taking only incremental steps is that the organization can land at a local optimum. That is why organizations need points where radical change happens. Radical changes or *Kaikaku* are usually introduced by senior management. A good example of a radical change is moving from component to feature teams.

> *It may be difficult to transition from functional teams or component teams to Cross-Functional Teams in a piecemeal fashion. Organizations might best be advised to put the right structure in place upfront with management support. Experience shows that it does not happen of its own accord, especially in large organizations.*[26]

Knowing that radical and incremental change come together, and that both are highly desirable, you can use this information to your advantage. How? One way is to create a change roadmap, as described next.

Create a Change Roadmap

Consider co-creating a roadmap with teams that includes both types of change and the speed of introducing the changes on a timeline. The roadmap may be strengthened by metrics that aid in understanding if a previous step has been completed successfully.

In a product group of 80-plus people, during the Go See effort, we collected many requests asking us to not change the composition of the teams. Employees were overwhelmed with constant changes during the last year and craved a period of stability. Thus, after consulting with management, we left the teams' composition intact. Transitioning to feature teams at once would be a radical approach, and we were not sure that people could absorb such a drastic change. Nevertheless, we got rid of proxy Product Owners and their local backlogs and introduced a professional Scrum with one Product Backlog ordered by one Product Owner (the CEO of the company) for 9 teams. Together with management and volunteers, we created a roadmap that reflected the speed of change and major activities on a timeline (see Figure 6.10).

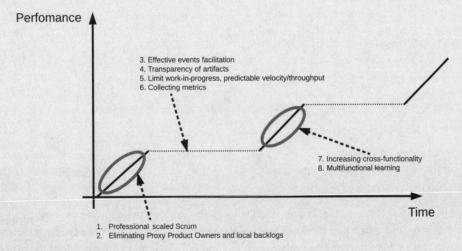

Figure 6.10
Example of a change roadmap.

Dissolve the Problems Instead of Solving Them

Instead of only thinking about how to get a little bit better, or improving the cycle time by 10% in a team, you should focus a meaningful amount of your time and energy on change initiatives that will produce a bold change in performance. A proven way of doing this is to consider dissolving the problems instead of solving them. What does this mean? To solve a problem is to change the effects of one or more undesirable causes; to dissolve a problem is to eliminate the causes and thereby eliminate the effects.

Effective management requires dissolving messes, not solving or resolving problems.[27]

For example, managing dependencies between teams would be a solving strategy, because the cause of the issue (e.g., lack of cross-functionality) remains intact. In contrast, creating perfect feature teams that are able to work in all architectural components and functions would be a dissolving strategy. A second example of dissolving a problem is eradicating the queues instead of managing them. We know that queues profoundly affect the economics of product development.[28] They hurt cycle time, quality, and efficiency. The dissolving approach would be to completely get rid of them. That means working in an ideal one-piece flow style with low transaction costs.

> **Note**
>
> There is a myth—a false dichotomy—that Agile teams need to choose between Scrum or *Kanban*. We share some thoughts about this in "Scrum and *Kanban*" in the Appendix.

Summary

In this chapter, we introduced and investigated nine guidelines that support a productive change. These guidelines, which can be applied to a product organization of any size, reinforce each other but can also be used independently. In all cases, however, you should start by creating the basic conditions for success. Certain conditions greatly increase the chance of a successful transformation, including having a senior leader who is the driver of the change and a clearly formulated problem that needs to be solved.

Guideline 1, "Influence people," is about human touch and maintaining a human-centric focus. Use corridor politics to your advantage, show individual benefits, build connections, and create lasting relationships. Guideline 2, "Co-create the change," is important if you want to arrive at decisions that are supported by the majority, even though this process will take more time. Guideline 3, "Voluntary participation," suggests viewing any change as a game with an agreed-upon purpose, rules, and internal feedback mechanism. Volunteers will inevitably design your change for success, overcome stress, and attract new followers. Success breeds success.

Every change comes with its own price. Respectful acknowledgment of the loss is necessary for people to move forward. That understanding leads to Guideline 4, "Acknowledge the Loss."

The human brain will filter messages that conflict with its existing mental models. That is why we suggest to continuously and patiently deliver the same messages many times (Guideline 5, "Deliver the message continuously"). We also offered two change models: edge theory (Guideline 6, "Help people to cross the edge") and Axes of Change (Guideline 7, "The Axes of Change").

From scientific research, we know that a change doesn't happen linearly. Instead, social change is better characterized by long periods of stability followed by short spurts of radical change (Guideline 8, "Find the right balance between radical/incremental change").

References

1. Melanie Franklin. *Agile Change Management: A Practical Framework for Successful Change Planning and Implementation* (Kogan Page, 2014).

2. Esther Derby. *7 Rules for Positive, Productive Change: Micro Shifts, Macro Results* (Berrett-Koehler, 2019).

3. Mary Lynn Manns et al. *Fearless Change: Patterns for Introducing New Ideas* (Addison-Wesley, 2005).

4. Peter Senge. *The Fifth Discipline: The Art and Practice of the Learning Organization* (Cornerstone Digital, 2010).

5. "How to Run Agile Perfection." www.youtube.com/watch?v=h0bOoOvUslU.

6. Management 3.0. "Happiness Door." https://management30.com/practice/happiness-door/.

7. Richard Kasperowski. *The Core Protocols: A Guide to Greatness* (With Great People Publications, 2015).

8. "Remove the Shade." https://tinyurl.com/RemoveShade.

9. Jim Collins. *Good to Great: Why Some Companies Make the Leap and Others Don't* (HarperBusiness, 2001).

10. S. Chris Edmonds. *The Culture Engine: A Framework for Driving Results, Inspiring Your Employees, and Transforming Your Workplace* (Wiley, 2014).

11. Jane McGonigal. *Reality Is Broken: Why Games Make Us Better and How They Can Change the World* (Penguin, 2011).

12. James B. Carse. *Finite and Infinite Games* (Free Press, 2013).

13. David W. Hutton. *The Change Agents' Handbook: A Survival Guide for Quality Improvement Champions* (ASQ Quality Press, 1994).

14. "Pop the Happy Bubble." https://tinyurl.com/PopHappyBubble

15. W. Warner Burke. *Organization Change: Theory and Practice*, 5th ed. (Sage, 2017).

16. Paul Ekman. "Basic Emotions." paulekman.com/wp-content/uploads/2013/07/Basic-Emotions.pdf.

17. "Griefwalking." https://tinyurl.com/GriefWalking

18. "Spiral Journal and the Uncomfortable Power of Self-Reflection." https://tinyurl.com/SpiralJournalExercise.

19. "Conversation Café." Liberating Structures. www.liberatingstructures.com/17-conversation-cafe/,

20. Tobore Onojighofia. "On the Theory of Mental Representation Block: A Novel Perspective on Learning and Behavior." March 12, 2021. https://tinyurl.com/TheoryMentalBlock.

21. "Lean Coffee Lives Here." Lean Coffee. http://leancoffee.org/.

22. "What, So What, Now What? W³." Liberating Structures. www.liberatingstructures.com/9-what-so-what-now-what-w/

23. "15% Solutions." Liberating Structures. www.liberatingstructures.com/7-15-solutions/.

24. Michael Hall. *Coaching Change: The Axes of Change, Meta-Coaching* (Neuro-semantics Press, 2015).

25. Esther Derby and Diana Larsen. *Agile Retrospectives: Making Good Teams Great* (Pragmatic Bookshelf, 2006).

27. Scrum Patterns Group. *A Scrum Book* (2019). www.scrumbook.org.

28. Russell L. Ackoff, *Re-creating the Corporation: A Design of Organizations for the 21st Century* (Oxford University Press, 1999).

29. Donald G. Reignersten. *The Principles of Product Development Flow: Second Generation Lean Product Development* (Celeritas, 2009).

PART II
APPLYING THE CONCEPTS

7

Group Facilitation

A meeting without a facilitator is about as effective as a sports team trying to
play a game without a referee.
—Ingrid Bens[1]

During the adoption and afterwards, there are many times where you need to facilitate a group
of people. Although we provide workshop examples and facilitation tips throughout this book, in
this chapter we focus on how to prepare and facilitate workshops in general and Scrum events in
particular.

Principles of Facilitation

Have you ever been in a meeting that was boring and not useful? Unfortunately, we have been in
lots of those meetings. We've noticed that in unproductive meetings, at least a few of the following
points are true:

- There is no clear goal.

- You do not know your progress against your goals.

- You cannot participate and contribute as much as you want.

- There is no facilitator.

- Certain types of personalities obstruct the collaborative process.

- There is social pressure to show up.

- You have to sit.

The sections that follow share a few basic facilitation techniques that help create a collaborative process. First, we'll start with a short overview of your role as facilitator.

The Role of the Facilitator

Your role as the facilitator is to foster a collaborative environment. More specifically, your role is designed to make sure the group reaches their goals, that people are given the chance to share the information that they have, and that the group does not go off track as they go through the workshop process.

Don't get too interested in what you have to say. The facilitator should not be talking too much. You want to intervene, but only at the right time. Keep the group on track and intervene when collaboration becomes unbalanced. Carefully monitor the group and choose which technique to use—continually reminding the group how they are progressing toward meeting their expectations and goals. Nothing frustrates the group more than setting goals and not meeting those goals, but not having that feedback during their meeting or workshop. They do not want to walk out feeling that they wasted their time. So, it is crucial that you set expectations with them. You should periodically track how they are doing against the expectations, and you should share how they delivered before moving to the next activity.

Meeting Goals

Ensure that the meeting goal states in clear and meaningful terms what people have set out to accomplish. Also, validate understanding and consensus with the group. Have the group acknowledge that the goal makes sense and that it is what they are trying to accomplish. Then revisit that goal as the group is going through the process to ensure that people remain aligned on what they are trying to reach.

You also want to be flexible if the original workshop goals change based on a new understanding. It is vital to make the group aware of that possibility to depart from the initial goals.

To create a feedback loop to keep the people engaged, try visualizing the workshop plan and progress.

Workshop Plan

You should use a plan to let the participants know which steps they will get through and to track progress as they move through the process—feedback helps to keep them engaged.

You'll want to ensure that the group keeps up with the plan and signal if progress is not as expected. If they fall behind, let them know, and ask them how they want to address that issue. Do they want to extend the meeting, move on to a new topic, or something else?

Try to create ground rules to help keep the collaborative process on track.

Ground Rules

It is difficult for people who do not know one another to determine how to normalize with the other parties' communication patterns. To clarify the desired patterns, you might want to lay out some rules that the group can agree to that are effective ways to communicate so that people do not get offended.

A facilitator is not there to tell people to be quiet or that it is time to move on. A facilitator's role is to remind people that they have a process that they have agreed to, to help them stay on track, and to ensure that people's opinions and considerations are included in the process.

Start with an initial set of ground rules, let the group determine if those rules make sense to them, and then let them change the ground rules they need. Example rules include the following:

- No side conversations, phones, or email. If some are speaking while others are having a side conversation, that will slow the group down.
- Reasoning rule: "I think so" is not good enough. Because that statement does not give information to the others, the speaker has to explain why—that is, their reasoning. If they do not know, that is also okay, but they have to share it with the group.
- No blame.
- Everybody is right, but only partially.

You might share these example rules and then ask the group if they want to remove, add, or change any rules.

Remember, the facilitator is not there to police the attendees, but rather to remind people that they have ground rules and to let the people validate if they are meeting those ground rules. A facilitator might say: "I want you to recognize that you set some ground rules, and I heard some people breaking rule X. Is that okay? Is it not disrupting anyone? And would you like to let it continue? It is your meeting."

Consensus

How will your group make decisions? One helpful way is by consensus. The consensus is a choice that "I" can live with and support when "I" leave today. It is not necessarily the choice that is most preferred by those making the decision.

You can validate a consensus agreement with these three tests:

- Can I live with the decision made here today? Or will I lose sleep over it? If you are concerned, lay your concerns out on the table.

- Can I refrain from behaving or speaking negatively to others about the decision? If not, make your concerns explicit here and associate them with your name. People need to share their concerns and support with the group, not say "yes" in the workshop and then share their concerns after the meeting with others.

- Can I support the decision and devote my time and effort to make the decision successful?

If participants do not satisfy the consensus agreement tests, that point must be documented. Make it explicitly understood so that those people who do not support the decision feel that their challenges have been considered and used in the decision-making process.

Parking Lot

How do you handle issues that people bring in that don't correspond to the workshop goals? Try a parking lot.

The parking lot is a way to ensure the group does not get too distracted by side issues. So, share that you have a parking lot to track issues that require further action outside the meeting. You should document all of these ideas and issues, and revisit, resolve, or define post-meeting steps for each item in the parking lot before completing the workshop.

Track and Prioritize Ideas

How do you handle a high-energy group with lots of input and ideas? Try tracking and prioritizing ideas.

An influx of too many ideas at once is challenging for a group to process. Imagine 10 people sharing ideas without giving time for others to react or even process those ideas. Good ideas might get lost. As a facilitator, you want to notice when people share ideas in the group, but those ideas are not acknowledged. When people have opinions that go unrecognized, they may disengage and stop paying attention. In such a situation, you can decide to track and prioritize the conversation:

- Stop the group.

- Mirror comments from multiple participants.

- Ask the group which idea they would like to address first.

Ensure that ideas are not lost in the dialogue.

Dealing with Specific Behaviors

The list that follows shares some tips for dealing with some typical challenging behaviors in your workshops.

- **The Expert.** When people are too smart in an area with which others are not too familiar, they can make complicated statements. If you notice this, it is important to summarize or exactly repeat what the person said. Ideally, participants will summarize their ideas themselves. This summary makes them hear their own words and forces them to stop and think if what they just said makes any sense. When you help Experts realize that they might not have been understood, then they will recommunicate their points to you, helping others understand them. If your summary is wrong, they will correct you and try to communicate their points more effectively.

- **The Whiner.** People who whine, "All is wrong," "Why is my idea not used," and "This will never work," should not be ignored. The more you ignore them, the more problems you can have.

  Often Whiners are whining because they feel disempowered. So, a good way to address this behavior is to acknowledge and repeat their concerns. Document each concern and then ask them for their recommended solution. This puts the responsibility back on the Whiners to address their concerns and gives them control. You can also add the matter to the parking lot and ask the Whiner to define actions to resolve it.

- **The Gorilla.** A Gorilla is a person who cannot stop talking. They have an idea and an opinion on everything. Usually, this is a person who likes to be recognized as a power player. They believe that the easiest way to express power is through a very vocal expression of their opinion on too many topics. Such behavior can easily prevent other people from sharing their input.

  A good way to deal with a Gorilla is first to acknowledge their comment: "John has a very good comment. Thank you very much. Let's record and be aware that John made that comment."

  If that person continues to dominate the discussion, you can ask others for comments: "John might have a good comment, but before we hear from John—and we have heard from him on a couple of topics—I'd like to hear from some other folks." In this way, you redirect the conversation and allow others to speak. You will need to come back to John and validate his opinions, too.

  Suppose it gets to the point that you just cannot get John to back off and allow others to speak. In that case, you can acknowledge John before requesting new comments: "John is a person who likes to express himself a lot, but we also like to hear from others." This makes both John and the group aware that he is the Gorilla in the meeting and creates a more balanced conversation.

Workshop Design

We were working with a large media company whose business structure included various divisions, each of which operated as a separate business. A part of the Agile adoption was to increase collaboration between the divisions and achieve more synergy for their top 10 accounts.

We were asked to facilitate a workshop for the shareholders and division directors that would lead to:

- Understanding why Agile works and how they could use it in their company

- Increased empathy among all directors

- A concrete plan to go from silo thinking to holistic thought

We planned a two-day workshop at a ski resort and invited the shareholders and all divisions' directors to attend. On both days, in the morning, we would enjoy the ski resort, and in the afternoon, we would facilitate the sessions. This was our initial plan:

First Session

Goal:

Understand Agile and how to use it in your organization.

Program:

Workshop: Which organization design and which leadership style support the Agile approach.

Second Session

Goal:

Create a concrete plan to go from silo thinking to holistic thought and increase collaboration and cross-selling.

Program:

Workshop: Create a shared vision.

Workshop: Develop the strategy.

We shared our workshop proposal beforehand for feedback, and apart from some small remarks they were satisfied with the setup.

The Plan Goes Awry

We started the first session after lunch. We intended to discuss organizational design and human operations. To our surprise, after a half-hour or so, the group started to disengage. Some started looking at their phones, others started having side discussions, and it quickly became an unpleasant situation for all of us.

We were experienced facilitators and had prepared an interactive workshop about the topics they proposed themselves. What were we missing?

We announced a 10-minute break to see if that would help. After the pause, we asked the group: "To what extent are things moving the way you expected?"

The biggest shareholder was not amused. He stood up and said: "This is a waste of my time. . . If I were at headquarters, I would leave and not come back."

Ouch!! We had hit rock bottom; the group had disengaged and was ready to leave and not come back. That would make the session a big failure.

We tried various actions to improve the situation, but unfortunately, they did not work. We decided to stop the workshop for that day and hoped to continue the next day.

In the evening, when they went out for dinner and late drinks, we stayed in the hotel to redesign the second-day workshop that desperately needed improvement.

The Magic of Engagement

In the book *Flow: The Psychology of Optimal Experience*,[2] Mihaly Csikszentmihalyi suggests that people have an optimal experience in what he calls the flow state. As depicted in the "flow chart" in Figure 7.1, the flow state happens when there is a balance between boredom and anxiety. Csikszentmihalyi uses four points as to how one can experience flow:

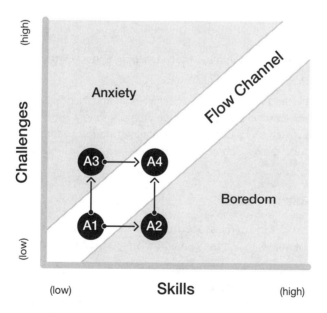

Figure 7.1
Flow diagram.

- **A1: Your starting point.** At this point, a person is experiencing flow, because the challenge of the activity is roughly equal to the person's skill level. There is focus on the task, gratification, and feeling of accomplishments.

- **A2: Become bored.** The person improves their skills to the point where they get bored. The challenge is now lower than the skill level, and the person no longer experiences flow.

- **A3: Become anxious**. The challenge is too hard for the current skill level and stresses the person, and the person no longer experiences flow.

- **A4: Get back to the flow:**

- *If the person is bored,* find a way to increase the challenge and get back to the flow.

- *If the person is anxious,* work on improving the skills needed to get back in the flow.

To get people in the flow zone during the workshop, we needed to redesign our workshop so that the group:

1. Had a clear goal

2. Moved without worrying

3. Were engaged in a doable task

4. Received fast feedback

5. Were able to focus

We concluded that we were likely doing too much teaching and too little working directly on their goals. Therefore, we decided to flip the workshop.

The new workshop would start with their concrete challenges and then work on possible solutions. When in doubt about how to solve a problem, we would propose to workshop on that specific topic. In this approach, we would teach topics only that were of direct interest to solve their problems. We opted to design the workshop using *serious games*[3] because they have all the ingredients to engage people.

What Is a Serious Game?

Chess is a game: The board is the game space, there are rules for playing the game, the chess pieces are the artifacts, and the goal is to win the game. You can play chess with your friends, just for fun.

Speedboat[4] is a serious game: You can use it to identify what your users dislike about your product or what's standing in the way of your organization meeting a desired goal. Many Agile teams use it in their Retrospectives. *Speedboat* is considered a serious game because it's played to make a business decision.

A serious game is a workshop format that uses game dynamics to answer questions, create insights, and find solutions about business problems. People play serious games to solve problems in a collaborative fashion. Each game has the following characteristics:

- Game space

- Rules of interaction

- Artifacts

- Goal

- Voluntary participation

The rules, game space, boundaries, and goals help people better express their creativity. Without these constraints, only about 5% of the people can come up with something creative. Because the games provide the participants with frequent feedback, and because you see progress and achievement, you experience playing as pleasant because of the dopamine released when you make progress. Working in a group of people increases creativity because they bring different perspectives to the same problem, so they explore a much larger solution space.

How can you use serious games in your product group? Let us explain how we used serious games to redesign the workshop.

The Flow of the New Workshop

After a few hours, we came up with the workshop design shown in Figure 7.2. We created a sequence of activities to maximize engagement and create an opportunity to teach what was of interest to the participants.

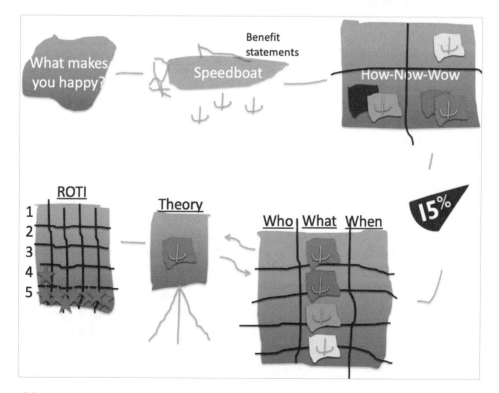

Figure 7.2
Flow of the workshop.

We started by asking each participant to share their expectations for the workshop. Next, we used the following sequence of serious game[3] formats:

- We used the *Speedboat*[4] game to identify anchors that were holding the group back from achieving their shared goals. After grouping similar anchors into themes, we ask the group to add benefit statements to each anchor—that is, to identify benefits that would arise if the anchors were lifted.

- Next, we decided to have the group weigh the anchor–benefit pairs along the dimension of impact and ease of implementation. We chose the *Now-How-Wow*[5] game for that.

- We then decided to use the output from the *Now-How-Wow*[5] game to develop and prioritize some initial action points. We used the liberating structure *15% Solutions*[6] and the *Who/What/When*[7] exercise for that.

- With the list of concrete actions in hand, we expected there might be questions on how to execute them. We could then teach exactly the topics related to their questions, thereby keeping the workshop participants engaged.

- We close with a *Return on Time Invested* exercise.[8]

Let us explain step by step how we came to this design using the five points for achieving flow.

Step 1. Have a clear goal.

We decided to start the workshop with a simple question to the group:

Imagine it is 8 p.m., and the workshop ended. While you are walking away to get ready for dinner, you look back to a great successful workshop. What will the workshop have produced that made it so successful for you?

We facilitated using a 1-2-4-All format and used affinity mapping to identify their common goals. Serious games have a goal, but the path to the goal is unknown and must arise through interaction.

Step 2. Moves without worrying.

We created the conditions for a safe environment by establishing clear, well-understood rules for each serious game. The rules set behavior expectations for each participant and also helped them make choices during the workshop. In a serious game, everyone is equal, so all participants can make an equal contribution to the result. In such an environment, people are more likely to participate and provide useful input. When everybody needs to play by the same rules, it creates an environment of safety.

Step 3. Is engaged in a doable task.

Each of the workshop activities had easy-to-understand rules and asked participants for their opinion, choices, and insights. For example, during the *Speedboat* game, we asked: "What's standing in the way of progress toward your goal?" This is a question about a personal view or experience; as such, the answer cannot be wrong.

Step 4. Receives immediate feedback.

> The participants received immediate feedback from the other participants on every action. The participants worked as a group and as individuals to create ideas and then merged and combined ideas into insights and conclusions. Typically, workshop attendees use sticky notes, sketches, and metaphors to support their discussion.

> For example, we asked all participants to first silently move the anchors from the *Speedboat* to the *Now-How-Wow* matrix and order them relative to each other. Each person could move any anchor as they wished. In doing so, the participants had to react to one another's actions in real time. After most anchors were in a stable position, we asked them to discuss the leftovers in small groups.

> Every action can be reacted to, built on, or undone during the game.

Step 5. Is able to focus.

> Each separate activity addresses a specific step in the process, captures progress, and shows the current action to focus on. Participants have to make choices to accomplish some goals, and there are certain rules they have to follow. This gives them focus on the current state, as participants consider the question, "What should I do and how?"

> Focus is further enhanced because the group works with external objects such as sticky notes or drawings on a whiteboard. These external objects, also called externalizations, allow the group to easily move from vague ideas to concrete representations, create a common memory as a group, create a common understanding of the situation, and focus on the task at hand.

The New Design Worked

Fortunately, the next day all participants showed up for the workshop. We explained the agenda and facilitated the day. The result was great, people were engaged and reached their goals. We closed with a *Return on Time Invested* exercise that showed everyone was satisfied with the results.

How to Design Your Workshop

Design your workshop as a series of interesting and meaningful activities with clear goals, rules, and feedback loops. The goals should support players as they make choices and encourage the invitees to participate in active decision making. The rules provide focus on the current goal and specific behaviors. Feedback is important because it gives the participants an intrinsic reward, promotes a sense of urgency, and creates focus.

The list that follows outlines the sections in our Workshop Design canvas, which were inspired by Luke Hohman's *Innovation Games: Creating Breakthrough Products Through Collaborative Play*.[4] You can use this template to design your own multi-activity workshop.

- **Your goals:** What do you want to accomplish when this workshop is done? What are the questions that need to be answered? What will you do with the answers?

- **Participants' goals:** What is motivating your participants? What makes it meaningful? Engaging? What do they get from this workshop?

- **Workshop activities:** What sequence of activities are needed to achieve your goals? How does the output of one activity serve as input for the next?

- **Opening activity:** Which activities do you need to diverge and generate ideas, data, or solutions?

- **Sensemaking activity**: Which sensemaking activity(s) do you need to pursue to organize and create meaning?

- **Closing activity:** Which activities do you need to converge the information by, for example, ranking, prioritizing. or selecting items for action?

- **Rules:** How do players interact with the game? (Examples: sticky notes, cards, sketching) Which actions can players take? (Examples: place items, group items, remove items) How are items placed? (Examples: hierarchy, flow, linked, cluster) How do the players interact with each other? (Examples: diverge–merge, turn taking, building in turns, agree act)

- **Physical design:** Consider the larger context. For example, physical game boards and games might need wall space and specific materials. How do you create the game boards? (Examples: printed, created by the players, created by facilitator)

There are many sources for serious games, including the excellent books *Gamestorming*,[9] *Innovation Games*,[4] and *The Surprising Power of Liberating Structures*.[10]

Facilitating Scrum Events

Some time ago, we were talking to a newbie Scrum Master who was going to launch a product group along with us. It was about a week before the first Sprint, and we were preparing to start the kick-off activities. The product group consisted of several Scrum teams working on the same product.

We asked the Scrum Master: "What is the first event or activity you would like to focus on and make it perfect in Scrum—Sprint Planning, Daily Scrum, or . . . ?" She thought for a while and responded that it was the Sprint Planning. This answer made sense because Sprint Planning is the first event in any Sprint. Well, is the answer so obvious?

Facilitating Sprint Planning

During Sprint Planning, the team selects Product Backlog Items (PBIs) and plans enough details to start the Sprint. In a single team setting, having a Sprint Goal and a Sprint Backlog works really well. If you're working with multiple teams, however, you still want to apply Scrum practices without sacrificing Scrum's empiricism.

Facilitating Single-Team Sprint Planning

Every event in Scrum can be fun, engaging, and collaborative. A self-managing team creates their plan and estimates work themselves without outside interference. The team owns its Sprint Backlog and feels confident that they will reach the Sprint Goal. Full team ownership means that no team lead or senior member creates most of the plan while other team members are merely bystanders. Instead, all team members create and understand the details of Sprint Backlog. Why? This shared activity fosters not only team ownership but also an intrinsic feeling of commitment to reach the Sprint goal.

You can try the workshop setup illustrated in Figure 7.3 and the guidelines that follow with beginning Scrum teams. (We understand that this might sound trivial but decided to include it for completeness.)

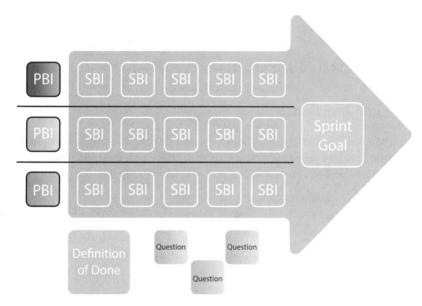

Figure 7.3
Setup based on the Graphic Game Plan game by Dave Gray, 2011.[11]

   Materials needed: Pens, sticky notes, a whiteboard, or flipcharts.

   Structuring the invitation: How do we reach our Sprint Goal?

We use the following facilitation steps:

1. Draw the Graphic Game Plan on a whiteboard and place the Sprint Goal at the end.

2. Post the selected PBIs at the left of each row and the Definition of Done (DoD) below it.

3. Ask the team to agree aloud on the first step required to accomplish the first PBI. Write their contribution on a sticky note—Sprint Backlog Item (SBI)—and post it on the same row next to that PBI.

4. Ask the team to keep going with the next steps, to keep writing their input on sticky notes and adding to the same row. Example questions that you can use in Steps 3 and 4:

   a. How do we know if a PBI is delivered correctly?

   b. What are the main concerns to be aware of when trying to reach the Sprint Goal?

   c. Which SBIs do we need to do to deliver the PBI?

   d. Which information, data, or resources do we need to accomplish the SBIs?

   e. What work is necessary to satisfy the DoD?

5. Repeat Steps 3 and 4 for every PBI until the Sprint Backlog is completed and the team is satisfied. Make a note of any unresolved questions or doubts that are not directly relevant to the plan and add them to the questions section.

6. Ask the team to order the SBIs and PBIs into a plan. Consider using the following questions for this:

   a. What, if any, dependencies exist between the selected PBIs or SBIs?

   b. How do we line up the dependencies between BPIs/SBIs? (Dependencies First pattern[12])

Facilitating Multi-Team Sprint Planning

At large scale, when many teams work on the same product, there is a single Sprint Planning event for the entire group of teams. We recommend facilitating this event by using timeboxes for each step and doing the best you can to start with a proper refined Product Backlog.

Consider facilitating the following steps:

Step 1. Recap
Step 2. The teams select PBIs
Step 3. Discover opportunities for coordination
Step 4. Closing summary

The sections that follow describe these steps in more detail.

Step 1. Recap

The Product Owner starts the session with the latest updates on the work to do and provides opportunities for asking questions. After that, the teams can either select the PBIs they want to work on or craft an overall Sprint Goal.

Consider crafting an overall Sprint Goal. Although each team has a local Sprint Goal, an overall Sprint Goal will support the whole product focus and stimulate collaboration among the teams for one or more Sprints.

A way to facilitate this is through the following sequence (see Figure 7.4):

1. **Find the overall goal.** Ask the question: "What will our product have done?" The Product Owner likely answered this question in combination with the teams prior to the Sprint Planning. Write the overall goal at the top of the wall.

2. **Find the team goals.** Ask the question: "How did the product do it?" Thinking of a future state as already completed reduces the possible outcomes that must be considered before suitable subgoals are selected. The teams work on this in parallel and select the Product Backlog Items required to achieve their team goals. We recommend using the 1-2-4-ALL liberating structure.

3. **Close.** Ask team representatives to come to the wall and post the goals and selected PBIs they came up with on the whiteboard; connect them to both the team goals and the overall goal. Keep everything nicely visible.

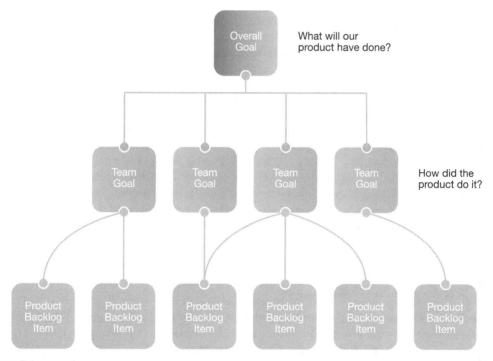

Figure 7.4
Overall and team Sprint Goals.

> **Caution**
>
> We recommend defining the overall goal ahead of Sprint Planning so that it can be used as the starting point and not slow down the larger group.

Step 2. The Teams Select PBIs

We let starting groups experience two options for PBI selection, before they create their own.

- In the first option, the teams select their PBIs in centralized collaboration. Each team has representatives approach the Product Backlog and divide the PBIs while working collaboratively. The representatives select PBIs according to their team's capacity and goals (see the Yesterday's Weather pattern[13]).

- In the second option, the PBIs are selected on a who-comes-first basis. The teams simply pick the PBIs they want. This approach has the advantage that the process goes faster, but has the drawback that lower-value PBIs might be selected over higher-value ones. When this happens, you can make the teams aware of that so that they can then coordinate and solve any issues.

After the teams have experienced both options, they can select which they prefer or, even better, develop their own approach.

> **Caution: Beware of the Efficiency Trap**
>
> Especially in the early Sprint Planning sessions, you can expect to see the teams select PBIs they can do most efficiently, even if that means choosing lower-value PBIs over higher-value ones. When this happens, you can remind the teams that a goal when scaling Agile is to increase agility at the product level, not local team efficiency. Working outside their area of primary expertise helps them learn new areas of the product and increases agility.

Step 3. Discover Opportunities for Coordination

We like the teams to own their coordination and to be aware of what other teams are doing during the Sprint. We do not want to assign the responsibility for coordination to a separate role. To create ownership and emergent self-coordination, the teams use Sprint Planning to discover the following:

- With whom they need to coordinate

- About what they need to coordinate

- When they need to coordinate

The teams understand the work and its details best and are therefore in the best position to identify coordination needs. But how do you create the conditions for emergent coordination?

You can facilitate diverge–merge cycles to identify work duplication, dependencies, and other shared work opportunities across the teams. Typically, we follow the steps illustrated in Figure 7.5 and described next:

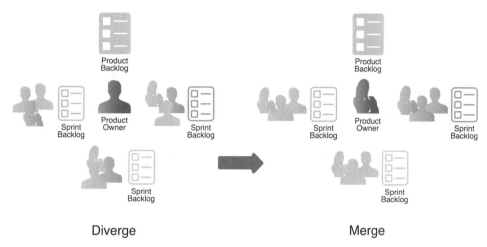

Diverge   Merge

Figure 7.5
Diverge–merge at Sprint Planning.

1. The teams start creating their Sprint Backlog for a period of time (usually 20 minutes).

2. The teams diverge.

   a. All teams at the same time send out a person to all other teams to inspect their Sprint Backlog. The teams explain their Sprint Backlog to the visitors to discover opportunities for coordination.

   b. We recommend starting with 5 minutes to ask questions.

3. The group merges the information: The people return to their teams and share what they learned.

4. The teams continue Sprint Planning and resolve any identified issues.

Usually, we do two or three diverge–merge cycles in total.

Step 4. Closing Summary

We recommend closing Sprint Planning by asking the teams to share the items they will work on with the whole group. Each team gets a few minutes to do this and visually place their PBIs where all can see. The group sharing creates a healthy peer commitment between teams instead of pressure between teams and the Product Owner.

Facilitating Product Backlog Refinement

Product Backlog Refinement (PBR) is an activity that Scrum teams regularly do to clarify potential upcoming PBIs. In single-team Scrum, the developers and Product Owner get together for one or more workshops during a Sprint to create and maintain a Refined Product Backlog.[6]

The teams add sufficient details to the PBIs on top of the Product Backlog—those they are most likely to work on in the coming Sprints—while avoiding wasting effort on detailing PBIs too far ahead that might change or never reach the top of the PBL. The details of the PBIs are added just in time. This can include performing detailed requirements analysis, splitting large PBIs into smaller ones, updating estimates, reordering the Product Backlog to handle dependencies between PBIs, and ensuring that the Product Backlog is updated with the latest information.

Teams that work together on a single product will benefit from doing shared PBRs in multi-team or cross-team formats.

Why Multi-Team Product Backlog Refinement?

In a multi-team setting, there is a single Product Backlog that is addressed by multiple teams. Providing teams with their own local Product Backlog reduces agility, diminishes overall product understanding, and makes interteam coordination difficult. Therefore, in a multi-team setup, two or more teams refine PBIs together without deciding as yet which team will implement which item.

Shared refinement can provide the following benefits:

- **Adaptability at the product level.** Why? Because all teams understand all PBIs on the Product Backlog, instead of each team understanding only its own PBIs (a subset) of the Product Backlog. If all teams understand all PBIs, then the Product Owner can put any PBIs deemed most valuable at the top without being constrained to the PBIs a particular team understands.

- **Improved self-coordination.** Why? Because the teams maintain a broad understanding of the whole product and the upcoming PBIs, and therefore are more likely to know about dependencies between PBIs.

- **Transparent measures of progress at the product level.** Why? Because all teams participate in estimating all PBIs, so there is one common velocity at the product level, instead of a distinct velocity per team that needs to be combined using voodoo statistics into a total.

How to Conduct Multi-Team Refinement

The activities for single-team refinement can also be used with multi-team refinement; the biggest change is in the facilitation of large groups.

When we work with teams, we show the teams four ways of doing multi-team refinement so that the teams can then choose the way they like most to continue with and improve. We work with the following formats:

- **Full roulette.** Each team picks a PBI for refinement and starts refining it at their station. After a timebox (we like 15-minute timeboxes), all teams move to the next station and continue refining where the other group left off; this is continued until the PBIs are refined or the workshop timebox expires. The full roulette approach motivates the teams to leave their work as clear and understandable as possible for the next group. Another benefit is that no one stays behind at a station to influence the next team.

- **Partial roulette.** This approach is just like full roulette, but instead of the whole group moving to other stations, one person stays at the station. This person then teaches the new group what was discussed before they continue with refinement. We use this approach in the beginning because it is easy to start with. After the teams have experienced the partial roulette method, we encourage them to try full roulette.

- **Diverge and merge.** In this approach, the groups do a diverge–merge action after each timebox. One person stays at each station and becomes the teacher. Then all groups send a person to each of the other stations. For example, suppose the participants include groups A, B, C, and D. One person from group A stays at the station to teach the new group, and one person from group A visits group B, another visits group C, and still another visits group D. After the teach-back, the visitors return to their original groups and share their learnings. Any puzzles and questions are then discussed as a group. We have applied this technique with as many as 35 people participating in the refinement. This approach is fast, but the teams do not develop a deep understanding of all PBIs.

- **Teach-back.** Each group picks a PBI and refines it. After the timebox is over, each group teaches their work so far back to the other teams and holds a Q&A discussion. This technique does not work well with a large number of teams, because the teach-backs will take too long for big groups, and it's harder to have a focused discussion with lots of people. Also, just as in the diverge–merge approach, the teams will not develop a good understanding of all the PBIs.

Role of the Users

During the refinement sessions, user, customers, subject-matter experts or other stakeholders play an essential role in clarification. Thus, the stakeholders and especially users will, ideally, participate in the detailed PBR sessions. When that is not possible, look for internal people closest to the users, such as people from the help desk, to serve as the users' proxies.

A Multi-Team Refinement Setup

For workflow administrative systems that have lots of user interaction, we like to use a setup that includes a story map, an example map, and a story board (see Figure 7.6). We use this setup as an introduction to multi-team refinement.

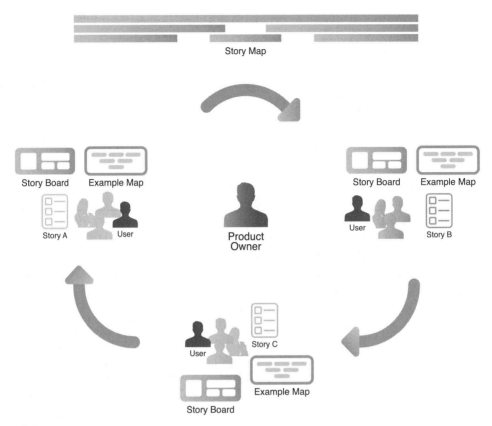

Figure 7.6
Initial setup for multi-team refinement.

Each team refines a story in parallel, while documenting their progress visually on a wall or flipchart. The steps are as follows:

1. The Product Owner tells stories about the PBIs using the story map.

2. Each team selects one story to refine in 10-minute roulette cycles.

    a. First, the teams create examples using the example map. Apart from the examples and questions for the Product Owner, the teams can also split items if needed.

    b. Second, the teams create interactions using the story board.

    c. Ensure each team passes each story at least twice with the example map and story board. Ensure that decisions and results are visually captured for all to understand.

3. Repeat with more PBI stories until the end of the timebox.

4. Close with a summary and capture the results in your favorite tool.

This setup works well with either partial or full roulette. We strongly recommend that you have the teams experience some example setups before building their own.

A Multi-Team PBR Example

The context for this example was a large product group (approximately 30 people) working on one product. Thus, there was one Product Backlog and one Product Owner. Two development teams were invited to the event along with the internal stakeholders. We wanted the developers to clarify the requirements directly with them.

The Goal and Working Agreements (5 minutes)

Any meeting starts with the definition of its goal, the desired outcomes, and working agreements. In our case, the goal was "Split a large feature" and the desired result was "Ordered minimum set of smaller features." The timebox was 2 hours, and we agreed on taking a break in the middle of the timebox.

High-Level Clarification (10 minutes)

We spent 10 minutes in open discussion, clarifying the giant feature in the following format:

- **Who:** Customer segment it relates to
- **What:** High-level scope
- **Why:** Business and customer value

Forming Mixed Groups (5 minutes)

We managed to form three small groups. Each group included at least one stakeholder and representatives of various teams.

First Round: Splitting (20 minutes)

Since the main aim was to split a large feature, we gave everyone splitting patterns. We asked them to come up with options for splitting the feature, and to capture those decisions in the form of a tree. At the top of the tree was the initial requirement that needed splitting. After the tree was defined, the groups used it for splitting. When a suitable pattern for splitting was found, the group applied it and moved to the next level, and so on. Figure 7.7 shows an example of a splitting tree.

Second Round: Rotation (5 minutes)

We asked each group to leave one representative at the station and the rest of the group to move clockwise to another station (partial roulette). The goal was to investigate what other teams were doing and receive feedback. One of the groups might have come upon an interesting option for splitting and it was important for everyone to find it out.

Third Round: Complete Splitting (20 minutes)

After the break, we took another 20 minutes to complete the split. Figure 7.7 illustrates a splitting option that one of the groups proposed.

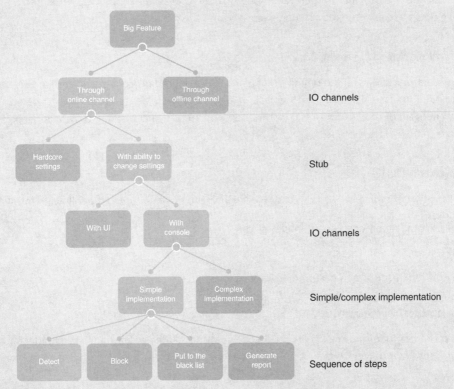

Figure 7.7
Example of a splitting tree.

Fourth Round: Merging (20 minutes)

The groups presented their results in an open discussion. It was interesting to see that they came to similar conclusions. The minimum feature set turned out to be surprisingly small. The main insight of the refinement was that the major business value could be achieved with relatively little effort.

Full Team or Team Representatives in Product Backlog Refinement?

On the one hand, having all teams refine all PBIs in large workshops might be too costly or ineffective. On the other hand, focusing on a subset of the total Product Backlog leads to reduced learning and alignment with the whole product. To balance these concerns, you should consider a cross-team refinement session where team representatives jointly identify related PBIs that are candidates for in-depth clarification at a multi-team PBR. In Large-Scale Scrum (LeSS), this exploration session is called Overall Refinement; it is a workshop in which team representatives and the Product Owner explore the work ahead by visioning, estimating, and splitting PBIs.

How to Facilitate Refinement with Team Representatives

We like to create new groups from the teams that participate in a cross-team refinement session instead of using the regular team setup. As an example, suppose there are four teams: A, B, C, and D. Then at cross-team refinement, we ask the teams to form four new groups, with each group consisting of representatives from teams A, B, C, and D. Why? When the groups include members from each team, all PBIs are refined by at least one person of every team. This setup creates shared ownership of the refinement results, and discussions between members from different teams can be a source of new insights.

The Role of the Product Owner

During the refinement session, the Product Owner plays an important role. The Product Owner should come prepared and explain what is needed from the business perspective. The following example illustrates this idea.

We worked with a product group that contained seven feature teams working on the same product. Team representatives collaboratively co-created a new process for refinement. Figure 7.8 shows the first combination of refinements they came up with.

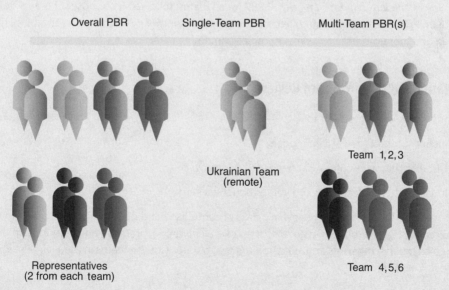

Figure 7.8
Example timeline for refinement activities.

The product group worked in two-week Sprints, and refinement started with an Overall PBR attended by team representatives. The Ukrainian team was the exception; it usually conducted a single-team PBR. The justification for this decision was the team's remoteness. The other six teams split into two groups of three, which held Multi-Team PBRs in parallel. The reason for selecting this approach was rather prosaic: The head office didn't have a big enough room to accommodate all of the teams at once.

Even though only the Ukrainian team had a separate single-team PBR, its coordination, dependency management, and fixing integration issues with the other six teams required more effort than for the other six teams combined.

Finding the Right Balance Between Single-Team and Multi-Team PBR

When you're considering whether single-team or multi-team PBR will be the best approach for your organization, we suggest starting with a minimalistic process and adding to that process only when it starts breaking down. There are two main reasons for this recommendation:

- The more process steps the teams need to follow, the less ownership they will feel over the process, and the less likely the teams are to care enough to improve it.
- Large, detailed processes tend to slow teams down and encourage a focus on the process instead of the product and the user.

Therefore, you should consider starting with the most minimal refinement process that (barely) works. For us, this often means an Overall PBR for all teams, followed by a subset of teams doing multi-team PBR for strongly related items. If the teams encounter problems along this path, then they can add more process and teams to multi-team PBR.

Facilitating Multi-Team Sprint Review

The Sprint Review is a moment to:

- Inspect progress toward your goals
- Discuss what works and what needs to be improved
- Incorporate that feedback into your Product Backlog

We recommend facilitating the review in cycles of centralized and decentralized activities. In the centralized parts, the Product Owner discusses overall planning, progress, and learnings. In the decentralized parts, the users and stakeholders collaborate with the teams in parallel. We typically use the following format.

1. The Product Owner starts and highlights what work was done; the Product Owner then introduces the teams and their features to the stakeholders. At this point, the stakeholders decide which team reviews they want to visit.

2. The teams engage in a first round of parallel Sprint Reviews. We usually facilitate rounds of fixed timeboxes, especially when people are new to this, and allow people to move between different teams. After a couple of rounds, there is a coffee break.

3. After the break, the review ends with a centralized gathering in which the Product Owner shares the plan for the next Sprints, discusses feedback that the teams received, and provides time for questions.

Figure 7.9 shows six teams holding Sprint Reviews in parallel. Users join the stations in which they are most interested and may move to the other stations in rounds.

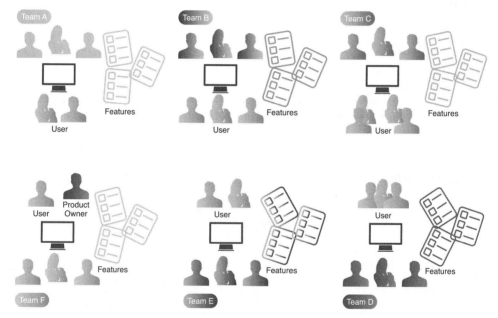

Figure 7.9
Typical setup for a Sprint Review.

The following tips are meant to help you prepare for a multi-team Sprint Review:

- Prepare the stakeholders about what to expect, especially those who are attending for the first time, before the review. Explain that they are in charge to ask all the questions they wish.

- The review is an excellent opportunity for the teams to learn from the stakeholders. So, encourage the teams to prepare questions for those stakeholders: What do the teams want to learn or validate?

- Put the teams on notice that they are accountable for what the stakeholders point out.

- Post the PBIs at the team stations so that the stakeholders know which team to visit.

- Post the team name or a number on a large sticky note or whiteboard at the team station.

- Encourage team members to rotate in collaboration with the stakeholder, and visit other team reviews.

Facilitating a Multi-Team Retrospective

The last principle of the *Agile Manifesto* states: "At regular intervals, the team reflects on how to become more effective, then tunes and adjusts its behavior accordingly."

In the Retrospective at the end of each Sprint, a Scrum team reflects on topics such as the following:

- Team dynamics

- Process

- Tools and skills

- The DoD

The end of a Sprint is an appropriate time for reflection because it provides a performance perspective on the team's plan, processes, and completed work. The team uses this full perspective to learn what can be improved. Next, we'll explain how this might work.

Proactive Learning Setup

In the Sprint Planning session, the team creates their Sprint plan. Then they execute it as best they can. In the Retrospective, they evaluate and analyze deviations from their Sprint plan. The key questions they consider are:

- Why did we deviate from the Sprint plan?

- What can we learn from these insights?

- How will we execute the next Sprint a little bit better?

The underlying learning loop is plan–execute–evaluate–analyze–improve. High-performing Scrum teams learn proactively and take changes—retrospective actions—into account in their Sprint Planning. They ask the following question at Sprint Planning:

How are we going to do this Sprint differently, so that in the next Sprint we are able to do it a little bit better?

Separate Local Issues from System Issues

The team must consider two types of issues in the Retrospective. On the one hand, there are local team issues—for example, a conflict between two people in a team or the lack of a particular skill within the team. These could very well be local matters to handle in the team Retrospectives.

On the other hand, there might be repeating issues that involve many teams—for example, a trend of decreasing product quality Sprint after Sprint, a super-linear increase in production issues over time, or just many teams struggling with clarifying requirements. These could very well be system-related matters to handle in a multi-team retrospective.

How to Facilitate a Multi-Team Retrospective

We facilitate the overall Retrospective in regular or in systemic mode.

Regular Mode

We facilitate the regular mode just like a single-team Retrospective. You do not need any additional workshop formats or techniques for that. The only difference is that you focus on issues at the group level instead of at the local team level. For example, at the beginning of your Agile adoption, the group may solve many problems relatively easily—the low-hanging fruit. After that, the problems become more challenging, but if they are not system issues, then the regular mode works just fine.

In the book *Agile Retrospectives: Making Good Teams Great*,[8] Esther Derby and Diana Larsen share five phases for structuring a retrospective:

1. **Set the Stage**

   - Encourage the team members to focus on the meeting. People's minds might still be filled with thoughts of their previous tasks.

   - Set up an environment where people are ready to contribute to the session.

2. **Gather Data**

   - Gather data on what happened in the last Sprint(s).

   - Identify the perspectives and data for the Sprint so that every participant has the same picture of what happened during the iteration.

3. **Generate Insights**

   - How do we make meaning from the data?

   - What are some root triggers for the selected problem?

4. **Decide What to Do**

   - You identified a list of possible root causes of the problem and potential solutions. Now you want to decide what you want to do differently in the next Sprint.

   - Which Testable Improvement are we going to try on and how?

5. **Closing**

   - Sum up the results of the Retrospective and point out what was achieved.

Systemic Mode

Prepare and facilitate the Retrospective in systemic mode when the group faces recurring problems that are hard to solve. We recommend using the Go See approach and spending a lot of time with the teams to identify system issues. When similar problems repeat in different teams or get worse over time, it might be a system issue that deserves further investigation. We also recommend gathering data, examples, quotes, and other relevant perspectives during the Sprints and using that information to prepare for a systemic-mode Retrospective.

Consider these questions when preparing for such a Retrospective:

- Which complexity factors are at play? What happened in the last Sprint(s)?
- What is the main focus of the Retrospective? Which recurring problems are addressed?
- Who is needed to give perspective or must participate in solving the problem? Do we need to invite people from outside the group? Do we need specific management to be present because solutions might be outside the group's authority?

Consider using Causal Loop Diagrams (CLD) to create a shared understanding of the issues. We provided many examples of the CLD technique in this and other chapters and will not repeat them here. (The Doom-Loop technique presented in Chapter 2, "Systems Thinking," is easy to use if the team is new to CLDs.)

System-level interventions focus on explaining and dealing with tough problems that keep coming back. Selecting and implementing such an intervention requires a thorough understanding of what has happened over time. Although we can never understand everything, you can use the iceberg metaphor (see Chapter 3, "Optimize for Adaptiveness") from systems thinking to create a thorough understanding of the system involved in your situation. In practice, that means taking a step back and considering the more extensive system of which teams are a part. Teams need to zoom out to understand how different parts of the system interact if they are to find more impactful solutions.

The three main steps you can take to guide your teams to formulate system-level interventions are as follows:

Step 1. Understand the current reality, the iceberg's visible part—the stories, data, and patterns.

Step 2. Understand the invisible part—the structures, and the mental models that create the current situation.

Step 3. Formulate an experiment to improve the system.

Before you start working with your teams, we invite you to consider two cautions.

Caution 1: Avoid Starting Without a Shared Vision

You can do yourself a big favor by establishing an agreed-upon goal beforehand. You may want to align that with the overarching company vision and expectations of teams. Such a shared goal creates pressure on the system to close the gap between the teams' current performance and their expected performance. You can then help the teams focus on this gap during the workshops.

Caution 2: Avoid Making "Expert" Proposals

The goal is to examine the problems and possible solutions as a group because all team(s) members and other related people are part of the system. Their collective mental models have created the current reality, so you must clarify those models together before thinking about solutions. To do so, avoid acting as the "expert" or interjecting your own proposals. If you propose a "solution" or, even worse, write a report, people will be ready to blame you when your solution does not work—and it probably won't.

The Appendix provides an extended example of a systemic-mode Sprint Retrospective.

Summary

This chapter first introduced the principles of facilitating groups. The role of the facilitator is to create a collaborative environment and help the group reach their goals. Setting goals, ground rules, and a plan for the workshop will support both you and the group during that activity. We also discussed the three typical behaviors of the Expert, the Whiner, and the Gorilla, and considered how you can deal with them to keep them engaged and keep the workshop productive.

Next, we described ways to design your workshops and discussed the importance of creating a workshop that engages all participants. Serious games are especially helpful for focusing the participants on the task at hand, as they contain all the ingredients for engagement.

Finally, we described how to facilitate some of the typical Scrum events—Sprint Planning, Sprint Review, Sprint Retrospective, and Product Backlog Refinement—in single-team and multi-team settings.

References

1. Ingrid Bens. *Facilitating with Ease!: Core Skills for Facilitators, Team Leaders and Members, Managers, Consultants, and Trainers*, 4th ed. (Wiley, 2017).

2. Mihaly Csikszentmihalyi. *Flow: The Psychology of Optimal Experience* (Harper Perennial Modern Classics, 2008).

3. "What Are Serious Games?" www.youtube.com/watch?v=JmG3fdptY_k.

4. Luke Hohmann. *Innovation Games: Creating Breakthrough Products Through Collaborative Play* (Addison-Wesley, 2007).

5. Dave Gray. "Now-How-Wow Matrix." GameStorming (January 5, 2011). https://gamestorming.com/how-now-wow-matrix/.

6. "15% Solutions." Liberating Structures. www.liberatingstructures.com/7-15-solutions/.

7. Dave Gray. "Who/What/When Matrix." GameStorming (March 30, 2011). https://gamestorming.com/whowhatwhen-matrix/.

8. Esther Derby and Diana Larsen. *Agile Retrospectives: Making Good Teams Great* (Pragmatic Bookshelf, 2006).

9. Dave Gray, Sunni Brown, and James Macanufo. *Gamestorming: A Playbook for Innovators, Rulebreakers, and Changemakers* (O'Reilly Media, 2010).

10. Henri Lipmanowicz and Keith McCandless. *The Surprising Power of Liberating Structures: Simple Rules to Unleash a Culture of Innovation* (Liberating Structures Press, 2014).

11. Dave Gray, "Graphic Gameplan." GameStorming (April 6, 2011). https://gamestorming.com/graphic-gameplan/.

12. "Dependencies First." https://tinyurl.com/DependenciesFirst.

13. "Yesterday's Weather." https://tinyurl.com/YesterdayWeather.

8

Preparing the Product Group

If you truly want to understand something, try to change it.
—Kurt Lewin[1]

Agile is all about learning and putting that learning back into your plan. Yet the traditional mindset about transformations leads many to believe that a grand plan is needed upfront about the future state and design of the entire enterprise. This assumes that we can know all of these details beforehand, and that such knowledge will increase the chance of success. A grand plan takes a lot of preparation time to create and contains a great deal of speculation about what could work. Such a massive program poses high risks for the company because it affects the whole organization. Strict processes, lots of discussions, and many time-consuming meetings are the result. Is all this elaborate preparation really necessary?

This chapter describes how to do just enough preparation to successfully start your transformation. We explain how to align management around the objectives, identify what needs to change, and define your product, and we consider how to identify the organizational elements to form the product group.

Areas of Concern for Successful Preparation

We usually take a few weeks to a few months to get from the first meeting with management to the product group launch. The reason is that the people involved need to participate in the preparation but also need to keep doing their usual jobs. If you can halt the people's work, you could probably finish the whole preparation within two weeks.

We have found the following topics crucial for an Agile transformation. We don't presume a hierarchical, orderable process because you're dealing with a complex system. Many of the activities occur in parallel, some of them happen before the product group launch, and some might happen later. In some contexts, you might consider some activities irrelevant. During the preparation phase, several areas of concern should be covered:

- **Area 1:** Involve the managers.

- **Area 2:** Understand the current reality.

- **Area 3:** Create a vision of the future.

- **Area 4:** Identify the product group.

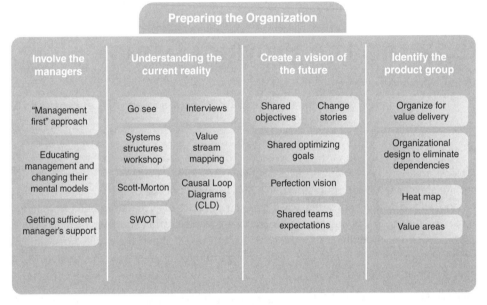

Figure 8.1
Areas of concern during preparation for the Agile transformation.

Note that the areas often overlap and do not have to be executed sequentially. That is why we explicitly call them *areas* instead of *steps*. The order of the activities is highly dependent on the context. The remainder of this chapter explores these four key areas in detail.

Area 1: Involve the Managers

The default approach to Agile adoption assumes that the organization starts with autonomous self-organizing teams. We call it a "teams first" approach. Our observation is that organizational coaches spend too little time involving and educating management before the actual adoption of the new organizational design. Ken Schwaber famously said that "Scrum is designed to disrupt the Hierarchy," and indeed, it is doing an outstanding job at that. From our experience, inadequate management support and sponsorship is the top challenge during most adoptions. With the "teams first" approach, the management comes into a conflict with the new organizational structure. Managers are then labeled as resistors and likely disengage from the adoption, creating a self-reinforcing loop of resistance to the changes.

It is difficult to grow effective Scrum Teams without senior management support, because these executives have the authority to change the system of work and resolve organizational impediments. Some potential organizational impediments include the following:

- The silo organizational structures that conflict with the cross-functional nature of the teams— for instance, teams organized around functions, components, or internal processes.

- Key performance indicators (KPIs) and bonuses that ruin the collaborative spirit of Scrum (The Spirit of the Game pattern[2])

- Human resources practices that stimulate people to choose narrow career paths

- Internal contracts with fixed cost, schedule, and scope constraints

We recommend that you start your adoption by making sure senior management is onboard. Though not an easy thing to do, it is a mandatory step before you consider moving further. From our perspective, activities for involving the managers fall into two broad categories:

- Educating and working with management to change their mental models about how to structure the system of work

- Getting sufficient managers' support to enable the necessary structural changes needed for successful Agile adoption

We'll explore these two points in subsequent sections.

Educating Management to Change Their Mental Models

Once we talked to one of the managers in a large service organization. We were discussing potential Agile adoption. We laid out our preferred approach to change and talked about the importance of an initial product definition. That's the focal starting point in any Agile adoption. Then we expressed a thought that senior managers should be well educated in systems thinking and Agile fundamentals before the product definition workshop took place. Our companion was surprised. "Why do you need the training?" he asked. He then continued: "We trust you and your experience, and we're ready to start with the solution that you define for us."

Have you seen senior managers outsourcing vital business decisions to consultants? We see it all the time, including outsourcing decisions about the company's strategy, which is sometimes developed by external consulting firms. That's a problem, from our perspective. Let us explain.

Senior managers are often the people who make organizational design decisions. From systems thinking theory, we know that the organizational design is derived from the managers' mental models—their perceptions of reality and their beliefs. And that's also why organizational coaching should start with the education of the senior managers. Changing mental models is the most powerful leverage with the highest impact in any Agile change initiative.

Once changed, the mental models of senior managers affect all subsequent decisions related to the system of work, and in turn employees' behavior patterns and hence the results of the adoption. Here are two stories illustrating this idea.

> The CEO of a medium-sized software company contacted us. The conversation happened on Friday night. He asked if we could help his company adopt Large-Scale Scrum (LeSS) straight away on Monday. We were busy and suggested that he postpone the decision for a couple of weeks; we also suggested that we start with the training for the senior managers and teams. Unfortunately, the training did not happen.
>
> Eventually, the company made an adoption decision on its own. In just a few days, the product group of 50 people adopted feature teams, and started working with one Product Backlog and one Product Owner. That was the fastest radical change we had seen. The CEO was very happy with the change. He told us the teams achieved a triple decrease in lead time in several weeks.
>
> After the change, one of us conducted a few multi-team Product Backlog Refinement (PBR) sessions for the product group and helped the Scrum Masters to properly facilitate multi-team events. That was it—we left the company and didn't support them for two years.
>
> What happened in that period of time? The product group gradually moved from one Product Backlog to just a few backlogs, and then eventually to six separate "backlogs"—which is exactly where they had been before the change. Teams gradually shifted their focus from the whole product to the product parts. Dependencies emerged once again, and transparency and adaptability tangibly decreased. This is a typical dynamic that you can expect when management adopts new structures without a deep understanding of the *why* behind them. When senior managers' thinking doesn't change, the old mental models eventually take their toll. The deeply ingrained approaches—"divide and conquer" and "work harder" instead of "work smarter"—start dominating.

The next story describes a lasting change in a big bank that happened after the senior managers vastly shifted their mental models.

A large bank had been experimenting with different Agile approaches for 5 to 7 years. Change initiatives used to be delegated down the hierarchy and predictably stalled at the lower levels of the company. Senior managers did not actively participate in change programs, and those programs barely scratched the surface. First, the company started with the *Kanban* method, but the initiative failed. The next one to go was the "Spotify" model, which yielded similarly unsatisfactory results.

When management approached us and asked to conduct training for the board and senior management team, we knew there would be a lot of skeptics in a classroom because of the past failures. Despite that, the training went smoothly and was worth every minute that we spent in the bank. Some of the topics that we covered during education were systems thinking, lean thinking, product definition, organizational design (structures, processes, and HR practices), and Scrum on a large scale. The senior management team was happy.

The next day after the training, the CEO and his team decided to initiate the most serious shift they had ever done. They decided to kick off a new experimental unit with feature teams as the building block and a broad product definition. They formed a transformation team for dealing with organizational impediments and to prepare the product group. It included both senior and middle management, a few internal Agile coaches, and external consultants. The CEO and the management team led the adoption. It took four months to launch the new product group. By the end of the year, the new unit was recognized as the "best unit in the bank." Inspired by the initial success, senior management started launching similar units one after another. In a few years, the retail products were developed and sustained by similar product groups based on feature teams working from one Product Backlog with one Product Owner.

The bank is still on its road to agility and sees the change as very sustainable. From our point of view, the pivotal moment happened after initial training that changed the mental models of the senior managers.

Commitment from senior managers is vital because they are people who have the authority to redesign the organization. The change cannot be delegated. Senior managers need to lead it in a visible, hands-on way. Thus, educating senior managers and shifting their mental models is indispensable.

Education Objectives

The following topics are some that you might consider exploring when educating senior managers (general managers and board members). The topics are presented in random order here and are not a comprehensive list.

- **Agile fundamentals:** Agile values and principles, *Agile Manifesto*, and business agility.
- **Organizational design:** Impacts on roles, structure, processes, and people—the and guidelines of Agile organizational design, pooled/sequential/reciprocal dependencies, HR practices and rewards, product definition, and product ownership and adoption.

- **Systems thinking:** Moving from local to global systems optimization, systemic effects in product development, circular cause-and effect relationships not close in space and time, nonlinear effects in product development, systems and collections, systems thinking theory, the iceberg of systems thinking, Causal Loop Diagrams, creative tension and organizational learning.

- **Complex systems:** Sensemaking and adaptive complex systems in product development.

- **Queueing theory:** Effects of queues on product development flow and effective strategies to work with queues—utilization and queues, batches, variability, and utilization.

- **Lean thinking:** Lean principles across all functions—the work of management, building teams of people, Go See, push versus pull, flow efficiency versus resource efficiency, perfection vision, one-piece flow, types of waste, stop the line, and value-stream mapping.

- **Scrum framework:** The Scrum framework to build your process—empirical process control, bottom-up intelligence, self-organization, Scrum values, framework overview, Scrum Team accountabilities, commitments.

- **Multiple-team Scrum:** How to use Scrum in large product development with many teams—copy–paste scaling, multi-team Scrum, Product Owner in a scaled environment, feature teams, and broad product definition.

- **Measures:** Outputs versus outcomes, lean budgeting, vanity and leading indicators, and evidence-based management (EBM).

- **Growing people and teams:** Role of management and HR—developing teams, theories of motivation, extrinsic/intrinsic rewards, empowerment, levels of delegation, and values-based management.

As you can see, there are quite a lot of educational objectives. It is naïve to think that you could cover them all during two or three days of intensive training. Instead, you'll want to deliver the education during a series of workshops. It's better to spread them over several weeks or even several months.

Getting Sufficient Managers' Support

There is no rigid rule on how to define how much support is "enough." Use your own intuition. Nevertheless, if you believe that the current level of support does not provide for enough structural changes for the adoption to succeed, continue working with the managers. The "Area 2: Understand the Current Reality" section later in this chapter provides additional ideas and tools for achieving the necessary support. In some extreme cases, if managers can't or won't provide the support, the board might decide to get new management.

> *With the four companies I have been chairman of, I have had to replace two of the CEOs to get a better push on Lean, and I have recently gone through a transition with a third in which the longtime CEO retired and we made sure that his replacement came with strong Lean credentials. We know the value*

that Lean can bring for our investors, so we can't afford to wait too long to get traction on the Lean conversion.[3]

According to the research of Richard Hackman[4] and Ruth Wageman,[5] 60% of the teams' success depends on intentional prework. They define a team's effectiveness as consisting of the following elements:

- The team's design (compelling purpose, real teams, solid structure, supportive organizational context, right people): 60%

- The way you launch the team (boundaries, working agreements, identity, connecting to the purpose): 30%

- The quality and level of team coaching: 10%

According to John Seddon,[6] culture change is free—people's behavior is a product of the system in which they work. For this reason, we prefer to implement as much of the structural redesign as possible before starting to work in the new setup. Significant structural changes can be implemented only with the support of senior management.

Table 8.1 is a checklist that includes both team design and supportive organizational context elements. Make sure that management is ready to support most of the items listed in the right column.

Table 8.1   Checklist to Evaluate Support for Structural Changes

Unsupportive Start Situation	Supportive Start Situation
Teams organized around product parts or siloed functions	Teams are organized around end-user features, products. or services that are purchased by the customers on the market (independent profit-and-loss [P&L] units)
Team members work in different locations	Team members physically sit in the same room, preferably around one large table
Hierarchy inside the teams (team managers, team product owners)	Team of peers; no hierarchy', the only title is Developer
The Product Owner, who has no real power, does not own the budget and cannot make strategic product decisions	The Product Owner is the product's CEO, with full ownership of the product
Internal contracts between the business and development department are in action, with deadlines and commitments	Business and developres work in the same business unit and success is measured by delivered value as assessed against established business criteria (e.g., profit, customer satisfaction, employee satisfaction, social impact)
Team members have functional managers who can influence their salary, vacation, and other rewards	Team members have cross-functional managers
There is a policy to rotate or regroup people frequently; the team composition is unstable	The team is stable, its core members stay for at least 1–3 years

We completed a Go See appointment in a retail bank. The primary goal was an evaluation of 30-plus Scrum Masters. The organization had been using Scrum for many years. We were not surprised to see another copy–paste Scrum[7] implementation with narrowly defined products, component teams, and fake "Product Owners." The organization suffered from long lead times, dependencies, coordination overhead, lack of transparency, and other natural consequences of a dysfunctional organizational structure. Management was questioning the effectiveness of the Scrum Master role and constantly blamed the people filling this role for the implementation's shortcoming.

From the top managers' perspective, the company had already successfully finished Scrum adoption on the team level. To their surprise, our observations were quite different from what they expected to hear. We pointed out the organizational design that conflicted with the goal of agility and speed of learning. From our point of view, the bank didn't have a Scrum Master problem, but mostly an organizational design problem. We presented the results of our assessment to the senior managers who hired us. We discussed component teams and the effect that the functional managers and centers of expertise had on developers, and how that prevented them from helping their teammates and becoming multifunctional specialists.

After the assessment, the executives asked us if we would be interested in helping their company—albeit without proper involvement of the board of directors—change its organizational design. We politely refused and still believe that was the best answer we could come up with at that moment.

The tricky question is, How much structural change can management handle at once? There's no easy answer. Here are some of the objections to a radical change you can expect at this point:

- Our company is simply too big to implement radical changes.
- You are describing the perfect state. Let's be pragmatic and tailor Agile to fit our current organizational design.
- We can start from where we are and take incremental steps, and eventually we will get there.

We urge you not to compromise on the Agile values and principles. We urge you not to take the safe route. Remember that your role as an organizational coach is to challenge the status quo and drive significant change and business results.

Area 2: Understand the Current Reality

In Chapter 2, "Systems Thinking," we discussed the importance of understanding the current reality in a context of creative tension. Too often, people start an Agile transformation without a deep appreciation of the current reality. They don't understand the deep reasons why the organization operates the way it does. As a result, the proposed solutions direct limited resources to changes that make no difference in the long run or even make matters worse. One of the principles of systems thinking is:

Small changes can produce big results, but the areas of highest leverage are often least obvious.[8]

To find the areas of highest leverage, we need to carefully investigate the Gemba, which means "actual place" in Japanese. Lean thinkers use this term to mean real place or the real thing, or the place of value creation. We use different approaches and tools to understand the current reality. Most of them are finely facilitated workshops. Regardless of whether you decide to use some of them or come up with your own, remember some of the keys to success:

- Inclusive, cross-level and cross-team activities are strongly recommended.
- Use small groups—for instance, triads—to gather data. That helps to converge on reality faster and drives out fantasies.
- Use low-tech tools such as whiteboards and sticky notes for discussion and collaboration.
- Experiment with formats—we trust in your inventiveness.

We want to mention a few tools and practices that we use regularly:

- Go See
- Individual interviews
- Value stream mapping
- Scott Morton diagram
- Weighted SWOT and confrontational matrix
- Finding system structures workshop

Go See

You need to focus on the work floor for a longer time to understand what's going on there. It isn't straightforward to understand the actual situation. Such understanding goes through different levels.

- **Level 1:** Walking around, observing a meeting, some visual management tools, and talking to some people. This gives some insights, though these observations are largely disconnected. Real problems are easily hidden from the visitor.
- **Level 2:** Observing for a few days, a couple of different meetings, different teams, and different product parts. One might think the process is understood, but only observe the normal process when things go well. It's still hard to understand what kind of problems can happen.

- **Level 3:** Observing a couple of complete iterations or a release, participating in meetings, and doing part of the work in pairs. Now there is a deeper understanding of the process and the work. Problems become apparent, and patterns of behavior can be observed.

One thing to look for is recurring events and patterns that keep coming back over time. Why? Because patterns are often the result of the organizational structure, processes, and policies the people work within. These issues can be addressed by redesigning the system of work. Contrary to popular belief, you cannot make substantial improvements in systemic matters by exclusively working on the people.

We recommend planning for various conversations and workshops with the developers and the management. Observe meetings and engineering practices, do pair programming, ask lots of open-ended questions, perform humble practice inquiry, and study worklists to understand the work.

Example: How to Perform Observation Sessions

Structuring the invitation: Explain that these observations are for you only. The observations are shared afterward so that others can provide comments and improve the observations. By doing that, people will also be more likely to accept your views.

Performing the observations:

- Show respect; be a fly on the wall. Ask questions only rarely, because you want to disturb the natural dynamics as little as possible. You're there to observe, not to have an opinion.

- Concentrate on observing without judging. Judging or creating an opinion takes the focus away from seeing, so that you become likely to miss out on important information.

- Observe the group, their interactions, the words they use, and the group dynamics. Look for recurring events in the meeting—these are precious.

- Make notes of all relevant information to process after the meeting.

- Finally, thank the people and share some observations.

After performing the observations, you could process your notes and offer your observations to the people for feedback. You can then process their input, and ultimately share some remarks on your findings in a face-to-face meeting. Optionally, you can make some recommendations for them to try.

Consider the following small excerpt from observing a team during their Sprint Planning and Sprint Retrospective events.

Example: Observations

Observations:

- There is no Sprint Goal.

- Looks like items are assigned in individuals; what about team ownership?

- Sprint Backlog seems not to be understood at Sprint Planning.

- They assign people to work on stuff during Sprint Planning; they could do assignment of tasks at Daily Scrums.

- Does not look like a team, but rather a group. "How many story points does person X have this Sprint?"

- People do not volunteer for the work themselves. One individual says that people have enough work and other people are overloaded. Why don't the people make the plan and decide for themselves?

- They do seem to use their average velocity.

- They seem to make a plan at Sprint Planning—which is good.

- It seems that some people plan work for others and also estimate work for others.

- They seem to want to avoid conflict; other team members ask few deepening/widening questions on a topic.

- It seems that the team forgets to look back at the Sprint and see what happened; they went right away into the start–stop–continue. They do not know what the problems were as a team.

Some events recur after a long delay of months or even years. It is hard to notice these patterns, especially if you can't be there for the longer duration. So instead of only practicing the Go See approach, also rely on stories and understanding of the people who work there to get insights into the system dynamics. Some practical ways to do that are discussed later in this chapter.

Individual Interviews

Learning from a diverse group of stakeholders in an organization provides several benefits:

- It not only builds understanding, but also develops relationships that will be helpful in the later transformation process. Lean thinkers usually say, "Go see, ask why, and show respect."

- It's a wonderful way of collecting events and searching for patterns of behavior. Hearing similar things from different people representing different parts of an organization means you have possibly come across a pattern. Now you can say. "Bingo!"

- The more accurately the system is presented, albeit often with polar views, the more chances you have to avoid bias.

For example, in a telecom company, we interviewed 30 people who contributed to the development of the product we were investigating. They included:

- Senior management, who provided us with the overall picture of the organizational structure and value stream. They helped us to find out which other groups of stakeholders needed to be interviewed.

- Engineers from different divisions involved in product creation firsthand.

- People from the sales function, who gave us lots of valuable information about clients and their needs.

- Clients who were using the company's service.

- People from the HR function, who helped us understand how the grading system worked.

- People from the marketing function, who created an actual business case and were responsible for the product success.

- Technical support people.

Interviews, whether one-on-one or in small focus groups, are preferable to surveys because they enable you to uncover not only what people think, but also which reasoning leads them to their conclusions.

The typical interview starts with establishing a safe environment. We discuss the purpose and why we are conducting interviews. We build trust by saying that whatever we find could appear as a quote in a final report, but anonymously. We ensure the interviewer gets a preliminary report to make sure we didn't distort the words and to provide us with feedback.

When doing interviews, it's important to show respect for the people and the way they work. Every organization has a unique history. Remember that you're there to help, and not to criticize their way of working. Be patient and show sincere curiosity by asking lots of open-ended questions. Some of the questions you might consider are as follows:

- What are your main duties and current responsibilities in the company?

- What are the main assets of the company and the product?

- If you could become twice as productive as you are now, what would need to be changed?

- What are the main impediments for the company in general, and for the product in particular?

- If you were the CEO of the company for a few days and could make any decision that would stick for a long time afterward, what would it be?

- What did we forget to ask you about that is critical for us to learn in the context of this product and/or company?

Remember, those questions are just openers for further inquiry. Use the click-down technique by asking an open-ended question about why the interviewees do what they do. An open question often asks, "Why?"; a closed question often asks, "What?"

Keep the goal of the interviews in mind: You're trying to discover repeating patterns that hinder adaptability and speed of learning.

Value Stream Mapping

Value stream maps (VSMs) are useful for evaluating the flow of any process. They show all the steps in the process, and identify whether each step is valuable, capable, available, adequate, and flexible. A value stream is the sequence of activities an organization undertakes with associated people and artifacts to deliver on a customer request. More broadly, a value stream is the sequence of activities required to design, produce, and deliver a good or service to a customer. The value streams are cross-functional: The transformation of a customer request into a good or service flows through many departments and divisions in a typical organization.

In our experience, VSMs become eye-openers for management. Sometimes the results are shocking because people are not aware of how ineffective their organization is. The usual flow efficiency range in an average service organization—the ratio between the value-adding time and the lead time required to complete a process— that we see is between 1% and 8%. The rest of the time, the work stays in queues.

> In product development, our greatest waste is not unproductive engineers, but work products sitting idle in process queues.[9]

We encourage you to learn more about the nature and economic consequences of the queues by reading *Managing the Design Factory*[10] and *The Principles of Product Development Flow*[9] by Donald G. Reinertsen.

The book *Value Stream Mapping: How to Visualize Work and Align Leadership for Organizational Transformation*[11] lists five main reasons why maps are so influential and significant:

- They offer a holistic view of how work flows through the entire system.

- They provide a macro-level perspective and help to avoid local optimizations.

- They offer a highly visual picture of how work progresses from a trigger to fulfilling the customer request.

- They deepen organizational understanding. which leads to better decision making and work designs.

- The quantitative nature of VSMs provides a foundation for data-driven strategic decision making.

> Value stream mapping forces an organization's hand to either make the difficult structural changes that are more in line with the cross-functional reality within which they exist, or continue to deny reality, stick with outdated structures, and continue to perform accordingly.[11]

Management often thinks in terms of functions and optimizes organizational structures around the utilization of people. This approach causes queues, delays, and long lead times. Unfortunately, the customer doesn't care if company functions were successful and employees got their bonuses or if service-level agreements between departments were respected. Much more critical to the customer is how much time it takes for their need to be satisfied. The value stream mapping approach reveals the true nature of work—the horizontal flow instead of the vertical flow (Figure 8.2).

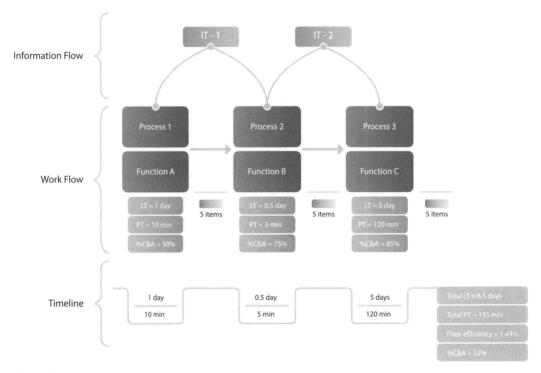

Figure 8.2
An example of a value stream map.

Metrics

With a value stream map (VSM), one evaluates the current state with three metrics: process time (PT), lead time (LT), and percent complete and accurate (%C&A).

The process time is the "touch time" to do the work. Process time doesn't include waiting time or delays.

Lead time is the elapsed time from the moment work is made available until it is completed and available to the next process step in the value stream. It is calculated as the queue time and delays plus process time.

Percent complete and accurate is the transformational metric because it highlights rework, which is the patent barrier to flow. This measure is obtained by asking the downstream unit what percentage of the time they receive work that is "usable as is"—meaning that there is no need to correct the provided information, add missing information, or clarify information that should have and could have been clearer.

Work-in-Progress

Good VSMs also include information about work-in-progress (WIP)—that is, the accumulation of work in different processes. It indicates started but not finished work. Intensive WIP is a symptom of overproduction and other waste in lean thinking terms.

Example: How to Run a Value Stream Mapping Workshop

We use a VSM workshop to create awareness of the main concerns for creating value. The goal is not to be very detailed, but instead to identify the primary concerns; the information obtained does not have to be very precise.

Materials needed: Pens, sticky notes, static-whiteboard cling sheets or a big wall covered with flipcharts.

Structural invitation: Invite a cross-functional group of stakeholders from different parts of the organization/product/value stream to the workshop. The optimal size of the group depends on the context. We find it comfortable to facilitate this workshop when the number of participants is between 8 and 16, and with multiple groups of 4 to 5 people each. Make sure that each part of the value stream is represented sufficiently. Consider inviting people from the sales, marketing, development, support, and management functions. For preparation, ask them to think about the process steps and to bring KPIs, percentages, and other relevant information.

1. Explain the purpose of the VSM exercise, the importance of understanding the current reality state, and probable benefits for the organization in the future.

2. Explain that some important event triggers the flow of value—perhaps a customer purchase order or a new feature request. This flow ends when some value is delivered.

3. Identify the core value stream with general questions like "How do external customers describe or perceive the flow of value they receive?" Write down the customers, the name of the value stream, the value received, and the triggers.

4. Agree on the process blocks that form the value stream. Determining how macro to go takes some practice. We aim for 5 to 12 serial process blocks. As VSMs are at the macro level, we recommend using a Pareto principle and mapping what happens 80% of the time so that you focus on improving most of the work instead of the exceptions. You might find a few parallel processes. In this case, stack them above one another.

5. Write descriptions of the activities, using the fewest words possible and a verb-plus-noun format, and the functions that perform them on the sticky notes.

6. Add information about WIP on the map.

7. Estimate metrics: PT, LT, and %C&A. When finished, calculate the total LT, total PT, and flow efficiency. Total %C&A is obtained by multiplying all local %C&A values and converting the result into a percentage. Remember, you are not looking for a very detailed description, but rather for an overview.

8. You are done!

Closing: Close the workshop by reflecting on the VSM. We recommend using the structure "What? So What? Now What?"[12] Capture the results using photos and keep the sheets for later use.

Scott Morton Diagram

A Scott Morton diagram (Figure 8.3) provides a macro view of the system and helps identify areas that need close attention during the individual interviews and later workshops. The Scott Morton workshop is often one of the first activities conducted during the Go See session. It also helps to evaluate the emotional state of the people in the system.

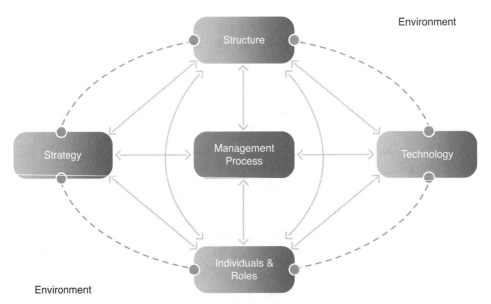

Figure 8.3
Scott Morton diagram.

During a Scott Morton workshop, we ask mixed cross-functional groups of employees to create drawings that comprise five forces (technology, individuals and roles, structure, processes, strategy) and the connections between them. What is especially interesting to notice is how employees evaluate the organization themselves. Notice and write down interesting or sarcastic expressions that pop up during the workshop and identify the organizational areas to which these expressions are related. Those are the focal points of interest during subsequent explorations.

The five forces in the Scott Morton diagram interact in response to the external environment within a company:

- **Technology:** IT that can be applied to facilitate business processes.

- **Individuals and roles:** People within the organization, the tasks they undertake, and the education and training they require to perform their functions.

- **Structure:** The way that the organization is partitioned and the way the partitions interrelate.

- **Management processes:** The standardized sequences of activities that organizations adopt to undertake the tasks they perform regularly. Their character reflects the power and control distribution within an organization, the structure, the people and their assigned roles, and the enabling technology.

- **Strategy:** General modes of doing business in pursuit of organizational goals.

There are many ways to facilitate a Scott Morton workshop. Next, we provide a concrete example of how we conduct this activity.

Example: Facilitating Scott Morton Workshop

Invite a cross-functional group of stakeholders from different parts of the organization, product, and value stream. We recommend that at least three levels of seniority be present in the room. That gives different perspectives and also covers the organization both in width and in depth. The subsequent steps are as follows:

1. Formulate the purpose of the meeting as being to get a macro view of the system and identify points of further exploration, agenda items, timeboxes, the parking lot, and so on.

2. Form mixed cross-functional groups with five or fewer members.

3. Explain the Scott Morton model.

4. Ask the groups to draw a model of the system that you are investigating (the product group or the company) using simple graphical symbols: arrows, lines, dotted lines, circles. The drawing could be a metaphor and have a storyline. There are no limits; tell the participants to go as far as they want.

5. Each group presents their drawing and explains it.

6. Have a discussion around patterns they have observed and conclusions they might have. What is similar in the groups' pictures? In what way are they different?

7. Thank participants and close the meeting.

> Once we organized a Scott Morton workshop in a telecom company. We had around 16 participants. What struck us was that all the groups produced similar drawings with lots of vertical lines that represented organizational silos. One of the groups presenting their creation and interpreted it by saying, "The organization is divided by thick walls. There are rare manholes between the walls, but only a few people in an organization know where they are located."

It's better to conduct a workshop with one or two co-facilitators. You will learn and hear lots of interesting things that would need further investigation during individual interviews. Be ready to write those points down. You could also use an audio recording and create a transcription afterward.

Weighted SWOT and Confrontation Matrix

A weighted SWOT analysis is a well-known technique to identify the strengths, weaknesses, opportunities, and threats (SWOT) for a business or product. A confrontation matrix is a tool used to further analyze the output of a SWOT analysis. It allows you to examine each different combination of strength, weakness, opportunity, and threat. The goal is to identify the most critical strategic issues the organization is facing.

Example: How to Run a Weighted SWOT and Confrontation Matrix Workshop

Invite a cross-functional group of stakeholders from different parts of the organization, product, or value stream. We recommend that at least three levels of seniority be present in the room. Here are the steps that we usually undertake:

• Use a 1-2-4-All[13] structure for gathering input from the participants. Work on one section (e.g., start with weaknesses) at a time before moving to the next section. For each section, ask the groups to produce a list of factors and give them weights from 1 (weak influence) to 5 (strong influence). When this step is complete, the result should look something like Figure 8.4.

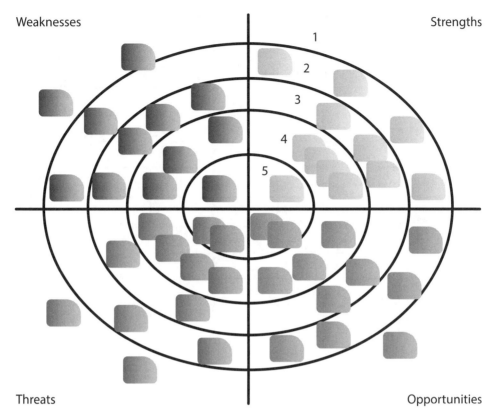

Figure 8.4
Weighted SWOT diagram.

- Next, ask the group to select the most influential factors from each section and create the *x*- and *y*-axes of the confrontational matrix: X (weaknesses, strengths), Y (threats, opportunities). See Figure 8.5.

- Ask the group to identify the intersections in the four resulting areas. The area where the weaknesses and threats meet is the most dangerous: In this area, the product group or organization will not be able to respond adequately. Those are the threats, and the company is weak there. In the weaknesses/opportunities and threats/strengths areas, the organization may need some help. They indicate the average risk. The area where strengths intersect the opportunities is safe.

Before closing the workshop, ask the participants about what was the most important and valuable for them. You could also use the *ROTI* or *Feedback Door*[14] techniques to see how useful the workshop was.

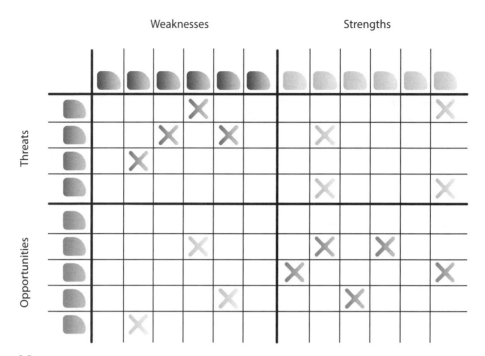

Figure 8.5
Confrontational matrix.

Finding System Structures Workshop

The structure is the network of relationships that creates behavior. By its very nature, the structure is difficult to see. As opposed to events and patterns, which are usually more observable, much of what we think of as structure is often hidden. We use the system structures workshop to uncover the organizational structures that produce the most critical patterns of behavior. The key to the workshop's success is inviting the right combination of stakeholders. After doing the activities described previously, you already should know where to search for them.

Example: How to Run the Systems Thinking Workshop

Materials needed: Pens, sticky notes, static-whiteboard cling sheets or a whiteboard/flipchart.

Structural invitation:

1. We start with a timeline activity, asking the cross-functional groups of stakeholders to remember as many events related to product development that happened during the time frame (up to a year) as possible. Then, we ask to divide these events into three groups: negative, positive, and significant. The size of the event could be both tiny ("sent a mail to marketing") and significant ("a major bug in production"). Make sure to prepare a few examples beforehand to get

the ideas across to the participants. Figure 8.6 provides an example of what your events trend could look like.

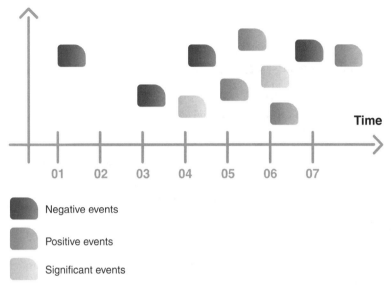

Figure 8.6
Events timeline.

2. After 10–15 minutes or so, the wall will be covered with events. Invite the group to find the patterns on the timeline. Consider asking questions like these:

   • What are the similar events that had been happening during the period?

   • What do you see on the timeline?

   • Which patterns can you identify?

   • What does this tell you?

3. Use a multi-voting system and give everyone 5 to 10 dots. Ask them to spread the dots all over the timeline to vote for the most critical recurring events that significantly influenced the product. Depending on how many participants you have, you can then create a few small, diverse groups (different departments, teams, business units). Each group should choose one of the top vote-getting recurring events to investigate.

4. Educate the participants a about the iceberg model (see Chapter 2, "Systems Thinking") and point out that the events and patterns have now been identified. They form the visible part of the iceberg. Now it's time to go deeper. Educate participants about the importance of systems structures, mental models, and Causal Loop Diagrams (CLD), and provide them with a simple technique to use—for example, the Doom Loop technique described in Chapter 2.

5. Equipped with this knowledge, let the small groups find the underlying structures and mental models behind the chosen events and patterns. A timebox of approximately 20–30 minutes is usually needed.

6. Support each group by walking around and answering their questions. Guide them, ask prob-ing questions, and help them to uncover the loops. When the timebox is over, ask each group to present their findings. Write down the insights that they have found.

7. Close the workshop by asking everyone to share what was most valuable for them.

Aligning on the Go See Results with the Systems Model

We discussed CLDs in Chapter 2, "Systems Thinking." These diagrams can be used as a tool for conveying observations after a Go See session and aligning people on the knowledge uncovered. For that purpose, organize a CLD workshop with a mixed set of participants, both management and team members. Invite everyone. Instead of presenting your own CLD, organize participants into small groups of three to five members, give them the most important variables that you had collected during the Go See activity, and suggest that they create their own models. After they complete their work, find common patterns, collect insights, and share your own CLD. Here is a preliminary plan for such a workshop:

1. Form three to five small mixed groups (5 minutes).

2. Hand out a list of the variables and ask groups to come up with their own models (20–30 minutes).

3. Each group presents their CLD and shares key insights (5 minutes per group).

4. Discuss emerging patterns and things the groups agree on (10 minutes).

5. Discuss where our perception of reality differs (10 minutes).

6. Present your own CLD and ask for feedback.

7. Close the session.

We completed a Go See activity in a product group of a telecommunication company. We cre-ated a final report and sent it to all interviewees and management (the customer for this ini-tiative). In the company. we observed a typical copy–paste Scrum adoption with multiple fake "Product Owners" and "Product Backlogs," component teams organized around platforms, lots of dependencies, and teams optimizing parts of the system and striving for local goals.

After completing the preliminary report, we conducted a collaborative session to present the results of the Go See activity and answer questions. We decided to kick off the session with the CLD exercise. We asked participants to create system models out of the variables:

- Number of Product Owners and Product Backlogs

- Number of local goals per team

- Transparency of the overall progress on a product group level

- Readiness to help other teams in a Sprint

- Local identification

- Average WIP

- Number of dependencies between teams

- Percentage of the most important features that teams were working on during the Sprint

- Ability to react to emergent work in a Sprint

- Probability that end-to-end features would be "done" by the end of the Sprint

- Time-to-learn from the market

- End-to-end feature spans over several Sprints

The result of the exercise was several CLDs, as Figure 8-7 illustrates.

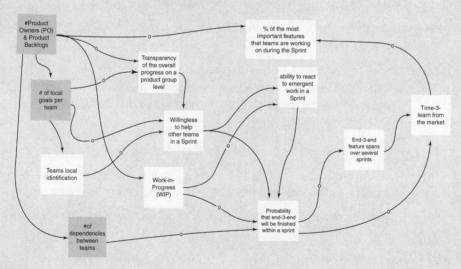

Figure 8.7
CLD created during Go See presentation.

We discussed patterns and differences. We well remember how easily and smoothly the rest of our presentation went. We still think that part of its success was the decision to start with the CLD exercise.

Example: Go See

The senior management of a telecommunication company was upset with the long lead times for their product development. They asked us to investigate the issue. We started our Go See investigation by conducting a series of telephone interviews, followed by a few days observing the activities in their office. After that, we shared our observations with the top managers; this created enough momentum for them to continue with an in-depth Go See. We then rushed to the headquarters for an assessment of the whole company. We held a two-day workshop with company senior management and employees focusing on company structure and the flow of value. Our goal was to create an action plan and set the next steps for a transformation. Some of the tools we used during the workshop were:

- **Scott Morton diagram.** Demonstrated the connection between crucial company building elements: strategy, processes, people, and structure.

- **Value stream mapping.** Gave us insights into the amount of waste in the product development flow (from customer request to the value delivery). Usually, it started from the first call to the customer support and finished with the new release.

- **Weighted SWOT analysis.** Created in mixed groups. All factors were weighted on a scale of importance from 1 to 5.

The detailed company assessment proved our first conclusions regarding component teams and their dysfunctions. The value stream mapping also showed that the average cycle time for a feature from start to finish was 6 to 7 weeks. We were happy that managers had some "Aha!" moments during the workshop:

- They agreed there was too much hierarchy for their medium-sized company.

- They understood that individual KPIs and bonuses locally optimized some departments in the company (sales and marketing) and pitted one function against another.

- Everyone in the room agreed that the company did not have a solid vision or a strategic plan.

The next steps we took were:

- Strategy planning workshop to create the company vision and strategy for upcoming years

- Simplifying the organizational structure and moving away from a functional organization to a team-based one

- Several Scrum training sessions in IT product groups to educate everyone

- Defining the product as broadly as practical

- Scrum training for the CxO people

- Kicking off the product group

Area 3: Create a Vision of the Future

A common pitfall of adopting an Agile way of working is to maintain a blind focus on implementing a favorite Agile method, rather than a focus on achieving the desired business objectives. In the preceding example, the business objective was to acquire new clients after changes in a federal law opened what the company's management saw as an opportunity window. When you focus on "implementing Agile," you tend to forget the reason behind the transformation—the real problems that need to be solved. In such a case, you run the risk of implementing a method but not solving the organizational challenges. The method becomes more important than the goal. The second problem is that the transformation activities become more about conforming to the rules of the method than about guiding people to create their own process that really works well. This pitfall is what we call "spreadsheet Agile adoption," wherein Agile coaches measure adoption progress by checking off the boxes in their spreadsheet. We do not recommend this approach!

It is crucial to align the management and the teams on the business objectives that they want to achieve with the transformation. Alignment creates a clear goal and focus. People remember—when times get hard—why there is a transformation in progress. A clear understanding of the gap between the current situation and the desired objectives creates a force to bring them together. Clear objectives also make future decision making more straightforward because they give you the context needed to evaluate different arguments during a discussion. Next, we provide you with tools for aligning the organization on the business objectives and organizational design goals.

Alignment Workshops

Management alignment is a process that can take numerous workshops spread out over many weeks to fully achieve. The exact duration, design, and facilitation techniques used are up to the workshop participants to decide. Apart from that, the main focus areas of the workshops are:

- A shared understanding of the objectives that are aimed for: the Shared Objectives Workshop

- A shared expression of the team expectations to be met: the Shared Team Expectations Workshop

- Definition of the organizational design optimizing goals: the Shared Optimizing Goals Workshop

- A definition of the perfection state: the Perfection Vision Workshop

Who should be present during these workshops? We prefer inviting everyone. Of course, the senior managers should be there. (Refer to the change guidelines in Chapter 5, "An Agile Adoption Approach.") Also, make sure that the results of the workshops are visible to the whole organization. You can get back to them when it's appropriate. Make sure that you establish a regular cadence to inspect and adapt the progress toward the objectives. We recommend starting with the Shared Objectives workshop.

The Shared Objectives Workshop

Any leadership team that leads the transformation needs to be able to share the reason and objectives for the transformation with the people involved—Peter Senge calls it the "shared vision" in his book *The Fifth Discipline*.[8] The shared goals bring into alignment the vision and the efforts of the organization's people. They create the conditions that enable process design, work design, and system-wide problem solving to flow in the same direction. The alignment is on what to move away from and what to move toward.

> *To empower people in an unaligned organization can be counterproductive.*[8]

Objectives are the specific results you want to accomplish within a particular time frame. Most objectives in our experience are related to one or more of the following:

- Decreased concept-to-delivery cycle time

- Increased financial results

- Increased employee satisfaction

- Cost reduction

- Increased customer satisfaction

- Improved reliability of service and product delivery

The idea is to find an organizational design that enables the company to achieve its objectives and expectations.

Example: How to Run a Shared Objectives Workshop

The goal is to create an initial set of alignment points to further refine in the next phase of the Shared Objectives workshop. Ask the participants to generate answers to the following questions individually:

- What is your biggest ambition for your group?

- What is so important about that?

- What are one or two things that work in your group?

- What are one or two things that do not work in your group?

After all participants have written, ask each person to explain their answers to their group, and post these items on the whiteboard. Use affinity mapping to identify common themes. Ask the participants to individually see which patterns or conclusions are emerging.

Questions that could be useful are:

- Given your perspective, what are the main points in this overview?
- What concerns does this raise for you?
- What does this suggest to you about the current situation?

After this warm-up exercise, you can move on to the next activity.

Facilitation Using the Shared Objectives Canvas

Four questions are at the heart of the Shared Objectives workshop (see Figure 8.8):

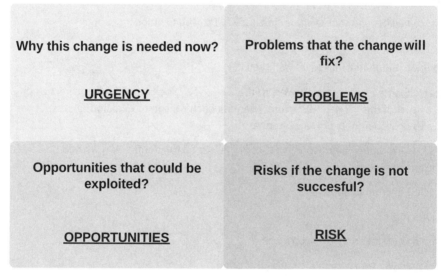

Figure 8.8
Shared objectives canvas.

- **Which problems will the change solve?** Creates alignment on what current systemic issues one will address. This question is about envisioning what the new situation would look like and which benefits it would bring to the product group. The gap between the current state and the vision—which leads to creative tension—creates energy for the change.

- **Which opportunities could we exploit that are presently out of reach?** Invites the partici-pants to align on the new opportunities that will be possible. What could we do in the future that is not possible now? For example, how will this change the way of working, product suc-cess, and employee satisfaction?

These first two questions align the group and create a pull toward the goal. The following third and fourth questions align the management on what to move away from.

- **Why is this change needed now?** Creates alignment on the urgency for change. What happens if we do not react quickly? Next to the alignment, it is most vital to clarify the urgency of the transformation at the beginning of this effort. Why? Moving too slowly in the first period can create the perception that this change is not so significant after all. In that case, people are more likely to give priority to other work over the needed work to move forward with the change.

- **What are the risks if the transformation fails?** What is currently making our group perform poorly? How is the current situation worsening our performance over time? Use these questions to align on all the bad things that will happen and that we want to avoid.

Progress cannot be generated when we are satisfied with existing situations.[15]

How to Facilitate the Shared Objectives Workshop

Ask the participants to generate answers to the "Urgency" block individually on sticky notes—for example, as part of the 1-2-4-All structure. Then ask each person to explain their responses to their group and to post their notes on a whiteboard.

Here are some examples of questions that could be useful for clarification when a person is presenting their answers:

- Can you say that in another way?

- Tell me more?

- What do you mean by the word . . . ?

- Do you have a story that illustrates your point?

As each participant shares their points, use affinity mapping to identify common themes. The common themes are where the participants are aligning.

When all participants are done, reflect with the group, using questions like these:

- What are the first words that come to mind when seeing this?

- What stands out?

- Which additional questions does this raise?

- On which points are we agreeing? Why are we agreeing on them (or why not)?

Then repeat the same process for the remaining three questions—*Problems*, *Risks*, and *Opportunities*. At the end, the various blocks of the canvas will contain areas covered by sticky notes. These areas point to where the participants align.

Next, reflect on the complete canvas and distill shared objectives statements about each area that the group aligns on. Questions that might be useful are:

- How does this all fit together?
- What are the primary outcomes we want?
- What are the implications for us?

The next step uses the shared objectives statements as a start.

Optionally Consider Creating Change Stories

The answers to the questions posed in the preceding section are used to write change stories. The building blocks for the stories are the points of alignment from the previous exercise. Each participant should write their own change story. This story should be short, to the point, and able to be quickly told at the coffee machine and meetings.

Some examples of change stories from companies of different sizes follow.

Example: Small Company

"We see that a lack of focus, shared values, and expert knowledge hinders us from developing end-to-end solutions, makes us waste resources, and causes us to lose good people.

We run a risk that this will cause our product to end. We need to deal with this now because we are losing control of our course. We have trouble completing our work and have reached the limit of our scale.

When we fix this, we will be able to respond to change fast with distinctive features, with little effort. We will become a cool and fun place to work."

Example: Medium-Size Company

"Before, we were agile and small. We liked it because we were autonomous; all information was transparent. Then one day, we grew and became bigger and received investments. This influenced our thinking and increased the amount of work to do. We need changes in structures and processes to become more effective and nimble, and improve quality."

Example: Large Company

"The world around us is changing rapidly—not only the technology, but also people's expectations. We used to be able to work with five-year plans and improve efficiency and predict long-term market effects, but those times are now gone.

Information is now transparent, and that opens all markets. A head start on competitors is no longer dependent on just information, but is much more about adapting rapidly to customer demands. Right now, during the era of digital transformation, intimate knowledge of our customers is more important than ever before.

Our main products have become commodities, and that means the competition will put pressure on our prices. If we keep doing things as usual, we will lose our visibility in the market.

Currently, sales and projects take too long because of many reasons. The fact is that this process has become routine for us, but not for our customers. Our customers are changing to Agile processes, and if we cannot join them, we may become a bottleneck in the supply chain.

We will be the first in our field to deliver customer value incrementally and stay ahead of our competitors by satisfying our customers through rapid cycles of high-value products."

Writing a story helps make the shared objectives more specific and puts things into context so that you can then have the much more important discussions—that discussion is what shapes the alignment. In addition to telling the stories, one can use them in other communications—for example, for creating an animation, in newsletters, or in other forms of contact with the larger organization.

How to Facilitate the Creation of Change Stories

Ask each person individually to use discoveries from the previous exercises to write an underlying story that:

- Addresses the sense of urgency: Why is this change needed now?
- Talks about the problems that the change will fix.
- Outlines the risks if the change is not successfully implemented
- Mentions the opportunities the organization can exploit as a result of making the change.

Then ask the participants to form pairs or trios. One person at a time can explain to the other(s) the urgencies, problems, risks, and opportunities. The others ask for clarification and provide feedback to improve the story. End the workshop with a presentation in which each story is read aloud.

Close with steps geared toward building ownership for follow-up. Questions that might be useful are:

- How interested are you in continuing your involvement with the next steps?
- Where and how could we let ourselves down concerning the next steps?
- Who needs to work with us in the next steps?

Another way of coming up with a change story is by employing a template. We often use a helpful tool from the lean change management movement called a "change story." It looks like a short and compelling message with critical points: "Before we . . . . We liked it because . . . . Then one day . . . and this influenced us . . . . That's why we want . . . . We will support . . . . We need help in . . . . That's why . . . ."

Shared Team Expectations Workshop

As mentioned in earlier chapters, self-managing teams are an important part of an Agile organization. But which team capabilities are needed to achieve the shared objectives? Use the Shared Team Expectations workshop to create a shared understanding of team expectations and the team characteristics, such as composition and skills, required to be successful.

The goal is to create a list of team and group capabilities that are needed to achieve the objectives. Ask the participants to generate answers to the following questions individually:

- Which team capabilities would you need to have that you don't have?
- How will these capabilities benefit you and the shared group objectives?
- What do we expect from the people in the teams in terms of skill sets and competencies?
- In what way do our current HR management practices support this?
- Which changes could be needed?

Then, ask each person to explain their answers to their group, and post these items on the whiteboard. Facilitate a discussion about self-managing Agile teams and Agile leadership and use affinity mapping to identify common themes.

Close this part of the workshop by reflecting and building ownership for follow-up. End by capturing the results for further processing and sharing.

Shared Optimizing Goals Workshop

Senior management has the power to design the organization. They need to align the business strategy with the organizational design. Before they can make informed decisions, it is necessary to understand how design decisions impact the capability of the organization to achieve the required goals. Although there are many goals one can design for, an Agile organizational design is primarily optimized for the goals of adaptability and speed of learning in order to deliver the highest value.

Use the Shared Optimizing Goals workshop to create collective insights and alignment at the management level on how the (current) organizational design decisions impact the organization's capability to achieve its agility goals. The approach we found very useful for this type of workshop is to co-create CLDs so that the participants can discover for themselves the underlying behavioral system dynamics within their organization.

Example: How to Run a CLD Workshop for Adaptability and Speed of Learning Optimizing Goals

When drawing a CLD, first focus on telling the story of the issue; do not focus too much on getting the correct variable names. In a good diagram, you should be able to easily tell the story by reading the variables as you go around the loops. Next, improve the variables' names by removing verbs and qualifiers, and by using nouns.

Use small groups to create a shared diagram. Remember that the goal of this exercise is to create alignment and shared understanding of how the system works. The discussion is more important than the actual diagram created.

Structuring the Invitation

Start by writing the key variables under discussion on a cling sheet. We use the following key variables:

- Adaptability at the overall product group level
- Speed of learning about a product feature

(In your specific context, the key variables could be different.)

Next, ask each participant to come up with a list of variables, one per sticky note, that affect or are affected by the key variables. (Consider using the liberating structure 1-2-4-All for this step.)

After all participants are finished, they should share their variables one at a time for recording on a flipchart and explain them to the group. You can facilitate this effort by removing duplicate variables and using affinity mapping to help the group discover common areas covered by variables. Give the areas a specific name—these area names become your variables in the CLD.

Variables to look out for are:

- Number of team worklists
- Shared understanding of work at the group level
- Functional dependencies between the teams
- Local team efficiency
- Cross-functionality of the teams
- The average end-to-end lead time of a product feature

Developing the Diagram

Have the group develop the CLD one variable at a time. Choose a variable from the list and add it to the cling sheet. Then discuss which cause or effect relationships they see with the other variables and draw the appropriate arrows. Here are some tips for successful facilitation:

- Rotate control of the pen every couple of minutes to keep everyone engaged.

- Make it clear that it is perfectly normal to have lots of tries before agreeing.

- Ensure that people understand that this exercise is about discovering each other's mental models and that all mental models are right for the person owning them.

Questions that might be useful during facilitation are:

- Which assumptions about . . . are you making with that response?

- What are some other options here?

- Which other factors might influence what happens next?

- What do you suspect is going on here?

- What is an example to support your position?

This discussion could result in a diagram similar to that in Figure 8.9.

Let's start the story at the "Number of team worklists." The more teams base their work on their worklist, the more likely it becomes that they will specialize in their own private area of expertise. An increase in "Number of team worklists" increases "Local team specialization." In this scenario, a team loses the understanding of the work of other teams, which makes it increasingly more difficult for the team to pick up work outside its specialization. A decrease in "Shared understanding of work at the group level" also decreases "Ability for a team to work outside its specialization."

At this point, when the work at the group level requires more work in a specialized area than the team can pick up, the other teams cannot help because they only know their specialty. As a consequence, "Adaptability at the group level" declines. In turn, the group cannot deliver the highest-value work, and the teams are likely to work on lower-value work instead. Thus, a decrease in "Team ability to pick up the highest-value work" decreases " Delivery of highest-value work at the group level." This will not amuse management. When their mental model is that "high utilization is better," a natural reaction to this scenario is to pressure the teams to work harder and to introduce more separate worklists so that the teams can specialize and be more efficient locally. This action again increases "Local team specialization"—a reinforcing loop that will worsen the adaptability.

Figure 8.9 also points out that having more worklists will likely increase the end-to-end lead time because a work item probably requires parts that are produced by different teams. Thus, these teams will have interdependencies that will cause delays, create queues, and introduce mistakes. Moreover, the time to integrate the work done across all teams—the end-to-end lead time—will likely increase.

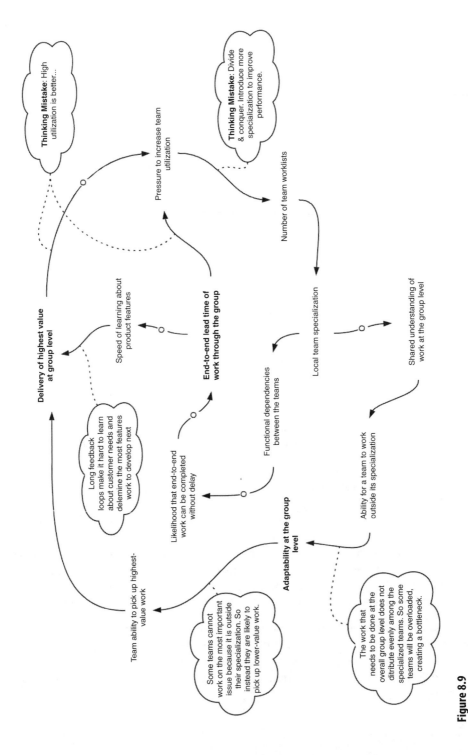

Figure 8.9
Optimizing goals diagram.

It is better to group related tasks and roles together. When you separate related jobs and roles into different teams, you introduce interdependencies over teams. In this situation, coordination will be costlier, as each team will need to coordinate and reach an agreement with people outside their own team to complete a feature. It can also lead to complicated coordination roles, as these roles will not have control over all the teams who perform tasks related to the work item. In addition, the end-to-end responsibility for a successful working feature becomes vague, as decisions made in one unit may impact some or all of the other units.

Closing the Workshop

After you have worked with the CLD, you can begin to generate insights and conclusions. In the end, a crucial understanding is that when the optimizing goals are adaptability, end-to-end lead time, and learning, it is better to reduce the number of team worklists and to not focus on local team efficiency.

With shared objectives, shared team expectations, and a shared understanding of optimizing goals, the next step is to combine all of that input into a concise perfection vision—the topic of the next step.

Perfection Vision Workshop

An Agile adoption does not have a static end-state as a traditional change program would have, but rather a dynamic end-state. You are not targeting an absolute performance that, once achieved, marks the end of the transformation. Instead, you seek a state in which your product group's value-adding capability tomorrow is higher than it is today. In that state, people naturally challenge the status quo and continually improve toward perfection. But what is perfection? We use the definition proposed by Aristotle.

That is perfect:

1. which is complete—which contains all the requisite parts;

2. which is so good that nothing of the kind could be better;

3. which has attained its purpose.

To Aristotle, "perfect" meant "complete" ("nothing to add or subtract").[16]

So, a system's perfection goal lies in its ability to achieve its purpose without the need to add or remove anything from it. In the context of Agile adoption, a perfection vision might include, but is not limited to:

- Processes

- Practices

- Organizational structure

- Behaviors, skills, and competencies we value in people

In other words, to fit Aristotle's definition, the perfection vision might answer the following question: What are the minimal processes, practices, organizational structure, and people capabilities required to satisfy the product group's purpose?

For example, a perfection vision might include statements like these:

- All teams in the product group can independently deliver the most valuable features into the hands of the end users in every iteration.
- Every day the whole product is potentially shippable.
- The teams share business KPI responsibilities and rewards.
- The teams work as closely with the customer as practical.
- Career paths encourage multi-skilled development paths and developers are highly skilled in multiple specializations.
- There are no projects, and all work comes exclusively from the Product Owner.

Why Use a Perfection Vision?

A perfection vision guides your continuous improvement efforts. Just imagine that you actually achieved your perfection vision—then what would you do? You would be perfect and there would be no possibility to improve anymore. That's not a good position to be in. Therefore, we use an unattainable perfection vision.

> Perfection is not attainable, but if we chase perfection, we can achieve excellence. —**Vince Lombardi**

How to Create a Perfection Vision for Your Product Group

The Perfection Vision workshop is the last alignment workshop. To make your product group perfect, you need to consider the whole product creation process:

Precondition: For this workshop, you need to have alignment on the business objectives, team expectations, and optimizing goals.

Participants: Invite the leadership.

Structuring the invitation: The goal is to define a list of concrete and measurable characteristics of the perfect product group.

We use the following question: What are the minimal processes, practices, organizational structure, and people capabilities required to satisfy the product group's purpose?

The steps for running this workshop are as follows:

Step 1. Share the example perfection vision statements.

Step 2. Ask participants to imagine that their product group is perfect, and that all business objectives, team expectations, and optimizing goals are achieved. Then ask them to go one month further out and look back at that moment of perfection. Ask them: Exactly what will your organization look like?

   a. What is the organizational structure?

   b. Which behaviors do you see?

   c. Which practices are you using?

   d. Which things do you value?

   Ask participants to write one idea per sticky note. When they are all done, ask them (using a round-robin approach) to put their sticky notes on the wall and explain their ideas to the rest of the group.

Step 3. Facilitate a group discussion using affinity mapping. Then, working in pairs, compile each theme into a perfection vision statement and present it to the group when done. Capture each statement on a whiteboard

Progress So Far

So far, we have described three areas of preparing a product group. In area 1, we described how to create management involvement and get a sufficient support. In area 2, we explained how to develop an understanding of the current reality. In area 3, we shared how to create alignment on shared objectives, optimizing goals, and teams' expectations, and how to develop a perfection vision. The last area uses the information from the previous areas to design a (sub)organization that can transform the current reality into the vision.

Area 4: Identify the Product Group

If a system is designed against this ideal, it can continually perfect the way it works to deliver value to the end customer.[6]

Now we are approaching a critical step in defining the boundaries of the product and the product group. In this step, you create a unit for a real product or service, while avoiding so-called internal products. In Chapter 4, "Agile Organizational Design," Guideline 2, "Decouple unit functions," states that a product group operates semi-autonomously within the larger organization and is measured on its financial performance. To design the product group, use the information presented in Chapter 4 and Chapter 6, "Coaching for Change," as a guide.

Of particular importance is the principle of revealing the reciprocal dependencies and containing them inside the product group. As a refresher, reciprocal dependencies are frequently encountered two-way interdependencies between the work of different units. They should be contained within the same unit, as they take twice as much time to coordinate compared to sequential or pooled dependencies. See also Guideline 5, "Contain reciprocal task interdependencies," in Chapter 4.

Organize for Value Delivery

This section provides an overview of defining a product in the context of software development with Scrum.

Most of our clients originally chose to organize their Scrum teams around smaller areas of function-ality with no clear customer or value proposition. We call this practice copy–paste scaling. In these cases, you find that the teams are working on just a part of the real product. This part is often a component or a specific activity in the development process; it is not a product in itself.

A broad product definition usually implies that the product spans lots of components and activi-ties, and provides solutions to the needs and problems of end users. We prefer to define a product as broadly as practical because that supports both adaptability and speed. In Figure 8.10, the CLD explains how the broadness of a product definition affects feature end-to-end time. A commonly used definition of a product is "something that is made to be sold."

> *A product is anything that can be offered to a market that might satisfy a want or need.*[17]

The product provides a way of making a profit or delivering another kind of value—for instance, social impact in the case of not-for-profit organizations. We use this definition and augment that with the following product properties:

- A product has users who are people.
- A product provides features to those users that address their needs and problems.
- A product has a business model; revenue stream, independent profit and loss (P&L) results, or return on investment (ROI).
- A product is developed and sustained by a system of people, components, and processes.

When teams work on a product-part (which they may erroneously call a "product") that does not have the properties from the preceding list, then they are probably not working on a real product. Of course, there will be exceptions to the rule—but as yet, we have not seen any commercial prod-uct without these properties.

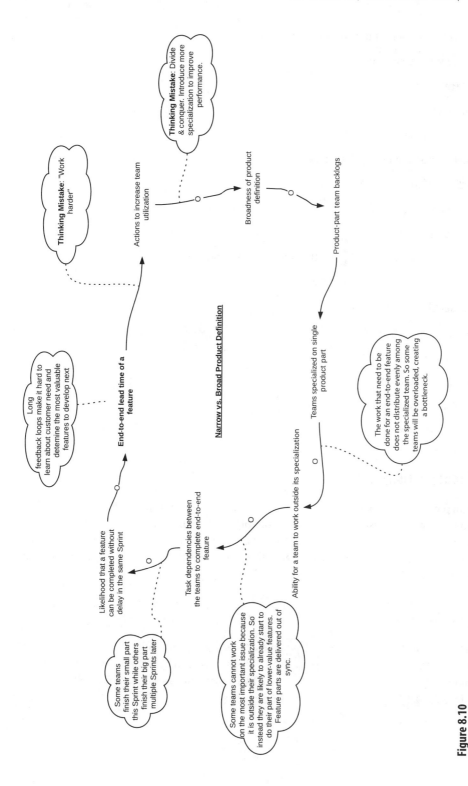

Figure 8.10

A broad product definition affects the feature end-to-end lead time.

Here are some examples of products from our clients:

- Energy trading system
- Surface radar
- Core banking services
- Business lending
- Small to medium enterprises banking
- Media platform
- Internet service
- Mortgage

And here are some examples of parts that aren't really products:

- Platform
- Internal CRM system
- Credit conveyor process
- Opening accounts process
- Website of the bank
- iOS application (in case of a bank)
- Loyalty program

What About Internal Products?

An internal product that does not have an end user outside of the company likely does not have an independent profit responsibility. Instead, it probably plays a supporting role related to, for example, reporting or administration. In large organizations, it is common to have a few internal products (often called shared services), and that is perfectly fine—as long as the majority of the company's outputs are real products.

Example: Internal Product

In one large company, we helped to launch a product group containing four teams that were working on the internal HR portal built for 30,000 factory employees. The Product Owner was a senior HR manager. The desired outcome of this initiative was reducing operational costs and simplifying HR-related activities for the employees.

In general, internal products should be avoided as much as possible when forming product groups in an Agile transformation. Why? The ultimate reason that any commercial company exists is to generate a profit. To achieve that goal, companies offer products and services to the market. Internal "products" may cause local optimizations at the expense of the whole. Internal groups run the risk of losing sight of the external customer and value, and instead start looking inward toward their own operational "efficiency." While this might be okay for some companies, it conflicts with the optimizing goals of an Agile organization when the internal product is actually a part of a real product. In that case, internal products can easily become a bottleneck in development when many real products depend on them to complete an end-to-end feature.

Product Definition from Different Perspectives

The product definition that marketing uses might not be the same as the product definition used by the development group, and that is perfectly okay. From a development perspective, the product definition is intended for optimizing adaptability and speed of learning so as to deliver value, as described in Chapter 1, "Organizing for Adaptability." From a marketing perspective, it might be beneficial to have a different product definition to address marketing goals. Marketing staff might differentiate their product definition to create a certain product identity and connect with certain types of customers.

For example, one of our banking clients has different kinds of loans with associated benefits and plans. These loans are presented as different products by the marketing department, but internally they are defined as a single broad product by the development group: From an internal perspective, the majority of functionality is similar for both products and they share the same architectural components and systems.

Another example could be the various smartphone models (product family) that a company offers, as they are presented as separate products for the end consumers. Internally, however, the smartphones share a lot of their development components and might be defined as a single product.

Where Does the Product Definition Fit in Your Transformation?

A systems approach considers the whole first, and then improves the parts only if doing so also improves the whole. The whole, in our case, is the product, and the parts are the teams and departments. Furthermore, as Russell Ackoff points out, the performance of a system is not the sum of its parts, but rather the product of their interactions.[18] Therefore, we first define the whole product with all its parts, and then we redesign the parts to improve their interactions.

A whole-product focus keeps the team locked on the value and enables them to work closely with the customers/end users. At the start of a transformation, the teams usually already work in an Agile approach such as Scrum, but the group wants to take the next step and evolve.[19] To do so, the product group must change from a series of teams that focus on small parts of the total product, to teams that have a whole-product focus.[20]

How to Define the Product

The product definition determines which organizational elements (people, components, processes, and systems) will be part of the first step in the transformation. The product definition determines:

- Who will be the Product Owner

- Which work items are on the Product Backlog

- Who the users of the product are

- Which organizational parts, such as teams and departments, you need to develop and run the product

For example, suppose you define your product as "the back-end." Then your Product Owner is a technical person who understands the back-end, and the items on the Product Backlog are likely to be technical (e.g., "extend domain model with . . ."). The users of your "product" are likely to be other developers. We call this a narrow product definition. Why? Because the back-end is just a part of a larger product and cannot produce customer value by itself.

In contrast, if your product is business loans, things are radically different. Your Product Owner is a business person who understands the market of business loans; the Product Backlog will have items like "Express loan offers to small businesses," and the users are likely to be paying customers. "Business loans" is a broad product definition. Why? Because it contains all the parts needed to produce an end-to-end solution to the end customer.

You can define your product by following these two steps:

Step 1.   Identify the required organizational elements to develop and sustain the product.

Step 2.   Clarify the revenue streams.

The subsections that follow explain these steps in more detail.

Step 1: Identify the Required Organizational Elements

You start with the elements—your component teams—that you currently call products, the activities, the people, and the processes you have presently in your group. You then study the workflow in your group so that you understand the types of dependencies that exist to develop, maintain, and sustain your product.

The typical steps to achieve this understanding are as follows:

1. Identify some typical external end users for your group.

2. Identify some needs that these end users often want to be addressed or tasks that they regularly need to complete.

3. Identify some features for each of the users that they consume to address their needs or perform their jobs.

4. Identify the boundaries through which the users consume the features to satisfy their needs and solve their problems (e.g., a browser, app, API, connector, or helpdesk).

5. Identify the organizational elements that are needed to produce the feature and satisfy the customer. You do that by studying how each feature flows through your organization into the hands of the customer. You start at the boundaries and work through the components, systems, people, and processes until completion.

There are numerous ways to facilitate these workshops. Our favorite is to use story maps, as described in the book *User Story Mapping: Discover the Whole Story, Build the Right Product*.[21] An example follows.

Example: Define Your Product Workshop

The Define Your Product workshop is run with a cross-functional group of people who understand the market, the customer, the technical landscape, the development work, the finances, and the management structure. Typically, more than 15 people participate in the workshop, including multiple people from at least the marketing, sales, (product) management, development, and operations departments.

> **Materials needed**: Pens, sticky notes, whiteboards/flipcharts.

> **Structural invitation:** The goal is to create a list of components, systems, activities, roles, and processes that define the product.

Ask the participants to self-organize into groups of people who work on the same or strongly related products and services but are from different departments.

Running the Workshop

Step 1. Identify the key users and required outcomes.

> Ask the participants to generate answers to the following question individually:
> - Who are the users of your current products and services? (e.g., internal users, partners, and external users)
>
> Ask them to write each user on a sticky note of the same color, and post it on their board. Use the liberating structure 1-2-4-table-group for gathering input from the participants. Use affinity mapping to cluster and remove duplicates.
>
> Then ask the participants to generate answers to the following question individually:
> - What are the most important wanted outcomes for your users? (e.g., What are your users trying to get done? Which savings in time, money, and/or effort are desired?)
>
> Ask the participants to write outcomes (one to three per user) on the same color sticky notes. Ensure that the color of these sticky notes is different from that used for identifying the users. Share the items among the various table groups. Each table group should have something that looks like Figure 8.11.

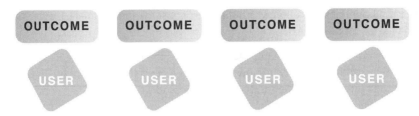

Figure 8.11
Outcomes and users.

Step 2. Identify the end-to-end activities to deliver the required outcomes.

Ask the participants to generate answers to the following question individually:

- Which activities are performed by the users to produce an end-to-end outcome?

    Write each activity that users do on separate sticky note of the same color. Use a different color than was used in Step 1.

    When participants are done, ask them to share their story with their table group. A story should start with a user and their need, then talk about the activities the user does, and end when the user attains the outcome.

    After everyone has shared their story, ask the table group to merge all activities into one story. Remove duplicates; create a most common story sequence and augment it with alternative stories.

    Use a diverge–merge technique to share ideas among the various table groups. Each table group should have results that look something like Figure 8.12.

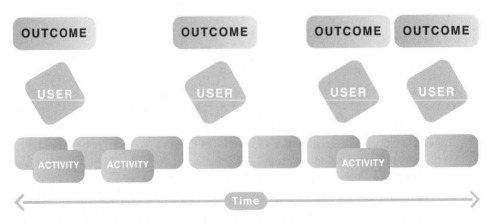

Figure 8.12
Activities for reaching outcomes.

Step 3. Identify required systems, groups, and individuals required to develop, maintain, and run the product.

Ask the participants to generate answers to the following question individually:
- Which systems/groups/individuals are needed to provide the outcomes?

Individually in your group: Follow the activities from left to right and write down which systems, components, groups, and individuals are needed to perform the activities (one per sticky note). Consolidate the sticky notes and add them to the bottom of the map.

Use a diverge–merge technique to share information among the various table groups. Each table group should have a result that looks something like Figure 8.13.

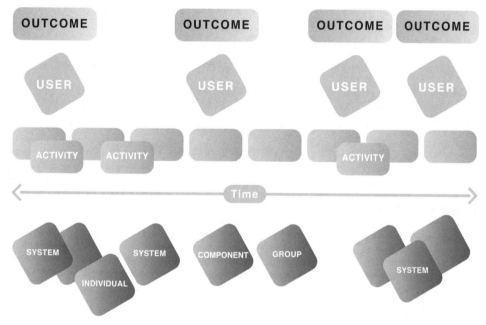

Figure 8.13
Organizational elements to produce the outcomes.

At this point, you laid the groundwork for your product definition. It has become clear who the end users are, which needs they have, the features they consume, and which organizational elements are required. The final step is to clarify if your product has a revenue stream, and if not to add the missing elements.

Step 2: Clarify the Revenue Stream

A proper product definition identifies a group broadly enough that it includes revenue streams. Without this element, the teams in the group will likely be disconnected from market concerns—where the real value lies—and instead focus on just a part of the whole product. Further, such a lack of linkage probably means decision making is divided among various parties. Typically, one party—the business—is responsible for financial considerations and requirements, while the other party—research and development—is accountable for delivering the product requirements on time and within the given budget. Each party will locally optimize for local concerns instead of adaptability (the so-called Contract Game[22(p. 106)]). In Scrum, the business-side Product Owner role avoids these local optimizations. The Product Owner owns the product and takes responsibility for both the vision and the P&L results for the product.

In this step, we ask the question: Do the identified organizational elements generate revenue for the organization? Or are we missing some parts needed to do so? The way we prefer to investigate this issue is to find answers to the following questions:

- How do the elements together generate cash? For example, is the product definition able to have usage fees? Asset sales? Subscription fees? Licensing? If not, what would need to be added to the product definition?

- Does the product definition have an independent P&L flow? If not, which organizational elements are missing?

- Which business KPIs can you assign to the product definition? For example, can you assign it an increase in gross income? An increase in new customers? Customer satisfaction?

If you cannot give meaningful answers to all of these questions, then your product definition is too narrow, and you need to expand it.

Product Definition Completed

At this point, you have identified a set of organizational elements that together produce value for end users and have an independent revenue stream.

The result typically includes tens of components, skills, and activities, and it can involve hundreds of people in total. With such a large group, you may want to ask, "How can I create effective cross-functional teams that include all these capabilities?" If more than 10 (or so) teams are involved, we recommend organizing the teams among value areas,[23] which could be dynamic in size depending on how the Product Owner oversees the market changes. In *A Scrum Book*, we defined a value area as follows: "A Value Area is a valuable product part that addresses the needs of a customer segment, but which has no useful value or identity apart from its inclusion in the product."[23]

In the next section. we describe how you can identify your value areas by using a value area heat map.

Organizational Design to Eliminate Dependencies

Some competencies are required more than others to develop the product features. For example, you might need the legal department only sporadically, while the website team might be necessary continuously. In this case, if you had to choose between including legal skills or website skills in your group, it would be better to select the website skills. Why? Because the website team dependency is the strongest and will give you the most benefit when included.

Start with the Product Features

We recommend using the features on the Product Backlog to study the dependencies. You should study the workflow (i.e., how the work works) and determine which organizational elements are needed to develop the features. The more often a particular element is required, the stronger the dependency is. We visualize this with a value area heat map. In this tool, where the more an element is needed, the more it heats up. Figure 8.14 provides a simplified example.

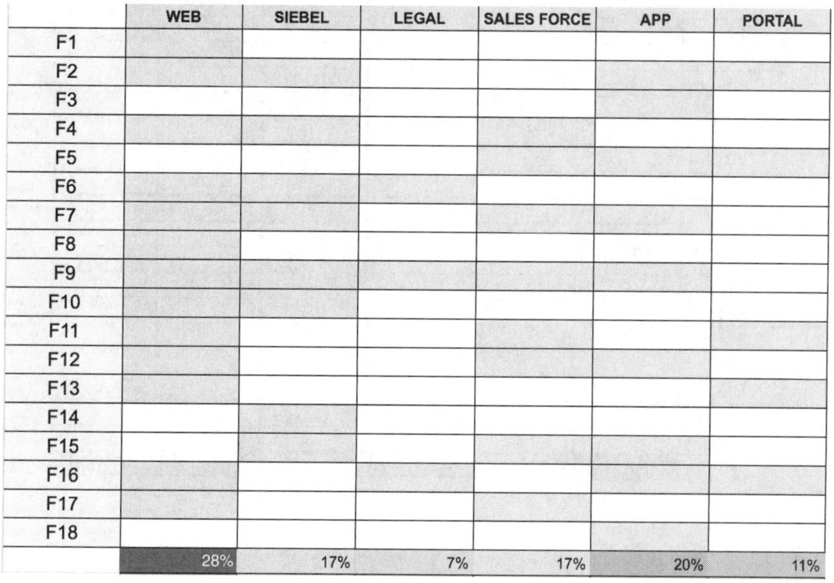

	WEB	SIEBEL	LEGAL	SALES FORCE	APP	PORTAL
F1						
F2						
F3						
F4						
F5						
F6						
F7						
F8						
F9						
F10						
F11						
F12						
F13						
F14						
F15						
F16						
F17						
F18						
	28%	17%	7%	17%	20%	11%

Figure 8.14
Heat map hotspot example.

The heat map has two dimensions. The *y*-axis shows the key features that you expect to develop. The *x*-axis shows the needed components and systems to create and sustain those features. A shaded area within the table indicates an element that is needed to deliver the feature.

In Figure 8.14, the Web component is used 13 times and the App component is used 9 times. The components that heat up the most—the hotspots—indicate the most frequently encountered type of work. The Web and App components are hotspots in Figure 8.14 and can serve as the starting point for further studying the types of dependencies present.

Using the Hotspots to Design Your Group

The heat map in Figure 8.14 shows a product containing six components. We assume that a single team is working on each element, so there are six teams.

Feature Specialized Team

When a team can work on all components but only one feature—that is, a team covers a complete row, as depicted in Figure 8.15—then the team is optimized for delivery speed at the single feature level but cannot adapt to work on other features. The team has no external dependencies for their specific feature; hence, there are no queues or delays.

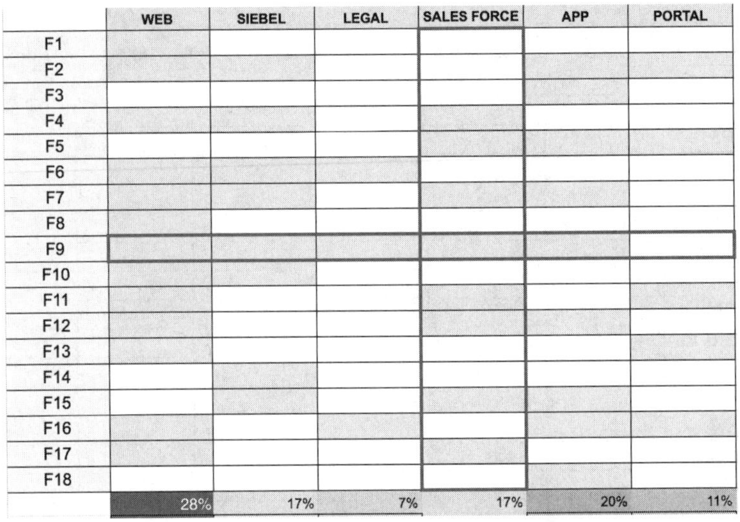

	WEB	SIEBEL	LEGAL	SALES FORCE	APP	PORTAL
F1						
F2						
F3						
F4						
F5						
F6						
F7						
F8						
F9						
F10						
F11						
F12						
F13						
F14						
F15						
F16						
F17						
F18						
	28%	17%	7%	17%	20%	11%

Figure 8.15
Specialized teams.

Component Specialized Team

In contrast, when a team covers all features but only one component, that team covers a complete column in the heat map. Such a team can work on all feature-parts; hence, it can adapt to all work that comes in but cannot deliver end-to-end customer value. Such a team is optimized for adaptability at the local team level but cannot work on other components to produce a complete feature.

Neither of these team configurations is particularly useful. On the one hand, if all teams are feature specialized, then it is hard for them to work in other functional areas. When the most valuable work is outside their expertise, they are unlikely to pick up that work, but will instead pick up lower-value work. They are maximized for speed for their work but are minimized in terms of adaptability to the work that needs to be done at the product group level.

On the other hand, if all teams are component specialized, then it is hard for them to work on other components to deliver value. When work spans multiple components, they are unlikely to deliver it completely. Such a team can work on all feature-parts—it is maximized for adaptability for working on all features, albeit only parts—but introduce hand-offs, queues, and delays to complete an end-to-end feature.

Therefore, the size of the heat map area that a team covers strongly determines its:

- Feature delivery speed
- Flexibility to pick up work from the Product Backlog

Finding the Optimal Balance

What if all the teams in the product group could pick up any work that comes in and could completely deliver it into the hands of the customer? In this case, the group would be maximumly adaptable to the incoming work, as explained in the CLD shown in Figure 8.10. The perfection goal is for each team to cover the whole heat map.

One problem with large products is that it can be hard for a cross-functional team to cover all features and component elements in the heat map. There may be just too many technologies and too much domain knowledge required. The solution is to let the teams learn this, and that can take many months or even years.

But what if you could redesign your organization? What would be your optimal starting configuration?

The optimal starting configuration is the largest area in the heat map that can be covered by all teams from the start. The challenge is to find the optimal balance between speed and adaptability in your context, and that depends on several variables:

- The value areas from the customers' perspective
- The teams' cognitive capacity and skills to cover elements and functionality
- The dependencies between the components for each feature to be developed

Specialize in the Customer Domain Using Value Areas

One of our clients had a large insurance system that was being worked on by many teams. We used interviews and questionnaires to determine where users spent most of their time when using the product. It turned out that there were two main groups of users. We noticed that segments of users would consume a specific subset of the total features. We identified a Claims area and an Evaluation area. In the graphics, we represented these areas in red and yellow. We structured the product group around these value areas. One benefit of this approach was that the teams that worked in the Claims area. for example, only needed to have a deep understanding of that domain. This reduced the required cognitive demand on the teams. The teams also needed to understand only a subset of the total elements, further decreasing the cognitive load. Note, however, that teams that work in a value area still deliver end-user features to the customer.

In our experience, organizations quite often find it challenging to recognize what their value areas are. We'll give a few more examples of such areas here:

- Areas "payments" and "money transfers" in a Daily Banking product

- Areas "EUR payments," "internal payments," and "lawns" in a Payment System product

- Areas "buying food" and "running business" in a Digital Food Service product

- Areas "I join," "I pay," and "I support" in an Energy Trading product

The main question is: "Which features do customers use most of the time?" When you answer this question, you will undoubtedly notice that certain groups use only a subset of the features most of the time. Those subsets are your value areas.

Suppose that in our example, we found through study that the users of the product spent most of their time using either the red-colored features (red area) or the yellow-colored features (yellow area), and that both groups of users used the orange-colored features (orange area). You can see this situation in Figure 8.16.

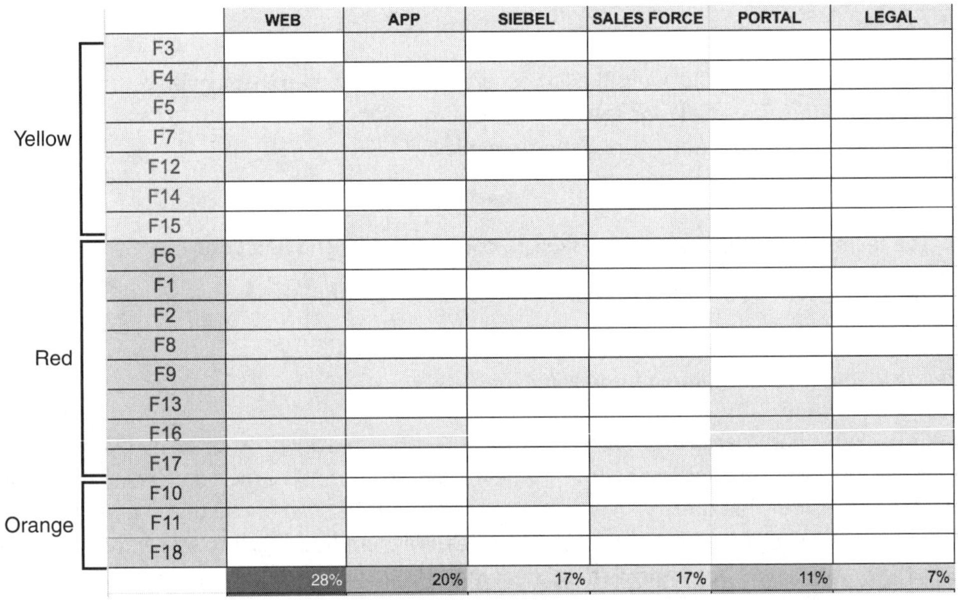

		WEB	APP	SIEBEL	SALES FORCE	PORTAL	LEGAL
Yellow	F3						
	F4						
	F5						
	F7						
	F12						
	F14						
	F15						
Red	F6						
	F1						
	F2						
	F8						
	F9						
	F13						
	F16						
	F17						
Orange	F10						
	F11						
	F18						
		28%	20%	17%	17%	11%	7%

Figure 8.16
Value areas per color.

The distinct value areas are indicated by the red (F6, F1, . . . , F17) and yellow (F3, F4, . . . , F15) features. The orange items depict features that are used by both sets of users—they overlap both value areas.

How to Use the Value Areas

The next step is to find the appropriate balance between adaptability and speed by finding the biggest area that can be covered by the teams and still deliver value. As a rule of thumb, we use the following criteria:

1. Maximize dependencies within a value area

2. Contain reciprocal dependencies within one value area

3. Ensure sequential dependencies between value areas

4. Manage pooled dependencies across teams and value areas

How big should a single value area be? We recommend creating a value area of no less than four teams. Otherwise, there will be lots of small value areas with a narrow product focus that reduces adaptability and affects speed. Please don't break this recommendation.

Figures 8.17 through 8.19 show an example result for each value area.

The Red Area

Figure 8.17 shows the red area. The Pricing, Web, App, Siebel, and Portal components are used often together, and their interdependencies are reciprocal.

		WEB	APP	SIEBEL	PORTAL	LEGAL	SALES FORCE
Red	F6					POOLED	
	F1						
	F2						
	F8						
	F9					POOLED	
	F13						
	F16					POOLED	
	F17						
		36%	14%	14%	14%	14%	9%

Figure 8.17
Value area heat map: red area.

The teams in the red area decided that they would need to cover at least these elements. Furthermore, you can see that the area has a pooled interdependency with the Legal function, and that it is a relatively strong dependency. The weakest interdependency is with Sales Force. We chose not to include Sales Force initially and only added it when the teams mastered the other elements. The Legal function was also not included in the teams because it was a pooled dependency.

The Yellow Area

The yellow value area has a different set of dependencies, as Figure 8.18 illustrates.

	APP	SALES FORCE	SIEBEL	WEB	PORTAL	LEGAL
F3						
F4						
F5					SEQUENTIAL	
F7						
F12						
F14						
F15						
	28%	28%	22%	17%	6%	0%

Yellow (bracket spanning F3–F15)

Figure 8.18

Value area heat map: yellow area.

The teams decided that they needed to cover at least the App, Sales Force, Siebel, and Web components—the hotspot. Furthermore, for this area, the Legal function was not needed at all, and there was a weak sequential dependency on Portal. The teams decided to not include Portal in the first step. In the exceptional case that a feature needed a change in Portal, the teams would coordinate with the red area to get it done. The teams also used these interactions as opportunities to learn more about Portal.

The Orange Area

How to handle the features in the intersecting orange area, depicted in Figure 8.19? A solution is to decide based on the feature itself.

	WEB	APP	SIEBEL	SALES FORCE	PORTAL	LEGAL
F10						
F11						
F18						
	33%	17%	17%	17%	17%	0%

Orange (bracket spanning F10–F18)

Figure 8.19

Value area heat map: orange area.

For example, F10 could be picked up by either the red or yellow area. F18 requires only the App component and can be picked up by the yellow area. The only complicated feature is F11. It requires the Sales Force and Portal, which neither the red area nor the yellow area possesses. So, how to handle this one? Well, remember the golden rule of Scrum Mastership: "Always ask the team."

The Final Result

The product definition included all elements, but we chose to not include legal skills in any of the teams from the start. Why? Because it was a pooled and weak dependency. Also, the teams felt they were not yet able to cover more skills right from the start. Instead, the Legal component became the next activity to include in their Definition of Done.

In the rare case in which a feature requiring legal skills would appear on top of the Product Backlog, we would plan for that by working together with the Legal unit in Refinement events and during the Sprint. At Sprint Planning, the team that selected this feature would then coordinate to work together with someone from Legal to get the feature done. Preferably, the Legal person(s) would also use the opportunity to teach the team so that they understood a little bit more about Legal at the end of the Sprint. If a team kept choosing to work on features with a Legal part, eventually they would learn enough to add Legal to their Definition of Done. Bas Vodde calls this *accidental specialization*.[24]

NOTE

Not all teams need to know everything about every element in the product definition right from the start. Teams can have their own specialty as long as all teams as a group can pick up all elements from the top of the Product Backlog.

Summary

This chapter described four areas, and some helpful activities and tools, that must be addressed to lay the foundation of a successful Agile transformation. Activities in the areas are not meant to be executed sequentially because their use is context-dependent.

The "involving the managers" area is about ensuring that you've obtained sufficient support from managers—a factor critical for a successful transformation. Managers can change the system and thus strongly influence people's patterns of behavior. You'll need to educate management and facilitate changes in their mental models to ensure that a supportive organizational context is created.

The "understanding the current reality" area emphasizes activities that create an awareness of why things work the way they do in the organization. You can perform such an investigation of the current reality with Go See, structural workshops, interviews, value stream mapping, and other tools.

The "creating a vision of the future" area aligns everyone around the business objectives. To reach the objectives, the group needs to develop specific capabilities and promote specific optimization goals. Agree on them, make them explicit, and refer back to them when needed. Creating a perfection vision generates a creative tension and lays the foundation for continuous improvement. Support transformation with change stories and shared team expectations.

The most critical area is "identify the product group," which deals with defining the boundaries of your product and deciding which competencies should be contained in a product group. An Agile organizational design is based on real products with a business model (P&L), customers/end users who are external to the organization, and delivery of features that cover specific needs.

The types of dependencies and the Value Areas pattern become important if the product is huge and has more than 10 teams. The heat map helps in identifying value areas and forming cross-functional teams.

The next chapter builds on this preliminary work and shows how to successfully launch the group and prepare to work in the new organizational design.

References

1. Kurt Lewin Quotes. https://www.brainyquote.com/quotes/kurt_lewin_170747.

2. "The Spirit of the Game." https://tinyurl.com/SpirtofGame.

3. Art Byrne and James P. Womack. *The Lean Turnaround: How Business Leaders Use Lean Principles to Create Value and Transform Their Company* (McGraw-Hill, 2012).

4. J. Richard Hackman. *Leading Teams: Setting the Stage for Great Performances* (Harvard Business Review Press, 2002).

5. Ruth Wageman. *Senior Leadership Teams: What It Takes to Make Them Great* (Harvard Business Review Press, 2008).

6. John Seddon. *Freedom from Command and Control: Rethinking Management for Lean Service* (Productivity Press, 2005).

7. Cesário Ramos. "Common Mistakes When Scaling Scrum." Agilix (June 7, 2016). https://agilix.nl/blog/the-problems-of-scaling-scrum/.

8. Peter Senge. *The Fifth Discipline: The Art and Practice of the Learning Organization* (Doubleday Dell, 1990).

9. Donald G. Reinersten. *The Principles of Product Development Flow: Second Generation Lean Product Development* (Celeritas, 2009).

10. Donald G. Reinersten. *Managing the Design Factory* (Free Press, 1997).

11. Karen Martin and Mike Osterling. *Value Stream Mapping: How to Visualize Work and Align Leadership for Organizational Transformation* (McGraw-Hill Education, 2013).

12. "What? So What? Now What? W3." Liberating Structures. www.liberatingstructures.com/9-what-so-what-now-what-w/.

13. "1-2-4-All." Liberating Structures. www.liberatingstructures.com/1-1-2-4-all/.

14. Loic Thomas. "ROTI and Feedback Door: 2 Methods for Getting Feedback." Beeckast (March 10, 2030). www.beekast.com/blog/roti-and-feedback-door-two-methods-for-getting-feedback/.

15. Taiichi Ohno. *Taiichi Ohno's Workplace Management: Special 100th Birthday Edition* (McGraw-Hill, 2012).

16. "Perfection." Wikipedia. https://en.wikipedia.org/wiki/Perfection.

17. Don McGreal and Ralph Jocham. *The Professional Product Owner: Leveraging Scrum as a Competitive Advantage* (Addison-Wesley, 2018).

18. Russell L. Ackoff, *Re-creating the Corporation: A Design of Organizations for the 21st Century* (Oxford University Press, 1999).

19. "Scale Your Product, Not Your Scrum." www.scrum.org/resources/scale-your-product-not-your-scrum.

20. Craig Larman and Bas Vodde. *Large-Scale Scrum: More with LeSS* (Addison-Wesley, 2017).

21. Jeff Patton. *User Story Mapping: Discover the Whole Story, Build the Right Product* (O'Reilly Media, 2014).

22. Craig Larman and Bas Vodde. *Practices for Scaling Lean and Agile Development: Large, Multisite, and Offshore Product Development with Large-Scale Scrum* (Addison-Wesley, 2009).

23. Scrum Patterns Group. *A Scrum Book* (2019). www.scrumbook.org.

24. Bas Vodde. Personal communications.

9

Launching the Product Group

A lift-off creates the positive force that moves a team toward successful delivery, time after time.
—Diana Larsen and Ainsley Nies[1]

Chapter 8, "Preparing the Product Group," showed you how you could prepare a product group for Agile adoption. We covered four essential areas of preparation:

- Involve the managers

- Understand the current reality

- Create a vision for the future

- Identify the product group

In this chapter, we build on that discussion and consider how to successfully launch the product group into its first iteration.

As you made it to this chapter, we assumed that by now you've made a thorough exploration of your product organization by implementing the Go See approach. You've discovered structures and mental models that underpin the system patterns that you have observed. You shared your insights with the larger group and created a shared understanding of the current reality. You worked with senior management to get sufficient support from them to undertake an organizational redesign. You have aligned a product group on several topics: why change is needed, business objectives, perfection vision, and optimization goals. You have created an initial definition of the product by examining organizational functions and components and taking into account the types of dependencies and principles of organizational design (Chapter 4, "Agile Organizational Design").

We also expect that during this preparation phase, you followed some change principles (Chapter 6, "Coaching for Change")—for instance, you found volunteers, and helped people to start crossing the edge.

Menu of Available Choices

This chapter provides details on how a coach/Scrum Master launches the product group into its first Sprint. We provide a list of activities and workshops that we find useful. It is a menu of available choices, not a prescribed method. Use the ones that fit your specific context.

- **Initial Product Backlog Refinement:** The initial set of features to start the first Sprints.
- **Define the Definition of Done (DoD):** Everything a team has to do to a feature so that the product is ready for delivery to end users with the new feature added to it.
- **Feature Team Adoption Map (FTAM)[2]:** Align on the feature team adoption first step and potential next steps toward the perfect cross-functional team.
- **Self-Designing Team workshop:** Facilitate a Self-Designing Team workshop where people volunteer to be part of a team.
- **Team lift-off:** Facilitate lift-off workshops to lay a solid foundation for team identity and success.
- **Facilitate decision making:** Create decision rules that will guide the product group and teams in their work.
- **Identify and launch communities:** Launch communities to address cross-cutting concerns within the product group.
- **Identify coordination mechanisms:** With the elimination of single-function teams, which coordination mechanisms are required?
- **Create useful checklists:** Reduce uncertainty by creating checklists that address typical problems in a large-scale environment.

From our perspective, the following items make up the Minimum Viable Launch (MVL):

- Create the product DoD
- FTAM
- Self-Designing Team workshop
- Team lift-off

You might consider running the other activities after the launch—for instance, during regular Sprint Retrospectives or at the first Sprint Planning; This is perfectly okay. For a small product group with three to five teams, you can even exclude the FTAM step if you understand that teams can work across the whole product right from the start.

Who Owns the Launching Process?

If you are an external coach, you should be working hand in hand or even behind the internal Scrum Masters and letting them "take the glory." Another critical point is that teams are the crucial stakeholders for the launch. Therefore, you should co-create a high-level plan with them beforehand. Failing to do so can result in disengagement and provoke challenging behavior, and it disempowers Scrum Masters and creates an addiction of the teams to the coach.

How Much Time Should It Take?

The launch duration varies from a single day to five consecutive days. Shorter launches feel more energetic, but some activities are inevitably postponed. Longer launches drain energy and might seem daunting for the teams, especially if they had gone through a long preparation period (see Chapter 8, "Preparing the Product Group").

We find two to three days to be a sweet spot and usually stick to this time frame. If you plan a more extended launch (e.g., five days), we recommend splitting it into two parts: Wednesday, Thursday, Friday, and Monday, Tuesday. People rest during the weekend in the middle and get back to the second part refreshed.

During the first COVID-19 spring, we prepared a large product group of seven teams in a telecommunication company for the launch. Usually, a preparation period takes no more than three months; otherwise, people start losing motivation and the drive for a change diminishes. This was an exception, and it took us four months. The launch was five days in a row. It was also 100% online, including the Self-Designing Team workshop. Now we think that was a mistake. People were too stressed and we had to keep it shorter.

Initial Product Backlog Refinement

A Product Backlog is an ordered list of what is needed to deliver a product. It aligns the team and stakeholders on the expected order of Product Backlog Items (PBIs) delivery. There are many ways to express PBIs, but each creates a change or addition to the product.

Try Features on the Product Backlog

Features refer to a piece of functionality in your product. They can be characteristics of a product, such as the "16-inch (3072 × 1920) display" on my MacBook, or they can be what a product does, such as "Facilitation Super Powers" on my favorite online collaboration tool. Features represent the outputs the teams deliver and may be composed of many smaller pieces of functionality.

For example, the feature "Facilitation Super Powers" has "Timer" and "Summon" functions, among other, smaller pieces of functionality.

An essential goal of a feature is to solve users' problems by helping them achieve a specific outcome. For example, the "Summon" functionality solves the problem of getting all participants looking at the same content.

How to Represent Features

The user value in a feature comes from the benefit it provides to a user. Therefore, it is crucial to understand the benefits the users seek and then identify which features could give that to them.

Sometimes the Product Owner has enough understanding if the user needs to add a feature as a solution to the Product Backlog. For example, you might add a feature to catch up with your competitors or because many customers request a specific feature. Although a proposed "solution" gives clarity and clear direction, it also constrains the teams to one particular solution. Furthermore, it is risky to express a solution without really understanding the problem first. Such an approach can lead to suboptimal solutions or, even worse, to solving the wrong problem.

The Product Owner can also express features in terms of outcomes or user needs. In that way, the Product Owner describes what a feature achieves rather than how it achieves it. For example, instead of putting "Timer" on the Product Backlog, the Product Owner could include "Users need to achieve focused and on-schedule activities for a group" in the Product Backlog. Although this provides less direction and clarity to the teams, it leaves options for the teams to develop innovative solutions. Also, the teams are more engaged as they can better contribute to solving the user's problem.

When the Product Owner has high confidence in product research data and a clear solution idea, define the feature as a solution. However, when the Product Owner is not so sure (which is most often the case in new product development), describe the features in terms of expected outcomes. One way to do that is through Product Goals—targets that can be used to plan against—and the Sprint Goal—the single objective of a Sprint.

Example of Creating an Initial Product Backlog with Product Goals and Sprint Goals

We were working with a group of 19 teams on a trading platform. The product was divided into three value areas[3] and had a large number of internal stakeholders, all of whom wanted to get their functionality yesterday. They were not aligned on the goals and did not understand why their features took so long to deliver.

To align the stakeholders, including the external users, we decided to run a 3-day initial Product Backlog Refinement workshop. We booked a hotel for 3 days and invited around 40 stakeholders to participate, including end users and customers.

We designed our workshop as follows:

Goals of Day 1: Create a roadmap of objectives for the coming year.

- Create a shared understanding of customer needs and key features.
- Co-create a sequence of objectives for the coming 6 months.

Goals of Day 2: Create detailed understanding about the first objectives.

- Create an ordered list of subfeatures for each key feature.
- Define acceptance criteria for each feature.
- Identify detailed measures for determining that goals are being met.

Goals of Day 3: Distill ready value area Product Backlogs.

- Split and size features.
- Identify acceptance criteria for each feature.
- Clarify features so that they are ready for Sprint Planning.

Our Workshop Flow

We created four groups to work in parallel and then used 1-2-4-ALL[4] to merge the individual group results (see Figure 9.1). Each group had one professional facilitator, internal and external stakeholders, and people from product development. The overall Product Owner and Area Product Owners also participated.

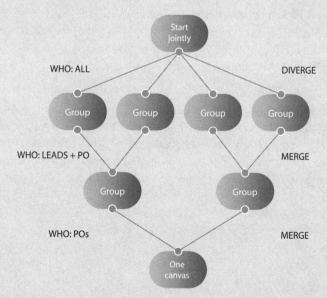

Figure 9.1
Workshop diverge–merge flow.

We started jointly to introduce the workshop. Then each group went to a separate room before merging the results with another group. We all then joined in the main room for final merging and discussion.

Our Workshop Sequence

We used the workshop plan shown in Figure 9.2.

Day 1: We started with the Value Proposition Canvas[5] to discover the customers' needs, pain points, and personal goals. This workshop produced two things:

1. A list of high-level customer needs and key features that we needed to develop to satisfy those needs

2. A set of high-level metrics that allowed us to see whether our customers' needs were met

We then used the discovered features, needs, and metrics to create product goals and possible options. We used a Roadmap canvas to facilitate the workshop. The goal of this workshop was to produce:

1. A brief description of the Product Goals

2. A cohesive set of key features that satisfied the Product Goals of each step

3. A set of high-level metrics that measured progress toward the goals

To merge the Roadmap canvases, customers and users would need to prioritize the various goals and features. As stakeholders have different needs and expectations, this was a critical part of the overall workshop. We asked the stakeholders to merge their Roadmap canvases with a Prune the Product Tree[6] workshop. Merging into a final tree was left for the next day.

Day 2: We started by merging the two trees into one larger tree in the main room. We used the rest of the day for story mapping[7] and to split large features per value area[3] and create acceptance criteria. The scope was the complete process from first contact with the system through all the steps in the chain needed for making the customers successful. After we developed a story map for the first three Product Goals, we still needed to get the top of the Product Backlog detailed and ready for Sprint Planning. That was the topic of Day 3.

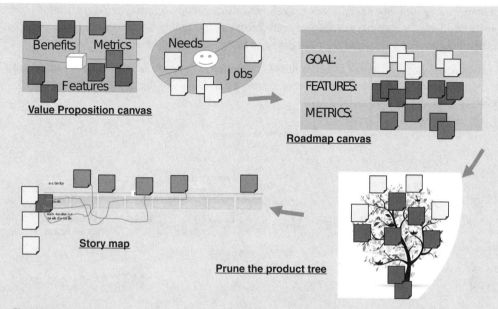

Figure 9.2
Workshop sequence.

Day 3: The last day was all about splitting, estimations, detailed clarification, and Sprint Goals. Those steps are described in Chapter 7, "Group Facilitation."

Define the Definition of Done

Scrum teams use the DoD to create a shared understanding of which work was completed in each Sprint. As Ken Schwaber (co-creator of Scrum) once taught us: Done means that there is no known work left to be done. Elements of DoD should be measurable and binary (yes/no). You can't be 80% done; Scrum treats such partial completion as 0%.

> *The Definition of Done is a formal description of the state of the Increment when it meets the quality measures required for the product.*[8]

The DoD includes measurable properties of the increment that developers need to conform to in every Sprint. It's assured through a series of activities, and execution is up to the developers. Activities can vary from Sprint to Sprint and should not be under any kind of extrinsic control. When your whole organization is just one cross-functional team, then there are no other options but for the team to perform all those activities themselves.

> *Scrum Teams are cross-functional, meaning the members have all the skills necessary to create value each Sprint.*[8]

Problems usually start when teams lack cross-functionality. That happens when organizations create teams around internal business processes, architectural components, and functions to pursue the goal of efficiency. For the sake of simplicity, we call such teams "component teams."

Let's have a look at the situation when multiple component teams are working on the same product. Each team performs only a subset—their product-part DoD—of the broader product DoD. Figure 9.3 shows an example.

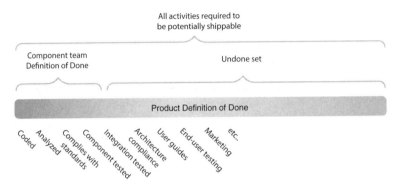

Figure 9.3
Product Definition of Done.

A component team that is organized around an internal business process or an architectural component considers "done" to have been reached when "their" component is tested—but that is not done at the product level! What remains are all the activities in the "undone" subset that still need to be performed.

The smaller the set of DoD activities that a component team performs, the more issues that will appear at the product level—for example, delays, handoffs between teams, and opaque measures of progress. The more component teams that are working on your product, the more partially done work that is created, and the higher the risk of running into unpleasant surprises later on becomes. To avoid this fate, when you develop one product with many teams, there should be a single, integrated increment by the end of each Sprint and a single, shared DoD.

Each component team needs to master all of the activities to produce a valuable and useful product increment every iteration. This is not a trivial task and can take many years, if it is even at all possible in your specific context.

Component Team Velocity?

Another issue with a narrow DoD is the notion of team velocity. Velocity can be useful in some cases; however, be aware that component teams have a *component* velocity, not a *feature* velocity. A component team velocity indicates the velocity at which partially done work—"inventory" in lean terms—is pumped into the system. So, the higher the component team velocity, the more waste you create in the form of work in progress, delay, and queues (inventory), for example. That's not a good position to be in when you want to be Agile. Some organizations try to manage these symptoms using *Kanban*, but we prefer addressing the root causes instead.

For these reasons, you should reconsider any policies that push the component teams to increase their velocity in isolation. Avoid using component team velocity as a measure of progress and try using feature velocity instead.

Next, we show a multi-team workshop format for defining your product DoD.

A Definition of Done Workshop

For this workshop, you need to have your product definition settled. How to define your product is described in Chapter 8, "Preparing the Product Group."

Participants

Invite the teams, people in coordination roles, product management, and other specialists that your product definition says are required. Consider adding sales, marketing, and general management participants as needed. The canvas illustrated in Figure 9.4 proposes a couple of sections for the teams to explore DoD activities. Adjust the sections as necessary to fit your specific context.

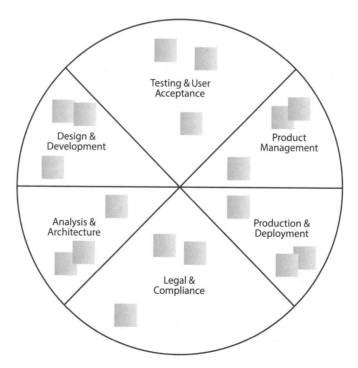

Figure 9.4
Definition of Done (DoD) canvas.

Structuring the Invitation

The goal is to define the activities that need to be completed so that there is no known work left to be done—the product DoD. We use the following questions:

- What do we need to do so that the product is in the hands of the stakeholders according to company standards, policy, and regulations?

- How shall we measure and make sure that each item in the DoD is done?

The second question focuses teams on the measures; otherwise, you might end up with a list of aspirations that never come to life.

Running the Workshop

Step 1. Each team/table group plots their current DoD on their canvas using sticky notes. Generate the DoD list of activities and corresponding measures. First work in pairs for 5–10 minutes; then consolidate the results onto the group canvas.

Step 2. Compare across the groups, using a diverge–merge technique, UX Fishbowl,[9] or the Shift and Share[10] liberating structure[4] to enrich each group's canvas. Ask the teams to update their canvas based on what was learned.

Step 3. Assign each section of the canvas (e.g., the Design & Development section) to a separate group and ask them to consolidate the results of all groups for that section onto the central canvas. Remove duplicates and combine similar items.

Step 4. Ask all the groups to take a few minutes to review the result, determine if it still acts as their DoD, and recommend how to improve or clarify it.

Step 5. Capture the result as the initial product DoD that everybody can live with.

Step 6. Close with a short retrospective and answer any open questions.

Once you have agreed on the product DoD, the next step is to determine how much of the DoD each team can pick up, and how they could broaden their component scope.

Feature Team Adoption Map

The book *Large-Scale Scrum: More with LeSS*[2] introduces Feature Team Adoption Maps (FTAM). An FTAM nicely expresses feature team adoption status and potential next steps for improvement.

An FTAM has two axes. The *x*-axis represents activities that teams need to undertake to conform to the DoD, while the *y*-axis represents the architectural decomposition of the product. Figure 9.5 illustrates a simplified example from one of our clients.

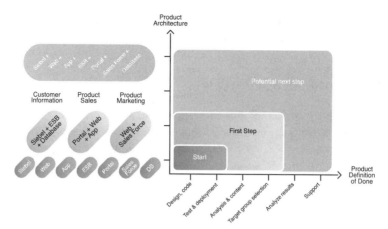

Figure 9.5
Feature Team Adoption Map.

At the bottom of the *y*-axis, you can find several components—for example, "DB" and "Web." Most teams work on one of these components. On the *x*-axis, you can see the activities obtained from the product DoD. The *x*-axis reflects the level of cross-functionality. Note that the component teams cover only the DoD subset—code, design, testing, and deployment; that's the "Start" situation. Several other single-function teams performed the remaining DoD activities—for example, one team does only "Analysis and content," another team does "Analyze results," and so on.

The "First Step" area in the FTAM shows how the teams broadened their architecture scope and DoD scope. They decided to combine several single-component teams into teams that cover broader subsystems:

- Customer Information teams, each mastering Siebel, ESB, and Database skills

- Product Sales teams, each mastering Portal, Web, and App skills

- Product Marketing teams, each mastering Web and Sales Force skills

This broadening of components was combined with a broadening of the DoD to include:

- Analysis and content

- Target group selection

The green area in the FTAM shows potential future steps. Its presence means that the teams will have an imperfect DoD.

Choose Subsystem Names Close to the Customer Domain

Note that the names of the subsystems are closer to the end-user domain vocabulary. We see this as a sign that the correct components are combined. When you cannot give a meaningful name to a combination, that's a sign that you could be on the wrong path. For example, the client called the complete product "Omni channel retail business." That's probably not so good, as this name describes the product from a technical perspective. An end user would likely give it a different name, like "Marketplace for financial products."

Ordering the Components and DoD Activities

If possible, you would like to add all components and all DoD activities to every team at once. This approach can work with smaller product groups that have a small number of technology stacks and components. When the number of components and technologies are too large for this all-at-once approach, we require an incremental approach. The main question then becomes: In what sequence should we combine components (y-axis) and DoD activities (x-axis)?

There is no single correct answer to this question because it depends on the following:

- The cognitive capability of the teams to master more components and DoD activities
- The preference of the groups regarding components and DoD activities
- The benefits of broadening the team's scope with particular components and DoD activities

Using the workshop that follows, you can find an answer to these questions.

A Feature Team Adoption Map Workshop

For the FTAM workshop, you need to have your product DoD and a heat map, and a description of three typical product features.

Participants

Invite the teams, product management, architects, and other specialists as identified in your product definition.

Structuring Invitation

The goal is to define the first broadening step in the FTAM that would give the product group the most benefits. Start with the existing team compositions.

We use the following question: What practical first step should we take in combining component skills and DoD activities?

Running the Workshop

Step 1. Remind the teams that the perfect feature team works across all components and performs all DoD activities. Then ask each team to select from the product DoD those activities they currently perform on their component(s). Consider performing a first round in pairs and then a second round with the whole team. Ask them to post the results on the canvas's x-axis. This is their current DoD. Figure 9.6 shows an example.

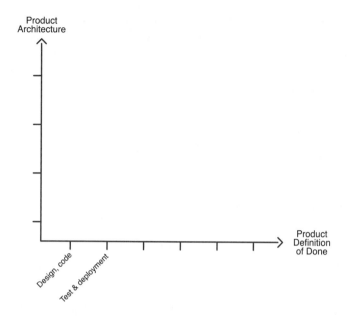

Figure 9.6
Start FTAM.

Step 2. Ask each team to identify which components they currently work on and to place them on the *y*-axis. This is their current component/activity stack. Ask the team to visualize their current state in the FTAM. Figure 9.7 shows an example.

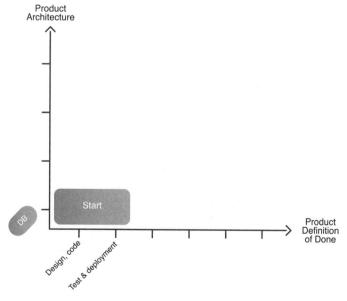

Figure 9.7
Current situation for DB team.

Step 3. Ask in which order they would like to add activities and components that give the biggest improvement. Provide the heat map to the teams so they can consider which components and activities are required most of the time to develop an end-to-end feature. You can facilitate this with the Now, Next, Later canvas illustrated in Figure 9.8 (based on the original idea by David Koontz[11]).

Figure 9.8
Ordering components and DoD activities canvas.

With this canvas, we typically use the following format:

a. Team members choose components and DoD items from the heat map and place them in the Now, Next, or Later section.

b. After all items are added to the canvas, the team evaluates the placements. Then anyone can place a DoD item onto an arrow to indicate they wish to discuss this item's placement.

c. Discuss the items on the arrows one at a time. Then move the item to the desired section.

d. Finish discussing all items, and then play additional rounds until there is agreement.

Ask the participants to group and add their component configuration on the *y*-axis and name it. Add the activities to the *x*-axis. Ask the team to visualize their first step in the FTAM. Figure 9.9 shows an example.

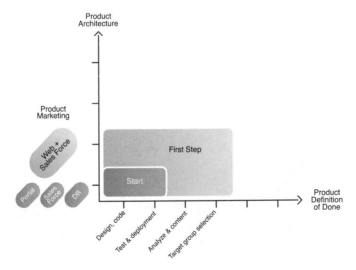

Figure 9.9
First step for DB, ESB, and Siebel teams.

Step 4. Ask the team to merge their FTAMs (two FTAMs at a time) until there are two FTAMs left. Then facilitate a centralized final merger on one canvas, as illustrated in Figure 9.10.

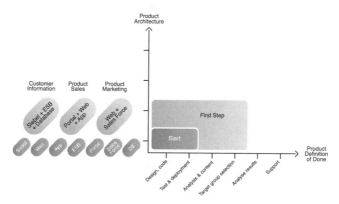

Figure 9.10
Merged FTAM for the product group.

This group agreed that the first step involved three areas: Customer Information, Product Sales, and Product Marketing. They also agreed that the teams that handled the "Analyze results" and "Support" functions would remain component teams for now.

Step 5. Ask all the groups to take a few minutes to review the result, determine if they still support the merged FTAM, and recommend how to improve or clarify it.

Step 6. Centrally debrief the workshop and visualize possible future steps of the FTAM and any open questions.

The end result is the FTAM. A good practice is to establish a regular cadence for updating the FTAM while your product group improves. You can package this activity as a part of the Sprint Retrospective.

The next step is to evaluate if redesigning the teams is required to actually perform the first step. If so, ask the teams to redesign themselves according to their FTAM. We facilitate that using a Self-Designing Team workshop.

Self-Designing Team Workshop

With the FTAM in place, the teams understand which activities and components each team should master. In the unlikely case that your starting teams already cover everything that is required, you are done. The teams can remain as they are. However, it is more likely that your starting teams are too narrowly specialized and need to be redesigned to match the required skills and capabilities. To do so, the teams need to answer the following questions:

- What is the best possible team composition?

- How can we create the best set of teams for the product group as a whole?

- Which factors should we consider when composing teams?

To answer these questions, we employ an approach consistent with the self-organizing principle of Agile organizations, moving from a command-control management culture to self-management. We prefer bottom-up knowledge and facilitate the team members to use their self-managing capability to design the teams themselves. The role of management is to set boundaries that optimize the product group—that is, to facilitate and to not constrain the outcomes to their own knowledge and references. The paradox of structure comes into play here.

> We might think at first that having no structure maximizes creative ability, but in fact the opposite is true! Some structure is needed.[12]

Of course, the amount and kind of structure is highly dependent on the teams' maturity. Managers may become too overoptimistic, delegating authority too early for a team, when it is not ready to take responsibility and showed no successes before. Investigate the authority matrix from the work of Richard Hackman in *Leading Teams: Setting the Stage for Great Performance* to make an informed decision.[7]

Before the Self-Designing Team workshop, we often run a Market of Skills exercise to help people get to know each other better. That activity becomes even more important in large groups where there are many strangers.

Consider a Market of Skills Workshop as Preparation

Market of Skills is an exercise that creates a broader picture across teams of the skills and abilities to which they currently have access, as well as skills and abilities that people would like to improve. It highlights blind spots that many are not aware of. The idea is simple: Everyone has a place in the "bazaar" where they sell their skills, talents, and traits, as well as buy them from colleagues.

To run the workshop, follow these steps.

Step 1. Distribute flipchart sheet, and ask each participant to write the following information on the sheet:

a. Personal information

b. What motivates you at work

c. Basic skills for sale

d. Secondary skills that are not directly related to the product, such as a hobby

e. What you want to learn from others

The standard timebox is 10–20 minutes to let people deeply dive into this activity.

Step 2. Depending on the number of people in the room, you can split the bazaar into several rounds. Let's say you have 80 people. Then you can divide them into three groups and organize three rounds of 15 minutes each. In the first round, the first group sells themselves, and others become buyers of their skills and traits. Other rounds follow a similar pattern. Make sure that you've defined the currency for the bazaar. It can be simple stickies.

It's up to you to decide whether you want to limit the number of them. We usually suggest that participants write the following information on them:

a. Skills to acquire

b. Skills the seller holds but forgot to mention

c. Skills to sell

You will see how engaging this exercise is.

Once we facilitated a market of skills for a large group of 90 people. We've run the bazaar in four rounds. We remember how loudly sellers were reaching out to the buyers and how passionately they were selling themselves. The big space was filled with the roar of dozens of voices. There were smiles and laughter everywhere. We took off the facilitator hats for a while and went for a walk around the bazaar, meeting people and handing out stickers. With each round, the energy level increased. And we were sorry to close the exercise—it felt great!

Step 3. Now it's time to close the exercise. You can do this in many ways—for instance, using the What, So What, Now What?,[13] Mad Tea,[14] 15% Solutions,[15] or Impromptu Networking[16] liberating structures.

Now you are ready for the Self-Designing Team workshop, the format of which was inspired by the workshop first described by Ahmad Fahmy and Craig Larman.[17]

A Self-Designing Team Workshop

Invite people who likely will be part of a team. Usually these are the team members and specialists who participated in the FTAM workshop.

Preparations

- **Flipchart listing the initial team constraints.** For example:

  - Between three and nine members.

  - Able to cover the "First Step" area of the FTAM.

  - Team members have the ability to learn their desired skills from each other.

- **Feature Team formation passport.** Ask each member to bring a filled-in passport like Figure 9.11 with information about themselves, including their current skills and which skills they would like to learn and improve. The passport uses the components and DoD activities from the FTAM. Extend and update it to fit your current context.

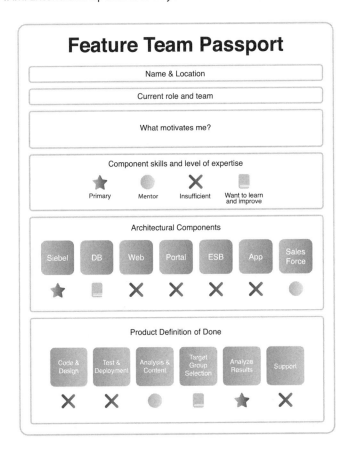

Figure 9.11
Example passport.

- **Evaluation checklist.** Prepare a checklist like Figure 9.12 to verify how well the team design meets the constraints and goals of the required feature teams. The teams will use this at the end of every facilitation round. Extend and update it to fit your team constraints and context.

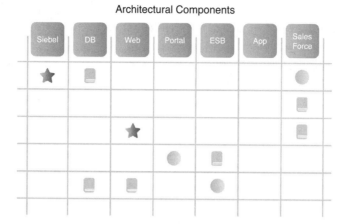

Figure 9.12
Example evaluation checklist.

- **Room setup.** Prepare various circles of chairs in the room. The number of chairs in each circle should correspond to the maximum team size. People will sit in free chairs and start a conversation with the people present using their passports. Place flipcharts with the team constraints and FTAM where they are clearly visible to each circle.

Structuring the Invitation

The goal is for participants to design themselves into feature teams. We use the following question: Which teams can we create so that each team covers the "First Step" area of the FTAM?

Running the Workshop

Step 1. Discuss the constraints, FTAM, passport, checklist, and room setup. Then facilitate the creation of one ideal prototype team that meets all the criteria on the checklist. Capture the prototype team on a wall for future reference. Communicate that the goal is to create *N* such teams as best we can. During this step, it's normal to change the initial constraints and expand or reduce them.

Step 2.   Ask the people to walk around the room, find a seat in a circle and introduce themselves, discuss their passports, and create a team in line with the prototype team. People are free to move around between circles as much as they like. Leave the room and return after the 20-minute timebox.

Step 3.   Upon returning to the room, ask the teams to complete their checklists and compare them to the prototype team. Each team identifies where they should improve (add or remove skills or people), communicates it to the complete group, and makes it visible on their flipchart.

Step 4.   Another round: Invite the people to improve the teams. Ask them to move around between circles as they please, and to join other circles that are in need of their expertise. Introduce themselves, discuss their passports, and see if the team comes closer to the ideal prototype team. Leave the room and return after the 20-minute timebox.

Step 5.   Upon returning to the room, ask the teams to complete their checklists and compare them to the prototype team. Each team identifies what they are missing and would like to add, shares it with the group, and makes it visible on their flipchart. Repeat the exercise beginning with Step 4 until the group is satisfied with the team designs.

Step 6.   Have each team create a name and present themselves to the group.

Step 7.   Debrief with a short review and open questions.

Once the team self-design is complete, the next step is to properly create the foundation for team success. You can do that by facilitating a team lift-off.

Team Lift-Off

The starting phase of a new team is the golden opportunity to lay the foundation for team success. People come together for the first time, and there is usually a good atmosphere. We call this the "honeymoon" phase, where things are amicable, conflict is low, and everything seems possible. People are curious to learn about others and want to be accepted in the group. Roles and responsibilities are unclear and all seem to get along well. After introductions, the group seeks structure and direction and requires clarification on the following issues:

- Deep introductions to each other

- Why they are here and what is expected from them

- How they will work together

- Team roles, tasks, and responsibilities

People also likely have concerns about safety and inclusion, so significant discussions are still avoided as much as possible.

This phase passes quickly into a phase characterized by much more conflict. Why? Because as the teams start to work, pressure to perform increases and the differences in perspectives and preferences create tension within the team. To maximize the chances of navigating this turbulent phase successfully (the storming phase in the Tuckman model[18]), we recommend laying a solid foundation during the "honeymoon" phase that the team can refer back to in times of need.

The Lift-Off to Lay the Foundation for Success

By the end of the lift-off, people should have a good sense of purpose, feel loyalty to the team, and want to belong to the product group. They should feel safe enough to contribute ideas and suggestions that will, in their opinion, help the group achieve its overall objectives.

Your Role as a Scrum Master

During the starting phase, a team is very dependent and reliant on its leaders. As a coach/Scrum Master, you will often assume the lead role initially, which is okay for a short time. The team looks to you for guidance and direction, and that's what you can give them. Remember that you lead only temporarily, and your first intention is to lay a team foundation for success. The sections that follow advise how you might do that by facilitating the teams to:

- Create a shared purpose

- Align on shared values and behavior

- Agree on a decision-making process

- Clarify the team goals

Discover a Shared Purpose

The first step is to discover a purpose, a sense of belonging, and the beginnings of predictable behavior to achieve that overall goal. Teams function better when they have a sense of purpose, and when they feel that group goals and tasks are meaningful, are interesting, and challenge them to think and work to their full capacity. When people have a sense of purpose, their commitment and performance increase.

Agile teams can find their purpose by answering the following questions:

- **What is the reason to do this work?** The product vision and our personal aspirations.

- **How do we contribute to achieving the product vision?** The team's actions and expected outputs.

- **How do we know that we are successful?** The team's measures for success.

Ways to answer these questions with your product group are described in Chapter 11, "Guiding the Product Ownership." The sections that follow provide a short overview and refer you to specific sections of Chapter 11 for more details.

The Product Vision

The product vision creates a shared purpose by clarifying the users, the user needs and problems to address, the business model, and the key features of the product. It provides a shared understanding of the future state.

In the section "Stakeholder Alignment" in Chapter 11, we share how you can facilitate Product Owners and teams to co-develop the product vision.

The Team's Actions and Expected Outputs

To further increase the sense of a shared purpose and team goals, teams should define their contributions to the product vision. This includes a common understanding of the users, the work of the teams, and the product or service the team delivers.

The Product Vision workshop conducted earlier covered the users and the delivered product. The FTAM workshop covered the DoD activities that are expected and across which components they will work. But, although it seems obvious that the team members should be clear about the team's actions and outputs at this point, we have seen too many teams in which this was not the case. Even if all the group members seem to know what the goals are, they often have different ideas about what accomplishing them entails. While people might be saying the same words, those words may mean different things to different people. To ensure shared understanding, we recommended going over the goals and the FTAM again with the individual team members and adjusting and extending those items to match the team-specific description.

We often conduct a private poll with the question: On a scale from 1 to 10, how sure are you that your team is capable of delivering an increment that conforms to the current DoD? You will be surprised to see that such a simple question leads to unexpected results and might result even in revisiting the DoD or restructuring teams. Why? We assume that some people are inherently shy and not used to expressing their opinions out loud. Without a poll, some important information could go away unnoticed and only be discovered after the first Sprint (or even later).

We facilitated the launch of a small product group with three teams. They had crafted the product DoD on the first day. During the second day, cross-functional teams emerged from a Self-Designing Team workshop. The launch went suspiciously smoothly, so we decided to ask a series of open questions, with answers being collected with private polls. After summing up the results, we found out that the average belief in the teams' conformance to the crafted DoD was 6 out of 10. That was too low. The rest of the four hours we spent facilitating a heated but very productive discussion that led to a revision of the teams' composition and an updated DoD.

The Team's Measures for Success

One of the important characteristics of a high-performing team is that its members are clear about the team's goals. We cover product measures and the creation of Product Goals and Sprint Goals in detail in the section "Product Ownership Measures" in Chapter 11. We recommend going over the measures again with the individual team members and adjusting and extending them to match the team-specific description.

Align on Shared Values and Behavior

Alignment on shared values, decision making, working agreements, and behaviors is crucial for team success. In this section, we discuss Scrum values and their impact on empirical process control. We also share an approach that you can apply to help teams use Scrum values to improve their teamwork.

Spirit of the Game, Empirical Control, and Trust

In response to the question "Why are Scrum values so important?" we have several answers. First, they determine the spirit of the game: the culture, the invisible component. They guide the Scrum Team in the absence of complete clarity. In other words, they are the ethical code of Scrum.

> Successful use of Scrum depends on people becoming more proficient in living five values.[8]

The Scrum framework doesn't cover all possible situations that teams might face. The values are similar to the principles of fair play in sports. The game rules in the Scrum Guide[8] describe artifacts, accountabilities, events, and link them together. The values are expressed at the level of specific, measurable behavior. It is people's behavior that determines the quality of relationships, affects engagement and motivation, and influences the desire to achieve team goals. Without values, Scrum quickly turns into a cargo cult, where one merely mechanically follows specific rules and ceremonies. You are probably familiar with such Scrum implementations. They go by many names: Fake Scrum, Mechanical Scrum, Pseudo-Scrum, and so on.

We have noticed that when most interactions in a team correspond to the Scrum values, an atmosphere of trust and psychological safety is more likely to emerge. As mentioned in Chapter 1, "Organizing for Adaptability," psychological safety is a main ingredient for a team's high performance. In social systems, people always assess potential interpersonal risks. For instance, they are prone to avoid looking stupid by expressing an unpopular idea or asking a question.

> Psychological safety means a climate where people can be themselves. When psychological safety is present, people calmly share problems and mistakes without feeling embarrassed and fearing punishment.[19]

We're all reluctant to engage in behaviors that could negatively influence how others perceive our competence, awareness, and positivity. Although this kind of self-protection is a natural strategy in the workplace, it is detrimental to effective teamwork. When people work in complex environments and develop innovative products, they inevitably make mistakes. But if they are blamed and punished for their daring, they become fearful and prefer to keep silent about the mistakes they made. Transparency and understanding of the current situation are reduced, and the organization loses the opportunity to learn and innovate.

We want to share the story of a Scrum Team whose boldness and openness influenced the entire organization. A few hours before another Sprint Review, the team realized that the functionality they had been working on throughout the Sprint wasn't working. There was a critical error on the server, and the team couldn't fix it. The Scrum Master asked what the team intended to do. The team said they were ashamed to go to the Sprint Review and were afraid to embarrass themselves. The Scrum Master explained that a lack of results was also a result, and promised to support the team. So, the guys decided to go to the Sprint Review after all. Their hearts pounding with anxiety, they stammered as they showed the screen with the critical error and explained how they intended to fix it. The CEO attending the Sprint Review said it was the best presentation he had seen that day. The CEO's support played a key role in making it a good tradition to discuss mistakes at subsequent Sprint Reviews. Later, teams began awarding a prize "for the biggest mistake made in a Sprint." This is an example of how Scrum values, especially courage and openness, have helped this organization maintain transparency, learn, and make appropriate decisions.

Working with Values

Values themselves are rather abstract by nature. Thus, people tend to understand them differently. Besides, we cannot know for sure the real intentions and motivations of people, as those are hidden; however, we can observe and measure their actual behavior.

> In general, all we can do is observe people's behavior—their plans, decisions, and actions—and try to gauge their attitudes toward those plans, decisions, and actions over time. Any attempt to determine their attitude is more a matter of guess-work than a reliable science.[20]

That's why we have found the following approach useful in our practice:

1. Find shared values.

2. Clarify values.

3. Agree on specific behaviors.

4. Create a 360-degree feedback loop.

In the upcoming sections, we'll describe each of these points in detail.

Find Shared Values

Scrum is based on five values: respect, openness, courage, commitment, and focus. Your team can use Scrum values out of the box, and that's fine. But if the Scrum Team you coach wants to extend the basic set or define their own set of values compatible with Scrum, please help them and facilitate this process. Otherwise, you can skip this section and move to the next.

We use a simple algorithm for defining team values; it is one of the many possible options for identifying these shared values. Some of the structures that are helpful here: 1-2-4-All,[21] Appreciative Interviews,[22] and Nine Whys.[23]

1. Give each of the team members a big list of 45 core human values for reference (see Table 9.1).

2. Ask each team member to pick three to seven most important values from the list and think about why they are so important individually. Firmly facilitate quiet self-reflection before moving on to the next conversations (5 minutes).

3. Form pairs/triads and ask them to share personal stories of how values manifested in their life and helped them to overcome life challenges. Give the pairs/triads 7–10 minutes to work in each direction (14–20 minutes).

4. Ask pairs to find a common set of values and bring them to the next round (5 minutes).

5. Bring the whole team together and facilitate an open discussion to select the final three to seven values from the sets that groups had developed in the previous round (10–20 minutes).

6. If you have multiple Scrum teams developing the product, you need one more step. Ask each team to share their set of values and help the product group to find common values. Different facilitation techniques can be helpful here: multi-voting, Conversation Cafe,[24] User Experience Fishbowl,[9] Shift & Share,[10] and open discussion.

Table 9.1   List of Core Human Values

Achievement	Adventure	Autonomy	Balance	Beauty
Compassion	Challenge	Community	Competency	Contribution
Creativity	Curiosity	Fairness	Faith	Fame
Friendships	Fun	Growth	Happiness	Honesty
Humor	Influence	Inner harmony	Justice	Kindness
Knowledge	Leadership	Learning	Love	Loyalty
Meaningful work	Openness	Optimism	Peace	Pleasure
Recognition	Respect	Responsibility	Security	Self-respect
Stability	Success	Status	Trustworthiness	Wisdom

Now you have shared values on different levels: personal, team, and product group.

Clarify Values

At the previous stage, the team selected values through deep conversations and life stories. We find it useful to consolidate this step further by writing down two- or three-sentence descriptions that clearly state what each value means in the team workspace. Here, we provide our own short descriptions for each of the five Scrum values; they were inspired by an article by Gunther Verheyen.[25]

- **Courage:** Doing the right thing; working on tough problems; supporting and adhering to Scrum values; not delivering undone; sharing even unpleasant information.

- **Openness:** Readiness to work in other fields and competencies; availability of information and challenges; sharing feedback and valuable information; interacting with stakeholders and the broader environment; readiness for change in the organization.

- **Commitment:** Teamwork and support; being focused on achieving Product and Sprint Goals; adhering to Scrum rules, principles, and values; continually seeking improvement; adhering to the DoD; doing the best work possible.

- **Focus:** Focusing on the simplest thing that can work; looking at what is essential now, without thinking about what may become important someday; directing efforts to optimize business value; focusing on creating a valuable and useful increment.

- **Respect:** Respecting people, their experience, and personal background; thinking about sponsors without creating unnecessary things and without wasting their money; caring about users and trying to solve their problems; perceiving one another as independent professionals; accepting the Scrum accountabilities.

Now let's talk about how to better facilitate this process for the team.

1. Form small groups and let them write down two- to three-sentence descriptions for each value. You can inspire the team with the descriptions we provided. Ask each group to write down descriptions in a bold and clearly visible way on big sticky notes or flipchart pages (20–25 minutes).

2. Hand out a number of voting dots and ask everyone to vote individually for the best descriptions in the room. Use the Gallery Walk technique to get the whole room on its feet to take a walking tour of posters or flipchart pages generated in the previous step (15 minutes).

3. Calculate the votes and pin down the most popular descriptions for each value. They become references for future conversations. (15 minutes).

At this point, you have a set of clarified values with short descriptions. Let's move on to identifying specific behaviors.

Agree on Specific Behavior Patterns

After the team has agreed on the same value definitions, you are ready to formulate specific behaviors that support (green area) and violate (red area) the values. It is vital to use "I" statements in the behavior descriptions to make them personal. To facilitate this step, we suggest creating several stations corresponding to each value, and then filling them with examples of measurable and observable behaviors in small groups.

Then use the World Cafe[26] or Shift & Share[10] technique to enrich each station with the wisdom of the crowd. Next, you can use Min Specs[27] structure or 20/20 Vision[28] to select the most striking examples for the team to follow.

Here are some examples of behaviors that were identified in one such session:

- **Courage:** I accept even those tasks that I do not know how to solve; I speak openly when I don't have time to implement the task; I forecast only the amount of work that I believe I can do.

- **Openness:** I voice current issues that stand in my way; I update information radiators (Scrum Board, Burndown) at least once a day; I don't work in the Sprint on tasks that the Scrum Team doesn't know about; I show only done features at the Sprint Review.

- **Commitment:** I strictly adhere to the DoD when working on PBIs; I perform testing tasks to help the team achieve the Sprint Goal; I fulfill team agreements; I learn new skills during the Sprint by working in pairs.

- **Focus:** I only work on the most valuable Sprint Backlog Items (SBIs) in a Sprint; I use pair and mob programming practices in the Sprint.

- **Respect:** I listen and don't interrupt colleagues, even if my competence is higher; I arrive on time for events; I don't blame other team members if the Sprint Goal isn't met; I don't raise my voice at colleagues.

Now, the team has calibrated the Scrum values and agreed on specific and measurable patterns of behavior (also called norms of conduct[29]). By this time, the team members should have the intention to commit to the values. But the mere intention is usually not enough. The team will enter a phase of high conflict—and at that moment you need to establish a feedback loop to adjust the patterns of behavior and maintain the agreements. See Chapter 10, "Coaching Teams," for details on how to do this.

Facilitating Decision Making

Teamwork requires making many decisions along the way. If decisions are to be implemented successfully, one needs to have "buy-in" from the people affected by them. It's hard to get this buy-in if people haven't been involved in the decision-making process. Servant leaders aim to build consensus in teams so that everyone supports decisions while avoiding groupthink.[30] During the launch, it's useful to define what exactly real consensus is, consider the necessity of the decision-making rules in teams, learn why people disagree, and employ simple techniques for building a consensus.

Why Consensus?

Many people think that consensus is equivalent to unanimity, but it's not. Otherwise, the discussions would potentially continue forever and would be a waste of time and energy.

> Consensus is a process in which all the team members agree to support a decision that is in the best interest of the whole.[31]

In consensus, the input of every member is carefully considered and there is a good-faith effort to address all concerns. But how to reach a consensus and avoid the trap of spending too much time on a decision? We observe that facilitators often struggle at this point. The process of reaching consensus is a challenge, and all too often a potentially great solution is watered down until we find something that everyone can live with. Another problematic issue is that facilitators under the pressure of the group may end up with a decision that is supported by the majority only. That decreases the overall buy-in and diminishes the implementation process.

We'll describe a useful and highly structured technique for building consensus that you can use during the launch. That is important because many vital decisions are made during several days: agreeing on a shared DoD, designing teams, crafting and clarifying shared values, and many more.

Five-Finger Consensus

Five-finger consensus[32] encourages the group to listen carefully when there is disagreement and encourages attentive listening to different points of view. It also helps to avoid a groupthink effect. But it doesn't permit a proposal to be watered down due to the fact some disagree. Here are the steps:

1. Once a decision has been proposed and discussed, and the team is ready to check for agreement, on the count of three, everyone holds up between one and five fingers indicating their level of support for the solution. An alternative is using a dot-voting system, but it has a weakness in this context: People are prone to change the level of their support as a reaction to how others vote. A 1–5 scale means:

   5: Strongly agree

   4: Agree

   3: See pluses and minuses, but willing to support

   2: Disagree

   1: Strongly disagree

2. If everyone shows a 5, 4, or 3, a consensus has been reached, and the team got the decision. In case 1s or 2s exist, those people are given the opportunity to explain why they gave the rating and make recommendations to enhance the proposal. The originator of the alternative accepts the recommendation or leaves it as it is.

3. The facilitator checks for consensus again. If all the team members show a 5, 4, 3, or 2, the choice is made, and we move ahead. If there are any 1s, those people are given another opportunity to explain why they gave the rating and make additional recommendations to

improve the alternative so as to make it more desirable to them. The originator of the proposal has the choice to withdraw the recommendation or accept it again.

4. In the final round, the majority rule is applied.

Decision Rules

The very simple question "What are your team's decision rules?" often baffles some Scrum Masters and leaders. And it's good if teams are able to respond to it easily. Agile values assume that decisions should be made collaboratively. For example, at the Sprint Retrospective the entire Scrum Team participates. Teams often use only one "default" rule, the majority rule, when solving any issues that arise in their work, without even considering that this rule can do more harm than good on some issues where the support of the majority of the team is needed. The possible decision rules with the corresponding pros and cons are as follows:

- **Majority rule:** A rule that is used by default in everyday life in many cultures.

  - *Pros*: Very easy to use; allows you to quickly make the decision.

  - *Cons*: After gaining 51% of the votes, you can simply ignore the minority position. Therefore, do not expect a lot of enthusiasm (if any) from the yielding side in implementing the decision. There is a high probability that the decision will be sabotaged. The majority rule divides the team.

- **Delegation:** Sometimes it's practical for a team to hand over the final decision to a group of people or one person as homework. After the group has completed their homework, the team can ratify or reverse the decision.

  - *Pros*: Delegation allows the team to move forward quickly, especially when the team trusts the person or group of people who are "given" homework.

  - *Cons*: The team may not ratify the decision made by the group afterward.

- **Super-majority rule:** The decision is made by the majority, as in majority rule, but the bar for passing the decision is raised. It can be 60%, 70%, or 80%.

  - *Pros*: The higher the percentage threshold, the more support we get, the less the team is divided, and the less possible resistance.

  - *Cons*: The time to make a decision increases significantly.

- **Multi-voting:** Often used when we need to prioritize a long flipchart list of possible problems or solutions. Dot voting is often used. Another option for multi-voting is the decision grid (more about it later in the text). Multi-voting is neutral. It does not divide the team into winners and losers. After all, everyone gives several votes and is directly involved in the decision-making process.

- **Consensus:** Many people mistakenly assume that consensus necessarily implies the best or most optimal solution. This is not true. Consensus also does not oblige the final decision to integrate all points of view (although this is undeniably good). For consensus, it is necessary and sufficient that the whole team is ready to live with and support the decision.

- *Pros*: A decision made by consensus will not meet with resistance and will be strongly supported by the team.
- *Cons*: Finding consensus can be time-consuming and requires an experienced facilitator.

- **Unanimous:** Used for critical decisions. Members must keep working to understand one another's perspectives until they integrate those perspectives into a shared framework of understanding. They can then create advanced proposals that are acceptable for everyone.

  - *Pros*: Has the best chance of producing sustainable agreements when stakes are high. You need to be careful here and distinguish real unanimity from fake agreement caused by groupthink.
  - *Cons*: Takes a lot of effort; difficulty in seeking "both/and" solutions; general tendency of teams to push for a fast decision.

Now let's discuss which rules are appropriate for a team in different contexts. We'll share a story first.

The Scrum Team had been working together for only a few days and members had just gotten to know each other. Working arrangements were discussed, and finally they reached the need to develop the DoD. Time passed, and the team still could not agree in any way as to what should be the percentage of code coverage by integration tests. Some team members began to rush the Scrum Master to make a decision. As a result, a decision was adopted using the "default" rule—the majority rule.

Needless to say, there were unhappy consequences. There were several more Sprints in the team, heated arguments did not subside, and a serious conflict was brewing. The developers split into two camps. Those who supported the adopted decision insisted on strict adherence to it (after all, the decision had already been taken), and the others, in every possible way, continued to sabotage the current DoD.

This is the typical example of how a majority rule has been misused. We suggest teams use at least consensus when dealing with such choices as the following:

- Establishing the DoD
- Creating working agreements
- Agreeing on the Sprint length
- Hiring/firing decisions
- Timing of the Scrum events

For less important issues, you could suggest that the team use multi-voting or super-majority rule. Finally, trivial issues can be resolved by a simple show of hands (majority rule) or delegation.

Teams do, indeed, benefit from having clear rules by which decisions will be made. Why? Because such rules decrease complexity and the level of ambiguity and are wheels for faster decision making. We recommend conducting a special alignment workshop with the team to create initial decision-making rules that they will use afterward. Here are the possible steps:

1. Discuss the importance of having clear rules for making decisions with the whole team (5 minutes).

2. Explain all types of decision making that can be used (majority, delegation, super-majority, multi-voting, consensus, unanimous). Answer questions if any pop up (10 minutes).

3. Brainstorm possible decisions that a team will possibly face in the future using the 1-2-4-All structure (15 minutes).

4. Use multi-voting if the list is too long and you want to limit the number of choices.

5. Create small groups (two to three members) and give each one a subset of the decisions that were generated during the previous step (10 minutes).

6. Decide on the meta-rule for the future decision-making process. We recommend it to be consensus, such as the five-finger consensus technique discussed earlier.

7. Ask groups to share the results of the discussions and place each sticky note in a proper cell in a decision matrix (see Table 9.2). Use the meta-rule for the whole group for making the final decision about which cell each sticky note lands in (15 minutes).

Table 9.2 shows an example of the decision matrix that was created by the product group (four teams) during their kick-off.

Table 9.2   Sample Decision Matrix

Majority	Delegation	Super-Majority	Consensus	Unanimous
Where we go to lunch	Order pizza	Firing a team member	PBI estimation	Hiring a new team member
	Buy coffee	Selecting a place for a team building	Feature team composition	
			Team seating	
			Format of the events	
			Selecting Scrum Master	
			Vacation days	
			Crafting a Sprint Goal	

Hang a decision matrix in the team room and use it as a guide when the team is required to make a decision.

In a product group, there had been long debates about how to make final decisions about some important decisions related to the enterprise architecture. Scrum Teams (seven of them working on the same product) were confused. The issue was solved when we proposed to create a decision matrix during the Overall Retrospective. Thus, the team representatives created one and filled it with content that bothered them. Some sticky notes went to delegation; others landed in the consensus column. From that moment, the speed of decision making increased, as confusion dissolved.

Additionally, you can develop a criterion (or several) according to which each decision will relate to one of the listed rules. For example, the criterion might be "importance" or "impact." How does it work? Suppose the team initially agreed that all-important decisions (more than 6 on a 10-point scale) should be made by consensus rule, 4–6 decisions on a 10-point scale by multi-voting, and anything less than 4 by majority rule (see Figure 9.13).

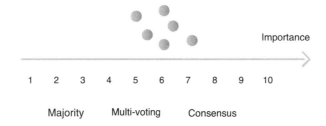

Figure 9.13
Consensus scale.

In this case, if it is necessary to make any decision, you can draw a scale on the flipchart, and the team votes, noting the importance of the scale. Then you calculate the mean and use one of the previously agreed-upon decision rules.

To this point, we've discussed the importance of the decision-making rules and how they deal with complexity and dissolve ambiguity. Let's move on to the process of consensus building. We'll share three useful techniques for creating consensus.

Identify and Launch Communities

Chapter 4, "Agile Organizational Design," emphasized that starting communities around cross-cutting concerns is important. A key building block of any Agile organization is a cross-functional team that optimizes the system for adaptability and speed of learning. As a side effect, developers in the same core specialization (e.g., architecture, testing, UI/UX) will work in interdependent but separate feature teams. This is considered normal, because we should not compromise the primary system goal. To align knowledge, develop common standards, and practice new approaches in a particular field of knowledge, however, we create communities of knowledge.

How do we start communities? That is relatively easy and is based on self-organization. To make it effective, you can follow these guidelines:

Step 1. Teach about the importance of communities. Use the principles from Chapter 4, "Agile Organizational Design," and Chapter 6, "Coaching for Change." Make sure teams understand that joining communities is voluntary. Also explain that communities don't have shadow backlogs from which teams might pull work. Community members might suggest items for inclusion in the Product Backlog, but they need to persuade the Product Owner before those items actually become PBIs. Focus teams' attention on the fact that communities do not have functional leaders or a formal hierarchy. Communities don't exist in a formal organizational chart. They naturally live and die, though some of them might be long-term groups. Communities cannot dictate any decisions to teams; they can recommend some decisions, but teams always have the last say.

Step 2. Identify potential communities. We use an Open Space Technology[33] structure for launching communities. For this structure, you need chairs in concentric circles, microphones for groups larger than 40 people, and large blank sheets of paper. Make sure you prepare in advance the large whiteboard with enough concurrent time slots.

We explain the "Law of Two Feet" that governs participation in the multiple sessions and the four principles of Open Space. The Law of Two Feet says: "Go and attend whichever session you want, but if you find that you are not learning or contributing, use your two feet!"

Then we open the marketplace and explain that anyone is able to propose a new community within the next few minutes. All you need is to get up on your feet, approach the center of the room, take a sheet of paper, write a community name on it, propose it to the group, and put it in a time slot on a whiteboard (see Figure 9.14).

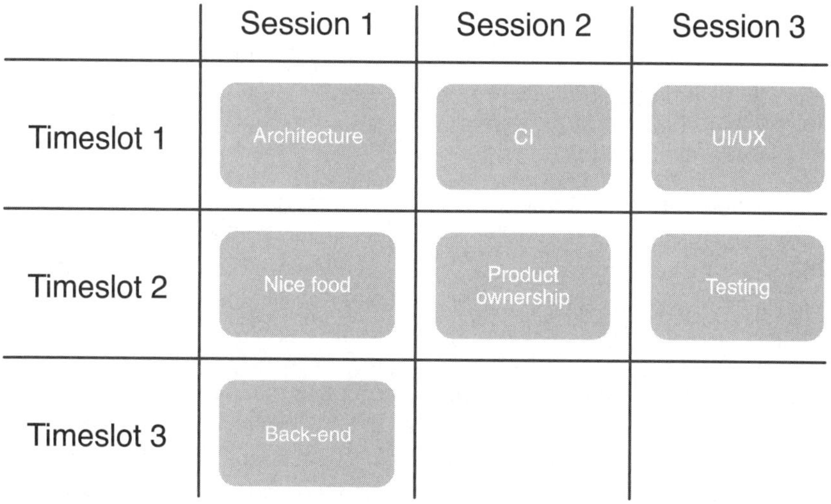

	Session 1	Session 2	Session 3
Timeslot 1	Architecture	CI	UI/UX
Timeslot 2	Nice food	Product ownership	Testing
Timeslot 3	Back-end		

Figure 9.14
Creating communities with Open Space.

Step 3.   Now it's time for multiple concurrent sessions to start. We hand out a template at each station that participants need to complete by the end of the respective timebox. Some major points that need to be filled in the template are:

    a. Official name of the community

    b. Community coordinator (optional)

    c. Date of the first gathering

    d. Preferable channel of communication (e.g., wiki, Slack)

    e. Participants

    f.   Any help you need?

    g. Something else important

When the time is up, let the groups present their templates and close any raised concerns. We love closing Open Space by using Impromptu Networking with three rounds of discussion on the question: "What did you get, and what are your hopes for the communities?"

> In a product group, the teams had launched 24 communities. Some of them were not related to product development at all. Examples of some fancy communities included "beer connoisseurs" and "food lovers." After several months, most of the communities had died and only six core ones were left: "architecture," "back-end," "Scrum Masters," "CI/CD," "testing," and "UI/UX."

Identify Coordination Mechanisms

In our experience, concerns related to coordination are at their hottest when the organization is introducing cross-functional Agile teams. People often don't believe in self-organization and are skeptical about decentralized approaches. This is fine as their mental models and assumptions are based on past experience; moreover, it's natural not to believe in something they have never seen before. Scrum Masters need to address these concerns, and to reduce uncertainty and teams' anxiety during the product group launch.

In Chapter 4, "Agile Organizational Design," we noted the importance of creating conditions for emergent coordination and introduced three techniques: communities, travelers, and component mentors.[2] This is not the final list. We also use some other decentralized methods of facilitation, such as multi-team events, Open Space, Lean Coffee, and UX Fishbowl. Here, we'll describe a typical workshop on coordination techniques that we conduct during a kick-off.

Step 1.   The purpose of the first step is collecting all concerns that need to be addressed through emergent coordination. We ask participants to form small groups, then hand each group an empty piece of flipchart paper divided into two columns. The columns are named: "What we need to coordinate" and "Coordination techniques," respectively. We ask the groups to put sticky notes with concerns in the first column. We also kindly ask them to not think about the second column for a while. The timebox for this activity is 5 minutes.

Step 2. The goal of this step is teaching. Put on your teaching hat and educate the teams about:

a. The principle of emergent coordination

b. Coordination techniques (communities, travelers, component mentors, Open Space Technology, Lean Coffee, UX Fishbowl)

See Chapter 13 of *Large-Scale Scrum*[2] for a list of additional coordination techniques.

Step 3. Now that participants know the techniques and the theory underlying them, ask the groups to fill the second column on the flipchart. This timebox is 10 minutes. Move around from group to group, answer any questions, and suggest techniques as you see fit. The groups should wind up with something similar to Figure 9.15.

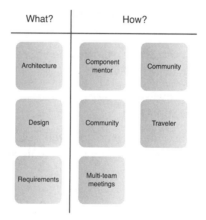

Figure 9.15
Example checklist.

By this time, teams are usually able to find the appropriate coordination techniques for all their concerns. If something is missing, help them by sharing your recommendations.

Well, now you are all set. The teams have figured out the coordination approaches for most critical concerns. You can suggest and refer to these approaches at any time in a Sprint. For instance, we usually remind the teams about the techniques at the Sprint Planning when two or more teams are going to work on tightly coupled items in an upcoming iteration.

Create Useful Checklists

In complex environments, we observe similar problems popping up during the Sprints. They are so common that we notify the teams about them beforehand and inquire if it makes sense to deal with them during the launch. If that's not the case or if we don't have sufficient time, the discussion can be postponed until the regular Sprint Retrospective.

Humans' physical and mental powers are limited. Scrum Teams work in highly turbulent and complex environments. They will benefit from strategies to overcome failures. And one such simple strategy is called a checklist.

> Checklists seem to provide protection against such failures. They remind us of the minimum necessary steps and make them explicit.[34]

By this time, you have already created the most important Scrum checklist—the DoD. You might encourage teams to create several other checklists upfront that address three challenges that they will likely face in future Sprints:

- **Sprint Goal challenge:** What should the team do when it sees the chances of reaching the Sprint Goal are low in the middle of the Sprint?

- **Underutilization challenge:** What should developers do when they face underutilization of their primary skills during the Sprint?

- **Emergent work challenge:** How should emergent work (e.g., bugs, sudden work coming from the Product Owner) be handled in a complex environment? Which team will pick up the new work and under which rules?

Sprint Goal Checklist

Somewhere in the middle of the Sprint, teams may realize that their chances of reaching the individual or even the overall Sprint Goal are low. From our experience, less mature teams often passively look at the Burndown dashboard or use some other visualization technique and do nothing about it. Therefore, we suggest that the product group use the Emergency Procedure[35] Scrum pattern and create a checklist of concrete steps upfront. It could be quite short:

1. Do something radically different and try to reach the Sprint Goal anywhere.

2. Notify and get help from other teams.

3. Collaborate with the Product Owner and agree on reducing the scope.

4. Cancel the Sprint.

How can you create such a checklist in your context? Follow these simple steps:

1. Educate the teams about Emergency Procedure and respond to their questions.

2. Use a 1-2-4-All structure to define the actual steps for the checklist. In the last step (All), you might need multi-voting or another decision-making technique.

One product group we worked with defined an interesting set of steps. The team whose local work affected the overall Sprint Goal, and potentially put it in danger, had to send an SOS message to a special Slack channel. After that, an emergency meeting with teams' representatives was conducted and they collaboratively decided on the next steps.

Underutilization Checklist

Individual underutilization in a cross-functional Agile team is one of the pains you'll have to deal with. After years working in companies where narrow specialization is incentivized and highly valued, a culture of narrow specialists is common. After structural redesign based on cross-functional teams, necessary conditions are created where multifunctional specialists may grow. But they don't emerge overnight and an acquired habit of making oneself busy is probably still there. Even if developers are willing to learn, we notice that in the short and middle terms, individual underutilization will be a strong stress factor.

We remember how stressful it felt after the first Sprint in a product group with six teams. There was so much tension in the air that we decided to cancel individual team Sprint Retrospectives and invite everyone for an Overall Retrospective. Almost everyone showed up. When the participants voted for the most critical issue to discuss, underutilization was it. The result of this discussion was the first underutilization agreement. Now we suggest creating such an agreement during the launch and warn the teams about the consequences of working in a cross-functional environment.

Create the checklist using the same steps described for a Sprint Goal. It is rather context-based but some items regularly pop up:

- Learning a new skill

- Pair programming

- Swarming/mob programming

- Product Backlog Refinement activities

- Helping other teams

- Removing technical debt

You'll have to inspect and adapt this checklist by adding and/or removing items, and perhaps changing the ordering. Chapter 10, "Coaching Teams," gives even more ideas on how to overcome the underutilization problem.

Emergent Work Checklist

Giving multiple Scrum Teams the same focus and asking them to work with a single Product Owner and a shared Product Backlog automatically makes all emerging work shared, too. Teams will benefit from crafting a set of guidelines that govern emerging work in the Sprints.

Here's an example of such a checklist developed by one of our clients:

- Emergent work appears in one of the preferred communication channels (e.g., Slack, or any other Information Radiator[36]) and teams volunteer for it.
- Emergent work complies with the rules defined on a *Kanban* board.
- Teams pick up new work one by one in a Sprint.

The creation of the checklist follows the same steps described in previous checklists.

Summary

This chapter showed how you can launch the product group into its first iteration. This effort starts by defining a common Definition of Done (DoD) for the product group. This step becomes possible after you've defined your product and appointed the Product Owner. Instead of focusing on component team velocity when defining metrics, each team should measure feature velocity, which reveals the whole system's capability to ship items to the customer.

Next, you can conduct a Feature Team Adoption Map (FTAM) workshop. During this workshop, the composition of the future teams is revealed, as well as the next steps to expand cross-functionality. Team design can start with a Market of Skills exercise and a Self-Designing Team workshop.

It's important to create teams' identities and an atmosphere of trust at the beginning. That's covered in the team's lift-off: creating a shared purpose, identifying measures of success, and performing actions and experiments. Agreeing on a concrete set of values and patterns of behavior is important, too. We provided a detailed algorithm for how to do that: selecting values, clarifying them, agreeig on specific behavior patterns and creating a feedback loop.

Teamwork implies making daily decisions. Crafting decision-making rules and having a shared consensus-building mechanism are useful. If secondary concerns pop up related to knowledge sharing and common standards, communities can be formed to deal with them.

In a scaled environment, coordination becomes more complex, but teams are still accountable for that; there's no need for dedicated coordination roles. Emergent coordination can be enabled with a set of simple coordination techniques (multi-team events, component mentors, travelers, and others). Finally, it's recommended to create some checklists for the most common challenges that teams face in a scaled environment: reaching a Sprint Goal, underutilization, and emergent work in a Sprint.

References

1. Diana Larsen and Ainsley Nies. *Liftoff: Start and Sustain Successful Agile Teams*, 2nd ed. (Pragmatic Bookshelf, 2016).

2. Craig Larman and Bas Vodde. *Large-Scale Scrum: More with LeSS* (Addison-Wesley, 2017).

3. "Value Areas." https://sites.google.com/a/scrumplop.org/published-patterns/value-stream/value-areas.

4. Henri Lipmanowicz and Keith McCandless. *The Surprising Power of Liberating Structures: Simple Rules to Unleash a Culture of Innovation* (Liberating Structures Press, 2014).

5. Jeff Patton. *User Story Mapping: Discover the Whole Story, Build the Right Product* (O'Reilly Media, 2014).

6. Luke Hohmann. *Innovation Games: Creating Breakthrough Products Through Collaborative Play* (Addison-Wesley, 2007).

7. J. Richard Hackman. *Leading Teams: Setting the Stage for Great Performances* (Harvard Business Review Press, 2002).

8. Ken Schwaber and Jeff Sutherland. "The Scrum Guide." https://scrumguides.org/docs/scrumguide/v2020/2020-Scrum-Guide-US.pdf.

9. "UX Fishbowl." Liberating Structures. www.liberatingstructures.com/18-users-experience-fishbowl/.

10. "Shift & Share." Liberating Structures. www.liberatingstructures.com/11-shift-share/.

11. David Koontz. "Defintion of Ready & Done." September 30, 2011. https://agilecomplexificationinverter.blogspot.com/2011/09/exercise-definition-of-done.html.

12. Darrell Velegol. *CENTER: A System of Six Practices for Taking Charge of Your Passions and Purposes in Self, Family, Work, and Community* (CreateSpace Independent Publishing Platform, 2013).

13. "What, So What, Now What? W3." Liberating Structures. www.liberatingstructures.com/9-what-so-what-now-what-w/.

14. "Mad Tea." Liberating Structures. www.liberatingstructures.com/mad-tea/.

15. "15% Solutions." Liberating Structures. www.liberatingstructures.com/7-15-solutions/.

16. "Impromptu Networking." Liberating Structures. www.liberatingstructures.com/2-impromptu-networking/.

17. Ahmad Fahmy and Craig Larman. "How to Form Teams in Large-Scale Scrum? A Story of Self-Designing Teams." Scrum Alliance. www.scrumalliance.org/community/member-articles/2030.

18. "Tuckman's Stages of Group Development." Wikipedia. https://en.wikipedia.org/wiki/Tuckman%27s_stages_of_group_development.

19. Amy Edmondson. *The Fearless Organization: Creating Psychological Safety in the Workplace for Learning, Innovation, and Growth* (Wiley, 2018).

20. S. Chris Edmonds. *The Culture Engine: A Framework for Driving Results, Inspiring Your Employees, and Transforming Your Workplace* (Wiley, 2014).

21. "1-2-4-All." Liberating Structures. www.liberatingstructures.com/1-1-2-4-all/.

22. "Appreciative Interviews." Liberating Structures. www.liberatingstructures.com/5-appreciative-interviews-ai/.

23. "Nine Whys." Liberating Structures. www.liberatingstructures.com/3-nine-whys/.

24. "Conversation Cafe." Liberating Structures. www.liberatingstructures.com/17-conversation-cafe/.

25. Gunther Verheyen. "There's Value in the Scrum Values." May 3, 2013. https://guntherverheyen.com/2013/05/03/theres-value-in-the-scrum-values/.

26. The World Cafe. http://www.theworldcafe.com/.

27. "Min Specs." Liberating Structures. www.liberatingstructures.com/14-min-specs/.

28. Dave Gray. "20/20 Vision." GameStorming (April 5, 2011). https://gamestorming.com/2020-vision/.

29. "Norms of Conduct." http://scrumbook.org/product-organization-pattern-language/norms-of-conduct.html.

30. "Groupthink." https://en.wikipedia.org/wiki/Groupthink.

31. Larry Dressler. *Consensus Through Conversations: How to Achieve High-Commitment Decisions* (Berrett-Koehler, 2006).

32. Julia Rozovsky. "The Five Keys to a Successful Google Team." Re:Work (November 17, 2015). https://rework.withgoogle.com/blog/five-keys-to-a-successful-google-team/.

33. "Open Space Technology." Liberating Structures. www.liberatingstructures.com/25-open-space-technology/.

34. Atul Gawande. *The Checklist Manifesto: How to Get Things Right* (Picador, 2010).

35. "Emergency Procedure." http://scrumbook.org/product-organization-pattern-language/emergency-procedure.html.

36. "Information Radiator." http://scrumbook.org/value-stream/information-radiator.html.

10

Coaching Teams

A successful coaching engagement will have a cascading effect, creating positive change beyond the person receiving the coaching.
—Dianna and Merrill Anderson[1]

In this chapter, we build on the work done in launching the product group and share how to further guide team development. We assume that the teams have formed and recently started working in the new setup.

We first share conditions that support effective team growth. Next, we delve into characteristics you can expect to see in Agile teams. We close by sharing coaching techniques to guide team development and facilitate healthy team dynamics.

The Building Blocks of the Agile Organization

Agile organizations regard the Agile team as an asset because they are the value-creating unit in the organization. For example, a Scrum team generates value by solving complex problems. To increase the chances that teams become and stay effective value-creating units, Harvard professor J. Richard Hackman proposes five enabling conditions that management can put in place to support team effectiveness:[2]

- **Real team:** Ensure that team members have a shared task, it is clear who is inside or outside of the team, the teams' authority is defined, and team membership is stable.

- **Compelling direction:** Provide the teams with clear goals, which are both challenging and consequential.

- **Enabling structure:** Ensure the team has the right people with the appropriate team norms, autonomy, technical and social skills to perform the work.

- **Supportive context:** Develop the organizational system to recognize and reward the team's performance, not just the performance of individuals.

- **Competent coaching:** After the preceding four conditions are in place, provide access to expert team coaching. This coaching can come from an external person, a manager, or a team member such as a Scrum Master.

This chapter focuses on the fifth condition—"competent coaching"—which is most likely to have positive effects only after the first four enabling conditions are in place. As a coach, it is up to you to work with management to facilitate these five enabling conditions for Agile team success.

From the section "What Is an Agile Team?" in Chapter 1, "Organizing for Adaptability," you can deduce how feature teams contribute to the conditions "real team" and "compelling direction." In Chapter 9, "Launching the Product Group," we shared activities such as the Self-Designing Team workshop, team lift-off, and creation of the Definition of Done that can help satisfy the "enabling structure" condition. Furthermore, Guidelines 1, 8, and 12 in Chapter 4, "Agile Organizational Design," show what can be done to support the condition "supportive context."

Observations of an Agile Team

With the enabling conditions in place, Agile development also needs an environment in which people jointly discover how to make the right product, quality and mastery are self-evident, and the current way of working is continually improved. It is up to you to work with the teams in meetings, teach them to navigate conflicts, and facilitate learning through workshops or training. Your hard work enables constructive feedback and healthy team dynamics to emerge. With that foundation in place, a group of people is ready to explore, evaluate, and adapt solutions on their journey to success.

Chapter 1, "Organizing for Adaptability," defined what we mean by an Agile team and identified such teams' structural and process characteristics. Now we will discuss the social dynamics of Agile teams. Why? Because to get an idea of how you might support your own teams, it can help to compare their dynamics with the dynamics of an effective Agile team. Based on your observations, you can then further work with the teams to define which kinds of help they require. It is like what happens when you go to the doctor: You know that you want to get better but have no idea how to do it, so you need the doctor's professional opinion and proposals.

What Makes an Agile Team?

If you've ever worked in a great Agile team, we are confident that you still remember this experience very well. We have been lucky enough to work in great Scrum teams several times, and that was fantastic. There was a strong feeling of belonging and a shared passion for reaching an overarching goal. We owned our process and stood by our decisions. A high level of respect and trust made it comfortable to share opinions, challenge decisions, and run the risk of making mistakes. We performed most of the work concurrently. For example, we also designed and tested when writing a piece of code. We worked closely with users to clarify ideas and validate our assumptions. More often than not, we worked in pairs or as a whole team on a single piece of work.

Looking back at our experiences working with and in teams, we conclude that these teams were highly collaborative. But what made an amazing Agile team was not only their collaboration, but also their ability to keep learning and use that new knowledge to keep improving their dynamics, process, and product.

The sections that follow share some social dynamics to look for when working with Agile teams.

Commitment

When people can say what they need to communicate and engage in a productive discussion with their team members, they feel heard and respected. Whatever the team then decides, everyone is more likely to respect and fully support the team's decisions, even if the solution is not necessarily the individual's idea. Each member is committed—to each other, to the organization, and to their growth.

Constructive Conflict

In an Agile team, it is not necessary that the members like each other personally. We have been in great teams where not everyone went out for beers together. However, the team should provide an environment where everyone can speak up without fear of embarrassment or rejection.

A healthy team considers different opinions on handling issues, performing work, and achieving the goal to solve complex problems. Its members discuss different points of view and enter into conflict about these matters—but it's constructive conflict. The goal is to learn from each other and find the best solution. Discussions are not about winning or losing, but rather about seeing problems from different perspectives and filling individuals' gaps in understanding. In this way, the team taps into its collective intelligence to come up with better solutions.

Integrity and Trust

Every Agile team should rely on a foundation of trust. Knowing that your team members are competent, are reliable, will behave according to expectations, and have your best interests in mind gives the team more time to focus on performing together. There's no more wasting time worrying about how things will get done.

Team members keep their commitment to each other and as a team to their stakeholders. As Patrick Lencioni pointed out in his book *The 5 Dysfunctions of a Team: A Leadership Fable*,[3] to feel committed to a decision requires the trust to engage in constructive conflict with your peers. Therefore, an Agile team seeks to get disagreements out in the open so the members can find the right answers. In poorly performing teams, you can expect to find people who hold on to their mental models, making learning difficult.

Integrity is the most crucial characteristic of an Agile team. Do the team members trust each other to do the right thing for the right reasons, even when no one is watching?

Respect

During meetings, everyone participates, and everyone's opinion is heard. People are respected, though not necessarily supported in their opinions. There is a thin line between respect for the person and respect for the person's opinion or work. One can completely disagree with an opinion but still respect the person. When people can separate these two types of respect, they can accept and act on feedback more efficiently.

During sessions, there are intense discussions about content. Senior people listen to junior people, and vice versa.

You should also observe an open feedback culture. People are providing and receiving feedback regularly, regardless of position, in a way that improves the team's dynamics and develops their relationships. People respond positively and use the feedback to change their behavior.

Utmost care is taken to keep team members together for an extended period so that they can grow into highly gelled and effective teams. Research points out that it can take a group up to 18 months,[4] if the team succeeds at all, to become genuinely productive. Therefore, it can be disastrous if you disassemble a team after a short period because the project is over. The team was just starting to get effective. When you form a new group for the next project, that new team must start all over again. Respecting the teams means that teams are no longer regularly reconfigured based on the work to do. Instead, the policy is to keep teams stable and ask the teams to learn and adapt to the ever-changing tasks (see also Guideline 12, "Multi-skill development," in Chapter 4).

Self-Control

Agile teams are self-managing teams. Researchers[2,5] point out that a self-managing team includes the following characteristics:

- The team plans and schedules its work.
- The team takes action on problems.
- It meets organizational goals and gathers information.
- There is a whole task for the group.
- Team members each have a number of skills required for completion of the work.
- The group has the autonomy to make decisions about methods for carrying out the work.
- Compensation and feedback about performance are based on the accomplishments of the team as a whole.

When you walk into the room housing the team, you can expect to find a noisy environment. If everyone is sitting quietly behind their computer doing their task, something is probably not right.

Why? Because Agile teams are fully aligned and work together around a shared goal. You should expect that they will work together more often than they work apart. Removing distractions is the first element in building alignment within a fully functional and high-performing team.

What You Can Do to Help a Group Become a Team

With the enabling conditions for team effectiveness in place, you might think that team leadership or effective communication is the cause of a healthy and good team. This assumption turns out to be false, as Richard Hackman explains in his paper "What Makes for a Great Team."[6] Good leadership and good communication and behavior are not prerequisites for an effective team, but rather are the results of a high-performing team; healthy dynamics are an emergent property. So, although a team's performance depends on how well the members interact, having success as a team creates the conditions for an effective team to emerge. You can start by helping the team achieve small successes.

> In fact, relational issues are one of the defining criteria of losing teams. They are the consequence of poor team results. One could therefore conclude that in order to have good relationships in any system, the prerequisite is to first focus the system on achieving extraordinary results. Indeed, when results are above expectations in any team, respect, pride, and motivation just seem to follow, as a direct consequence.[7]

Work with the Teams

We'll share some practical tips that you can start using with your teams in the remainder of this chapter. Your role and actions will depend on the team's context, their product, and the team's needs. But before we dive into the practical topics, there is one crucial aspect we discussed in many ways in previous chapters that bears re-emphasizing here: the role of the leadership in shaping the environment that the team needs to be effective.

Role of the Leadership

Agile teams do not exist in isolation. They are part of a larger organization that strongly influences their performance. You can work with the leaders in an Agile organization so that they support the teams in the following ways:

- Improve the organizational design to better support the teams.

- Communicate to teams what is expected of them—their purpose, and how success is measured at the product group level.

- Repeatedly encourage people to reflect on what they learn, apply it to their work, and then pass their learning on to others.

- Be confident in their ability to create an atmosphere of trust and vulnerability.

- Create transparency by sharing relevant information. The teams need to understand why they do what they do to take ownership of their process and results.

- Ensure everyone understands the importance of their role to the team, how they contribute to the organization's success, and how each team member positively impacts the team.

- Reward team behaviors that build effective teams and encourage team members to lead by example.

Building on the Team Lift-Off: Coaching Multifunctional Learning

Cross-functional or feature teams are the foundational blocks of an Agile organization. They break down the functional silos and improve communication. They optimize product organization for learning, speed, and flexibility. Cross-functional teams are meant to be cross-component, too. For example, in software development, that means teams share a common codebase and are able to work through numerous architectural components. In other areas of development, it might mean that the teams share a common complete product. Thus, we intentionally remove the coupling between the organizational structure and architecture and use Conway's law[8] to organize the team around the primary units of delivery. (You can find more information about feature teams and their advantages at featureteams.org, Chapter 4, "Agile Organizational Design," and Chapter 8, "Preparing the Product Group," discussed how to structure your product organization with feature teams in detail.)

In this section, we focus on a topic that is both very important and very sensitive for any Scrum Master—coaching the team in multifunctional learning and supporting people in growing their skills after the team has been formed and lifted off. We explore the foundational theory, which might seem rather controversial, and show how multifunctional learning is connected with business agility. Then we give you a bunch of practical tools that you can use in your own context.

Busy Teams

Once, we observed 10-plus teams in a large service company during an extended enterprise Go See effort. We attended various Scrum events, watched how teams collaborated, noticed how they dealt with conflicts, and much more. We undertook this effort for a very sound reason—to uncover the underlying system structures and develop deep interventions. What immediately caught our attention was the focus on resource utilization during Sprint Planning, including these phrases uttered by team members:

- "Do we have enough work for the designer in this Sprint?"

- "Seems like testers are already filled up with work."

- "Can we pull another item for our iOS developer to make her busy?"

What we observed was not unique to that company. We have noticed similar sentiments in many organizations. Teams often cannot respect the order of the Product Backlog and instead select work of lower order to keep team members busy. The reason for this behavior is a painful gap in knowledge and organizational structures/policies that value individual performance over the team performance.

Individual and Team Performance

There are a number of professions in which one person can be partially or even completely independent from others—for example, writers, scientists, bank clerks, gymnasts. How do these people become effective? For example, professional gymnasts are supported by a range of people, from personal trainers to dietitians, but eventually it all comes down to the individual's talent, training mentality, and performance. Their success depends mainly on themselves; they rarely have to wait for others during training or game performance.

A Scrum team is multidisciplinary and contains a whole arsenal of skills and competencies needed to deliver value to users. The workload on a single specialty is mostly uneven in a complex environment, which means such teams are highly susceptible to bottlenecks. Peak loads on a specific specialty may vary from iteration to iteration. For example, in Iteration N, the team may have a peak workload in the business analysis skill; in Sprint $N + 1$, the peak workload might shift to testing.

> The theory of constraints implies that the system's performance is going to be limited by the bottleneck. If there is no change to the bottleneck, the system will not improve. When the bottleneck is influenced, the system changes.[9]

Note that a bottleneck determines a system's throughput, and that spending time optimizing non-bottlenecks will not provide significant benefits.

Let's see what happens if we apply an individual performance strategy to a cross-functional team. Figure 10.1 shows what a typical team board could look like at the end of the iteration if everyone is equipped with an individual performance strategy.

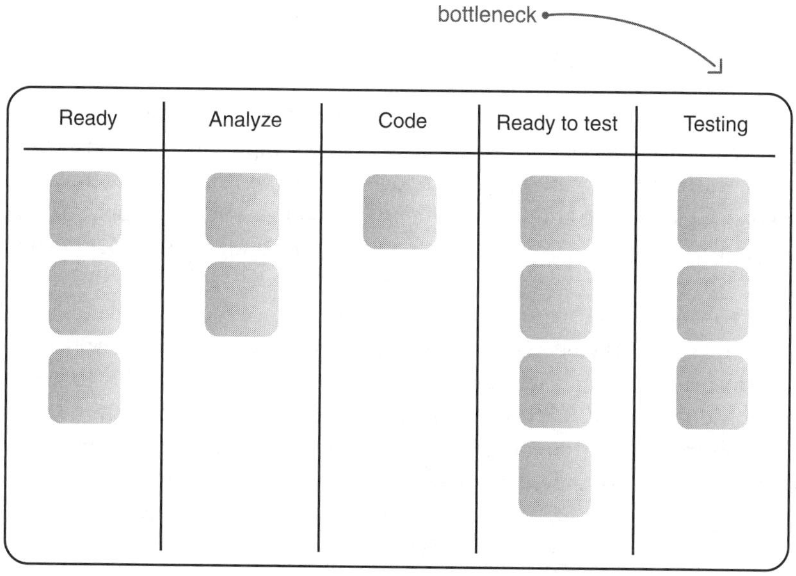

Figure 10.1
Visualizing the bottleneck in a flow.

As you can see in the snapshot in Figure 10.1, the bottleneck at that moment is in testing, because the largest queue is right before this point. If such a picture is consistently observed in a team, then testing is considered a system bottleneck. When the rest of the team continues doing more analysis and coding tasks, this will overload the bottleneck even more. This is pointless (a suboptimization) if we want to optimize the system performance.

> When a subsystem's goals dominate at the expense of the total system's goals, the resulting behavior is called suboptimization.[10]

In other words, team members can be productive on their isolated expertise at the expense of the team performance. Therefore, using the strategy of maximizing individual skill utilization in teams is not optimal in a team context. Instead, you will want to create a team whose members can work on multiple kinds of tasks—a team of multi-skilled individuals. An optimizing team performance strategy can be described as follows:

1. Reveal the bottleneck—for instance, by visualizing the flow of work with Scrum/*Kanban* boards over time.

2. Improve individual performance at the bottleneck—for instance, by taking away the distractions from experts.

3. Help the team influence and expand the bottleneck—for instance, by taking away simple work from experts at the bottleneck and letting them concentrate on more critical stuff.

4. Most importantly, learn to develop secondary skills to help others effectively.

5. Repeat.

Multifunctional Learning and Agility

When an Agile team preserves the goal of maximizing utilization of single-skill specialties, it has multiple implicit backlogs, not one. The existence of multiple implicit backlogs in a team with interdependent tasks, which is a common case in product development, leads to a serialization of the team's work, which increases the end-to-end time to get it done. The typical phrase you can hear is, "I will do this task because I can do it most efficiently." At the end of a Sprint, some team members must process the remaining tasks, while the others sit idle, or even worse start working ahead. Working ahead might sound like a good idea, but it makes sense only when the tasks are independent; if not, it will make things worse by creating more inventory, delay, and rework. A focus on individual skills also forces the business to change the order of the Product Backlog to ensure there are tasks for each individual's single specialty. Thus, the team doesn't work on the most critical features from a customer perspective and suboptimizes value delivery. Let's investigate this dynamic with the Causal Loop Diagram (CLD) shown in Figure 10.2.

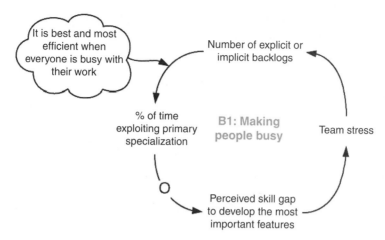

Figure 10.2
Exploiting the primary specialty.

The first balancing loop is B1, "Making people busy." The greater the perceived skill gap to develop the most critical features from a customer perspective, the more stress the team will feel, and the more pressure it will face to increase the number of implicit backlogs ("These are my tasks, those are yours"). That makes developers locally efficient at the cost of suboptimizing the whole. Pay attention to the mental models: "I don't know this stuff. I'm not a 'XXX' developer"; "It's the best and most efficient when everyone is busy and doing 'his/her work." This dynamic doesn't happen at the single team level only. When a knowledge gap becomes large, then new teams with separate backlogs emerge.

Let's investigate this dynamic further. We have another story for you.

Number of Backlogs Increases over Time

A company that a friend of ours launched began as a small startup a few years ago. Five people were sitting in the same room, working on one product. They worked by swarming[8] most of the time. They were nimble and Agile at that time. Everyone was engaged in the most crucial work, regardless of the primary specialization.

What happened after several years? The company grew over time, and it decided to create specialized teams and give each team a separate backlog. The company ended up having 13 "Product Backlogs": iOS backlog, Android backlog, UI/UX backlog, and more. Homogeneous teams were composed of narrow specialists who worked very efficiently locally. The average feature work-in-progress (WIP) of the product group increased because developers focused on starting and finishing work in the local backlogs. This amplified the lead time and caused organizational stress. The product organization couldn't deliver value to the market fast enough. Management reacted to the organizational stress by asking people to work harder. That led to even more specialization, more backlogs, more WIP, and more organizational stress.

The dynamics in this story are quite typical in many of today's organizations. Figure 10.3 provides a graphic depiction of the story components.

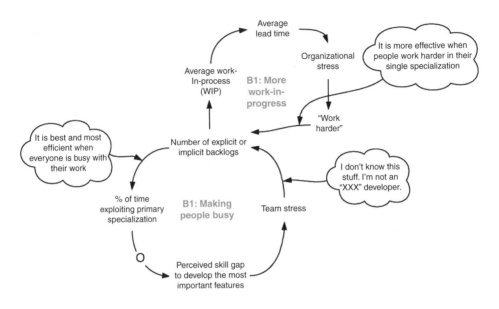

Figure 10.3
Increased work-in-progress (WIP).

Pay attention to the mental model: "It is more effective when people work harder in their single specialization." The system diagram shows how focusing on making people "busy" impacts the speed of delivering value in the long term. More backlogs also mean more dependencies and reduced value delivered. Let's investigate why. When an organization introduces more team backlogs for the same product, then teams tend to focus on a part of the whole product and become less cross-functional, as Figure 10.4 illustrates. That inevitably leads to artificial dependencies between feature parts across multiple teams.

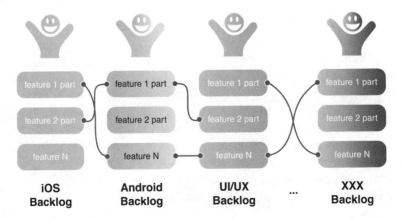

Figure 10.4
Feature dependencies between teams.

The organization starts managing the dependencies, instead of eliminating them.[11] The more dependencies, the less probability that a customer-centric feature will be "done" in an iteration. Dependencies affect the feature lead time, which in turn introduces a new form of organizational stress, because now the speed of development is slowing down. Furthermore, teams working on their own team backlog have a narrow view of the whole product and do not realize when they are working on low-value work from the customer's perspective.

The Team Did Not Work on the Most Important Features

In 2019, we worked with a product group that contained three feature teams. They were working on a complex banking solution. By the time we joined them, they had already kicked off three cross-functional feature teams with local backlogs. We asked the "Product Owners" and "Chief Product Owner" to create a single Product Backlog as an experiment. It became evident to us that work was not distributed evenly in a single Product Backlog, as you can see in Figure 10.5.

Figure 10.5
Single Product Backlog.

The sticky notes' colors represent different parts of the product from the customer's perspective. Having three backlogs meant that teams were suboptimizing the whole and working on the less critical features. That experiment convinced the Chief Product Owner that having three local backlogs was suboptimal. Fake "Product Owner" roles were eliminated, and the teams started working with a single Product Backlog.

Let's add loops R3 and R4 to the diagram in Figure 10.3. R3 is about the increasing number of dependencies that result from the growing number of local backlogs. The more dependencies between backlogs, the less probability that a feature can be completed ("done") during the Sprint. This inevitably affects average lead time, leads to more stress, and triggers more "work harder" behavior. The loop R4 is about the potential value delivered to the market, which decreases with the increasing number of backlogs. Less value means more organizational stress and again, more "work harder" behavior. The three reinforcing loops R2, R3, and R4 create a triple "fixes that backfire" archetype with B1 (see Figure 10.6).

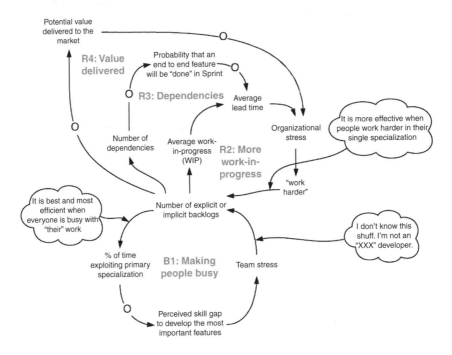

Figure 10.6
Making people busy fix that backfires.

The central theme of the pattern "fixes that backfire" is that people take reasonable measures to remedy an unwanted situation. Still, after the "fix," the problem comes back—sometimes in a different form—and is more robust than before. Taking more of the same actions just worsens the situation: More backlogs → more problems → longer lead time → more organizational stress. Now let's see how to redesign this system to optimize value instead of aiming to make people busy.

Optimizing Value and Multifunctional Learning

The fundamental obstacle to optimize for value delivery while maximizing throughput and minimizing cycle time is the absence of multi-skilled specialists, which allows the team to balance the workload across its members.

You can consider implementing an optimizing value strategy in two steps:

Step 1. Create a single customer-centric Product Backlog that reflects the current understanding of the most important features from a customer perspective.

Step 2. Ask the team(s) to respect, in general, the order of the customer-centric Product Backlog in development.

Working from a single Product Backlog creates an inevitable knowledge gap in single-skilled team members. The larger the knowledge gap, the more that the developers need to work together and help others in the team acquire additional skills. Over time, team members develop secondary or even tertiary skills and become multi-skilled specialists. Look at the diagram in Figure 10.7.

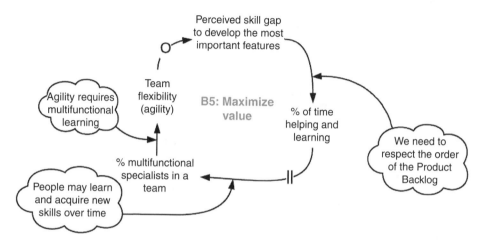

Figure 10.7
Optimizing value requires multifunctional learning.

Pay attention to the mental models: "We need to respect the order of the Product Backlog," "People may learn and acquire new skills over time," and "Agility requires multi-skilled team members."

Frankly, there is nothing new about the concept of multifunctional specialists and cross-functional learning. In the famous "The New New Product Development Game" paper,[12] multifunctional learning is identified as one of the main characteristics of highly effective teams. Multifunctional specialists were introduced in Toyota a long time ago by Taiichi Ohno.

We often hear the argument: "We understand the idea behind that. But still, a deep specialist will be more effective and knowledgeable than a cross-trained one." And we agree with this argument. But Agile organizations do not train people to create efficient resources. Instead, they form teams capable of embracing change and minimizing bottlenecks. Remember, when the system is heavily loaded, even a small change in capacity can lead to a significant difference in cycle time. We investigated this issue in depth in Chapter 3, "Optimize for Adaptiveness." In *Managing the Design Factory*, Donald G. Reinertsen writes:

> *This ability of autonomous teams to align resources to bottlenecks is extremely important because it minimizes queues in the development process. Since these bottlenecks can shift rapidly and unpredictably during a program, the flexibility of team members to work outside of specialty is a critical tool for dealing with such bottlenecks.*[13]

Culture of Narrow Specialists

We have seen many Agile teams apply fixes by having each member work efficiently on their own single specialty—the resource utilization strategy. The quick fix of increasing the number of backlogs has a side effect that weakens the system's natural ability to implement the more fundamental correction. When an Agile team adopts the resource utilization strategy and maintains it for some time, a culture of narrow specialists is installed. It takes a lot of effort, leadership support, and patience to overcome the resistance to apply the fundamental solution instead. In the CLD in Figure 10.8, the reinforcing loop R6 corresponds to the culture of narrow specialists.

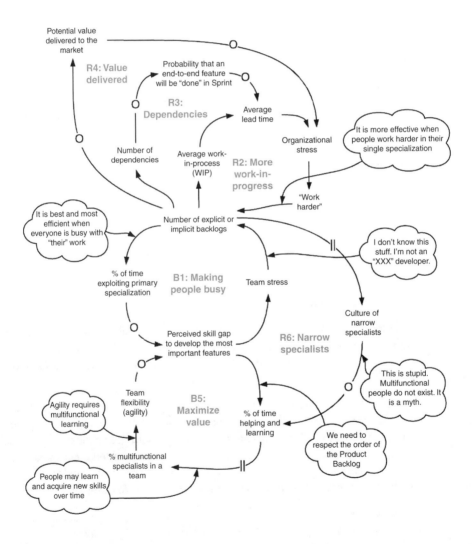

Figure 10.8

Culture of narrow specialists dynamic.

Pay attention to the mental model: "This is stupid. Multifunctional people do not exist. It's a myth." With the help of CLDs, we've investigated the implications of learning disability in teams. Quick fixes have long-term consequences. The act of increasing the number of explicit or implicit backlogs spawns lots of problems: intensive WIP, queues, long lead times, organizational stress, less value delivered. The solution to those negative consequences is multifunctional learning.

Multifunctional learning is the heart of agility.

How to Optimize for Multifunctional Learning

We often face similar questions and objections related to the concepts of multifunctional learning. Let's go over some of them.

- "I've been learning . . . for several years in a row. It is impossible to become a deep specialist in a short time." We agree immediately. It's true. But the goal is *not* to clone a unique specialist, but rather to influence the bottleneck.

- "We will slow down a lot if we start helping each other and learn." Helping coworkers expands the bottleneck, reduces WIP, shortens lead time according to Little's law, and improves performance in a system level. People must make the trade-off between short-term benefits and the more speculative benefits of long-term investment.

- "We don't have time for training." The best way to learn, from our point of view, is continuously working in three modes: pairing, mob programming, and swarming. Thus, you can start learning tomorrow by sitting next to an expert and doing some pair work with that person.

- "A drop in quality is inevitable." This might happen, and the team can remedy that problem by engaging in pair development, swarming, and mob development. These techniques involve constant feedback loops and continuous reviews. Engineering practices are also important— in particular, automated testing, test-driven development, and, in case of software development, writing clean code and emergent architecture practices, without which you cannot flourish in Agile development.

- "You require a five-year university study to do this work. There's no way you can learn this with a two-week training and some pairing." Yes, there are exceptions that cannot be addressed easily by multifunctional learning.

There are many options to deal with the situation when Agile teams are used to working in "make people busy" mode. But first of all, you need to reveal the system to itself and create awareness. How to do that?

1. Point out the tendency of the team to focus on resource utilization instead of increasing agility.

2. Conduct a system modeling workshop and let people gain insights into the "making everyone busy" strategy and the consequences associated with it. Use the system diagrams presented in this book for inspiration.

3. Create an awareness that people are working on the less critical stuff from a customer per-spective by creating a single queue of requirements (Product Backlog). When possible, use the "cold turkey" strategy and move to a single queue overnight.

4. Gradually reduce the number of queues (backlogs) over time if there is a painful knowledge gap.

We'll also provide some other practical tools and techniques that can help Agile teams to enable multifunctional learning.

Provide Enabling Structures

Once we were asked to observe the product group in a midsized service organization. Management complained that developers were not willing to learn new skills and help each other. Another point of concern was features that usually spanned multiple Sprints to become "done." Sometimes the teams were able to reach a Sprint Goal, but that happened only rarely. We rushed to the headquarters to see the situation for ourselves. Table 10.1 shows the results of our observations, organized according to the iceberg model.

Table 10.1   Observation Results

Patterns of behavior	Features are spanning multiple Sprints
	Scrum Master is balancing the workloads of team members during Sprint Planning
	Developers do not help each other in a Sprint and exploit their primary skills
	Developers identify the main skills bottleneck during Sprint Planning and pull technical debt into the Sprint instead of finding ways to alleviate the bottleneck
System structure	No slack time for learning
	Functional managers (Java, QA, etc.) heavily influence salaries and perform performance appraisals
	Tech leads make key architectural and technical decisions
	Scrum Masters take part in a performance appraisal along with tech leads
Mental models	"Scrum Master is just a manager"
	"People should be busy in a Sprint"
	"Shared team accountability is a myth"
	"The team is productive when its members are productive individually"

We presented this iceberg to the product group—it was quite an eye-opener. From our point of view, the current organizational structures did not support multifunctional learning and improving cross-functionality in teams. So, which actions should one undertake in this situation? First, don't try to push harder to influence people's behavior. Most likely, you will encounter compensating feedback. The system is in a stable state. The second law of the fifth discipline is:

The harder you push, the harder the system pushes back.[14]

The more effort you expend trying to improve matters, the more effort that seems to be required. Instead, remove forces that are responsible for undesirable behavior. Not surprisingly, some of our recommendations to the product group were as follows:

- Remove the functional manager roles and establish a cross-functional manager position (Guidelines 11 and 12 from Chapter 4, "Agile Organizational Design") so that managers encourage multi-skill growth.

- Reduce the number of titles and leave one "product developer" title for everyone so that people can't use it as an excuse to work on something else.

- Introduce multifunctional career paths (Guideline 12 from Chapter 4, "Agile Organizational Design") so that the organization properly values multi-skilled people.

- Plan additional slack time for education and training.

It took a while to introduce the recommended changes, but slowly teams started acquiring additional skills. The flow smoothed out, and eventually management was happy with the changes.

Learning and mastering is a natural trait for human beings. But organizational structures may impede learning and generate dysfunctional behaviors. The prevailing mental model might suggest that people do not care or want to learn, but the organizational system often makes it hard to do so. Resolving organizational impediments and creating enabling structures creates the necessary conditions for cross-functional learning.

Visualize Flow of Work

Visualization is critical for any Agile organizations—it reveals the queues and helps to optimize the flow of work. In digital service and development organizations, in contrast to production and assembly lines, inventory is invisible. It is stored on hardware disks, and walking along the office doesn't give you an overview of how much waste is really being created.

Queues are the hidden source of most development waste. They are concealed from view in our financial systems. Because they are composed of information, not physical objects, they are hard to spot in the workplace.[15]

If we could do just one single thing when coaching a team, we would visualize the flow of the work. By visualizing the flow of work, one can see the bottlenecks and create awareness. Let us share one story that illustrates this idea.

Coaching the Busy Team

We were coaching an overgrown (20 individuals) team in an outsourcing software company. The group was always behind the schedule and had a poor track record in the department. Management was dissatisfied, blamed developers, and constantly pushed them to work harder.

When we started working with them, morale was way down. We observed that the team wasn't really a team. They operated in strict silos. Subgroups were formed within the team (business analysis, testing, coding, etc.) that made themselves locally efficient at the expense of the performance of the whole. Everyone just "threw their work over the wall" and felt responsible just for the piece of work that they personally owned.

We guessed that inventory was enormous and suggested that the team visualize their work first. A board photo (Figure 10.9) shows a vast WIP that became apparent after the team created a simple visual tool with several columns that reflected the team's workflow.

Figure 10.9
Work-in-progress (WIP).

We asked the group what they noticed on the wall during the first Daily Scrum that happened after this exercise. The answer: "A huge amount of work that is started but not completed." They also detected that testers had been overwhelmed with work and were the bottleneck. That wasn't something they didn't notice before. But now, after we visualized the flow, it created awareness for everyone. We revealed the system to itself.

The next question from us was "What are you going to do about it?" We got a predictable answer: "We need more testers." We responded: "Okay! But before we get them, what is the point of starting new work—for instance, in Java—that stays in a queue in front of the QA column?" We received another predictable answer from programmers: "We're not able to test. Unfortunately, we cannot help." And then a wonderful moment happened. The QA people spoke up and pointed out the areas of work where they would love to receive help from others. They said they would create scripts for exploratory testing and provide them to the rest of the team so that programmers could help.

Soon the group returned to their places and attacked the bottleneck. In a while, the flow improved, and lead times decreased.

Introduce a Star Map

A *star map* is a simple competency matrix that visualizes the cross-functionality of the specific team. It reveals gaps in knowledge and uncovers potential bottlenecks. The rows of the matrix are just a list of team members; the columns contain the competencies and skills needed to deliver value. You can use various symbols to fill the matrix, but the simplest set that we used were as follows:

- "Star" is a deep expertise in a particular skill.

- "Dot" is an intermediate skill.

- "Book"—I want to develop this competence to help the team later.

- "Skull"—In no case do I want to do this, just do not count on me.

Figure 10.10 provides an example of a star map.

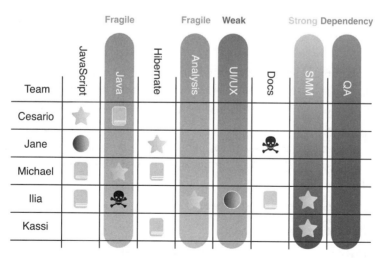

Figure 10.10
Example star map.

Ideally, we would like to see two or more stars in each column, because then the team becomes truly flexible and can fight the peak loads. The combination of a star and a dot is a good one, too. If we find columns with no stars, this is a wake-up call. The team needs coaching and assistance; otherwise, they might have quality problems with work in this competence. But the most problematic columns, in which there are no designations (except for books), indicate dependence on external expertise. Dependencies rob the team of autonomy and prevent the delivery of value. Dependencies block work and significantly increase lead time and, as a result, reduce organizational flexibility.

You can conduct a workshop with the team to initialize the competency matrix. Here are the steps to follow in this workshop:

Step 1. Tell the team about the tool and what it is used for.

Step 2. Gather all the skills and competencies to deliver a releasable increment. Bring the Definition of Done (DoD) and Product Backlog as needed. Use the 1-2-4-All[16] structure to collect the various skills.

Step 3. Cluster the acquired skills and remove duplicates.

Step 4. Agree on the symbols ("star," "book," "shard," "dot") and ask team members to change or expand this set. Define the concrete criteria for each symbol if needed.

Step 5. Create a large paper rectangle on the floor (don't skimp on paper and space) and draw the columns and rows. Fill in the team members' names and skills (we often use stickers for this).

Step 6. Set the timebox (15–20 minutes) and let the team organize themselves by filling in the matrix.

Step 7. Discuss your findings. Ask questions: "What do you notice?" "What are we best at?" "What are the weak links?" "What should we pay attention to?" "What surprised you?" "What is worth clarifying?" "What is puzzling?" You can use the What, So What, Now What[17] structure for this purpose.

Based on the results of the workshop, invite the team to identify further steps to strengthen their cross-functionality. You can use the Testable Improvements[18] Scrum pattern for planning the next steps. Agree when you will do the next inspection and adaptation of the matrix.

Each time we conduct this workshop, we are surprised with the volume of book symbols that are placed on the matrix. People want to learn! By conducting the workshop, we just create the conditions where the natural desire of people to improve and learn and become better versions of themselves is revealed.

Here are a few guidelines for using the star map:

- Inspect the tool at least once per quarter.

- The workshop should end with concrete steps to improve cross-functionality. Remember that inspection without adaptation is useless.

- Post the star map as an Information Radiator in a team room.

Use Three Modes of Development

We are convinced that there is no better way to strengthen cross-functionality and simultaneously reduce WIP in an Agile team than by continually working in one of three modes illustrated in Figure 10.11 and described here:

Pairing
(WIP>1)

Mob programming
(WIP=1)

Swarming
(WIP=1)

Figure 10.11
Three modes of development.

- **Pair programming:** Working on one or more features in parallel in pairs.

- **Swarming:** Working on one feature at a time (WIP = 1), but not in a structured way; teams self-organize their work. They could work in several pairs or triads or any other way.

- **Mob programming:** Working serially on one feature—a technique that has been gaining momentum in recent years. The team can work on one feature at a time by using one computer and a large screen/projector.

Mobbing is a single-piece flow activity. From a flow efficiency perspective, it is the most efficient way to develop, if the team can reduce the transaction costs to the point where it becomes economically feasible to work on one feature from the start to done states. Let's describe what a typical day for a team that works in single-piece flow looks like.

The Day of a Team

During the Daily Scrum, the team discusses the next important feature that is needed to achieve the Sprint Goal. The team briefly discusses the plan for the day and decides to start with parallelization and pair programming. Multiple pairs of developers start to set up a test suite by writing acceptance tests and implement a thin slice of functionality for each test. Another pair focuses on the user interface, while another pair further clarifies the requirements by adding more acceptance tests. The team works in pair programming mode for several hours, and then everyone gets together to discuss the next steps and share what they have learned. The team agrees that now there is no way to effectively parallelize the work, so they decide to continue with integrating their work in a mob programming mode. At the end of the day, the feature is tested, and one hour is left to write the documentation. The developers go into swarming mode, forming two subgroups that work on the documentation in parallel and complete the feature by the end of the day.

Working in three modes has many advantages. Here, we list just some of them:

- It is one of the best ways to enable multifunctional learning in a team.

- No or little extra code review is needed.

- Trust increases, as the team is forced to learn to negotiate and listen to different points of view, to come to a consensus.

- No transfers or losses of information occur.

- There is collective code ownership.

- High-quality decisions are made, because everyone knows what is going on.

- With perfect flow, the team works on one feature at a time—that is, in one-piece flow (WIP = 1).

Team Working in Three Modes Continuously

One company that works in this way continually is a payment systems company with which we collaborated. From the very first Sprint, 35 developers in 6 feature teams began to work in the format of pair programming, mob programming, and swarming every day. The visualization of the work of such teams looks surprisingly simple, as Figure 10.12 illustrates.

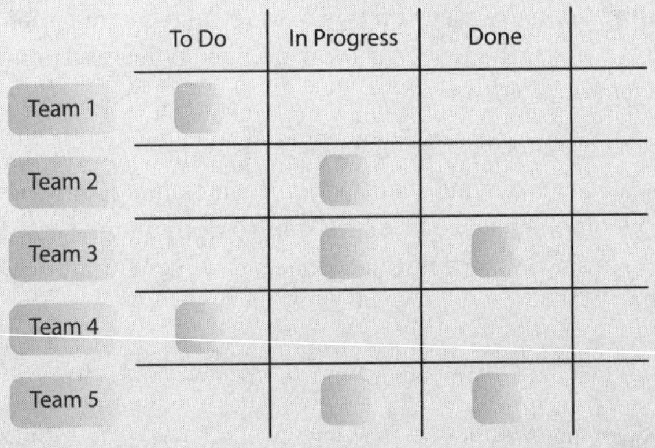

	To Do	In Progress	Done	
Team 1	▢			
Team 2		▢		
Team 3		▢	▢	
Team 4	▢			
Team 5		▢	▢	

Figure 10.12
Simple visualization when using three modes of development.

It's just three columns that are crossed by the team swim lanes. Each team pulls a couple of features at the Sprint Planning and converts them to a "releasable" state at the end of the Sprint.

The three modes of development are so counterintuitive that it takes a lot of patience and training to initially implement them. To ensure that your approach to the three modes is successful, we suggest that you follow these guidelines:

- Start with short mob-programming sessions of no more than two hours, several times a week. Involve volunteers—there is nothing worse than people who are forced to do something they don't like. Try to not break this rule.

- End each session with a retrospective.

- Present the three modes as an experiment. This will create an atmosphere of psychological safety and trust.

- Conduct the first sessions with no more than three to five people to reduce stress and go through the storming stage faster.

- The best places to hold the first few sessions are meeting rooms, where nothing distracts from work.

- Have a large whiteboard or flipchart sheets available to visualize ideas and diagrams.

- In the first sessions, use typical code *kata*—code challenges focused on improving skill and technique—before moving on to more complicated tasks.

- Install a familiar working environment and editor for writing code in advance on the machine you will be using.

- Set up a large visual timer for timeboxes—for example, on a tablet.

- Introduce the *pomodoro* technique and take frequent breaks every 20–30 minutes to relieve fatigue.

- Use the "two legs" rule. If someone doesn't like the session or is just tired, they can just leave, switching to something more useful.

We often invite teams to actively experiment with the three modes for a month. After that, they can decide for themselves whether to return to their previous style of work or continue. As a rule, a month is enough for the main benefits to become visible for any Agile team. Most teams continue to work this way.

Introduce Slack Time

Full utilization does not lead to better system performance. Under full utilization, there is no room to absorb variation in work. Suppose an urgent bug crops up during a Sprint. If a team is operating at full capacity, they will have no capacity available to handle that bug. Under pressure, the team might neglect writing tests, avoid refactoring, or create some other form of technical debt to complete the work on time.

Under full utilization, there is also no space for innovation, creativity, or learning. Why? If a team has a tight schedule, muscle memory makes people exploit their primary specializations and current skills instead of sharing knowledge and looking for innovative ways to solve the problem. You can read more about this issue in the documentation for the Scrum pattern "Teams That Finish Early Accelerate Faster."[19]

In recently formed cross-functional teams, people are actively unlearning previous experiences and learning unfamiliar approaches like pairing, mob programming, and swarming. Quite often they are experiencing stress. For this reason, we recommend using the Slack Time practice described in eXtreme Programming. It is a time buffer that a team explicitly designates in an iteration for unexpected work and multifunctional learning.

> Slack is the time when reinvention happens. It is time when you are not 100 percent busy doing the operational business of your firm. Slack at all levels is necessary to make the organization work effectively and to grow. It is the lubricant of change.[20]

A slack task is:

- A valuable task that helps the team work more effectively
- A task that can be instantly postponed for an iteration without doing lasting damage

Slack time has many forms and could be used for the following activities:

- Book clubs
- Self-directed discovery and exploration time
- Adding tests to legacy code
- Paying off technical debt
- Architectural redesign
- Participating in communities of practice

Develop Explicit Agreements

When multiple Agile teams are working on the same product, some people inevitably experience knowledge gaps. This is expected and normal. In our experience, creating an explicit agreement about how teams will handle periods of underutilization helps them a lot and decreases ambiguity. We've already described this process in Chapter 9, "Launching the Product Group." Here we provide an example.

Underutilization Agreements

In one of our clients' product groups, five teams were restructured into feature teams after two months of preparation. They were properly educated before the lift-off and knew in advance they would encounter knowledge gaps. The Scrum Master facilitated a workshop and teams came up with a concrete algorithm for how to deal with underutilization. Here it is:

1. Help the team using three modes (pairing, mob programming, swarming).

2. Help other teams.

3. Learn new skills.

4. Resolve technical debt.

5. If the other points are irrelevant, talk to the Product Owner and take a new item from the Product Backlog.

We also observed some Agile teams using WIP limits to enable learning. For instance, a team pulls at least one unfamiliar item (different technology, business domain) into the Sprint.

Coaching Multifunctional Learning Summary

The work of solving a complex problem (for example, a feature) with interdependent tasks is rarely distributed evenly among the people in a cross-functional team. In general, when team members cannot handle tasks outside their specialty—because of a knowledge gap—some will be over-loaded while others are idle. The usual response to this challenge is for the idle people to start new work that corresponds to their primary specialization. Developers become efficient individually, but this process increases rework, leads to more handovers, and decreases the overall feature cycle time.

The solution is a team of multi-skilled specialists. A team of multitalented people will experience fewer bottlenecks, as they can help overloaded team members and thereby reduce the end-to-end time needed to solve a complex problem. The team develops multi-skilled members by working in the three preferred modes—pairing, mob programming, and swarming—continuously. Some other techniques they can use are the star map, visualization of the workflow, and slack time.

Dealing with Recurrent Complex Problems in Teams: Systems Team Coaching

As Russell Ackoff reminds us, "The performance of the system depends on how its parts interact, not on how they act taken separately."[21] Thus, you can improve the performance of a system by improving the interactions of its parts. Applying this wisdom to teams that solve complex problems with interdependent tasks—a social system—suggests that you can improve the performance of a team by improving how the team members interact.

Systems coaching for teams takes a systems approach and focuses on how team members' interactions and relationships influence the performance of the team as a whole. How does a team keep itself stable while revisiting the same problems over and over and not improving performance?

Working in a team means communicating, and that means influencing other people in the team. Rather than focusing on individuals or the content of what is said, ideally you will take a holistic approach to identify the circular relationships to help the team understand how their thinking and behavior led to their current reality.

Working with an individual outside their team reduces the possibility for overall improvement. Consider, for example, a group of rock-star developers who individually possess the necessary competencies to a large extent, but are nevertheless not effective when working collectively as a team. The mechanistic approach is to look at which individuals might cause these problems and then work with those people. Such a practice is undoubtedly not systemic in nature and assumes there is a root cause of the issues. Diagnosing individuals also does not account for team dynamics, team synergy, the added value of cooperation, or the dysfunction that can arise when working together.

For example, when a team member comes late to meetings, repeatedly slowing the team down, do you focus on that individual? Or do you instead focus on the whole team? In the systems approach, we address the entire team and make transparent to the team how it allows the individual to come late to meetings: *If you're part of the system, you're part of the problem.* There is no root cause for complex problems; there is no blame, because all team members play their role in creating their current reality. Therefore, the golden rule of systems team coaching is simple: Address the team as a whole (see Figure 10.13).

In team coaching, the system or the team is perceived and addressed as one unitary and coherent client whole.[7]

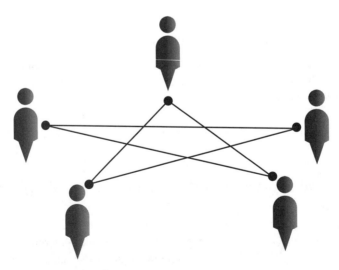

Figure 10.13
Interactions and relationships.

That is why the client of a systems coach is the system and its relationships. By improving the interactions, you enhance the synergy between individuals in the teams.

Insights from Systems Coaching

Before we describe our preferred techniques for systems coaching, we would like to share some essential insights upon which we build. When we work with teams, we rely on the following systems insights:

- An Agile team is a social system. A social system has a tendency to remain in a stable state, called *homeostasis*. Homeostasis ensures that the internal conditions remain relatively stable while the environment changes. The team wants the internal conditions to remain stable because that satisfies the outside expectations of the team.

- The stable interaction patterns in a team come mainly from the individuals' mental models and resulting behaviors.

- Observing the team's interactions can uncover interaction patterns that show how a team keeps itself in a stable/blocking state.

- You can probably never determine the root cause of a complex problem. And even if you could, others will likely bring in alternative explanations and you could end up assigning blame instead of solving problems. Therefore, do not look for root cause explanations, but instead help the team discover how their structures and thinking may be contributing to their current problems.

- A team can define systems improvement actions when team members understand how they keep themselves in the current problematic state.

- Each team is part of a larger system that influences its performance.

Next, we describe techniques that you can use for the following purposes:

1. Perform circular observations to identify patterns of interactions

2. Assess the current team situation

In these techniques, the overarching theme is to not think about linear cause-and-effect relationships and explanations, but rather loops of influence. These feedback loops help to make transparent the patterns and underlying mental models.

Perform Circular Observations to Identify Patterns of Interactions

The following dialogue describes a typical dynamic we have experienced many times in one form or another, where emotions are running high in a team during Sprint Planning. Consider the conversation that might happen between the Product Owner and the developers.

Product Owner: This feature is important to us. Can you get it done in the coming Sprint?

Team Member 1: It's too vague . . .

Product Owner: When can you pick up the feature?

Team Member 1: We need to make an estimate, so we need more details to understand exactly what to build.

Product Owner: I will detail it some more this afternoon. Can you then tell me what you will deliver in the current Sprint?

Team Member 3: It does not matter. Let them develop it, then I'll test it, and we will see how it goes . . .

Product Owner: This is unacceptable. I have to know when the feature will be done.

Team Member 2: We use Agile, so calculate the date using our velocity, and you'll know.

Based on this dialogue, which, if any, of the following actions would you take?

1. Focus on what's being said to understand the argument and explain who is right and who is wrong?

2. Work with the people to analyze what is going on and analyze the root cause?

3. Point out how each individual behaves in the current situation?

4. Look for patterns in interactions and make them transparent?

5. Ask the team which actions they would take?

Options 1 and 2 are about analyzing and finding explanations for the behaviors. One could expect to find "explanations" such as the following:

- The Product Owner believes that the team can predict the future. If the Product Owner would prepare better and add more details, then everything would improve.

- The team members are unprofessional. If they were committed, they would give good estimations.

- The Product Owner is not capable. We need to replace the Product Owner.

Taking such positions assumes there is a root cause and will likely increase conflict. People will defend their positions, and in the end there will be drama instead of an improved situation.

Based on the systems insights previously discussed, we would most often choose option 3, 4, or 5 and avoid looking for linear explanations. Instead, we would seek to reveal patterns of low-quality interactions. But how do you help the team discover these patterns?

Revealing Patterns of Interaction

We like to say that when you listen and observe a particular interaction three times, you can consider it potentially to be a systems issue. At the third observation, you can think "Bingo!" and ask yourself: What is going on here? Which thinking is generating this recurring behavior? How does the team keep repeating itself? What are the loops that keep this team from progressing? Figure 10.14. shows a simple interaction loop.

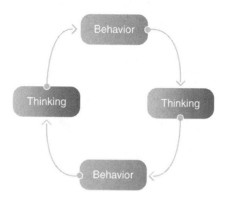

Figure 10.14
Simple interaction loop.

Loops produce stable patterns of behavior, and they are very powerful. A loop for the previous example dialogue can be discovered using the following thinking format:

The more the Product Owner shows behavior <A>, the more the team thinks <B>.

The more the team thinks <B>, the more the team shows behavior <C>.

The more the team shows behavior <C>, the more the Product Owner thinks <D>.

The more the Product Owner thinks <D>, the more the Product Owner shows behavior <A>.

Let us use this thinking format in our example and discover a potential loop. If you look back at the example dialogue, what do you notice? We observed at least three remarkable points:

- The team does not answer the Product Owner's question three times in a row. Bingo! That could be a pattern!

- The Product Owner is active, pressuring the team to make a commitment and promising to add details.

- The team is reactive, not taking responsibility.

Based on the conversation, one could imagine the following loop.

The more the Product Owner shows behavior <Pressure the team to commit>, the more the team thinks <We have to be careful>.

The more the team thinks <We have to be careful>, the more the team shows behavior <Hold back and ask for more details>.

The more the team shows behavior <Hold back and ask for more details>, the more the Product Owner thinks <The team is passive and is not committed>.

The more the Product Owner thinks <The team is passive and is not committed>, the more the Product Owner shows behavior <Pressure the team to commit>.

Figure 10.15 illustrates this dynamic.

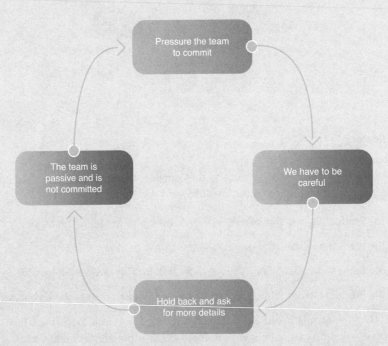

Figure 10.15
Example interaction loop.

If such a loop is present, your goal is to help the team discover its existence by asking questions and sharing observations. Let's see how this dialogue progressed further and how we helped the team become aware of their situation:

> **Me:** You are a team. Does your organization expect you to provide your customers with an estimate?
>
> **Product Owner:** My manager expects commitment. (*speaking for the team*)
>
> **Me:** (*interrupting the Product Owner*) Can't the team answer for themselves?

Product Owner: Yes, but . . .

Me: Great. Team, please go ahead.

Team Member 1: You know, it's impossible to predict the future isn't it? (*not answering*)

Team Member 2: Exactly, and they always hold us accountable for it. (*not answering; who is 'they'?*)

Me: I notice that you are not answering my question. Back to my question again, it is important that we understand what is expected of the team. So, do you know if your organization expects you to provide estimates?

Team Member 1: We can only commit to an estimate when the Product Owner provides us with enough details. (*not answering, not taking ownership of the issue*)

Me: (*Bingo!*) I asked you a question three times, and you keep avoiding to answer. Do you recognize this as well? Maybe there are other stakeholders whose questions you do not answer?

Team Member 1: No, that almost never happens.

Me: (*what about others?*) Do others think so, too?

Team Member 3: I am not so sure. I think it happens quite often. I agree that it is our responsibility to provide answers to our stakeholders when they ask us.

Me: Great.

Team Member 1: Okay, but we cannot do anything about the estimates. The Product Owner needs to provide us with clear requirements.

Me: (*speaks in the third person about the Product Owner*) I see you are talking to me, but the Product Owner is sitting there. Please tell him directly.

Notice that instead of focusing on the content of the interaction, we focused on its quality. The question is not "What do the people say?", but rather "How are they saying it?" You are not looking for linear cause–effect relationships, but instead looking to make transparent the circular behaviors, the quality of the interactions, and the underlying thinking.

Some Example Questions for Preparing a Session

We close this section with some example questions you can consider asking the teams to help discover patterns of interaction:

- What is happening now?

- What stands out in your communication?

- What assumptions are you making when you say that?

- How do you as a group keep this situation intact?

We end this section with a few remarks about the function of *undesired behavior*.

Undesired Behavior

Undesired behavior often has an important function. Instead of "getting rid of it as quickly as possible," you can instead use it to discover:

- What this behavior shows that so desperately needs to be brought to the organization's attention
- What issue is carefully hidden in the system

Persistent undesired behavior could be a symptom of a team or system under pressure that guides you toward an obstacle to the team's progress. You can discover the system dynamics by exploring the following questions:

- What is so bad about that behavior?
- For which problem is this undesired behavior a good solution?
- Which disaster would happen if the undesired behavior stopped?
- What remains out of the picture for as long as this behavior continues?

There are many more types of questions you can consider that go beyond the scope of this book. We strongly recommend the book *Making Questions Work* by Dorothy Strachan[22] for a deep dive into the art of asking questions. For a deep dive into systems coaching, we recommend the book *Systemic Team and Organizational Coaching* by Alain Cardon.[7]

Team's System Assessment

We have had many conversations with managers about their challenges in working with Agile teams. To our surprise, we noticed the following recurring problem: "We want the team to do X, but they do not want to do X or seem to care about X. We have been at problem X for a long time and we are not making any significant progress."

In such a situation, there can be many different dynamics at play. For example:

- X does not provide any value for the team or its members.
- The team does not feel ownership of the problem that X is intended to fix.
- The team thinks that X is not the right solution and might have a much better one.
- And many more . . .

What stood out during these conversations was that the organization and team can be stuck in the same situation for a long time. A systems assessment might provide ideas for finding a way out.

The Systems Assessment Workshop

The goal of the Systems Assessment workshop is to help the team understand the systems forces that are keeping them in a stable but suboptimal state. With that understanding, the team can then generate actions for improvement.

In the workshop, we do the following:

1. Understand the current situation of the team in the organization's context. Why? Because the team is part of a larger system and has to take into account the inseparable relationship with its context.

2. Investigate why the team is blocked. Why? This gives ideas about what can be done to get things moving again.

   Materials needed: Pens, Post-Its, a whiteboard/flipchart and large prints of the systems assessment canvas.

   Systems assessment canvas: Use the canvas to discover relevant information about the team's current state (see Figure 10.16).

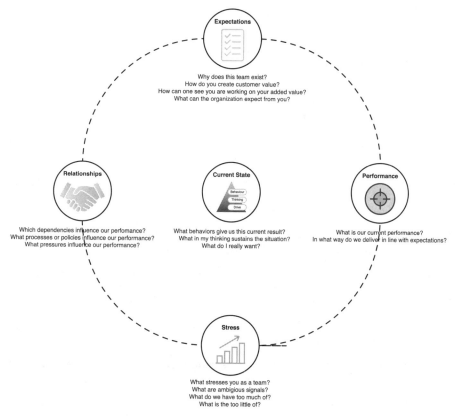

Figure 10.16

Assessment canvas.

In the middle of the canvas is the iceberg model. We use this to visualize the team's current behavior, thinking, and drive. Around the iceberg model, you can see four areas that influence the current state. These areas represent the context of the team.

- **Relationships:** Captures the external dependencies, pressures, policies, or processes that influence the team.

- **Stress:** Captures the imbalances in interactions with the surrounding environment.

- **Expectations:** Captures the team's understanding of their role or function within the larger organization.

- **Performance:** Captures the team's current performance in relation to the expectations.

The systems assessment investigates how the context (expectations, stress, performance, and relationships) and the current team's iceberg keep the team in a stable state regarding their problem. By answering and discussing the questions on the canvas, the team starts to understand what is keeping them in their stable state.

Structuring the invitation: Invite the team to express their current team challenge using the canvas.

Sequence of steps: Introduce the canvas by describing the steps:

Step 1. Understand the current context.

Step 2. Understand how the team keeps itself blocked.

Step 1: Understand the Current Context

In small groups explore the current situation using the questions on the canvas section. Form small groups and ask them to fill the canvas one section at a time.

- When they're done, invite the group to share their results using a diverge–merge technique.

- Ask each group to refine their section based on new insights.

- Merge the canvases of the whole group into one. Use affinity mapping to identify common themes, group similar items, and remove duplicate items.

- Ask the whole group, "What does the canvas reveal?" Use 1-2-4-All with larger groups.

With those data in hand, the team then looks for circular cause–effect relationships in Step 2.

Step 2: Understand Why the Team Is Not Making Progress

Use the canvas in Figure 10.17 to reflect on how the current expectations, relationships, behaviors, and thinking prevent the team from being successful.

What keeps us blocked?

What is the problem?
How does the context/mental model/goals relate and support/block the team from making progress?
What do we gain from remaining in this state?

Actions to break free

Where can we bring change?

Figure 10.17
Reflection canvas.

Capture the end result and insights as input for future sessions. The last activity is to generate actions to break free and move toward their future state. Invite the team to identify further steps by, for example, using the liberating structure 15% Solutions[23] and the serious game Now, How, Wow.[24]

Possible Next Steps

A follow-up exercise could be for the team to clarify where it wants to be in the future. Why? Team members need a goal to determine if they are making progress. Without a learning goal and a performance goal, it becomes very difficult to coach the team.

Let us share an example from one of our clients.

Teams Stuck Arguing with Management

We were working with a group of 17 dev-ops teams in an energy services company. Some teams repeatedly delivered low-quality products with lots of bugs. Customers were complaining and management was convinced that the teams were at fault. So, they asked us to come over and "fix" the teams. Early on, we decided to perform an assessment of the situation.

We started by joining some of the teams in meetings to get an overview of their behaviors. Using the iceberg model, we found:

- Sighing and puffing in meetings

- Many people acting as observers in meetings instead of as participants

- Disengagement from discussions when the ideas of others did not match their ideas
- People assuming that they understood what the others meant
- People not asking each other for the reasoning behind statements
- People not confronting each other

Next, we invited the team to do the Systems Assessment workshop. We started with the Performance and Expectations blocks. We stressed the need to focus on facts and to leave thinking about solutions or causes for later in the workshop. Following is a summary of the results.

Performance	Expectations
What is our current performance?	**What can be expected of us?**
- We create a lot of functional errors. - Currently, we measure success by delivering story points and components. When we connected these components to each other a couple of months ago after building for a year and put something in the process, everything broke.	- Ensure that we deliver good quality to our customers. - Solve user problems, including second-line support calls. - Implement new functionality that makes users trade more effectively. - Solve our own impediments. - Provide reliable forecasts to our Product Owner.
In what way do we deliver in line with expectations?	**How do we add value?**
We deliver way too slowly compared to what management expects.	- Ensure users can trade in the short term. - Improve the trading process in the long term.

After this, the team was eager to explain why their performance was so bad. We used the Stress and Relationships blocks for that. The results are summarized in the following blocks.

Stress	Relationships
What are ambiguous signals?	**Which dependencies influence our performance?**
• Management wants to jointly come up with better solutions, but is not open to what the team thinks.	• The requirements are unclear to us, so we have to make lots of business domain decisions by ourselves. But we do not understand the domain well enough to make the right decisions. When we ask the business for clarification, we have to wait days to weeks to get an answer.
• Management wants good quality and no technical debt, but focuses on delivery on a certain date at all costs.	
• Management wants ownership in our team, but imposes a lot of prescriptive processes and command and control on us,	
• Management wants team responsibility, but appeals to people individually instead of as a team.	• For most of our user stories, we need other Scrum teams to deliver their parts.
What do we have too much of?	• We deliver software and after many weeks we finally get feedback. Most of the time the feedback includes lots of defects.
• We have too much work, too many rules, and too much micromanagement.	
What do we have too little of from the organization?	
• Overview of direction and release goals, clarity about the business vision, clarity about the architecture direction, room for self-management, respect, appreciation.	

With the context information on the walls, the next step was to make sense of it. We invited the team to discover how they kept themselves in this current state without improving. We did that using the blocks Iceberg and What keeps us blocked?

Iceberg	What keeps us blocked?
What behavior gives us the current results?	**What is the problem?**
• Taking decisions and not supporting them or acting accordingly.	• Uncomfortable in discussions with each other and with hierarchically higher people.
• Not daring to show lack of understanding of requirements.	

- Not daring to confront the Scrum Master or managers.
- Giving in to pressure to ship low-quality software.
- Not daring to address each other.
- Little self-management and self-correction.

What in our thinking sustains the current situation?

- Management follows a command-and-control structure that leaves little room for our own ideas.
- I don't really care about quality because management makes all the decisions and does not listen to us.
- "I" know better and "I" have the overview; "you" don't.
- "I" am working constructively and those who disagree are not constructive.
- My behaviors and feelings are perfectly okay, because others do not fully understand the situation as I do.
- The Scrum Master is useless because he does not understand software development.

- Challenging each other and hierarchically higher people is scary.

How do the context and iceberg keep us blocked?

- Management pressure and control makes us disengage and lose ownership of our decisions and product quality. Performance goes down and management puts more pressure on us.
- Accepting requirements that we do not understand and not asking for clarification makes us ship low-quality product. This then gives more work to fix defects and creates lower confidence in management.

Based on this understanding, we facilitated a workshop with the team, management, and the Product Owner to come up with action for improvement. It resulted in the following actions.

Actions to break free

Where can we bring change?

Regarding behavior:

- Disagree and commit based on a thorough discussion.
- We give the reasoning to our position and ask someone else for their reasoning if it is not done.
- It is a sign of professionalism if you share your genuine opinions about the topic in question.

Regarding management pressures:

- Each Product Backlog Item must be testable and understood by the team before the team can take it as a candidate for the Sprint.

- The team makes work decisions free from management control, and governs itself during the Sprint without outside intervention.

Regarding decision making:

- The team is involved in decisions that affect them.

- We trust our Product Owner to make the final decision.

The systems team assessment takes a local view of the team and its closest surroundings. It helps the team improve locally. However, you may observe repeating issues across multiple teams when you work in a large product group. In that case, the systems team assessment is of little use. You likely need to address the larger product group as a whole. Later in this chapter, we share a workshop format for that.

Improving Team Dynamics: Trust

Despite the significance of trust for team performance, it's often overlooked in organizations. So, why is trust so important indeed? According to scientific research, trust directly affects a team's effectiveness.

> Interpersonal trust can be defined as an individual's willingness to accept vulnerability based upon positive expectations of the intentions or behavior of another. By extension, intrateam trust refers to the aggregate levels of trust that team members have in their fellow teammates.[25]

In cross-functional teams, the impact of trust is amplified because Agile teams are characterized by the interdependence of work, large diversity in skills, and high team autonomy. More trust means that more energy is spent on valuable discussions and actual problem solving instead of on political issues and interpersonal conflicts. Trust is a component of psychological safety, which is necessary for people being themselves.

R. M. Kramer defines psychological safety as follows:

> [I]ndividuals' perceptions about the consequences of interpersonal risks in their work environment. It consists of taken-for-granted beliefs about how others will respond when one puts itself on the line, such as by asking questions, seeking feedback, reporting a mistake, or proposing a new idea.[26]

If people can fully express themselves, they can easily take interpersonal risks, openly share their mistakes, and ultimately learn from them. We discuss in this detail in the section "Align on Shared

Values and Behavior" in Chapter 9, "Launching the Product Group," how trust increases transparency and upholds the empirical process. How do you facilitate conversations about trust in your teams? In the "Trust" section in the Appendix, we share two workshop formats. Here, we briefly share two practical tools that you can use in your team coaching to unleash and build trust in your team.

ORID: Focused Discussion

ORID is a specific facilitation framework that enables a focused conversation with a group of people to reach some point of agreement or clarify differences. It was developed by the Institute of Cultural Affairs (ICA) in Canada.

The ORID method can be applied in many contexts. It can be used for group conversations, individual application, and even as a backbone structure for larger events (conferences, meetups). Agile teams might benefit from ORID by using it for problem-solving workshops, debriefing processes, Retrospectives, training, team lift-off, coaching and mentoring, decision making, celebration conversations, crafting a product strategy, conflict resolution process, and more.

Focused dialogue honors the different perspectives people maintain instead of searching for a single "truth." It is helpful in stopping criticism and avoiding a rush to false conclusions. It provokes team participation. It also stops blaming and demanding, and helps people take responsibility for making changes. The result is better meetings, more effective dialogues between people, and more understanding and empathy.

The ORID method is based on a four-phase model. Each phase addresses a specific area to get a better understanding of reality and collect different points of view. The four levels of reflection form a pattern from which innumerable conversations can be drawn. It simply flows from a natural internal process of perception, response, judgment, and decision.

Here is a short description of the phases:

- **Objective:** Perceptions—what we often call "objective reality."
- **Reflexive:** Feelings, emotional reactions to information received from the outside.
- **Interpretation:** Analysis, understanding of the information and why it is important.
- **Decision making:** Next steps and conclusions.

We share the ORID workshop format in "The ORID Framework" section in the Appendix.

Radical Candor

Often, people don't confront organizational impediments and tolerate the status quo. Sometimes Scrum Masters choose the safe route and spend most of their time drawing on flipcharts, managing sticky notes, passing a microphone from one participant to another during a "demo," keeping the Scrum Board up to date, updating burndown charts/cumulative diagrams, creating tickets in Jira, performing administrative tasks that the management and team "dump" onto them, and managing team dependencies. When the "Agile leaders" do not challenge teams, the management, and the whole organization, they become useless. The most effective Agile leaders whom we have seen had the courage to ask the uncomfortable questions, and to keep advocating for the principles and values of Agile. In our experience, they are mature individuals with clear goals and strong backbones. Furthermore, they practice radical candor.

To clarify how leaders can best provide feedback, Kim Scott developed a simple model entitled *radical candor,*[27] as illustrated in Figure 10.18.

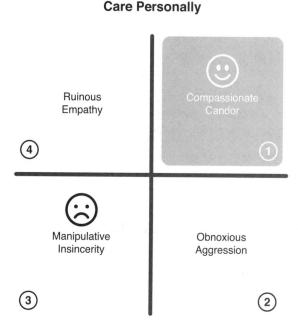

Figure 10.18
An example of radical candor.

Radical candor is the type of feedback in which we challenge others directly while simultaneously showing care for those people. How can you use radical candor yourself and with the teams? We share workshop formats in the "Radical Candor" section in the Appendix.

Facilitating Conflict

As complex adaptive systems, teams will inevitably face conflicts and disagreements. The ability to effectively deal with a conflict is an attribute of the high-performing team. If the team agrees that constructive conflict is normal, it can get over the conflict and work toward a resolution. By doing so, the team becomes stronger, more mature, and more collaborative.

Facilitating conflict is an advanced topic. Team coaches often overestimate the team's capability for resolving the dispute themselves. They let the conflict reach the point where emotions go too high, and people are divided into warring camps. At this point, teams need a professional mediation process. This level of conflict goes far beyond the constructive one encountered in high-performing teams.

To handle conflict in teams, we use a three-step model:

1. **Align conflict strategies.** Team members have different life experience and personal preferences when handling conflict. They will benefit from sharing their preferences and discussing which type of conflict is good/bad for them.

2. **Create a conflict protocol.** Conflict often feels painful. Concrete rules for handling conflict, attitudes, and specific behaviors will decrease ambiguity and stress. Such an agreement creates commitment and a healthy peer pressure.

3. **Coach the team.** Sometimes despite your best efforts, the team is not able to resolve the conflict. At this point, the coach should step in and act as a mediator to help them reach an agreement. This can be the last chance to fix the issue.

The "Facilitating Conflict" section in the Appendix shares guidelines to help you lay solid groundwork for handling and facilitating conflict.

Facilitate Feedback Loops for Learning: Learning New Practices

Agile adoption, like any other significant change in organizations, involves unlearning practices and processes that worked in the past and replacing them with new practices that enable agility. Organizations create an Agile culture by changing "the way we do things here" into "the Agile way we do things here." A critical factor is the organization's learning capability. Learning new skills takes engagement, clear goals, and a measurement of progress.

People and teams that follow through their own learning path feel more ownership of the new processes and support the adoption. Therefore, you cannot simply copy someone else's model, because you would then miss out on the crucial part: the learning journey.

> **Note**
>
> Next, we share an approach to plan, do, and measure learning new skills. Although we present this process as a series of discrete steps and exact numbers, the format is not the most important point to remember. The real value of the proposed approach is that it helps the team's thinking to discuss and clarify their learning goals and how to achieve those goals.

Teams can take three steps to set up themselves up for effective learning:

Step 1. Determine the goal and quantify it.

Step 2. Break down the overall goal into specific actions that the team can practice.

Step 3. Define measures that create a feedback loop on how well the team is performing.

Let's delve into each of these steps in more detail.

Step 1: Determine Your Goal

The first step is to capture what the team wants to learn about and improve. At the level of the product group, a goal could be: *We want to have more reliable product deliveries.*

This measure is rather vague. The team would need to quantify it so that it becomes clear what this goal means and how the team will measure "reliability." For example:

What do we measure? Number of production issues after a release

How do we measure? Monitoring reports and incoming helpdesk calls

Past: [January–April 2020] Average of 71 issues at the end of the Sprint

Goal: [June–August 2020] Average of 5 issues at the end of the Sprint

Even though this measure is now quantified, it is not very useful for the team to drive their improvement. What is missing are concrete actions the team will try and a feedback loop.

Create a Feedback Loop for Learning

Feedback is essential for learning. Usually, the faster one receives feedback, the better. However, not all feedback is useful. Useful feedback helps you:

- Understand what exactly is *not* going as you would like it to go.

- Analyze why there were deviations from your perfect plan and determine actions for improvement. That information, in turn, might point to either required training (e.g., in feature coverage test development) or learning (a path to discovering new ways to make code more reliable).

The team needs to think about which specific actions they can take to support the group to reduce production issues and become more reliable.

Step 2: Create Specific Actions

Deliberate practice is often used in sports and musical training to learn and improve players' performance.

> In the late 1970s, psychologist K. Anders Ericsson was interested in how many numbers one of his students could keep in his head with consistent practice. They started with a random 5-digit string, which the student had to remember. If he got it right, the length of the string was increased by 1. If he got it wrong, the length of the string was reduced by 2. After a few weeks, the student succeeded in remembering an 11-digit string. The average person can only remember 7 digits.

Deliberate practice requires practicing a task that you can repeat many times, like the task of remembering the strings of digits. To practice in their daily work, a team can plan for learning time in the Sprint, or use their usual work to practice.

Continuing with the preceding example, which actions can the team take to move toward zero known defects in the Sprint? A key point is to break down the larger goal into concrete, smaller specific actions to improve through focused practice. Some measurable actions for the team could be:

- We solve defects immediately after discovery.
- We automate acceptance tests for x% of the features during the Sprint.
- We perform exploratory tests of y% of the features with the whole team.
- We write z% of the code in pairs.

These are concrete actions the team can objectively measure to determine how well they are doing them during the Sprint. In *A Scrum Book*,[8] we find that process improvements should be testable.

> Write improvement plans in terms of specific concrete actions (not goals) that the team can measure objectively to assess whether the team is applying the process change.[18]

So, consider using improvement measurements that are process-focused, not outcome-focused. Step 3 explains how to do that.

Step 3: Define Measures That Drive Learning

Agile teams own their process and measure their progress. Therefore, the measures for improvement are created by the teams themselves. Don't let anyone else create the improvement measures—if you do that, you remove ownership from the teams. Furthermore, the measures should follow directly from the work of the team, so that the team gets insights into where to improve. In other words, avoid management indicators that are not directly generated by the work of a team because they are not useful to drive learning.

For example, the team could define a measure for "We solve defects immediately after discovery" as follows:

> **Name:** Solve defects immediately after discovery
>
> **What do we measure?** Percentage of defects that were solved within one day after discovery.
>
> **How do we measure?** Capture the situations where we did not solve a defect immediately after discovery.
>
> **How can you take action with it?** What are we doing/not doing to solve defects within one day? Which, if any, competing commitments are driving our actions?

In general, the team creates a hypothesis about how their process works in perfection and maximizes their intended outcome. Then they run the Sprint and test for deviations from perfection, evaluate and analyze them, and determine new improvement actions. When you measure the performance of concrete actions toward concrete goals, you drive learning! The "Example Workshop to Define Measures for Improvement" section in the Appendix provides an example of how you can run a workshop to define measures for improvement.

Summary

We began this chapter by defining a cross-functional team as being the main building block of any Agile organization. We examined five conditions for team effectiveness and identified characteristics of a successful team: constructive conflict, commitment, integrity and trust, respect, and self-management.

We devoted quite a large number of pages to multifunctional learning, which is a necessity when creating a flexible team. By creating CLDs together with a team, you can help the developers to take responsibility for their actions and have a deep understanding of the system. Approaches that facilitate learning include the three modes of development, slack time, star maps, and explicit agreements.

Systems team coaching starts with performing circular observations, and is then followed by a systems assessment. Applying techniques that help in building trust can improve communication within the team.

References

1. Dianna and Merrill Anderson. *Coaching That Counts* (Routledge, 2016).

2. J. Richard Hackman. *Leading Teams: Setting the Stage for Great Performances* (Harvard Business Review Press, 2002).

3. Patrick Lencioni. *The 5 Dysfunctions of a Team: A Leadership Fable* (Jossey-Bass, 2002).

4. Ralph Katz. "The Effects of Group Longevity on Project Communication and Performance." *Administrative Science Quarterly* 27, no. 1 (1982): 81–104. www.jstor.org/stable/2392547.

5. Susan G. Cohen and Diane E. Bailey. "What Makes Teams Work: Group Effectiveness Research from the Shop Floor to the Executive Suite." *Journal of Management* 23, no. 3 (1997): 239–290. doi:10.1177/014920639702300303.

6. J. Richard Hackman. "What Makes for a Great Team." *Psychological Science Agenda* (2004). www.apa.org/science/about/psa/2004/06/hackman.aspx.

7. Alain Cardon. *Systems Team and Organizational Coaching: The Systems Coaching Collection* (www.metasysteme-coaching.eu, 2014).

8. Scrum Patterns Group. *A Scrum Book* (2019). www.scrumbook.org.

9. Zoe McKey. *Think in Systems: The Art of Strategic Planning, Effective Problem Solving, and Lasting Results* (2019).

10. Donella H. Meadows. *Thinking in Systems* (Chelsea Green Publishing, 2008).

11. Illia Pavlichenko. "Eliminate Dependencies, Don't Manage Them." 2018. www.scrum.org/resources/blog/eliminate-dependencies-dont-manage-them.

12. Hirotaka Takeuchi and Nonaka Ikujiro. "The New New Product Development Game." *Harvard Business Review* (January 1986). https://hbr.org/1986/01/the-new-new-product-development-game.

13. Donald G. Reinersten. *Managing the Design Factory* (Free Press, 1997).

14. Peter Senge. *The Fifth Discipline: The Art and Practice of the Learning Organization* (Doubleday Dell, 1990).

15. Donald G. Reinersten. *The Principles of Product Development Flow: Second Generation Lean Product Development* (Celeritas, 2009).

16. "1-2-4-All." Liberating Structures. www.liberatingstructures.com/1-1-2-4-all/.

17. "What, So What, Now What? W³." Liberating Structures. www.liberatingstructures.com/9-what-so-what-now-what-w/.

18. "Testable Improvements." https://tinyurl.com/TestableImprovements

19. "Teams That Finish Early Accelerate Faster." https://sites.google.com/a/scrumplop.org/published-patterns/retrospective-pattern-language/teams-that-finish-early-accelerate-faster.

20. Tom Demarco. *Slack: Getting Past Burnout, Busywork, and the Myth of Total Efficiency* (Currency, 2002).

21. Russell L. Ackoff, *Re-creating the Corporation: A Design of Organizations for the 21st Century* (Oxford University Press, 1999).

22. Dorothy Strachan. *Making Questions Work: A Guide to What and How to Ask for Facilitators, Consultants, Managers, Coaches, and Educators* (Jossey-Bass, 2007).

23. "15% Solutions." Liberating Structures. www.liberatingstructures.com/7-15-solutions/.

24. Dave Gray. "Now–How–Wow Matrix." GameStorming (January 5, 2011). https://gamestorming.com/how-now-wow-matrix/.

25. B. A. De Jong, K. T. Dirks, and N. Gillespie. "Trust and Team Performance: A Meta-Analysis of Main Effects, Moderators and Covariates." *Journal of Applied Psychology* 101, no. 8 (2016): 1134–1150. https://doi.org/10.1037/apl0000110.

26. Roderick M. Kramer. *Trust and Distrust in Organizations: Dilemmas and Approaches* (Russell Sage Foundation, 2004).

27. Kim Scott. *Radical Candor: How to Get What You Want by Saying What You Mean* (Pan Books, 2019).

11

Guiding the Product Ownership

Product Owners, not proxies.
—Ken Schwaber[1]

As Product Owner, you evolve the Product Backlog, reordering the existing items and adding or removing items based on learning. Product ownership comprises many vital areas of activity. First, there is customer understanding to discover which problems to solve for maximized value delivery. Second, there is providing vision and direction that enable the teams to self-manage toward a common goal. Third, there is collaboration with stakeholders about investments, schedules, and expected outcomes. The Product Owner maintains transparency by keeping the Product Backlog visible to all stakeholders, such as senior management, the team, and customers.

In this chapter, you find techniques and practices to set up each of these areas of product ownership in your product group.

What Makes a Team Product Owner?

When we coach organizations on product ownership, we teach them about the Product Owner (PO) role and its responsibilities. Why? Misconceptions about the PO role often lead to reduced agility, development bottlenecks, and teams that do not understand the customer domain. Let us unpack this for you.

Avoid Product-Part Owners

A common mistake in large product development is having POs who work on a product part instead of the complete product. Although people call such a person the PO, they still act as managers or requirements engineers and often play the PO role for one team. Such a team PO—usually a requirements person such as a business analyst (BA) or project manager (PM) relabeled to the PO role—works on a part of the product, manages a team product backlog, and acts as a liaison between the development team and the users, customers and other teams.

The liaison role introduces the dynamics described in the Causal Loop Diagram (CLD) shown in Figure 11.1. In that CLD, you can see how having team POs could easily lead to unnecessary hand-offs, overhead documentation, and poor user-problem understanding by the teams.

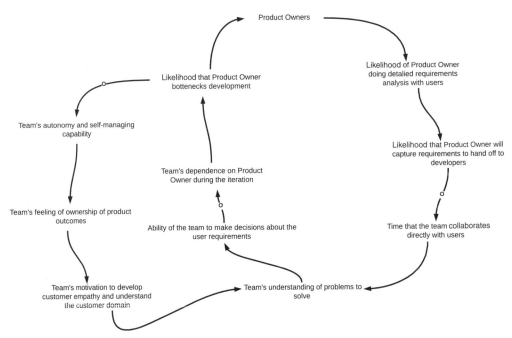

Figure 11.1
Typical systems dynamics in large-scale development with team Product Owners. (Inspired by Craig Larman).

Let us explain the CLD in Figure 11.1 with a short story. We start the story at the variable: **Product Owners**. A team PO **likely does detailed requirements analysis** with stakeholders (users/customers). The PO will **capture requirements and then hand them off to the team**, typically as user stories. The more the team PO acts as a go-between handing off the user stories, the less time **the team collaborates directly with the users**. Instead, the developers must read the requirements to understand the users' problems. When the team works with the user stories instead of the actual users, they miss out on asking questions directly to the users, developing user empathy, and obtaining a good **understanding of the problems to solve**.

Although it is the real PO's job to understand the problem space and to develop a solution space that drives the team, a team with a poor understanding of the users' problems has little **ability to make decisions about the user requirements** and becomes dependent on the team PO. Also, it is very hard to write clear, complete, and consistent requirements. So, the teams usually ask many clarification questions to the team PO. The team PO likely does not know all details or answers and has to go back to the stakeholders to clarify the issues. Usually, the stakeholders are busy people, so it can take some time before they answer. During that time, the team either works on something else, waits, or makes a guess and continues. All these options make the team less effective.

Over time, without direct interaction with the users, the **team's dependence on the PO during each iteration** increases. Over time, it is **likely that the PO bottlenecks development**. With the team unable to make progress by themselves, the **team's autonomy and self-managing capability** decrease (the "shifting the burden" archetype, introduced in Chapter 2, "Systems Thinking"). With less self-managing ability, its **feeling of ownership of product outcomes** and planning commitments likely decrease over time. Eventually, the **team's motivation to understand the user domain** is further reduced to the point that they focus mainly on the requirements and technical work. The PO tells them the details of which problem to address, and they just execute it without really understanding the user's problems. All of this slows down the development loop and makes it harder to change direction quickly.

These dynamics are the result of working with many teams on a single product, but using a separate team PO and backlog for each team; it's the familiar copy–paste scaling[2] setup (see also Chapter 1, "Organizing for Adaptability"). When you have a single product, you need a single strategic PO and a single Product Backlog for all the teams.

Replace Product-Part Owners with a Real Product Owner

A business analyst (BA) with the right market understanding, skills, and mandate can play the role of a PO—but it's still generally a bad idea to have them play this role for the team. Why? Business analysis and requirements elicitation is just one of the activities required to solve a customer problem. So, you would like to avoid local optimizations of BA (single specialists) with cross-functional teams. We recommend eliminating the team Product-Part Owner role, and considering promoting team POs to become development team members. The team PO is then no longer responsible for "the requirements," but rather is responsible (just like all other development team members) for delivering a valuable working product increment.

As a team member, the team PO can now:

- Contribute to the team's feeling of ownership of product outcomes.
- Increase the team's understanding of customer problems to solve.
- Avoid seeing business analysis as the goal, and instead keep the focus on delivering a valuable product.
- Help validate whether requirements are valuable and help the team adapt their plan accordingly.
- Take the lead during team–customer understanding sessions.

After eliminating the team PO roles, all the teams work with one real strategic PO.

How to Promote the Team Product Owner to Team Member

Team POs usually do not like it when they are promoted to team member. The PO role made them feel somewhat special, and being a team member does not really feel like a promotion. We usually take one of two approaches to handle this.

In the first approach, we leave the team PO role in existence, but we also take these steps:

- We ensure that everybody knows who the true PO is, and that this person makes the final decisions.

- We ensure that the team and team PO together clarify Product Backlog Items (PBIs) with the users. So, there's no more team PO clarifying items individually and handing them off to the team.

In this configuration, it becomes obvious that the team PO is not the real PO, and that clarification of PBIs is the whole team's responsibility. The real PO may identify user needs, discover deficiencies in their process, and envision what they want. It is the PO's job to identify product increments that provide value by addressing those problems, but it is the team's responsibility to clarify the details. Basically, you end up with an additional skill name in your team. Over time, nobody really cares about the special skill name of the team PO, just as they do not care about the special skill name for the programming or testing functions. Eventually, the promotion of the team PO to team member comes more gradually.

We were working with a group of seven teams, all of which had team POs. We had already defined a broader product, found a new PO, and helped develop the self-designed feature teams. The leadership was doubting how to deal with the team POs. After much discussion, it was decided that the elimination of the team PO roles would be too much of a change at once. So, we started working in the new setup with team POs. After the first Sprint, we had a Retrospective with the team POs, and they unanimously proposed to eliminate their own role, as it was no longer useful.

In the second approach, you remove the role of team PO. This approach creates the most resistance, so it requires a more delicate coaching process. The approach we take is based on the Axes of Change model[3] described in Chapter 5, "An Agile Adoption Approach."

With the elimination of the team PO, the next step is to identify the real PO.

The Product Owner in a Senior Position

As noted in the previous section, the PO at scale does not work with a single team. Rather, the PO has the full accountability for the whole product and is shared between multiple teams. Product management is the essential practice for POs.

> *Product management's job will change and will be harder. Product managers and customers are now Product Owners. They are responsible for managing the projects, Sprint by Sprint, to maximize value and control risk. They are accountable to senior management for the success or failure of the project.*[4]

Successful product ownership requires the ability and mandate to decide on the following:

- Product vision
- Product strategy
- Overarching product goals
- Which features to develop
- Order of feature delivery

The PO has the final say and provides leadership regarding which ideas to pursue, features to develop, enhancements to make, and stakeholder proposals to accept or reject. A PO's decisions significantly impact product success and the organization's economic results. So, to be successful in large-scale Agile development, the PO needs:

- An understanding of the organization and its market, customers, and users to make informed decisions about investment, priority, and release dates
- The mandate to make decisions that will have a substantial impact on product success

Given these characteristics, we recommend placing the PO role at a senior management level. In companies with a board of directors, that PO role would be at the board-1 to board-2 level. At this level, the PO can be accountable for product success and responsible for, among other things, the profit and loss (P&L) results for the product.

We've been coaching a midsize company that creates houses for the U.S. market using 3D printing and innovative materials. Senior management invited us to conduct a Go See effort. They had some concerns regarding scaled Scrum implementation. During the Sprint Review, we observed how the team-level POs presented individual increments and reported progress toward team-level objectives and key results (OKRs) to the CEO. Despite their efforts, the main business objective that senior management aimed for was not reached. The team-level POs had a limited market understanding, did not communicate directly with investors, and were not responsible for product strategy. In our Go See report, we suggested eliminating the team-level PO roles. From that moment on, the CEO of the company took over the PO role.

Avoid Product Owner Committees

The PO is one person, not a committee. On the one hand, people in a committee bring diverse perspectives on a subject. This is a good thing, as it challenges people to discover hidden assumptions and explore alternative views on a subject. On the other hand, many bad things can happen when the perspectives come from different organizational units that have opposing goals. As described in Chapter 4, "Agile Organizational Design," coupling between units is associated with an increase in coordination costs, goal conflicts, ineffective or dysfunctional government, loss of productivity, and, most importantly, decreased ability to respond to change. To avoid these negative outcomes, you'll need to ensure the PO has the mandate to make final product decisions when needed.

Outward-Focused Product Owner

The PO role is often a new, full-time role in an organization owing to its accountabilities, responsibilities, and reporting, rather than the addition of activities to an existing role. Many senior roles comprise general managerial activities. In organizational role descriptions, you can find activities such as the following:

- **Vacations**
- **Hiring**
- **Resource allocation**
- **Conflict resolution**
- **Talent development**
- **Appraisals**
- **Culture**
- **Coordination**
- And many more.

Although these activities are all important, not all are directly related to product ownership. We therefore recommend removing most of the managerial activities from the PO role so that the PO can focus on the product. All product-related activities are performed by the PO or the teams, and the remaining general managerial activities are done by—yes, you guessed it—managers. The work of management is to create the conditions for the teams to succeed.

> *A manager knows that improving the company is not his job but the job of the people themselves. The manager's job is to help the people understand this and make it possible for them to do so.*—**A senior Toyota manager**

Typical recommended PO activities are as follows:

- Customer research to understand customer segments, motivations, and purchase behaviors of the targeted customers

- Product research to understand what the customers really want, so that the product can be tailored to match their needs

- Creating, updating, and refining the product vision

- Driving the direction of development through ordering of the Product Backlog

- Stakeholder management and alignment

- Budgeting to obtain resources needed to develop the product

- Funding the learning infrastructure and activities to develop the teams

- Hiring people to develop the product group.

Try to separate the PO's activities from the general management activities so that the PO is outward-focused on customer understanding. Leave the inward-focused management activities for managers.

Workshop to Separate Product Owner Activities from General Managerial Activities

We often use the following simple workshop format to separate inward-focused management activities from the outward-focused PO activities.

Preparation: Ensure all participants understand the role of the Product Owner and Manager before the start of the workshop.

Materials needed: Pens, sticky notes, whiteboard or flipcharts.

Structural invitation: Invite representatives from different parts of the organization that work as, for example, program managers, project managers, line managers, senior managers, and team product owners. Explain that the purpose of the workshop is to separate managerial activities from PO activities.

The steps we usually take in this workshop are as follows:

Step 1. Ask to write down the tasks (one per sticky note) that you and your management do? You might, for example, use the liberating structure 1-2-4-All[5] for gathering input from the participants.

Step 2. Ask the participants to place the tasks from the previous step along the scale Managerial Focus ↔ Product Focus. Use relative ordering and affinity mapping to identify clusters of similar tasks. When complete, the result should look something similar like Figure 11.2.

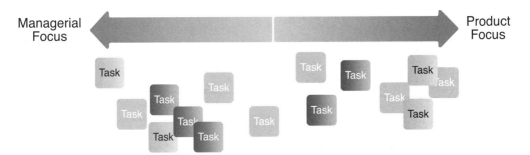

Figure 11.2
Product versus management task focus.

Step 3. Using a Q&A format, divide the tasks between the PO, developers, and general management as illustrated in Figure 11.3. We actively facilitate this step and take the opportunity
to clarify details about the PO activities.

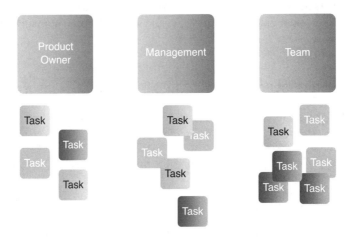

Figure 11.3
Task separation per role.

Step 4. Facilitate a group discussion using the What? So What? Now What? structure.[6] Consider the
following questions:
  a. How are the current management's and PO's activities impacted?
  b. What changes, if any, are implied for the PO role activities?
  c. What first actions do we need to take to implement this new setup?

Product Ownership Measures

Many organizations think about which measures they should use to quantify their product development. Here are some questions that we often hear:

- Which financial product performance measures should we use?

- How do we measure performance of the teams?

- How do we measure customer value?

All of these questions become easier to answer once you have a broad product definition and a PO in a senior position. Let us explain how we answer these questions.

Measuring Business Impact

The product group where you are adopting the Agile approach already exists at this point, so it likely already has measures for success, strategic goals to reach, and financial expectations to meet. For example, a bank product could have the following goals:

- Number of new clients: **10,000**

- Gross income from new clients: **$67 million**

- Cost to serve: **maximum $9000**

- NPS: **35%**

Why not just reuse these measures? Usually your current product measures do not need to be altered and you are good to go. Now, if your current "product" measures are, for example, velocity, planned versus actual, or number of defects, then you are likely working with a narrow part of the product and a Product-Part Owner. Therefore, you should extend your product definition as described in Chapter 8, "Preparing the Product Group," so that you can connect it to the business measures and end users.

What About Budgets and Costs?

In the context of large-scale development, you will likely have many teams working on your product prior to your Agile adoption. This means that the existing salaries of full-time equivalents (FTEs) are known and can be considered a fixed cost. There is no need for people to book hours on various project numbers because all the people in your product group work on the same product. So, you can eliminate project budgeting in your product group altogether.

A PO influences cost by:

- End-user engagement to reduce opportunity costs (potential benefits that a business misses out on when choosing one alternative over another).

- Reducing rework through upfront planning and rapid feedback to reduce rework costs.

- Reducing overproduction (the main category of waste) by having customers "pull" features. The Product Backlog is used to smoothen the introduction of work to the teams. A quality Product Backlog reduces variability (a main source of waste) by having similar-sized, high-quality PBIs ready for the teams to pick up.

- Clarifying details of PBIs in a just-in-time manner, thereby avoiding upfront speculative, months-long specification efforts.

- Addressing impediments that lower quality, because good quality increases the flow of features. The more features flow smoothly, the more resources that are freed up and can either be released to reduce costs or be reinvested elsewhere.

We once were in a discussion with the CEO of a bank and one of his POs who was starting in her new role. Coming from the traditional mindset, she told the CEO that she wanted to add many more teams to her product group, and asked if he would approve that. The CEO responded: "Well, that decision is up to you. If you think that will make you more successful and you can afford it, then go for it."

Once your product definition is broad enough to have a P&L, then the PO can adopt an entrepreneurial mindset. That's Agile as it should be.

A note on contracts: To enable the PO to continuously replan to maximize product success, consider avoiding contract types that impedes agility. For example, a fixed-price, fixed-scope contract would limit the PO's possibilities to replan based on feedback from the market; it would also limit possibilities for investing more in areas of interest and defunding other areas.

Measuring Team Performance

When teams are working on a part of the product—that is, they are component teams—with team POs, then which kind of team measure could you use? We often observe that teams use output or activity measures, such as story points, tasks done, or cycle time. Why? Because it is not fair to use the financial performance measures for a component team. For example, you likely would not measure the performance of a database team based on the increase in the number of new clients, because such a team cannot directly influence the number of clients.

When teams can deliver features that solve user problems, then team performance can be connected to product performance measures related to economic impact and user value. The output and activity measures are still very important, though, and we recommend using them as measures for the improvement of the team processes and flow of features across the large product group. See the section "Multifunctional Learning and Agile," in Chapter 10, "Coaching Teams."

Measuring Product Qualities

Perceived value is the perception of what a product is worth compared to alternatives.[7] The more benefits a customer experiences for what they paid, the higher the perceived value is. The question is how to identify the right problems to solve, and then to solve those problems better than the current available solutions do. In consequence, there are two main measurement parts to consider:

- Are we solving the right problem?

- Are we solving the problem better than the current solutions do?

Answering these questions starts with a thorough understanding of the users and customers—the topic of the sections that follow.

Customer Understanding

One significant tactic for the PO is early validation of assumptions about problems worth solving and solutions worth implementing. If you don't understand whether you are solving the right problems, you could end up with a lot of high-quality features that have no customer value. Let us give you an example from one of our clients.

> On a Monday when we were working at a large bank, the PO nervously approached me. He had just released a new version of the lending product. The helpdesk was getting tons of calls from unhappy users to the extent that they had to roll back the release to the prior version. What had happened? After some investigation, we concluded that the release solved many problems for the users, but they were not the problems the users wanted to be solved. The release had solved the wrong problems and decreased the usability of the product. Why did this happen? The teams assumed they deeply understood the users' problems, but they did not!

When Agile teams start to move fast, the development problem shifts to the customer understanding:

- How can we determine the most valuable features to develop next?

- How can we validate whether we created the right features?

Agile development no longer assumes that product management knows exactly what the customer wants. Instead, the Agile strategy to minimize risk is learning fast and putting that knowledge back into the plan.

Validate Assumptions Early and Often

Agile mechanics reduce risks by learning what works and what doesn't work as early as possible. The PO breaks down a large plan into a sequence of smaller parts that focus on learning by experience about the best path to reach a goal. The PO can consider four different types of uncertainties:

- **Value uncertainty:** You reduce value risk by validating whether you are solving the right problems for your users. Are you addressing the right user needs? Are you solving the right problems?

- **Solution uncertainty:** Solution risk is decreased when, for example, you verify that you correctly solved the customers' problems or that you can build your product with the suggested technology. Are you solving the problem right?

- **Investment uncertainty:** Investment risk is reduced when, for example, you validate your expected financial estimations. Do customer behaviors or growth match the estimations? Are the development costs within the expected boundaries to be profitable?

- **Schedule uncertainty:** Schedule risk is reduced when, for example, you verify that you can deliver the product within the time frame of opportunity. Which features should not be included in the release? What are alternative faster implementations for reaching the Product Goals?

Instead of financing the large development initiatives upfront based on speculation, opinions, and unvalidated business plans, funding is provided for just the first part that gives information about the highest risks. With that new information, the PO will make informed decision about further steps. The PO can decide to stop the initiative, continue as planned, change direction, or invest even more than initially planned.

There are many techniques that the PO can consider to reduce these uncertainties—for example, end-user workshops, competitive analysis, pilots, prototypes, set-based design, and thorough upfront analysis, to name a few possibilities. All these techniques help to shorten the feedback loop from assumptions to validation. Shorter feedback loops help the team to learn faster.

Caution

Innovation is complex and requires time. For a complex system, cause and effect are separated in time and space. The PO needs to take into account a broad range of data points over a period of time to develop a thorough understanding of the system.

The Product Owner Process

Validating assumptions by developing software can be costly. So, you'll want to ensure that the teams develop features that have been adequately studied and shown to be valuable. Discovering which features to develop depends on your product context and life-cycle stage. It can include a vast array of product research activities, such as the following:

- Customer interviews

- Customer understanding workshops

- Advertising

- Writing hypotheses

- Designing Wizard of Oz experiments

- Prototyping

- A/B testing

- Live product

In the new-product development context, the PO starts with low-cost tactics that quickly reduce uncertainty, such as interviewing customers and running small experiments. Over time, the PO applies bigger, more expensive tactics such as experiments, prototyping, and shipping an actual product. The "truth curve" developed by Giff Constable shows the level of believability for different kinds of experiments,[8] as illustrated in Figure 11.4.

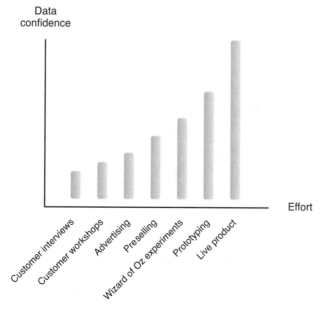

Figure 11.4

Truth curve. (Adapted from Giff Constable, Talking to Humans: Success Starts with Understanding Your Customers.[8]*)*

The PO starts with low-cost methods because they can provide quick insights, albeit at the expense of lower confidence. The data from those methods are subject to the judgment and interpretation of the PO. The more expensive methods lead to higher confidence, but they take more time to prepare and run. For example, live product data about usage, purchases, or retention are unquestionably valuable, but shipping a live product takes longer and therefore increases the validation loop.

A bank with which we worked wanted to increase the number of its customers. Many potential customers started buying a product on the bank's website, but only about 16% actually completed the purchase. How was this possible? The bank studied what kept 84% of its customers from buying its products by conducting the following activities:

- Customer understanding workshops: We organized an afternoon of customer workshops in a hotel. We facilitated customer discovery using the SpeedBoat and ProductBox serious games.[9]

- Customer questionnaire: We designed a set of six questions that we sent out digitally to customers.

After analyzing all the data, the PO came to the conclusion that the main problems were:

1. The duration between submitting the request and getting approval or rejection from the bank was too long.

2. Users had to submit their financial information multiple times to different parts of the bank.

With these conclusions and the data from the funnel, the PO formulated the following assumptions, among others:

- I believe that by decreasing the approval time, we can acquire at least 5000-plus new clients.

- I believe that by simplifying the approval process for "easy" customers, we can increase our revenue by 40%.

The next question was how to validate these assumptions. The development teams and PO got together and formulated the following goals:

- Decrease the approval time for "easy" customers from an average of 120 hours to an average of 1 hour.

- Increase straight-through processing from 50% to 90%.

In the last step, the teams and PO created a Wizard of Oz[10] experiment for the still uncertain features, and decided to build the high-confidence features.

Serious Games for Customer Understanding

As mentioned in Chapter 7, "Group Facilitation," serious games are very useful to engage team members as well as your users and customers. A subset of serious games called innovation games[9] are specifically designed for customer understanding. The "Example: Customer Understanding with Serious Games" section in the Appendix provides a detailed example of using innovation games and other serious games to create an initial value proposition.

Stakeholder Alignment

Different stakeholders need different information to make decisions. A senior manager might be primarily interested in strategic progress, while an end user is more concerned with feature delivery dates. During a Sprint, the teams focus on a short-term Sprint Goal that aims to get the product closer to the longer-term Product Goal.

How can the PO align all of these stakeholders? And how can the PO provide product guidance and create a sense of purpose? Start by aligning the stakeholders on the product vision, and then create a cascading set of objectives on which to align them.

Align on the Product Vision

A product vision describes a future state and helps to align and inspire your teams and stakeholders. A product vision answers a bevy of questions: Why are you creating the product? What does your company hope to accomplish with it in the future? And how the product will change the user's world? Many roads can lead to the desired future, but unfortunately it is impossible to know which route to take upfront. A PO can use a product roadmap to align with stakeholders on alternative roads toward the vision.

> The Product Owner owns the Vision and sets out to realize it by creating a Product Organization as well as by defining a Value Stream. The Product Owner articulates a path toward the Vision as a Product Roadmap, and works with stakeholders to reduce it to a concrete, specific Product Backlog.[11]

A big idea is to use the team's intellect to discover solutions to customer problems. An effective team does more than design and implementation; they also refine PBIs, propose and test new ideas, and help the PO make informed decisions. Ideally, then, the teams should develop customer empathy and deep customer understanding. But how to do that? First, consider removing artifacts, processes, and roles between the teams and customers so that the team focuses more on customers and users than on intermediate artifacts! Also, consider not giving the teams a fixed list of work to execute; instead, ask the teams to solve customer problems.

Second, consider starting by co-creating the product vision with the teams and facilitate team–user refinement workshops during the Sprints for detailed Product Backlog clarification.

Consider Co-Creating the Product Vision

Consider developing the product vision together with the teams. The teams will have better buy-in to the vision, but this collaboration will also increase their understanding of both organizational and user goals. The PO remains the main person who develops the product vision, and retains the final decision-making power over the vision and the content of the product.

Typically, you should consider clarifying the following matters:

- Who are the targeted users and customers?

- Which key user needs will the product satisfy?

- What are the most important features?

- How will the product change the user's world?

- What are our business goals? And how is the product expected to benefit our organization?

How can you co-create the product vision with the teams? We conduct a workshop focusing on the preceding questions, but there are many other formats and canvases you can choose (e.g., Roman Pichler's Product Vision Board[12]).

The steps we generally take are as follows:

Step 1. The PO shares the initial product research results and the draft product vision with the teams.

Step 2. Organize the participants into table groups. We like to include the PO in a team, too.

Step 3. Provide them with a flipchart list of questions, or select a canvas and ask them to answer the questions from their perspective and share the results. We like to use 1-2-4-ALL for each question. Encourage participants to build upon, rephrase, or extend the draft vision created by the PO.

Step 4. Ask each table group to write their answers to the questions and prepare to share them with the rest of the teams. Invite the other groups to provide feedback.

Step 5. Create new mixed groups by selecting one person from each team. Give each mixed group one of the product vision questions and ask them to merge all the answers. Consider using team 1-2-4-ALL; also consider using affinity mapping

Step 6. Summarize all answers on a single canvas and capture the initial product vision. The PO has the right to include or refuse any of the team's findings.

The product vision is a good place to start, as it provides the reason for creating or enhancing the product. For example, the vision statement "Effortless business collaboration" captures the essence of the vision. It is likely a multi-year goal that is too abstract to measure directly, and that is okay: Its purpose is to align, inspire, and guide decision making about what to build and what not to build. A key point is that you use the vision to derive smaller steps representing a path, as shown in Figure 11.5.

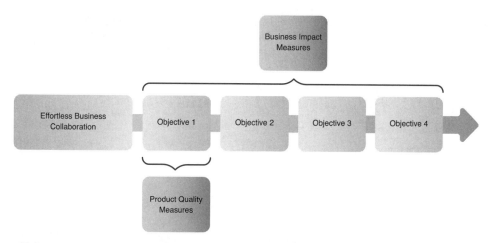

Figure 11.5
Example vision and its breakdown into objectives.

Each objective is concrete and measurable, and should indicate if and how the product initiative is progressing toward the vision. The product quality measures suggest whether you are solving the problem right. The business impact measures suggest whether you are solving the right problem. For example:

> *We believe that by reducing the duration between applying for a business loan and receiving a proposal from 2 weeks to 1 day, we will increase our closed loans by 40%.*

A business impact measure like "Percent **increase in closed business loans**" indicates whether you're solving the right problem. A product quality measure like "Percent **decrease in processing duration**" suggests whether you are solving the problem right.

Align on the Objectives

In contrast to the product vision, an *objective* is a goal that is directly measurable, which is key for inspecting progress, learning, and adapting the team's plan accordingly. We recommend aligning on the following objectives:

- **Product Goals:** Describe a future objective of the product.
- **Sprint Goals:** Describe the single objective for a Sprint.

A market change or change in customer understanding can give birth to a Product Goal. It could be related to a large new feature or a significant redesign with a time frame of a couple of months to a year. Also, consider early validation of the most risky assumptions. What are the high-risk speculations that you have, that if proven wrong, will put you in a bad position?

With a Product Goal in hand, consider starting with a list of the Sprint Goals as your initial Product Backlog. Each Sprint Goal represents a product increment and takes the product in the direction of the overarching vision.[13] Figure 11.6 shows a breakdown of a Product Goal into a first optional solution, and possible follow-on Sprint Goals. The PO can use such a setup as an initial Product Backlog.

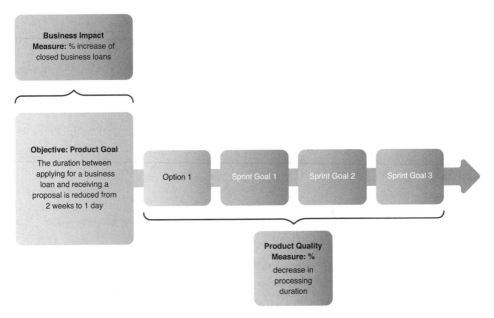

Figure 11.6
Example Product Goal and its breakdown into Sprint Goals.

Product Owner Leadership

In large-scale development, many people and teams develop the product. When the PO masters only product management techniques such as customer understanding, prioritization, and market analysis, but lacks leadership skills, it will be hard to effectively drive product development and growth. The following sections help reflect on leadership behaviors and offer some practical techniques.

Try to Keep the Teams Stable

When you put people together in a team, they will not immediately perform at high levels. It takes time for people to develop trust, working habits, and effective collaboration. Furthermore, if team members know that they will stay together for a short period, they are less likely to care about the process used during the team's lifespan. In contrast, if they will work together for many months or even years, they are more likely to care about building the approach that works best for them.

Every time a team changes, the team performance is affected; the larger the change, the more significant the potential decline is. New members might have to learn about the design, code, and domain, and how to work with new team members.

Reliable Forecasts

Maintaining stable teams can improve the organization's forecasts. As team members get to know one another's capabilities, they can learn how much work they can do together. Shared mental models and psychological safety comes with time and reduces the fear of conflict—a key ingredient for creating commitment to results.

Ideally, you will avoid resource pools, people who work on multiple teams, and re-creating teams to match the work. Instead, keep the teams stable as much as possible, and ask how they can learn whenever a knowledge gap needs to be bridged to complete the job. Also, enable the teams to freely determine how much work can be done and prevent the PO from forcing more work onto the team.

Avoid Micromanaging the Team

We observe many teams that rely on the PO to make team decisions, be they decisions about tasks, estimates, solutions, conflicts, or team membership. Maybe stepping in to manage the team might help in the short term, but stepping in over and over again reduces team autonomy. Every time a decision is made for the team, the PO is actually removing an opportunity for the team to grow. Self-managing teams plan their work, create their tasks, make all estimates, if any, and own their decisions. There is no need for others outside the team to do that for them; this also applies to the PO. In short, the teams own and manage their work.

We recommend clarifying:

- Which decisions are up to the PO

- Which decisions are up to the team

- Which decisions are made together

- How each decision is made

You know you are doing the heart of Scrum if nobody allocates assignments and ensures they are done in time. [14]

Collaborate as a Peer with the Teams

When teams struggle to manage their work, it is very tempting to step in and "help" the team. For example, suppose a team seems to not be making enough progress. The PO might be worried and the team might not seem concerned. In such a situation, it is perfectly okay to talk to the team. But this discussion should occur on a peer-to-peer level, not on a hierarchical power level. The PO can ask awareness-type questions to help the team realize that there might be an issue, or share their view and explain the concerns. Ultimately, though, the PO should leave it up to the team to decide the details, if any, about what to do. The PO might not agree with the team's decisions, but lets the team take full ownership and responsibility and then hold each other accountable at the end of the Sprint.

For such a constructive collaboration to happen, consider removing any formal appraisal authority from the PO role so that teams and POs are peers in that respect. Consider connecting team performance to product performance measures related to economic benefit and user value.

Being peers does not mean that team members and POs cannot hold each other accountable. Recognize the challenges inherent in dealing with complexity and unstable requirements and emerging insights; however, as a PO, you should not accept teams that repeatedly overcommit. An Agile team should learn about their capacity and be able to provide reliability in delivering on the Sprint Goal. Repeatedly overcommitting and wishful thinking usually do not help and if the teams show such behavior, it is professional to hold them accountable for that. Similar situations can occur where the teams hold the PO accountable.

Stakeholder Committees

Many products have internal users, stakeholders, and external users. For example, a lending product can have external users who apply for loans and internal users who assess risk and offer lending proposals.

We have noticed that POs often struggle to convince and align larger groups of users and stakeholders. Individual stakeholder negotiation and prioritization can lead to excess workload and, more importantly, a lack of understanding and trust among stakeholders. This makes it hard to establish shared goals and commitment to the plans among stakeholders. To avoid this dilemma, consider creating a stakeholder community whose members regularly discuss priorities and strategies and align with the PO's decisions.

Connect the Teams with Users

The PO does not precisely describe the functionality to develop. A PO is not a user story writer. As we showed in Figure 11.1, having a PO who serves as a requirements engineer reduces the team domain understanding and ownership of the product outcomes. Instead, the PO should help the team learn about the user domain and allow the team to take full ownership of its solutions. Consider connecting the team directly with users, as this enables the team to learn about the user problems and to influence product decisions.

Summary

This chapter focused on the Product Owner role. At large scale, a senior manager with deep understanding of the market and stakeholders should fill the PO role. The PO should spend most of their time working on the product, stakeholders, users, and teams, but should not focus on general managerial activities; that is the responsibility of management.

To work effectively with a large group, you need a strong product vision to drive the self-managing teams, and the teams need to work closely with the end customers to clarify Product Backlog Item details so that the PO has more time for strategic work. Measures of success are based on outcomes, rather than outputs, as product success is key, not the amount of work the team gets done. Multi-team event facilitation techniques will prove invaluable for the group, and PO leadership should be attuned to collaborating successfully with the teams.

References

1. Ken Schwaber. "Product Owners Not Proxies." January 31, 2011. https://kenschwaber.wordpress.com/2011/01/31/product-owners-not-proxies/.

2. Cesário Ramos. "Scale Your Product NOT Your Scrum." Agilix (2016). www.agilix.nl/resources/ScaleYourProductNotYourScrum.pdf

3. Michael L. Hall. *Coaching Change: The Axes of Change Meta-Coaching)* (Neuro-semantics Press, 2015).

4. Ken Schwaber. *The Enterprise and Scrum (Developer Best Practices)* (Microsoft Press, 2007).

5. "1-2-4-All." Liberating Structures. www.liberatingstructures.com/1-1-2-4-all/.

6. "What, So What, Now What? W³." Liberating Structures. www.liberatingstructures.com/9-what-so-what-now-what-w/.

7. Raquel Sánchez Fernández and M. Ángeles Iniesta-Bonillo. "The Concept of Perceived Value: A Systematic Review of the Research." *Marketing Theory* 7, no. 4 (2007): 427–451. doi:10.1177/1470593107083165.

8. Giff Constable. *Talking to Humans: Success Starts with Understanding Your Customers* (2014).

9. Luke Hohmann. *Innovation Games: Creating Breakthrough Products Through Collaborative Play* (Addison-Wesley, 2007).

10. Jeff Gothelf and Josh Seiden. *Lean UX: Designing Great Products with Agile Teams*, 3rd ed. (O'Reilly Media, 2021).

11. Scrum Patterns Group. *A Scrum Book* (2019). www.scrumbook.org.

12. Roman Pichler. "The Product Vision Board." www.romanpichler.com/tools/product-vision-board/.

13. "What Is a Product Backlog?" www.scrum.org/resources/what-is-a-product-backlog.

14. Ken Schwaber. Heart of Scrum for Software Development. https://heartofscrum.org/quote/nobody-allocates-assignments-and-ensures-they-are-done-in-time.

APPENDIX

Case Studies and Workshop Examples

A. Reference to Case Studies

- **Large-Scale Scrum at Large Dutch Bank:** https://agilix.nl/case-study/large-dutch-bank-our-journey-towards-agility-at-scale/?lang=en

- **Large-Scale Scrum at MTS Kassa:** https://agilix.nl/case-study/mts-kassa/?lang=en

- **Large-Scale Scrum at Surface Radar:** https://agilix.nl/case-study/voorbeeld-case-study/?lang=en

B. System Improvements with Scrum Patterns

We seriously thought about whether we should include this section on Scrum patterns, but we think they are so important that we prefer to give a short, incomplete overview of Scrum patterns rather than omit them altogether.

We like to use Scrum patterns[1] for systemic improvements. A Scrum Book contains 94 Scrum patterns. Contrast that to the Scrum Guide of a few pages. Knowing the rules of Scrum does not make you a great player of Scrum, in very much the same way that knowing the rules of chess does not make you a great chess player. So, while the *Scrum Guide* provides the rules of Scrum, the Scrum patterns explain how to solve systemic problems in a specific context.

What Is a Scrum Pattern?

A Scrum pattern captures proven solutions that were distilled from observing many Scrum teams across the planet—both their successes and failures. Here, we've provided a simplified and short summary of the pattern for the famous Daily Scrum.

A Scrum pattern consists of the following parts (we show some examples of these parts):[2]

- **Initial context:** The Development Team has created a Sprint Backlog and is working to achieve the Sprint Goal.

- **Problem statement:** The team makes progress in a Sprint by finishing Sprint Backlog Items, but given the complexity of the work, the characteristics, size, and quantity of tasks change frequently—sometimes minute by minute.

- **Forces:** There are 3,628,800 ways to order 10 tasks, yet only a few of these ways will put the team "in the zone." … Too much replanning and re-estimating wastes time and suffocates developers.

- **Solution:** Have a short event every day to replan the Sprint, to optimize the chances first of meeting the Sprint Goal and second of completing all Sprint Backlog Items.

- **Resulting context:** Daily Scrums have additional benefits as well: reduce time wasted because the team makes impediments visible daily; help find opportunities for coordination because everyone knows what everyone else is working on; and so on.

A Scrum pattern:

- Is only applicable in a specific context (**initial context**). If your context does not match, consider if the Scrum pattern is useful in your context.

- Describes a problem in that context (**problem statement**). If you do not have the problem, then you probably do not need the solution, either.

- Explains the forces that need to be considered when applying the pattern (**forces**). The forces guide you to come up with your specific solution that works in your specific environment.

- Offers a canonical solution to a problem in that context for inspiration (**solution**). You can implement the solution in many different ways. It also explains why the solution solves the problem and balances the forces so that you can create your implementation of the solution.

- Describes the new systemic state and points to new Scrum patterns to consider applying (**resulting context**).

Scrum patterns help you identify which problems you want to address and provide a proven solution that will point you in the right direction.

How to Use Scrum Patterns

You can use Scrum patterns to build and improve your Scrum team, your product organization, and your value stream.

The patterns in *A Scrum Book*[1] organize into two pattern languages: Value Stream and Product Organization. The Value Stream language structures the time needed to deliver a product, and the Product Organization language structures the relationships between people to build Scrum teams. (You can access the pattern and the languages for free at the scrumbook.org website.) These two pattern languages form the two wholes of Scrum. Now, how to use these languages?

A Systemic Approach

How do you design a house? Russell Ackoff explains it this way[3]: The architect designs to satisfy the needs of the residents and first draws the house (the whole). The architect then divides the house into rooms (the parts). A room is only improved if it also improves the house, and it can be the case that the architect chooses to make a room worse to improve the house as a whole. So, you start with determining the function of the larger whole and then improve the whole by refining it with parts.

We apply the same approach with the Scrum patterns. You start with the most extensive pattern (the whole) and then refine it with subsequent patterns. You are always keeping in mind the goals of the whole.

You might be thinking, so what? First, it is crucial to understand the boundaries of your system and the goal you are striving to reach because you are unlikely to improve the performance of the whole by improving the parts taken separately.[3] Let us explain using a simple example.

Using Systems Thinking and Scrum Patterns to Build Your Team

Suppose a team is having trouble aligning during the Sprint because of the complexity of the work. Thinking about the Scrum framework, what does Scrum offer to help the team members align? Yes, you are right, the Daily Scrum event. You can determine that the Daily Scrum might be appropriate for this team by verifying that the pattern's problem statement matches your current problem. The problem statement of the Daily Scrum pattern states

> *The team makes progress in a Sprint by finishing Sprint Backlog Items, but given the complexity of the work, the characteristics, size, and quantity of tasks change frequently—sometimes minute by minute.*[2]

A good match! So, let's apply the pattern, right? Well, maybe. Let's look at the Daily Scrum pattern position on the Product Organization pattern language (see Figure A.1).

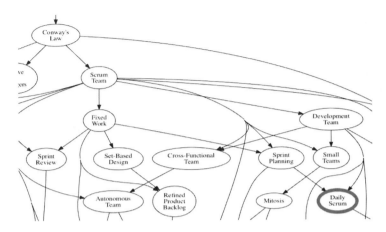

Figure A.1
Pattern language graph: single pattern selected.

You can see the location of the Daily Scrum pattern in the language. The Daily Scrum pattern has two incoming arrows, one from Sprint Planning and one from the Development Team pattern. The arrows mean that the Daily Scrum pattern refines both of these patterns. In other words, it improves the larger system's Sprint Planning and Development Team.

What use is having a Daily Scrum if the team did not do Sprint Planning? Exactly! Not very useful. The team will improve its performance with the Daily Scrum pattern if it already works from a Sprint Backlog created at Sprint Planning. Sprint Planning is the more extensive system, and Daily Scrum is a smaller part of that system.

So, before applying the Daily Scrum pattern, the language suggests investigating if you need first to apply the Sprint Planning pattern. If you have not implemented the Sprint Planning pattern already, then do that first.

Expanding the System Boundaries

In Figure A.1, Sprint Planning has an incoming arrow from Scrum Team, an even larger system. So, how do you create a Scrum team? What is the first step? Do you first need a development team? A Product Backlog? A Scrum Master? Or maybe a Product Owner? When we put this question to people, they usually choose a temporal approach. For example, they suggest starting with the Product Owner or development team and then add them to make up a Scrum team. This approach focuses on the parts, Product Owner, development team, or Scrum Master instead of focusing on the whole, the Scrum team. Figure A.2 illustrates that Daily Scrum is a part of Sprint Planning, which is a part of the larger system Scrum Team.

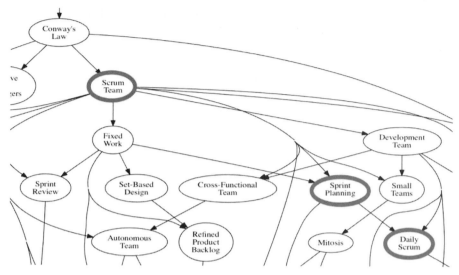

Figure A.2
Pattern language graph: expanded boundaries for Daily Scrum pattern.

Again, the language points you in the right direction. The Scrum Team pattern text suggests having a product vision and gathering people who can make and deliver the product. After you have that, you might refine the Scrum team by, for example, creating a development team when you face the problems it solves. The key is that you start with the whole, the Scrum team, and improve the parts if doing so also improves the Scrum team.

Pattern Sequences

The initial context and problem statements of the individual patterns help you identify if a pattern could be helpful for your specific situation; the pattern language enables you to determine the sequence of patterns you might need to implement. A pattern sequence is the order of patterns application. Organizations create their pattern sequence by selecting the patterns that are most appropriate in their context.

But how can you determine the context? And how do you handle the pattern relationships depicted in the pattern languages?

Handling the Pattern Relationships

There are two relationships between patterns:

- A pattern can be an alternative to another pattern. Alternative patterns refine a common larger pattern.

- A pattern refines another pattern. The refinement relationship defines a dependency between patterns.

For example: In Figure A.3, you can see that Sprint Burndown Chart, Scrum Board, and Yesterday's Weather refine the Sprint Backlog—a dependency relation. Before applying the Sprint Burndown Chart, we recommended using the Sprint Backlog first.

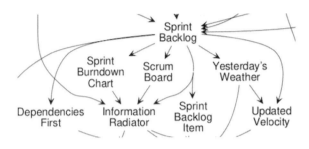

Figure A.3
Pattern relationships.

Also, the patterns Sprint Burndown Chart, Scrum Board, and Yesterday's Weather are alternatives to each other. You can try any of those after you implement the Sprint Backlog. For example, these are some valid sequences you can generate:

- Sprint Backlog → Sprint Burndown Chart → Scrum Board

- Sprint Backlog → Sprint Burndown Chart → Yesterday's Weather → Scrum Board

- Sprint Backlog → Sprint Burndown Chart → Information Radiator → Scrum Board

Finding Your Starting Context

As mentioned previously, you need to understand your current context to select patterns and form a sequence. A way to determine that is to perform Go See sessions (see Chapter 8, "Preparing the Product Group").

The list that follows shows a subset of Go See results that we developed when working with a client to understand the current context.

The team's conclusions:

- We do not break the stories down sufficiently; a lot of work remains hidden during the Sprint, which gives us unpleasant surprises. Also, team members find it hard to help each other during the Sprint.

- There are no acceptance criteria for the stories, and the teams do not understand what to achieve.

- There is no clear goal for the Sprints. Sprint Planning is about "fixing 50% of the errors," and the team is not involved in deciding on this plan.

- It's unclear what the improvement actions are, what problem we want to solve, and how we know that the problem is solved.

- Work is not transparent to team members or the Product Owner. For example, a team member spends three weeks on test suite updates, and we just discovered this in a Sprint Review.

- In many Scrum events like Sprint Planning, the team lead asks most of the questions; there is a poor shared understanding of the work.

This excerpt portrays some of the contexts in which the teams operate.

With this context, you can facilitate a workshop to help the team build a pattern sequence.

C. Example of Building a Pattern Sequence Workshop

The goal of this workshop is for the team to select the patterns they want to implement and create their pattern sequence. It consists of three steps:

Step 1. Select the patterns to try.

Step 2. Create a sequence of patterns using the pattern languages.

Step 3. Select which pattern to implement first.

Materials needed:

- One set of pattern cards per group of four participants. Download your pattern card deck at scrum-patterns.org.

- Prepare a set of flipcharts to remind the team of the Go See results and their identified problems and current context. We use just a simple bullet point list to visualize the Go See results for discussion.

- For each group, a printed Value Stream and Product Organization pattern language graph.

- Pens, sticky notes, a whiteboard/flipchart, and large prints of the systemic assessment canvas.

Structuring the invitation: Invite the team to select the patterns that match their context and create a pattern sequence.

Select the Patterns to Try

Step 1. Use the prepared flipcharts to facilitate a summary of each of the identified problems. Then use serious game 35[4] to prioritize the cases. The result is a prioritized list of problems the teams want to solve.

Step 2. Briefly explain patterns and pattern languages and provide an example of a pattern sequence—the workshop's goal.

Step 3. Provide each table group with a preselected subset of the pattern cards that best fits the team's context. We recommend using a maximum of approximately 20 cards. (You need to select the pattern subset upfront.)

Step 4. Use the 1-2-4-All[5] liberating structure on the top three to five problems. Go down the list of problems, and for each, ask a question such as "What patterns do *you* see for making progress on our points?"

Each table group individually determines the top three patterns they would like to implement, and then all groups share their selection. In a workshop we facilitated, the teams selected the following patterns to try:

Definition of Done

Sprint Goal

Dependencies First

Enabling Specification

Definition of Ready

Visible Status

Swarming

Refined Product Backlog

The next step is to create a sequence to decide with which pattern to start.

Create a Sequence of Patterns Using the Pattern Languages

Give each table group a printed Value Stream and Product Organization language graph. Use the selected patterns to create a sequence in the following steps.

Step 1. Each table group marks the selected patterns in the language graphs.

Step 2. Starting at those patterns, draw a path through the other selected patterns in the order you might apply them. Continuing with our example, the team came up with the graph shown in Figure A.4.

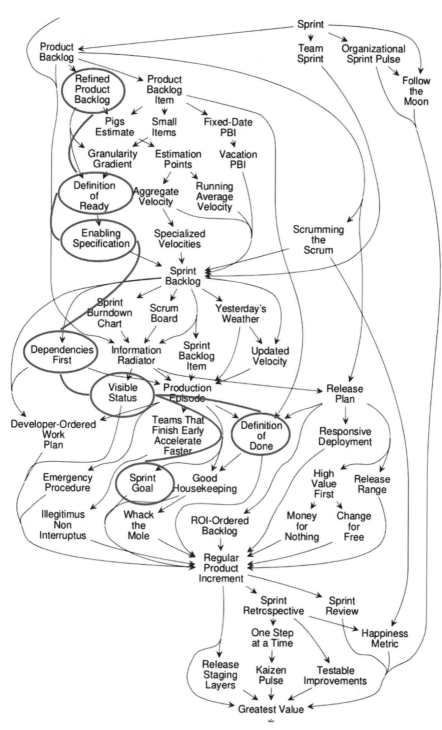

Figure A.4
Identified pattern path.

Step 3. Ask the teams to reflect on the pattern path: Which larger patterns could be needed? Which smaller patterns could be added? Continuing with our example, the team came up with the graph shown in Figure A.5.

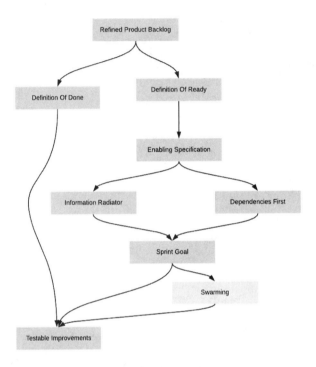

Figure A.5
Pattern sequence created using the language graph.

The orange-colored patterns are from the Value Stream language; the Swarming pattern (the blue one) is from the Product Organization language. The initial context of Swarming expects Sprint Goal to be adopted—that is why it is positioned after Sprint Goal.

Step 4. Use 1-2-4-All to determine the first pattern to start with (see Figure A.6).

Continuing with our example, the team started with this sequence: Refined Product Backlog → Definition of Done → Testable Improvements.

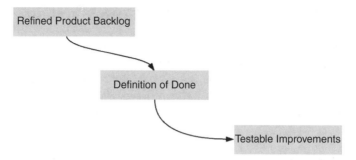

Figure A.6
Selected patterns to start with.

Apply One Pattern at a Time

A sequence is your best guess on how to improve the system at that moment in time. When you adopt a pattern, you will learn if it works or not. If it works, you keep it; if not, you backtrack and try another pattern. The basic process is as follows:

Step 1. Find your current context.

Step 2. Choose the pattern in that context that will most strengthen the whole.

Step 3. Apply the pattern.

Step 4. If it makes the system more whole, then recognize your new context and go to Step 2.

Step 5. If not, undo the pattern and try another at Step 2 instead.

Keep an experimental mindset, be ready to learn and adjust, and understand that there is no "best" sequence. A sequence shows a path, but the teams have to do the walking and discover how to implement it.

Create Your Own Pattern Language and Share in Your Organization

You can find the patterns mentioned in this section at scrumbook.org. If you decide to make use of the patterns, we look very much forward to your experience. You can create your own sequences, augment with your patterns, and create a language that works in your organization.

D. Example of Systemic Mode Sprint Retrospective

A Sprint Retrospective can be conducted in two modes: regular and systemic. The first mode is usually shorter and addresses minor or well-known issues that do not need deep analysis. A systemic Retrospective is used when teams meet with chronic and complex problems with no obvious solutions, when stakes are high. Often people have unsuccessfully tried to solve the problem before. Systemic mode broadens thinking and helps to articulate problems in new and different ways.

Step 1: Discover the Stories, Data, and Patterns Related to the Problem

The first step is about understanding the current reality. Why? Because we want to avoid premature conclusions. Improvement starts with accepting the reality of the current situation. When the team creates a thorough understanding of their current reality together, they share and agree on their condition. Based on this common understanding, the team can then start investigating how this situation is created and what they can do to improve it.

> If I had an hour to solve a problem, I'd spend 55 minutes thinking about the problem and 5 minutes thinking about solutions."—**attributed to Albert Einstein**

Gather Data Workshop

Avoid thinking about solutions in this workshop. Instead, begin by gathering data, emotions, and essential events in the form of stories. You want each of the participants in the situation to describe the problem from their point of view.

Steps You Can Consider

Consider trying one of the following workshop formats for capturing data, emotions, and essential events.

- Show and Tell: https://gamestorming.com/?s=show+and+tell
- HistoryMap: https://gamestorming.com/history-map/
- Timeline[6]

Facilitation

- Invite the team and stakeholders from different areas who play a role in the problem. Various perspectives are essential for a thorough discussion.
- Every stakeholder tells their story from their perspective.
- Focus on gathering facts; prevent discussing whose fault it is. Ensure people understand: It's nobody's fault, or everybody's, whichever you prefer.
- Focus on gathering concerns, doubts, and emotions.

Example Facilitation Questions

- What are the crucial facts that make this a problem?

- What are the critical events that happened?

- Which people's emotions were present?

- How do different stakeholders view the situation?

Caution

People tend to present a "solution" while explaining the problem. It's tempting to express a concern as, for example, "There is too little focus on product quality," instead of "Our product quality does not match the customers' expectations." Ensure that people do not jump to solutions or actions and instead focus on describing what happened.

Let's look at an example of one of our clients.

We worked with a group of nine teams developing a hardware and software product. The group suffered from low forecast reliability and low productivity. After a Gather Data workshop, the group had identified their most critical data:

- Large features that cannot fit into a Sprint

- Unacceptable product at the end of a Sprint

- Stakeholders are unhappy with the reliability of our progress reporting

- Complaining and heated discussion about the sequence of work within teams and with stakeholders

- Feature velocity is zero for many Sprints in a row

We jumped to conclusions and suggested they should work with features small enough to fit into their Sprints. At first sight, we thought that the solution was to teach them how to split large features into smaller ones. After some small success in the early Sprints, gradually the features became bigger and bigger again, not fitting into a Sprint.

We decided to follow up with a workshop to identify patterns.

Identify Patterns Workshop

You use the Gather Data workshop's result to identify important events that keep recurring over time. When problems or events happen only once, they are likely to be contextual and not systems.

So, recurring events are your friend in discovering undesired trends and patterns, but how do you discover them as a team? Try behavior over time graphs (BOTG). As explained in Chapter 2, "Systems Thinking," a BOTG can help the group better understand the trends and patterns in their situation.

We often use the canvas shown in Figure A.7 and facilitation to gather the information to construct a BOTG.

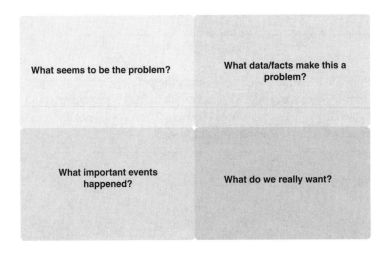

Figure A.7
Story canvas.

Steps You Can Consider

Use the story canvas to come up with the pieces for the story.

- For a multiple teams session, we use structures such as the Shift & Share[7] liberating structure or the World Café[8] method.

- At each table, ask participants to individually write answers for each area of the canvas on sticky notes.

- Discuss the results at the tables for 10 to 20 minutes. The table groups update/rewrite the stickies based on this discussion on their table canvas.

- At the end of the timebox, one person stays behind and the rest move to different tables for the next round. We do one round per question.

- After all rounds are done, use affinity mapping to merge and cluster the items of the table canvases onto one canvas.

Next, use the answers on the canvas to create more stories.

- Ensure the stakeholders agree on the stories.

- Take note of essential nouns and post them next to the canvas. These nouns will be candidate variables to use in the next steps.

Once you have shared stories about what happened, you are ready to build a BOTG. Ask the group to use the story and the nouns next to the canvas to choose the top three to four variables that influence and describe their problem. You can, for example, use the liberating structure 1-2-4-All for that.

Now that they have the critical variables in hand, ask the participants to draw the BOTGs and discuss these graphs using the following questions:

- Why are these series of events important?

- Based on the graph, what do we want to focus on?

Once your team(s) understands the data, patterns, and behavior over time, they can decide their *leading question* to address: What change in the current reality do we desire? A frequently used format for the leading questions is as follows:

"**Why are we** *<observed dynamic>* **despite our** *<previous actions for improvement>* **while our goal is** *<desired reality>?*"

We performed an Identify Patterns workshop that resulted in the following story and BOTG.

"Our problem seems to be that we are not able to deliver customer value every Sprint. The features are just too big. Although in the beginning, most features were delivered in a Sprint, over time most features started to span multiple Sprints despite our constant focus and awareness of management. When splitting items, emotions run high between developers and we get few features small enough. Management pressures us to increase productivity."

The group identified three main variables: features per Sprint, pressure on productivity, and transparency on progress. Plotting these variables over time showed the trend illustrated in Figure A.8.

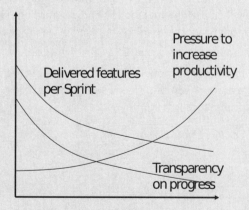

Figure A.8
Behavior over time graph with the top three variables.

As expected, the teams realized that as features per Sprint and added value decreased, the pressure from management increased. Our leading question became: ***Why are we*** *getting bigger features that cannot be finished every Sprint **despite our** training and coaching **while our goal** is to deliver value every Sprint?*

To answer this question, we needed to understand the driving forces that made the teams behave in this way. We needed to discover the mental models and group dynamics that generated this behavior over time.

Step 2: Discover the Structures and the Mental Models

Specific forces and factors generate and sustain the structures and patterns in a system. These structures create most, if not all, resistance when one applies a change intervention. So, the better the team(s) understands the underlying structures, the more likely it is to define useful intervention experiments.

One key force that generates the structures are mental models. You can use the Causal Loop Diagram (CLD) technique to discover the mental models and the structures at play (see Chapter 2, "Systems Thinking," for details on how to run such a CLD session).

Facilitation for Discovering Mental Models

People behave and make decisions based on their mental models. These models help them react efficiently to situations they face in their daily lives. Mental models are developed over time and are shaped by our experiences in life and the groups in which we participate.

As a facilitator of systems sessions, it is essential to realize that each person will describe the situation from their viewpoint based on their mental models and assumptions. Because different people likely have different mental models, another person's thinking or behavior can seem irrational or hard to understand.

Let us give you an example. In my mental model, most big dogs are dangerous. Therefore, when going for a walk, I avoid them as much as I can. When I see a big dog, I do not have to think about how to react anymore; I just automatically follow my script.

Our mental models give us stability by protecting us against all kinds of ideas.[9]

On the one hand, knowing what to do gives me a feeling of security and structure; on the other hand, it makes my behavior predictable and may limit my ability to discover that my mental model is incomplete or wrong. So, each mental model brings a perspective that can challenge other mental models. When people are open to different perspectives, sharing mental models creates a better team understanding of the current situation.

When facilitating the session, try to focus the group on discovering the mental models at play that explain the current behavior, decisions, situations, and emotions. Try the following questions while the teams draw their CLDs.

- Why do things go as they do?

- What is my/our personal responsibility?

- How do I/we support the current dynamic?

- To what extent am I a part of the problem?

- What are the dominant mental models that people use to create this situation?

- Which group dynamics are at play?

- What do people do and why?

Pay Special Attention to Confirmation Bias

In reality, all of us are susceptible to a tricky problem known as confirmation bias. Our beliefs are often based on paying attention to the information that upholds them, while tending to ignore the information that challenges them.

For example, whenever I encounter a big dog that barks, I place greater importance on this "evidence" supporting what I already believe: Big dogs are dangerous. I might even seek proof that further backs up my belief while discounting examples that don't support my idea.

As a facilitator, you can use the Five Whys method to explore possible confirmation bias. By asking "Why?" multiple times, you identify cause-and-effect relationships underlying a particular issue. The technique's primary goal is to discover the loops and variables in your CLD by repeating the question "Why?" Each answer forms the next question's basis and helps you ask questions to generate dialogue, discover mental models, and identify confirmation biases.

Back to the example of one of our clients.

With our main question and current understanding of the key variables, we conducted various CLD sessions. One of our first result was the CLD illustrated in Figure A.9.

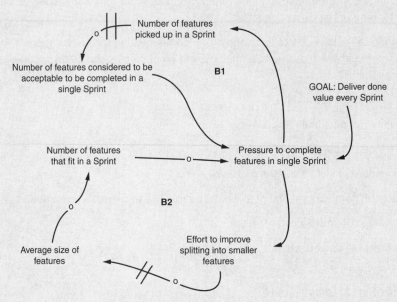

Figure A.9
First Causal Loop Diagram.

The bottom causal loop: The goal "to deliver value" put pressure on the teams to complete end-to-end features in every Sprint. The teams put extra effort in discovering how to split features, but splitting was very difficult in their context of hardware and software development. It was taking a lot of time to split and get end-to-end features in a Sprint.

The top causal loop: Surprisingly, the pressure to complete features also made the teams pick up fewer features. Over time, the acceptable number of features to complete in a Sprint became smaller and smaller, and that reduced the pressure (as shown in the CLD).

What we discovered was that the group often chose to work with fewer large features instead of making the effort to split features into multiple small ones. But why did they do this?

As a facilitator, we guided the teams through various discussions during the CLD sketching. Some of their answers were as follows:

- **What do we really want/shared vision?**
  "Deliver value every Sprint."
  "We must meet our estimations."

- **How do I support the current dynamics?**
  "I let everybody just do the thing they are good at."
  "I am not as productive as I could be, so I want tasks that I can do efficiently."

- **What are the current mental models?**

  "You just cannot split these things."

  "It takes too much time to split features that can better be used for developing."

  "Shipping features every Sprint does not make sense because we cannot test it until after all hardware is also done."

- **What do people do?**

  "Create technical features."

  "Late component integration works and is more efficient."

- **Why aren't we learning?**

  "We have no leadership commitment to measures and expectations."

After another round of modeling, the group produced the CLD shown in Figure A.10. We discovered the real reason behind the team behavior. Although the spoken goal was to deliver value in every Sprint, in reality the old system goal of "meeting estimations" was still in place. This implicit goal, created by pressures in the larger system, made the teams focus more on individual efficiency instead of choosing to invest time and effort to improve splitting so that many small features could fit in a Sprint. It was easier to lower the norm and fit only one or two features inside a Sprint and have many other features span multiple Sprints—the top balancing loop in the CLD in Figure A.10.

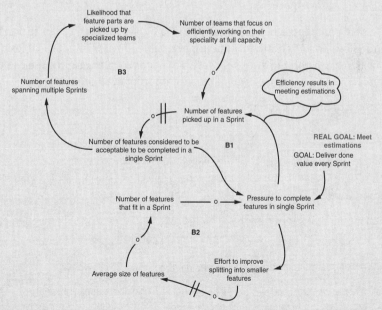

Figure A.10
Second Causal Loop Diagram.

By having features that spanned multiple Sprints, most teams and individuals could still work on feature-parts within their specialty and be locally efficient. This particular dynamic is also expressed in the "drifting goals" systems archetype.

Step 3: Formulate an Improvement Action

Interventions are meant to change an undesired rising trend into a downward trend or to change an undesired downward trend into a rising trend. There can also be a fluctuating trend in the BOTG that you might want to stabilize.

As described in Chapter 2, "Systems Thinking," only four types of systems interventions are possible:

- Adding a variable to establish a new causal relationship

- Establishing a new causal relation between current variables

- Reducing delays to improve feedback and learning

- Breaking or weakening of an existing cause-and-effect relationship

Most of the time, you'll want to intervene in a balancing loop because a balancing loop is keeping your current situation stable. It's important to realize that your current thinking and actions actually create this exact balancing loop, so to intervene you will likely need interventions that are radically different from your previous ones!

Intervening in a dominant loop is most likely to yield the biggest impact. Variables that have a lot of outgoing arrows can point to a strong influencing variable, a major cause. Variables that have a lot of incoming arrows can point to a strong effect, a major effect. Because you are dealing with systems issues, interventions are likely to require broad support or even organizational design changes.

Back to the example of one of our clients.

We identified the balancing loop B2 as the main loop in which to intervene. Our question became: What can be done to turn the downward trend of the number of features in a Sprint into an upward trend?

A key mental model that supported the dynamic was "Efficiency results in meeting estimations." From that, the teams came up with a set of possible interventions that might help:

1. Management stops expecting the teams to plan to 100% capacity.

2. Create awareness that delivering end-to-end features increases transparency into progress and that value starts with usable features.

3. Move to feature teams using the AB-BA model.

4. Management values cross-team results and devalues individual results.

5. Lead by example and show how to split a feature.

6. Debunk the myth that testing is only valuable after the complete large feature is done.

Eventually, the teams and management came to the insight that planning for the teams to work at full capacity does not increase efficiency at the overall feature level. They agreed to perform interventions 1 and 2. Management made it possible for the teams to plan work for approximately 60% capacity and use the spare capacity to learn how to work outside their main specialization, but on end-to-end features. The CLD in Figure A.11 shows this intervention.

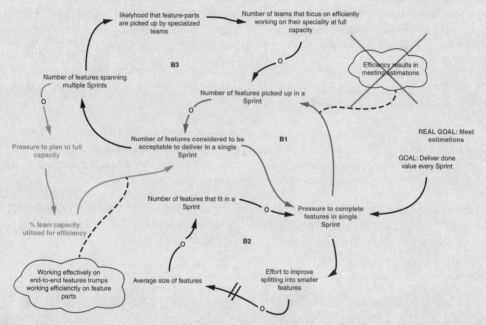

Figure A.11
Final Causal Loop Diagram.

Although some people were still skeptical, especially management, the teams were fortunate, and by planning less work in the Sprint, they became more reliable the next Sprint. This small success was the stepping stone to implement other interventions. Within a year, the whole group managed to finish a few features per Sprint regularly. The focus shifted to quality and finishing features, and as a result, their reliability significantly increased.

E. Scrum and *Kanban*

There is a myth that Agile teams need to choose between Scrum or *Kanban*. This is a false dichotomy. Regardless of which definition of *Kanban* that you use, it complements Scrum, and does not contradict it. The *Kanban* Method, as formulated by David J. Anderson, is an approach to incremental, evolutionary process and systems change for organizations. It is framework agnostic and can be used with any underlying process.

> *Kanban is not a software development lifecycle methodology or an approach to project management. It requires that some process is already in place so that Kanban can be applied to incrementally change the underlying process.*[10]

Scrum.org defines *Kanban* as "a strategy for optimizing the flow of value through a process that uses a visual, work-in-progress limited pull system." The original *Kanban* from Toyota is a tool for managing the flow and production of materials in a Toyota-style "pull" production system.

We perceive *Kanban* and Scrum as helpful tools for organizations to identify their problems and learn, then solve problems and improve. That is the key. Bear in mind that the perfection goal is a true one-piece-flow system with zero inventory.

> *The challenge is to develop a learning organization that will find ways to reduce the number of kanban and thereby reduce and finally eliminate the inventory buffer. Remember: the kanban is an organized system of inventory buffers and, according to Ohno, inventory is waste, whether it is in a push system or a pull system. So kanban is something you strive to get rid of, not to be proud of.*[11]

That is why we recommend using a swarming pattern [Swarming: One-Piece Continuous Flow] (dissolving the problem) at the start if possible. However, sometimes that is not an option because of the high transaction costs.

Once we worked with a product group that had a poor-quality codebase and lacked automated tests. The manual regression took them almost 2 weeks. They used to accumulate a big batch of features for 2 months and then do the manual testing. Working in a one-piece flow approach would be too much stress for them and impractical. Thus, we started with 1-month Sprints and asked the teams to come up with a releasable increment by the end of each timebox. In essence, we challenged them to work with a twice smaller batch. That resulted in quite a lot of pain and resistance from several people. Eventually, though, it created the necessary conditions for increasing test automation. In a year, the product group moved to 2-week Sprints and reduced technical debt significantly. They are still on their one to one-piece flow.

In this case, Scrum teams may use *Kanban* and temporarily manage the queues (solve the problem) instead of eradicating them (dissolve the problem). Nevertheless, your focus should remain on the perfection vision, lowering transaction costs in the long term to make one-piece flow possible, and eventually getting rid of *Kanban*.

F. Example: Splitting Product Backlog Items

The items on a Product Backlog (PBL) are of different sizes. The Product Backlog Items (PBIs) nearer to the top tend to be smaller, while those closer to the bottom tend to be bigger. There are two main reasons for this.

First, a PBI closer to the bottom of the backlog has a lot of uncertainty—uncertainty in value, uncertainty in details, but most of all uncertainty about whether it will ever reach the top of the PBL. New items may emerge, or further information may lead to a different prioritization. Therefore, you shouldn't waste too much effort in these uncertain PBIs; instead, try to add its details just in time.

Second, there is no right size of a PBI. Stakeholders more readily identify with features that make sense in their domain. Features are usually too big to complete in a single 2-week Sprint and, therefore, are not very practical for the teams. Teams prefer splitting a large feature into smaller items for the following reasons:

- **Risk mitigation:** Better slicing means a more detailed analysis of the items. Thus, there is a big chance that the team identifies and mitigates risks that otherwise would have surfaced in the upcoming Sprint.

- **Postponing less valuable work:** Splitting a large item makes it possible to separate the most valuable parts from the less valuable parts. The most valuable stories can go to the top and the rest go more to the bottom of the PBL. The Scrum team does not waste any time on performing something that has less value from the Product Owner's perspective.

- **Better forecasts:** Smaller items improve understanding and cause fewer surprises in Sprint. A team that stably finishes, on average, the same number of stories from Sprint to Sprint, becomes more reliable for the Product Owner and stakeholders.

- **Saving time on estimations:** When the team delivers 6–10 small stories during a Sprint, it is very likely that those stories are approximately equal in size. This means that over time the team will not have to estimate each story individually but can provide good forecasts by just counting the number of them.

- **Less process variability in a Sprint:** Taking on a large PBI comes with increased unknowns and surprises in the Sprint. In terms of production flow, it corresponds to working with large batch sizes. Large batch sizes increase the process's variance, which leads to queues and all of their associated problems. To reduce variance, reduce batch size or, stated otherwise, split big PBIs into smaller ones.

- **Better distribution of work within the Sprint:** Teams that take in large PBIs are often overloaded at the end of each Sprint. This problem is complex, but a finer slicing of stories is one of the ways of dealing with it. Small stories in the Sprint lead to better parallelization of the work, better measures of progress, and more opportunities for team members to help each other.

- **Fast feedback:** The team can obtain feedback from the Product Owner and stakeholders during the Sprint without waiting until the end of the Sprint.

- **Better spirit:** Feedback on progress toward a goal motivates people. People like the feeling of accomplishment. Think about it, which are your favorite football (that's soccer, for you Americans) matches—those that end with a score of 0–0 or 3–2?

Helping the Team Become Masters in Splitting PBIs

Many Scrum teams have difficulties with splitting user stories. Often, we hear people saying, "It's absolutely impossible to split this PBI." That's not true, as you can always split off a failure case. The failure case is both valuable to an end user—you want good information when things go wrong—and, by definition, smaller. For the teams to learn how to split PBIs, we recommend organizing a workshop on story splitting for every Scrum team.

Next, we share a workshop format for splitting items. It consists of the following steps:

Step 1. Discuss the importance of PBI splitting.

Step 2. Share the principles of PBI splitting.

Step 3. Split a big PBI as an example.

Many Scrum teams prefer to use a user story format when working with PBIs, so we'll use the terms "stories" and "PBIs" interchangeably here.

Discuss the Importance of Splitting

Before the meeting, make sure you get the Product Owner onboard. First, ask everyone why it is important to learn how to split big PBIs. Ask the team to form small groups and let them discuss this question for a couple of minutes. Then, start an open discussion and write down the answers on a flipchart. Add your own ideas if necessary.

Share the Principles of Story Splitting

Count off the whole group in twos. Give participants with odd numbers printed techniques for splitting user stories,[12] and those with even numbers a cheat sheet of examples of each technique.[13] Ask everyone to read the documents thoroughly for 10 minutes.

A very effective way of learning is teaching others. When the 10 minutes are up, ask the even numbers to pair up with the odd ones. Give them another 10 minutes to teach the material they have just studied to each other (5 minutes in one direction and 5 minutes in the opposite direction).

Move from one pair to another and answer their questions if needed. We recommend avoiding an open discussion as much as possible. It is better to answer the same question several times in small groups than to get stuck in an open discussion for a long time and drop the group dynamics. A main principle of facilitation, and one to which we adhere, is preferring to work in small groups over an open discussion.

Split a Big Product Backlog Item

We ask the Product Owner to bring a story that they would like to split in advance.

To ensure that discussion doesn't take forever and help maintain the focus, consider working in timeboxes. Ask how much time the team will need from the Product Owner to answer all the clarifying questions about the story the Product Owner has chosen. Depending on the answer, start a timer and facilitate an open discussion. Help the discussion to stay focused. The developers often delve into less important themes and digress.

After the Product Owner has clarified the details, form small groups of no more than four. Make sure every group includes a domain expert or a business analyst. Give them 20 minutes, provide the necessary materials (flipcharts, boards, markers), and ask to split the story into at least 10 smaller ones. Move from one group to another, answer any questions that arise, and provide support in every way possible.

Put the Results on One List

Return to open discussion and ask each group to present the results of their work. After each presentation, help the team to make sense of the facts and implications by asking questions such as "What's the most interesting thing that you have noticed?" and "What new stories have you discovered from this group?"

After each group has presented their splitting options, make the final list with the whole group. If you followed the algorithm, you could come up with a list of 10–20 stories. These stories have not been described in sufficient detail yet. You will have to deal with this at the next Product Backlog Retrospective activity.

G. Example: Increasing Customer Understanding with Serious Games

Serious games enable groups of people to come up with creative and supported solutions to problems together. They take advantage of fun, involvement, and collaborative creativity to find a supported answer to a business problem. From the Product Owner's perspective, serious games help gain insights into customer needs, user motives, product usage, and desires.

How can you use serious games in your product group? Let us provide an example.

We worked with a company that wanted to develop a new enterprise collaboration product. It already had some ideas about the users' problems, their needs, and the desired product features and wanted to start development. We proposed to first fine-tune their current ideas before starting iterative development. We identified the following approach to validate their ideas:

1. Product vision validation: Validate and adjust the initial value proposition and product vision.

2. Continuous discovery and development: Iteratively validate the most fundamental assumptions and develop a first release.

Product Vision Validation

We wanted to address three main goals:

- Identify the needs and problems of the users to determine the required outcomes.
- Understand user tasks and goals as input for developing potential solutions.
- Validate our initial value proposition and determine the highest risks.

With these questions in mind, we organized a customer understanding session to "Envision our next product." That involved the following steps:

- Invite key external users and customers from different client organizations.
- Invite internal people from product management and R&D.
- Mix external users and customers with internal people into three table groups.
- Facilitate a day of serious gaming.

The mixed groups put the internal people in direct collaboration with the users to maximize customer empathy and understanding. In addition, we placed a silent observer in each table group to take notes about anything the customers/users said that was interesting for further analysis.

We designed our game plan using the "Design Your Workshop Canvas" we shared in Chapter 10, "Coaching Teams."

Our Game Plan

Figure A.12 shows the sequence of serious games we used for the workshop.

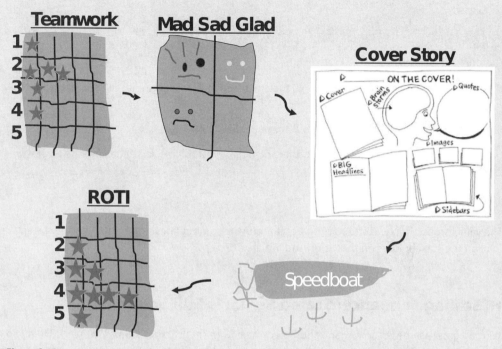

Figure A.12
Game plan for customer understanding.

After opening activities, we started with a warm-up using a Histogram[14] to identify how the participants felt about collaboration effectiveness in their organization. After that, we identified their daily problems, tasks, and needs by playing the Mad Sad Glad game.[15]

To identify their ideal product and wanted outcomes, we built on the Mad Sad Glad results with Cover Story.[16] The group discussions and presentations gave us detailed insights into the users' desired outcomes. In the last step, we wanted to understand what would prevent them from realizing the ideal product in their organization. The product group would also need to find solutions to these problems to be useful. We used the Speedboat[17] game to identify the issues to solve. We closed with a Return on Time Invested Histogram.[16] After that we had a great dinner!

Analyzing the Game Results

The next day, the internal people got together to post-process the game results. We compiled the results and clarified the initial product ideas using the Value Proposition canvas.[18]

Results

This session provided the Product Owner with better insights into:

- The tasks of the users

- The problems and impediments the customers had in realizing their tasks and solving their problems

- The goals the users wanted to achieve by doing their tasks

- How the customers thought about solving their problems and achieving their tasks

The value proposition was the starting point for further product development. A key next step was to align the stakeholders on the vision and initial next steps.

H. Scaling Sequence: Scaled Scrum Is Still Scrum

You can grow a large Scrum organization piecemeal from small Scrum teams that work. Doing so requires the development of a product organization and a process for delivering the product. Each team builds its local process first. As the group adds more and more teams, they create their inter-team coordination process and product organization.

A typical Scrum pattern build sequence that you might want to consider in your organization is as follows (relevant Scrum patterns appear in brackets):[1]

- **How do you start?** Create a working [Scrum Team].

- **How do you grow one team?** Add people to your team and split into two teams when it becomes too big. Both teams share the way of working. The new team might hire a Scrum Master to guide the team in the use of Scrum.

- **How do you organize the teams?** Organize the teams so that they work across components and keep delivering end-user functionality. Beware of [Conway's Law].

- **How do you deal with product cross-cutting concerns like architecture or UX?** People form into communities.

- **How do you keep the team focused on the whole product and working on the most valuable work?** All teams work off a single [Product Backlog].

- **How do you identify dependencies across the various teams?** Hold multi-team events like [Sprint Planning] and Product Backlog refinement where the teams identify opportunities for coordination during the [Sprint].

- **How do you keep all the teams aligned and have a consistent view on progress?** All the teams work in the same Sprint and deliver a single working product.

- **How do the teams handle interteam coordination during the Sprint?** The teams figure out the best way to coordinate their efforts based on the identified dependencies during multi-team events and community meetings.

- **How do you keep transparency at the product level?** All the teams work according to a single [Definition of Done].

- **How can you plan delivery at the product level across all the teams?** All teams share a common estimation scale and aggregate their velocity for the single product's progress.

- **How can you evaluate progress on the full product?** Produce a single product increment and hold a single [Sprint Review] for all the teams.

- **How do you deal with systemic problems?** Hold an overall Retrospective in systemic mode (see Chapter 10, "Coaching Teams") to solve systemic issues.

- **How can each team keep producing end-to-end customer features when the size and complexity of the product keep increasing?** Specialize the teams along [Value Areas].

- **How can the single Product Owner keep a deep and broad understanding of the market and product details?** Form a [Product Owner Team] with an expert for each [Value Area] that works under the leadership of the single [Product Owner].

So, scaled Scrum is still Scrum. For each part of the Scrum framework, we:

- Keep it as simple as one-team Scrum
- Keep all teams focused on the customer
- Keep all teams focused on the whole product
- Keep all teams autonomous and self-managing

Scrum is a framework that builds a process, not a method that produces products. We use the Scrum framework to build the complete product development process. Nothing needs to be added to the Scrum framework.

I. Example: Workshop to Define Measures for Improvement

Let's see how you could facilitate a measure-for-improvement workshop.

A useful measure:

- **Enables you to take action:** Provides concrete process data about behavior.
- **Is testable:** Allows for performance analysis and the generation of improvement actions.

- **Is aligned with a greater goal:** The purpose of the system
- **Drives learning:** Shows deviations from your perfect process.

How to Facilitate the Workshop

Materials needed: Pens, sticky notes, a whiteboard/flipchart, and the Measure for Learning canvas.

Structuring the invitation: Suppose that the goal is to determine how the teams will learn the organization's selected Agile practices. To do that, start with identifying the list of learning goals and associated measures.

Ask the participants to generate answers to the following questions individually:

- Which practices do we need to learn as a team/group/organization to achieve X?
- Which current measures do we use to measure progress?

Then, after all participants are done writing, ask each person to explain their answers to their (table) group, and post them on the whiteboard (see Figure A.13). Use affinity mapping to identify common themes.

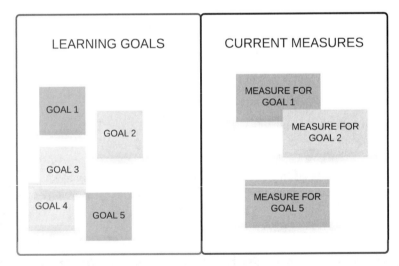

Figure A.13
Goals and Measures canvas.

Facilitate a group discussion so that the participants discover patterns and create insights. Consider a What? So What? Now What?[19] format. With a common understanding, along with the lists of goals and measures, you start to create measures for learning.

Using the Measure for Learning Canvas

The goal of this activity is to improve current measures and create new measures for the practices the team wants to learn and improve on. At the core of this workshop are the four questions outlined in Figure A.14. You use these questions to improve on the learning goals and measures of the first exercise.

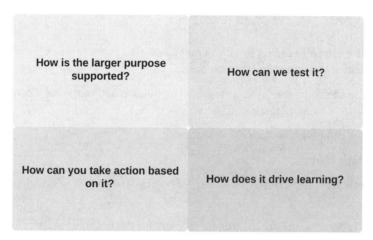

Figure A.14
Measures for Learning canvas.

How to Facilitate?

Select a learning goal and related measure(s) from the first exercise. Then assess and improve your selection by answering all questions on the canvas. We recommend to follow the following sequence, one at a time:

- How does it support the purpose?

  With which greater goal is it aligned?

- How is it testable?

  Which concrete performance can we analyze?

- How does it drive learning?

  Which deviations from your perfect process does it show?

- How can you take action with it?

  What are concrete process data or observations about behavior? And how can we generate improvement actions from that?

Steps

Step 1. Ask the participants, working in pairs, to generate answers to the first question on sticky notes.

Step 2. Ask each pair to explain their responses to their group and to post their notes on a whiteboard. (You can use the 1-2-4-All liberating structure, for example.)

Step 3. Repeat the same process for the remaining three questions.

Next, reflect on the complete canvas and distill measures and actions for each learning goal. You can use notice, meaning, and application questions.

Let us give an example of the canvas using the goal mentioned in Chapter 10, "Coaching Teams": *We want to learn how to be more reliable.*

- **Name:** Solve defects immediately after discovery
- **Stakeholders:** Team
- **How is it testable?** Capture the percentage of defects that were solved within 1 day after discovery.
- **How does it drive learning?** The situations where we did not solve a defect immediately after discovery.
- **How can you take action with it?** What are we doing/not doing to solve defects within 1 day? Which competing commitments are driving our actions?
- **Past:** [Week 31] 0% of defects were solved within 1 day after discovery.
- **Goal:** [Week 32] 30% of defects are solved within 1 day after discovery.
- **How does it support the purpose?** Solving defects earlier reduces the total known defects at the end of the Sprint. That improves reliability.

The overall goal can be captured as follows:

- **Name:** Zero known defects at the end of the Sprint
- **Stakeholders:** Team
- **Scale:** Percent decrease in known defects
- **Meter:** Build reports
- **Past:** [April 2022] 45 known defects at the end of the Sprint
- **Goal:** [June 2022] 0 known defects at the end of the Sprint

J. The ORID Framework

The ORID method is based on a four-phase model. Each phase addresses a specific area so as to get a better understanding of reality and collect different points of view. The four levels of reflection form a pattern from which innumerable conversations can be drawn. It simply flows from a natural internal process of perception, response, judgment, and decision.

Here is a short description of the phases:

- **Objective:** Perceptions, what we often call "objective reality."

- **Reflexive:** Feelings, emotional reaction to information received from the outside.

- **Interpretation:** Analysis, understanding of the information, and why it is important.

- **Decision making:** Next steps and conclusions.

Some examples of the questions for each phase are shown in Table A.1.

Table A.1   ORID Framework Questions

Objective	Reflexive	Interpretation	Decision Making
What happened?	Where were you surprised?	What is the significance of this?	What are we going to do?
What did people hear or see?	What annoys you?	What options are open to us?	What are the next steps?
What facts do we know?	What was easy or difficult?	What insights are beginning to emerge?	Who will do it? By when?
What did you notice about this?	Where were you engaged or not engaged?	What underlies these issues?	How will we apply what we just learned?
	When were you excited?	What leverage does this give us?	What are we really committed to now?

A great learning resource is an article by Brian Stanfield entitled "The Art of Focused Conversation."[20] Another great resource is his book *The Art of Focused Conversation: 100 Ways to Access Group Wisdom in the Workplace.*[21]

Rational and Experiential Aims

A good discussion will benefit from having both a good facilitator and an intention. The intention creates a foundation for the facilitation process and helps you find the appropriate questions. When thinking about the intention, it is useful to think from two angles: rational aim (RA) and experiential aim (EA). Rational aims are related to the "head" aspect. There is often more than one rational aim for each meeting. Here are some examples:

- Arrive at a consensus decision about which tool will be used for the Sprint Backlog.

- Establish working agreements for our team that we can use for all future meetings.

The experiential aim means defining the experience you want people to have as a result of being in this meeting or workshop together. It focuses on how you want people to sense each other, reflect on the data, experience the moment, and feel about a certain topic. These concerns are related to the "heart" aspect of your meetings. An experiential aim is often the most important part of the meeting—never leave it out. It will make the difference between whether people return invigorated to the meetings you lead, arrive in an uncooperative state, or just not attend at all. Here are examples of such aims:

- Build trust among team members.
- Motivate the team to try one new technique during the next iteration.

We recommend that you establish rational and experiential aims and write them down before starting to brainstorm the questions.

Using the ORID Framework

We like checklists. They can give sufficient structure to a meeting and help you remember important stuff you might otherwise have forgotten. Here is a short checklist in case you want to use the ORID framework:

1. Gather relevant data and trends to understand the situation.
2. Establish the rational and experiential aims.
3. Identify key stakeholders and key participants and validate the topic and RA/EA with them.
4. Brainstorm questions that achieve the RA/EA.
5. Select and order questions that you will ask.
6. Prepare your opening and closing carefully.
7. Facilitate a meeting and learn from your experience.

To understand the checklist better, refer to the template in Table A.2. It reveals each point of the checklist in more detail.

Table A.2   ORID Checklist

Topic: General topic at hand married with the needs of the team	
Rational Aim (RA): The "head" aspect of the meeting	**Experiential Aim (EA):** The emotional aspect of the meeting
Opening/Context: An invitation that explains why the team is having this conversation and the purpose of it. Focuses on the topic and serves as a reminder of any previous agreements.	
Objective: Objective questions, at least three or four, to get a good sampling of data from which to draw conclusions	**Intent:** Should link to RA/EA
Reflective: Reflective questions, at least two, a positive and a negative to let people express the full range of emotions	**Intent:** Should link to RA/EA

Interpretive: Interpretive question. Sometimes several subquestions are needed to dive to a deeper level. You might even need the additional ORID questions to explore each option here.	**Intent:** Should link to RA/EA
Decisional: Decisional questions (at least two or three)	**Intent:** Links to RA/EA
Closing: The words you use to bring the conversation to an end. Thank people for their time; sum up the results of the meeting.	

Retrospective Example

This is an example of using the ORID method as the framework for the Agile Retrospective. We came up with two rational aims: "Inspect the past iteration in relation to team relationships, processes, and tools" and "Come up with at least one improvement for the next iteration."

The experiential aim was "Experience a productive Agile Retrospective and build trust." We communicated the aims to the whole team beforehand.

Then we came up with a metaphor of a butterfly, in which each part of the butterfly wing corresponded to the specific phase of the method (blue—objective; red—reflective; yellow—interpretive; green—decisional). We created four hand-drawn flipcharts with butterfly wings and questions for each phase. There were 14 questions in total.

Objective	Reflective	Interpretation	Decision Making
1. What was the Sprint Goal?	5. What surprised you?	8. What are we doing really well, and what should we keep doing the same way?	13. What are the next SMART steps?
2. What was the forecast and how many items are "done"?	6. What annoyed you and made you mad?	9. What is the most important aspect of work we need to improve? (dot-voting)	14. Who is responsible for the improvement?
3. What were the major events?	7. What made you laugh?	10. What could be the underlying root causes of the issue? (Nine Whys)	
4. What are the key metrics/data available?		11. How to make sure that the problem doesn't recur?	
		12. What is within our circle of influence? (Circles and Soup)	

We opened the flipcharts one by one. Objective and reflective questions were discussed as batches in small groups, and the answers then shared in an open discussion. We clustered similar ideas with stickies on the wall. In the interpretation phase, we used two additional techniques, Nine Whys[22] and Circles and Soup,[23] to ensure the potential decision was a systems one and in the sphere of team influence.

ORID Summary

ORID is a focused and highly participative conversation with the whole Agile team that builds on a natural internal process of perception, response, judgment, and decision making. ORID can be used as a subsidiary tool for a meeting or as a general framework for larger events. Start with the intention (RA/EA) and use the ORID checklist and template to get a better outcome.

K. Trust

Trust Canvas

The Trust canvas is a powerful vehicle for a team to have a conversation about trust and generate the next steps for its growth. The original Trust canvas was created by an old friend of ours, Alexey Pikulev. Here, we present an updated version based on recent research results. Christina Breuer and her colleagues have identified the most frequently occurring factors that positively influence trust in teams.[24] The following is a short description of the factors they describe:

- **Ability:** Task-related ability factors such as reputation, expert knowledge, experience in the field of work, ability to perform a task successfully, and accuracy and thoroughness of work. Team-related ability factors include being able to offer positive and negative feedback, proactivity, friendliness, and high participation in decision making. How do we grow our ability?

- **Benevolence:** Trust develops when people help others in the team to get the work done and when members make autonomous decisions on their work processes. Team members need to care about each other. Are members ready to listen and take into account the concerns and problems of others? Are members loyal and supportive of other members' or team decisions? How can we connect and engage with each other?

- **Predictability:** Team members with consistent and regular team behavior gain trust. For example, such members keep their commitments, are promptly available and socially present to other members, and act in consistent, predictable ways. How do we take responsibility and fulfill it?

- **Integrity:** Teams with strong ethical principles, team values, and team interactions build trust. Members who behave according to the shared team values and treat private information confidentially build trust with the team. How can we align team values? Which principles and behavior are essential to us?

- **Transparency:** A team experiences trust when no information difference exists between its members; it experiences mistrust when things are ambiguous. Trust in the team increases when all relevant information is shared openly—that is, when there is information transparency. Clarity about work, roles, responsibilities, and deadlines also increases trust within the team. How can we build and support clarity, openness, and transparency? How can we avoid uncertainty and vagueness?

The Trust canvas helps create mutual expectations in a team and supports conflict resolution. We have found that teams use this tool in three main contexts:

- During the team's lift-off to establish working agreements and expectations.

- In Agile Retrospectives, where team highlights areas that need special attention and improvement.

- As an indicator of the team's health and gathering data. For instance, we observed team members placing red stickies on Trust canvas areas that failed from their perspective in a Sprint.

Facilitating the Trust Canvas Workshop

We regularly start the Trust Canvas workshop by collecting positive experiences of the team associated with high levels of trust. We do this with storytelling. Stories are important to humans. Throughout time, we have always shared stories. Stories have been important for humanity, for learning and passing on knowledge through generations.

Based on the stories collected and storytelling, we create a unified picture of why trust is important for the team. To evoke storytelling, the following questions are useful:

- Describe a time when you were part of a team with a high level of trust and respect among team members and those outside the team. How was trust and respect built and communicated?

- How did it feel to be a part of this community/team?

- What made it possible to establish such a high level of trust in that team?

- Which aspects of trust were the most valuable for you?

- What have you learnt from this experience?

You can use several facilitation techniques to aid in collecting stories[25]:

- Appreciative Interviews[26]

- Conversation Café[27]

- Anecdote Circles[28]

- Drawing Together[29]

- Rory Cubes [30]

Collect insights and patterns for the whole team to see on a flipchart. Summarize them if needed. Now you can proceed to the Trust canvas.[31] Use a simple 1-2-4-All technique for generating ideas and filling the canvas with stickies.[5] Finish with What? So What? Now What?[19] and/or 15% Solutions[32] to generate insights and next steps.

Trust Constellation

Constellations is a coaching technique for identifying system elements and their relationship to each other. This technique enables us to see a situation from different perspectives, understand dependencies, and reveal influential factors. As a result, the team becomes aware of its relationship dynamics and can make informed decisions.

The default way of facilitating constellations is to place a problem statement or topic in the middle of the circle on the floor. The coach asks the team a series of questions related to the topic discussed. Team members move toward the center of the circle or backward depending on how they agree with the statement. Another approach is to identify objects that represent team members and spatially orient them on a table or a flipchart. Here are some example statements that you can use to investigate the trust theme:

- "Trust is important to me."

- "I trust myself."

- "I trust the team."

When team members stop moving and positions are stable, ask the system revealing questions. Be comfortable with silence and give the team ability to respond thoughtfully:

- What do you observe?

- What are the patterns you notice?

- What does this constellation reveal about the team?

- What does your position mean?

- What would it take for you to change your position?

- What does the team need?

- What should the team avoid?

- What can the team do to improve the constellation?

Questions are usually asked in an open discussion format. Additionally, you might prefer forming small groups with team members representing different positions in a constellation. Give the groups several minutes to discuss the question, then return to the open discussion format and ask each group to present their findings.

L. Facilitating Conflict

The following exercises will help you to establish a solid ground for handling conflict. We recommend using them in a sequence. However, if you see fit, you can change the order. Feel free to refine and change the exercises to make them more appropriate for your context.

Exercise: What Color Is the Conflict?[33]

The goal of the exercise is to create an awareness of how team members deal with conflict. People identify and share their outlook on the conflict.

Step 1.   Individual work. Provide a team with sticky notes of different colors: red, blue, white, orange, green, and so on. Let everyone choose any color that meshes with their personal view on conflict. Even if people choose the same color, they may do so for different reasons—and those reasons are interesting for a team to know. Give participants several minutes to write down why their chosen color is associated with the conflict. Additionally, you can ask them to explain how their view of conflict was shaped by their childhood and major life events.

Step 2.   Sharing views on the conflict. Go around the table and ask everyone to explain why they picked their color. Show respect, curiosity, and use active listening. Strive for equal participation. Alternative formats are Appreciative Interviews,[26] 1-2-4-All,[5] Drawing Together,[29] Conversation Café,[27] and Shift & Share.[7]

Step 3.   Debrief. After everyone shares their personal views, debrief them on the exercise to build a foundation for adjusting conflict agreements. Here are some of the questions you might consider:

    a. What was the most striking thing for you?

    b. Which feelings did you have when you listened to other people?

    c. What is the importance of this exercise?

    d. What needs to be changed in our conflict agreements?

Exercise: Five Conflict Strategies

Kenneth Thomas and Ralph Kilmann identified five conflict resolution strategies that people typically use to handle conflict[34]:

- **Avoiding:** People just withdraw from the conflict when the discomfort of confrontation for them exceeds the potential reward from resolution of the conflict. One might think that it is easy to get the facilitator's help, but people aren't really contributing to the conversation and withholding ideas. When conflict is avoided, it is not resolved.

- **Competing:** This strategy is used by people who are planning to win. It is an assertive and not cooperative mode. The assumption is that one side wins and the others lose. It doesn't let diverse perspectives emerge and prevents understanding of the full picture. Competing is suitable for sports or war, but not for team problem solving.

- **Accommodating:** One party gives in to the wishes/demands of another. This is a cooperative but not assertive mode. Sometimes it is a gracious way if a person figures out they have been wrong. It's less helpful when one person accommodates another just to preserve harmony or to avoid confronting the issue directly. Accommodation can result in unresolved issues.

- **Collaborating:** In this method, people are both assertive and cooperative. They are able to actively defend their positions and are still open to other opinions at the same time. A team allows each participant to make a contribution and co-creates a shared solution that everyone can support.

- **Compromising:** Team members are partially assertive and cooperative. Everyone gives up a little bit of what they want, and no one gets what they want. Compromise is often perceived as being fair, even if no one is happy with the outcome.

People choose how cooperative and how assertive they are in a conflict. Everyone has preferred ways of responding. In fact, we generally use all methods depending on the circumstances, though of them are our primary preferences. Figure A.15 illustrates the five strategies for dealing with conflict.

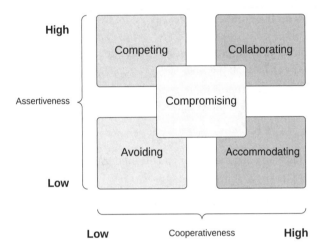

Figure A.15
Conflict strategies.

The following facilitation steps are based on the microstructure Appreciative Interviews.[26]

Step 1. Individual work. Give the team a couple of minutes to think about their preferences in handling conflicts. When they're done, ask them to rank those strategies from the most to the least frequently used.

Step 2. Sharing strategies in pairs. Team members conduct interviews and tell stories about how they dealt with conflict and which strategies they used (5–7 minutes in each direction, 10–15 minutes total).

Step 3. Sharing strategies in groups of four. In groups of four, each person retells the story of their pair partner. Ask team members to listen for patterns in strategies and make note of them (15 minutes).

Step 4. Collect patterns. Collect insights and patterns for the team on a flipchart (10–15 minutes).

Step 5.   Debrief and find the possible action steps.

    a. What surprised you?

    b. What have you learned about the team?

    c. Which potential problems might hold us back?

    d. Which decisions do we need to take?

    e. What should be included in our conflict protocol?

Use 1-2-4-All to discuss the questions if needed (10 minutes).

Team Toxins

Relationship expert John Gottman, in his best-selling book, *The Seven Principles for Making Marriage Work*,[35] has identified four behaviors that get in the way of communication and strong, collaborative relationships: blaming, defensiveness, contempt, and stonewalling. When used frequently, these toxic communication patterns are so lethal to human relationships that Gottman calls them "The Four Horsemen of the Apocalypse." In the context of teams, they are regularly referred to as "The Four Team Toxins" (see Figure A.16).

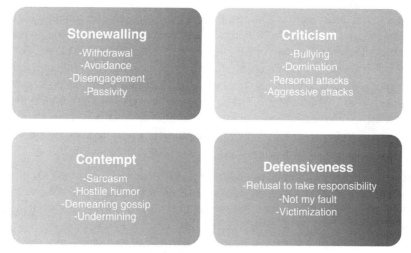

Figure A.16
The Four Team Toxins.

Team toxins can wreak havoc on the teams and organizations if left unchecked. They can lead to team conflict if people are not aware of and able to deal with them. Understanding the concept of team toxins is the proactive way to deal with conflict and helping the team be antifragile:

- **Criticism:** There is a big difference between a criticism and a complaint. A complaint focuses on a specific behavior or event. An example of a complaint is "I'm upset that you didn't check with me before you committed code to the repository. I wanted to make sure that the code style is fine. Could you check with me next time?" In contrast, when criticizing, people express negative feelings about the other's character and become judgmental. An example of the criticism is "Why are you so forgetful? I always ask you to check with me before you commit code. But nothing changes." Pay special attention to the words "you always," "nothing," and "you never" that accompany criticism.

- **Contempt:** Contempt is born when one has a sense of superiority over others. It can take many forms: sarcasm, hostile humor, disrespectful comments, undermining attempts of colleagues to resolve the conflict, sneering at other suggestions, making rude jokes, interrupting, and not listening to each other.

  Once we were facilitating a session with four Scrum Masters working in the same product group. Jane, one of the Scrum Masters, was hostile and showed disrespect toward John, another Scrum Master. John said: "I suggest that we prepare together for the joint events like Sprint Planning and Overall Retrospective for several teams. That will help us to share knowledge." Jane responded in a mocking tone: "To be honest, I'm not sure it helps. Teams do not accept you and it's a waste of our time. You are desperate as a facilitator." Contempt causes physiological damage. When Gottman and his colleagues observed it in relationships, they aborted the research because they couldn't expose people to conditions they knew could be damaging to their health.

- **Defensiveness:** Defensiveness escalates the conflict, because it's just another way of blaming. The defender sends a message: "The problem isn't me, it's you." Defensiveness assumes that the problem lies somewhere outside there, so the defender is not able to fix it. For example, team members might list numerous external circumstances that prevent them from learning or delivering value. You can run into phrases such as "That's just how we do it here"; "That's our culture"; "It's such bad code, that there's nothing I can do"; and "The traffic's terrible in the morning, so I can't be at the standup on time." Both criticism and contempt often lead to defensiveness, and vice versa. Eventually there's someone who tunes out—and that means the arrival of the last toxin, stonewalling.

- **Stonewalling:** People stonewall when they feel psychologically and physically overwhelmed. Stonewalling means acting as if you don't really care. In a dialogue, the stonewaller doesn't give any visible feedback to what is being said. They don't nod in response, but rather just look down or away. The stonewaller is completely "out of it." People don't disengage at once, of course; it takes time for a stonewalling toxin to arrive. Therefore, long periods of criticism, contempt, and defensiveness usually precede the appearance of stonewalling.

  Once we were observing a team Retrospective where one of the participants completely disengaged from the conversation. Finally, she stood up and silently left the room. Rather than confronting the arguments, she avoided the fight—but she also avoided her team.

When the four toxins are present, the team's ability to process information is reduced. It's harder to pay attention to what others are saying, because the most ancient part of the brain (amygdala) is activated. This leads to the most reflexive and least intellectually sophisticated responses: to fight (criticism, contempt, defensiveness) or flee (stonewalling). It leaves no chance for creative problem solving.

Exercise: Team Toxins[36]

The goal of this exercise is to raise awareness of the team toxins and their impact, and to help the team come up with solutions to address their presence in the team's work.

Preparation. Start by putting a matrix on the floor with tape and creating floor labels (we prefer A4 size paper) for each toxin. Introduce each toxin one by one while putting the corresponding floor labels down: Criticism, Contempt, Defensiveness, Stonewalling.

Recall experience. Ask the team members to express how other people behave in each zone. Be playful and encourage participation. Ask them to recall situations when they recognized the toxins. Use the ORID questions for deep investigation at this point (Table A.3).

Table A.3   ORID Questions for the Team Toxins Exercise

Objective	Reflective	Interpretation
In what situations do you come across the toxin?	What is your reaction here?	What do you think is behind this toxin?
	What surprises you about people's reactions? Why?	What are the unfulfilled human needs here?
What words do you hear?		What do people really mean?
What is the typical facial expression?		What benefits do people get when the toxins are present?
What is the typical body posture?		

Find "home." After the team has experienced all four toxins, ask them to find the one that feels like their "home." It is the default toxin that an individual probably adopted and used through the years as a coping mechanism. Invite everyone to physically step into the zone labeled with the toxin on the floor and stand there. Most likely, you will encounter small groups forming in each quadrant. Now ask groups to conduct interviews by sharing stories of how they used toxins to their advantage in their life or working environment. In 5–10 minutes, get back to open discussion and ask the small groups to share their insights and most interesting stories. Collect insights and patterns for the whole group to see on a flipchart. Summarize if needed.

Find a signal. Now suggest that the team come up with a code word or a signal so that team members know that a toxin may be present in the room. Emphasize the phrase "may be present." Explain to the team that the signal is supposed to open up a conversation about team behavior, as simply labeling someone with a specific toxin would evolve into blaming. The signal could be a particular word, sound, or movement/gesture that everyone in the team agrees to use. For instance, one team that we were coaching decided to choose the word "toxins" whenever they thought they were present in the room. Another team created a graphic poster with a short description of all four toxins and brought it to every Scrum event. Some of the decisional questions that you could use here are as follows:

- What's the next step in implementing what we agreed on during this workshop?

- What name would you call this workshop?

- What unfinished business on toxins do we need to pick up tomorrow?

- Which kind of follow-up would help you apply more effectively what you have learned?

- Who else should take this workshop?

Create a Conflict Protocol

Conflict protocols are helpful guidelines that effective teams develop to manage conflict constructively. They provide clarity to the team about how they expect one another to engage in discussion and debate. The contract comprises examples of acceptable and unacceptable behaviors and how the team members keep each other accountable. Use the following steps to create the conflict protocol.

Step 1. Ideal team. Ask the team to think about their ideal team. How would that team handle conflicts and disagreements? Use 1-2-4-All or silent brainstorming to capture ideas.

Step 2. Behavior patterns. This is the core part of the conflict protocol. Put two questions in front of the team:

   a. What are some behaviors you want to have happen when conflict occurs?

   b. What are some things you do NOT want to happen when conflict occurs?

   This part can be effectively facilitated using Min Specs.[37] First, generate the list of acceptable and unacceptable behaviors individually. Then, form small groups and consolidate the final lists to make them as complete as possible (6 minutes). Proceed to testing each behavior listed on a sticky note. If the behavior can be violated and the conflict still remains productive, the sticky is dropped from the list (15 minutes). Compare the lists across small groups and consolidate to the shortest list (15 minutes).

Step 3. Creating accountability. Inappropriate behaviors must be confronted if the conflict protocol has been violated. When teams avoid confronting issues, that increases resentment among the team members who play by the rules and affects the entire team.

   a. How will you hold one another accountable for following these agreements?

   b. What will you do if someone breaks an agreement?

   Use 1-2-4-All or a simple round-robin technique to gather ideas; use voting if needed.

Step 4. Finding consensus. The portrait of the ideal team, accompanied by a minimum list of acceptable and unacceptable behaviors plus a plan for how to keep the team accountable, is a team's conflict protocol from now on. Check the agreement for consensus.

We were working with a product group consisting of eight teams over the course of half a year. The teams experienced a massive turnover and had lots of conflicts. At the Overall Retrospective, the team representatives suggested a formal set of steps that everyone should follow if they had a conflict with any member of the product group. This is what they came up with:

1. Talk with the other person.

2. Focus on behavior, not on personality.

3. Use active listening.

4. Identify points of agreement and disagreement.

6. Develop a plan.

7. Set up meeting times to continue your discussions.

8. Follow through on your plan.

Some concepts that we have covered elsewhere can also appear in the conflict protocol: radical candor, team toxins, Scrum values, nonviolent communication approach, context/observation/impact/next (COIN) technique, and others.

Coaching the Team

Inevitably, despite the existence of clear conflict protocols, there will be conflicts that exceed the team's current abilities to handle them, and you might want to step in. Before you decide to act, prepare by observing the team to answer the following questions:

- At which conflict level is the team?

- Should the team, based on their maturity, be able to solve the conflict by themselves?

- Why are they not able to solve it themselves?

- What if I do not intervene? Will the conflict likely escalate further, or will they fix it?

- Do they have ideas on how to solve the conflict?

Based on the answers, you can decide whether to intervene. Of course, ideally the team should solve the conflict themselves without your help. Every time you solve a problem for the team, you take away an opportunity for them to learn and grow. When the observed team behavior and conflict level make the conflict too hard for the team to resolve, you need to act.

Useful Guidelines for Resolving Conflict

You can know a lot of theories about conflict coaching, but the key is asking the right question at the right time. The following are some guidelines that might help you during the session.

- **Guideline 0: Ensure there is a common interest to resolve the conflict.** Otherwise, you don't have to start.

- **Guideline 1: Emphasize the common interest rather than the positions.** A sensible solution requires uniting interests, not positions. It is the interests that (re)define the problem. If a person takes a position of "working outside my main specialty" and "not working outside my main specialty," these two perspectives seem to be incompatible. If the person instead focuses on interests, then the problem is redefined: "I want to develop my main specialty further" and "I don't want to learn skills that do not contribute my main specialty." So, the solution lies in working outside the main specialty and still contributing to the person's main specialty. The advantage of such an approach is that in addition to the conflicting position, it is seen that there are conflicting interests, but also joint and compatible ones.

- **Guideline 2: Create multiple options.** People tend to look too quickly for the best answer; in this way a more sensible decision-making process, in which a choice is made from many options, is avoided. All too often, the situation is stated as "Either you're right or I'm right." Room to negotiate can arise only if many clear ideas have been developed, which can be elaborated in the negotiation (brainstorming and only then criticizing and selecting). The alternative solutions must be mutually beneficial: The interests must be known, and the consequences of the decisions taken must be considered.

- **Guideline 3: Use objective criteria instead of subjective/emotional criteria.** However much understanding there is for the other party and however much people look for means to reconcile interests, the harsh reality is usually that some interests remain in conflict with each other. In such cases, a much better solution is to discuss the issue on a basis that is independent of the will of both parties—that is, based on objective criteria.

- **Guideline 4: Identify and acknowledge the emotions at play.** Most of the time, the conflict in this state is no longer about content, but rather about emotions such as lack of recognition, lack of respect, or ensuring that one is right by vigorously defending one's position.

- **Guideline 5: Agree that the team uses "I messages" instead of "you or they messages."** When in the midst of conflict, people are more likely to take things personally, making communication difficult. Make sure that people speak in "I" terms, saying something about themselves instead of about the other.

- **Guideline 6: Keep responsibility for the conflict and its resolution in the team.** Consider asking questions like "What is preventing you from solving this?"

- **Guideline 7: Ask for permission.** Consider asking questions like "Is it okay if we go further into this?" and "May I ask a question about this?"

The Conflict Coaching Session

The goal of this session is for the team to understand how they keep themselves in a stable state of conflict. Once that is clear, they can formulate steps to break the loop and leave the row behind.

How do you approach conflict coaching of a team? We will review the four most important points one by one.

1. Discuss with the team whether you will immediately have a plenary session with all team members or have individual conversations first. There are pros and cons to both approaches. If the team members are already very suspicious of each other, separate conversations can reinforce that distrust. But you also increase curiosity: What emerged in those conversations? And in separate conversations, you often learn a lot more, which can help with the analysis.

2. Make sure everyone knows how the process will go. Clarity is priceless. If you want to have individual conversations with the team members first, start with a short plenary session. In this session, you can explain how the process works and indicate that a discussion with everyone will follow. Make it clear that the conversations are entirely confidential.

3. You are engaged in conflict coaching for the purpose of helping the team to achieve better cooperation. Investigate thoroughly whether the team *wants* to be coached by you. And consider the issue from the other way around: If the team has explicitly asked to be coached by you, investigate why they asked you to help them.

4. If you start with individual conversations, you will have a joint analysis of your findings. If you immediately start with a plenary meeting, you analyze on the spot. Always check whether the team members support your conclusions.

5. Close with a brief look into the future as an instrument to make the team more robust.

We do not provide a detailed example of a workshop here, as many can be found elsewhere in this book.

M. Radical Candor

The strategy of *radical candor* can be useful for all kinds of leaders including Scrum Masters, Agile coaches, change agents, and others. Let us provide you with an example.

Before opening a Sprint Retrospective, the Scrum Master noticed that one of the developers was sitting with their notebook open and writing code. The Product Owner stated that this was her personal request, so that she could respond to an inquiry from the stakeholder as fast as possible. The Scrum Master reminded the Scrum Team about the importance of the event and said firmly that she would not start the event until everyone was fully focused. After a short conversation, the developer closed the notebook and the Scrum Master started facilitating a productive Sprint Retrospective.

It is difficult to provide feedback and simultaneously challenge management and teams. But part of an Agile leader's job is to ensure everybody is able to point out mistakes and celebrate victories with equal frankness. Moreover, this balancing act is an ethical obligation if you support Agile values and principles. For instance, a Scrum Master cannot passively look on while the rules of Scrum are being broken and empirical control suffers. While providing feedback, you should show sincere care for other people. You should be congruent above all. Sometimes you show care by shouting at someone. When teams and management know that an Agile leader is acting in their interests, they are prepared to accept feedback. Here's another example.

At a Sprint Review, the Product Owner thanked the developers for the work they had done. The developers were about to demonstrate an increment to the stakeholders, but the Scrum Master pointed out that not all the PBIs met the current Definition of Done (DoD) precisely. The team acknowledged that two features did not meet the DoD. The Scrum Master supported the team, saying that he had observed their work and commitment to the Sprint Goal during the Sprint. Nevertheless, to uphold the principles of empirical control and transparency, they should not demonstrate work that is not "done." The Scrum Master shared an example from his own experience and outlined possible negative consequences. The Product Owner and developers were disappointed, but acknowledged that the Scrum Master was right. After the Sprint Review, they conducted a Sprint Retrospective, where they decide to pull fewer features into a Sprint next time, and instead focus on making them "done."

Let's have a look at some other strategies in the model.

Obnoxious Aggression

If you cannot show radical candor, the next best thing is not to be so nice. Why so? Despite the tone of the feedback, people will see their mistakes and weak points. That means that they can improve. Here's an example of obnoxious aggression in action.

An organization hired an external Agile coach to assess its Scrum Teams' maturity. After the Go See session, the Agile coach organized a meeting with management and tore the organizational processes to shreds. He didn't mince words; he was arrogant and rude. Management was distraught, although they agreed with the overall conclusions. It wasn't the content, but rather the form that provoked animosity. Management did not see the Agile coach's desire to improve the situation, but only his desire to criticize. The organization didn't continue the contract. Nonetheless, during the following months, the organizational processes improved significantly.

Ruinous Empathy

This is where the majority of mistakes are made. In this case, Agile leaders do not challenge, but only show sincere empathy. But that actually does a great disservice to the teams and organization, because people cannot improve without honest feedback and a clear understanding of where they should be heading to. Here's another example.

The speed of development had turned out to be lower than expected. The stakeholders started putting pressure on the Scrum team and their management. One of the managers met with the Scrum Master personally and asked him to "reduce the quality for a while, so the team can just hand over the result." The developers weakened their DoD with the Scrum Master's permission. The Scrum Master had sincere sympathy with the team and management and wanted to relieve them of the pressure, even though he realized that the technical debt was growing. Within a few months, the Product Owner decided to release the product onto the market. It turned out that the team couldn't do so, due to the amount of undone work that had accumulated.

Manipulative Insincerity

The worst possible option, manipulative insincerity is present when an Agile leader exerts influence using manipulation. In this case, the leader is thinking more about themselves than about the team: how to save face and retain their position in the organization, and about what other people think and say. In this instance, there is no challenge, and no care for others. Here's an example from the field.

The stakeholders were requesting that the Scrum team stick to the "committed" dates. The Scrum Master avoided getting into a direct dialogue with those concerned and educating them on how planning is conducted in an empirical environment. Instead, he started meeting with different groups of people and pitting them against one another. After some time, the developers started to express a negative attitude toward the Product Owner and to consider all representatives of the business to be enemies. The Scrum Master wore the hat of "team protector," though he was actually the real cause of the problem.

Start Practicing Radical Candor

Up to this point, we have examined four strategies: radical candor, obnoxious aggression, ruinous empathy, and manipulative insincerity. Only one of these is optimal. So, how can you start practicing radical candor? We shall give you several recommendations.

- Be well balanced. That means taking care of your physical and moral health. An Agile leader is like a rock amidst turbulent waves. If you don't take care of yourself, then you cannot care for other people.

- Build trusting relationships. Show genuine interest in people's lives and personal interests. Take an interest in how their last holiday went and what they remember best. Ask how a colleague's ill child is feeling and how you can help. If you do this and people know that you care about them, they will react more favorably when you challenge them.

- Show openness and vulnerability. Ask them to provide direct and honest feedback, and listen to it with a desire to understand and not to give a quick answer. Ask, "What can I start doing or stop doing, so as to become an even more effective leader?"

- Start practicing radical candor tomorrow.

- Find useful feedback techniques. Use it yourself and teach those around you. For example, nonviolent communication (NVC), situation/behavior/impact, context/observation/impact/next (COIN), and others.

- Don't talk behind people's backs. Avoid taking on the role of intermediary in a conflict. Insist that the people involved in the conflict resolve it by themselves. Only if they cannot do so should you step in as a mediator.

- Familiarize your team with the model of radical candor and use it in a Sprint.

- Practice radical candor in relation to everyone in your organization: senior and middle management, Product Owners, teams, and so on. If this is impossible and unsafe, consider changing your place of work.

The most effective Agile leaders possess the heart of a lion and bravely advocate for the principles and values of Agile. Furthermore, they practice radical candor. Radical candor is the type of feedback in which we challenge people directly while simultaneously showing care for them. While providing feedback, one should show sincere care for other people. When teams and management know that an Agile leader is acting in their interests, they are prepared to accept feedback. Be well balanced, build trusting relationships, and show openness and vulnerability. Don't talk behind people's backs and start practicing radical candor tomorrow.

N. Cost of Delay

Is it possible to quantify the impact of the queues? Many organizations are now using the concept of *cost of delay*, which has gained traction over the years. It recognizes the loss of a benefit due to the delay and/or penalty. In product development, we aspire to get some benefit from the result of our work. The cost of delay depends on urgency and value.

$$\text{Cost of delay} = \text{value} \times \text{urgency}$$

Just because something is more urgent than something else doesn't necessarily mean we should give it the highest priority. The first step in using the concept of cost of delay is to agree on a model that best describes how the value is affected. Figure A.17 illustrates some of the most used models.[38]

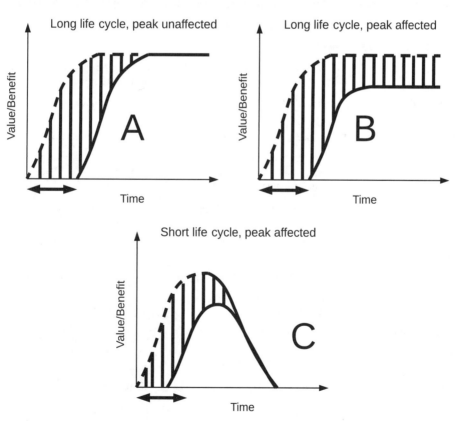

Figure A.17
Cost of delay models.

An example of Model A is a monthly late penalty incurred by not implementing some requirement requested by a regulator. Model B is the case where a delay limits the long-term revenue. When a competitor beats your organization by becoming the first to introduce an innovation to the market, it can get traction so fast that your organization won't be able to acquire as many customers as it could if it released a product earlier. Model C illustrates an opportunity with a short lifetime, so that a delay significantly limits potential revenue.

References

1. Scrum Patterns Group. *A Scrum Book* (2019). www.scrumbook.org.

2. Jeff Sutherland et al. *A Scrum Book: The Spirit of the Game* (Pragmatic Bookshelf, 2019).

3. Russell L. Ackoff, *Re-creating the Corporation: A Design of Organizations for the 21st Century* (Oxford University Press, 1999).

4. Dave Gray. "35." GameStorming (February 26, 2013). https://gamestorming.com/35/.

5. "1-2-4-All." Liberating Structures. www.liberatingstructures.com/1-1-2-4-all/.

6. Esther Derby and Diana Larsen. *Agile Retrospectives: Making Good Teams Great* (Pragmatic Bookshelf, 2006).

7. "Shift & Share." Liberating Structures. www.liberatingstructures.com/11-shift-share/.

8. The World Cafe. www.theworldcafe.com/.

9. Jaap Schaveling and Bill Bryan. *Making Better Decisions Using Systems Thinking: How to Stop Firefighting, Deal with Root Causes and Deliver Permanent Solutions* (Palgrave Macmillan, 2018).

10. David J. Anderson. *Kanban: Successful Evolutionary Change for Your Technology Business* (Blue Hole Press, 2010).

11. Jeffrey Liker. *The Toyota Way: 14 Management Principles from the World's Greatest Manufacturer* (McGraw-Hill, 2004).

12. Richard Lawrence and Peter Green. "The Humanizing Work Guide to Splitting User Stories." Humanizing Work. www.humanizingwork.com/the-humanizing-work-guide-to-splitting-user-stories/

13. "Story Splitting Cheat Sheet." Humanizing Work. http://agileforall.com/wp-content/uploads/2009/10/Story-Splitting-Cheat-Sheet.pdf

14. Mike Lowery. "Chart Your Happiness." Nomad8 (October 22, 2012). https://nomad8.com/articles/chart-your-happiness.

15. "Mad Sad Glad Retrospective." Retrium. www.retrium.com/retrospective-techniques/mad-sad-glad.

16. Dave Gray. "Creating a Sharepoint Vision Using the Cover Story Game." GameStorming (December 13, 2011). https://gamestorming.com/?s=cover+story.

17. Dave Gray. "Speed Boat." GameStorming (April 5, 2011). https://gamestorming.com/?s=speedboat

18. Alexander Osterwalder. *Value Proposition Design: How to Create Products and Services Customers Want* (Wiley, 2014).

19. "What, So What, Now What? W³." Liberating Structures. www.liberatingstructures.com/9-what-so-what-now-what-w/.

20. Brian Stanfield. "The Art of Focused Conversation." ICA Associates. https://tinyurl.com/ArtFocusedConvo.

21. Brian R. Stanfield. *The Art of Focused Conversation: 100 Ways to Access Group Wisdom in the Workplace* (New Society Publishers, 2000).

22. "Nine Whys." Liberating Structures. www.liberatingstructures.com/3-nine-whys/.

23. Dave Gray. "Circles and Soup." GameStorming (August 15, 2011). https://gamestorming.com/circles-and-soup/.

24. C. Breuer, J. Hüffmeier, F. Hibben, and G. Hertel. "Trust in Teams: A Taxonomy of Perceived Trustworthiness Factors and Risk-Taking Behaviors in Face-to-Face and Virtual Teams." Human Relations 73, no. 1 (2020): 3–34. doi:10.1177/0018726718818721.

25. "Liberating Structures Menu." Liberating Structures. www.liberatingstructures.com/ls/.

26. "Appreciative Interviews (AI)." Liberating Structures. www.liberatingstructures.com/5-appreciative-interviews-ai/.

27. "Conversation Cafe." Liberating Structures. www.liberatingstructures.com/17-conversation-cafe/.

28. "The Ultimate Guide to Anecdote Circles." Anecdote. www.anecdote.com/pdfs/papers/Ultimate_Guide_to_ACs_v1.0.pdf.

29. "Drawing Together." Liberating Structures. www.liberatingstructures.com/20-drawing-together/.

30. Rory's Story Cubes. https://www.storycubes.com/en/.

31. Philip Rogers. "The Team Canvas: Building Trust via Transparency." January 29, 2021. https://medium.com/agile-outside-the-box/the-team-canvas-building-trust-via-transparency-cf88ac05c66d.

32. "15% Solutions." Liberating Structures. www.liberatingstructures.com/7-15-solutions/.

33. Adapted from "Colour Conflict." SafetyCare. www.safetycare.com/ohs-pdf/Colour%20Conflict.pdf.

34. Kenneth Wayne Thomas and Ralph Killman. *Thomas-Kilmann Conflict Mode Instrument* (CPP, Inc., 2002).

35. John Gottman. *The Seven Principles for Making Marriage Work: A Practical Guide from the Country's Foremost Relationship Expert* (Harmony, 2015).

36. Adapted from "Exercise: Team Toxins ." Team Coaching International. https://teamcoachinginternational.com/wp-content/uploads/2019/12/Team-Toxins.pdf

37. "Min Specs." Liberating Structures. www.liberatingstructures.com/14-min-specs/.

38. Magnus Dahlgren. "Determining Value Using Cost of Delay." April 6, 2017. https://medium.com/@MagnusDahlgren/determining-value-using-cost-of-delay-266cd94630c6.

Index

Symbols

%C&A (percent complete and accurate), 210
1–2–4-All structure, 214, 224, 228, 275, 392, 394, 397
The 5 Dysfunctions of a Team (Lencioni), 293
15% Solutions structure, 151, 176, 267, 325, 392
20/20 Vision, 277

A

ability, trust and, 391
accidental specialization, 249
accommodation, 397–399
accountability, 397
acknowledgement of loss, 144–147
    loss aversion bias, 146–147
    volume of loss, assessment of, 143
Ackoff, R. A. 79
Ackoff, Russell L. 21, 79, 80, 118, 315–316, 361
actions
    creating, 334
    feedback loops, 334
    improvement, 375–379
adaptability, 51–68
    definition of, 53–54
    flow efficiency, 54, 65–66
    importance of, 51–52
    operational strategy, 63
    as optimization goal, 5, 6, 62
    queueing theory

        algorithms, 54–62
        behavior of queues, 54–61
        queueing system structures, 61–62
    resource efficiency, 64–65
adoption, Agile. *See* Agile adoption
Adventures in Complexity (Kuhn), 117
aggression, obnoxious, 401
Agile adoption
    common mistakes in, 107
    conditions for success, 113–115
        change leaders, 114
        feedback loops, 115
        goals and objectives, 114–115
        safe spaces, 115
    expansion of
        continual improvement steps, 118
        discontinuous improvement steps, 117–118
    individual and organizational learning, 115–117
    leading groups, 111–112
    organizational interventions, 124–130
        BOTG (behavior over time graph), 29–30, 124, 126, 371
        CLD (Causal Loop Diagram), 31–35, 124, 126–130, 194, 218–219, 375–377
        experimentation, inspection, and adaption, 130
        high-leverage interventions, 130
        stories, creating, 125–126
    overview of, 109–111

B

C

Product Backlog Items (PBIs), splitting, 381–383
   benefits of, 381–382
   importance of, 378–383
   principles of, 382–383
   results of, 383
   story splitting workshops, 378–383

Agile Development
Books, eBooks & Video

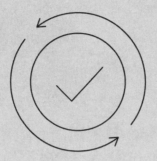

Whether you are a programmer, developer, or project manager, InformIT has the most comprehensive collection of Agile books, eBooks, and video training from the top thought leaders.

- Introductions and general Scrum guides
- Culture, leadership, and teams
- Development practices
- Enterprise
- Product and project management
- Testing
- Requirements
- Video short courses

Visit **informit.com/agilecenter** to read sample chapters, shop, and watch video lessons from featured products.

Register Your Product at informit.com/register

Access additional benefits and **save 35%** on your next purchase

- Automatically receive a coupon for 35% off your next purchase, valid for 30 days. Look for your code in your InformIT cart or the Manage Codes section of your account page.
- Download available product updates.
- Access bonus material if available.*
- Check the box to hear from us and receive exclusive offers on new editions and related products.

Registration benefits vary by product. Benefits will be listed on your account page under Registered Products.

InformIT.com—The Trusted Technology Learning Source

InformIT is the online home of information technology brands at Pearson, the world's foremost education company. At InformIT.com, you can:
- Shop our books, eBooks, software, and video training
- Take advantage of our special offers and promotions (informit.com/promotions)
- Sign up for special offers and content newsletter (informit.com/newsletters)
- Access thousands of free chapters and video lessons

Connect with InformIT—Visit informit.com/community

the trusted technology learning source

Addison-Wesley · Adobe Press · Cisco Press · Microsoft Press · Pearson IT Certification · Que · Sams · Peachpit Press

 Pearson